COMPUTER AIDED ENGINEERING GRAPHICS

COMPUTER AIDED ENGINEERING GRAPHICS

(As per the new Syllabus, B.Tech. I year of U.P. Technical University)

RAJASHEKAR PATIL
B.E., M.Tech., (Ph.D.)
Faculty, Department of Mechanical Engineering
Vijayanagar Engineering College
Bellary, Karnataka

PUBLISHING FOR ONE WORLD

NEW AGE INTERNATIONAL (P) LIMITED, PUBLISHERS
New Delhi • Bangalore • Chennai • Cochin • Guwahati • Hyderabad
Jalandhar • Kolkata • Lucknow • Mumbai • Ranchi
Visit us at **www.newagepublishers.com**

Published by New Age International (P) Ltd., Publishers
First Edition: 2009

Branches:

- 36, Malikarjuna Temple Street, Opp. ICWA, Basavanagudi, **Bangalore**. © (080) 26677815
- 26, Damodaran Street, T. Nagar, **Chennai**. © (044) 24353401
- Hemsen Complex, Mohd. Shah Road, Paltan Bazar, Near Starline Hotel, **Guwahati**. © (0361) 2543669
- No. 105, 1st Floor, Madhiray Kaveri Tower, 3-2-19, Azam Jahi Road, Nimboliadda, **Hyderabad**. © (040) 24652456
- RDB Chambers (Formerly Lotus Cinema) 106A,1st Floor, S.N. Banerjee Road, **Kolkata**. © (033) 22275247
- 18, Madan Mohan Malviya Marg, **Lucknow**. © (0522) 2209578
- 142C, Victor House, Ground Floor, N.M. Joshi Marg, Lower Parel, **Mumbai**. © (022) 24927869
- 22, Golden House, Daryaganj, **New Delhi**. © (011) 23262370, 23262368

ISBN : 978-81-224-2568-0

Rs. 125.00

C-08-08-3031

Printed in India at Ajit Printers, Delhi.
Typeset at Inhouse.

PUBLISHING FOR ONE WORLD
NEW AGE INTERNATIONAL (P) LIMITED, PUBLISHERS
4835/24, Ansari Road, Daryaganj, New Delhi-110002
Visit us at **www.newagepublishers.com**

PREFACE

The communication of the ideas through the graphical language is the oldest form of communication among humans; all it requires is some kind of equipment to form an image. We might recall the prehistoric era where mankind used the stick to scratch out a message on the sand or certain ancient alphabets were in the form of the pictures. Engineering graphics is a study which requires special equipment or tools to form the images. The tools can be simple pencil and draft board or a computer controlled drafting device.

From time to time several attempts were made to make the creation of the objects by graphical means. The Engineering Graphics has evolved from primitive hand drawing to instrument drawings to present computer 2D find 3D drafting. Today the default industry standard is to use computerized drawings. The computerized drawings have their advantages of storage and retrieval, ease of modification, transmission. Further the most important factor is the accuracy of creation of overall design and specially curves which no hand drawing can match.

Educational institutions are aware of the present needs of the industry and slowly switching from the drawing boards to computers in their classrooms. With the introduction of computer drawings the students are able to create better and faster drawings more accurately, be it any complicacy in the engineering drawing. Further, there is less likelihood of making mistakes and at the same time avoid the conventional time consuming procedures in creating the drawings. Many engineering institutions worldwide have adopted this approach to increase the employability quotient of the students.

Think3 Company is working hard to make students friendlier to the industry by introducing CAD software complementing the existing course curriculum at the universities. Think3 is committed to provide the required training to the trainers on the software for use in the classroom.

Think3 is proud to present the Engineering Graphics module for the ITI, Diploma and engineering students. The module presented here will not only align with the existing Engineering Graphics subject for various university students but the format of the course will also support the e-learning for the students. Now the students can learn the basics of Engineering Graphics by using Think3 software from ITALY. The subject matter and the material coverage is the same as what they would like to cover in the regular curriculum.

This is an attempt to make students learn how to use world's most advanced graphical software to create engineering graphics.

Although enough care has been taken in preparation of the book, yet some errors might have crept in. Healthy suggestions/comments/feedbacks are welcome in this regard.

Last but not the least, I am thankful to New Age International (P) Limited Publishers for taking interest to publish the book in a short span of period with a nice get up.

Author

Syllabus

U.P. Technical University

ECE-151/251 : COMPUTER AIDED ENGINEERING GRAPHICS

L T P
0 1 3

Unit-I

1. Introduction to Computer Aided Sketching

Introduction, Drawing Instruments and their uses, BIS conventions, lettering Dimensioning and free hand practicing.

Computer screen, layout of the software, standard tool bar/menus and description of most commonly used tool bars, navigational tools. Coordinate system and reference planes. Definitions of HP, VP, RPP & LPP. Creation of 2D/3D environment. Selection of drawing size and scale. Commands and creation of Lines, Co-ordinate points, axes, poly-lines, square, rectangle, polygons, splines, circles, ellipse, text, move, copy, off-set, mirror, rotate, trim, extend, break, chamfer, fillet, curves, constraints viz. tangency, parallelism, inclination and perpendicularity. Dimensioning, line convention, material conventions and lettering. **2 Sheet**

2. Orthographic Projections

Introduction, Definitions- Planes of projection, reference line and conventions employed, Projections of points in all the four quadrants. Projections of straight lines (located in First quadrant/first angle only), True and apparent lengths, True and apparent inclinations to reference planes (No application problems). **2 Sheet**

3. Orthographic Projections of Plane Surfaces
(First Angle Projection Only)

Introduction, Definitions-projections of plane surfaces-triangle, square rectangle, rhombus. pentagon, hexagon and circle, planes in different positions by change of position method only (No problems on punched plates and composite plates.) **1 Sheet**

4. Projections of Solids (First Angle Projection Only)

Introduction, Definitions-Projections of right regular- tetrahedron, hexahedron (cube), prisms, pyramids, cylinders and cones in different positions. (No problems on octahedrons and combination solid) **2 Sheet**

5. Sections and Development of Lateral Surfaces of Solids

Introduction, Section planes, Sections, section views, Sectional views, apparent shapes and True shapes of Sections of right regular prisms, pyramids, cylinders and cones resting with base on HP. (No problems on section of solids) **1 Sheet**

Development of lateral surface of above solids, their frustums and truncations. (No problems on lateral surfaces of trays, Tetrahedrons spheres and transition pieces).

6. Isometric Projection (Using Isometric Scale Only)

Introduction, Isometric scale, Isometric Projection of simple plane figures; Isometric Projection of tetrahedron, hexahedron (cube), right regular prisms, pyramids, cylinders, cones, spheres, cut spheres and combination of solids (Maximum of three Solids). **1 Sheet**

Note: At least 3 drawing assignments must be on AUTOCAD.

BASIC SKETCHING COMMANDS

The commands used are of windows based. Just by selecting the icon of the command, the operation can be executed. Three modules commands are used they are Drawing (draft) environment.

Sl. No.	Drawing (draft) environment commands	Think3 Commands	Tool (Icon)
1.	Select tool	**Select Entity**	
2.	Point	**Absolute/Delta Point**	
3.	Line	**Two-Point Line**	
4.	Curve	**Insert Curve through Control Points**	
5.	Arc by 3 points	**Three-Point Circle**	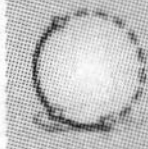
6.	Arc by center point	**Radius Circle**	
7.	Circle by center point	**Center Circle**	
8.	Rectangle	**Rectangle**	
9.	Fillet	**Fillet**	
10.	Chamfer	**Chamfer**	
11.	Trim	**Trim/Extend Curves**	
12.	Trim corner	Operation performed by **Trim/Extend Curves**	
13.	Extend to next	**Trim/Extend Curves with Limits**	
14.	Split	**Split Curve**	

15.	Offset	**Offset on Plane**	
16.	Fill	**Cross Hatch**	
17.	Move	**Move/Copy Entities**	
18.	Rotate	Operation performed by **Move/Copy Entities**	
19.	Mirror	**Mirror Entities**	
20.	Scale	**Scale Entities**	
21.	Stretch	**Multistretch Entities**	
22.	Smart dimension	**Smart Dimension**	
23.	Distance between	Operation performed by **Smart Dimension**	
24.	Angle between	Operation performed by **Smart Dimension**	
25.	Leader	**Label Dimension**	
26.	Text	**Insert Text**	
27.	Character map	No similar command in think3	
28.	Connect	**Join Curve**	
29.	Parallel	**Parallel Line**	
30.	Perpendicular	**Snap to Perpendicular**	
31.	Concentric	No similar command in think3, but the same result can be achieved by **Snap to Arc Center** command	

32.	Collinear	**Collinearity Constraint** But cannot be used in Drawing	
33.	Rigid	No similar command in think3	
34.	Tangent	**Snap to Tangent**	
35.	Equal	**Equal Length/Radius Constraint** But cannot be used in Drawing	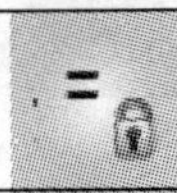
36.	Lock	**Ground Constraint** But cannot be used in Drawing	
37.	Symmetric	**Symmetry Constraint** But cannot be used in Drawing	
38.	Zoom	**Zoom Window**	
39.	Pan	**Pan View**	
40.	Fit	**Fit View**	

■■■

CONTENTS

1

INTRODUCTION TO COMPUTER AIDED DRAWING

INTRODUCTION

- One of the best ways to communicate one's ideas is through some form of picture or drawing. This is especially true for the engineer. The purpose of this is to give you the basics of engineering sketching and drawing.
- "Sketching" and "Drawing": *Sketching* generally means freehand drawing. Without using any drawing instruments. Ex: Sketch the face of human being. *Drawing* usually means using drawing instruments. Ex: Draw the chair which is used to sit.
- Engineering Drawing is a document that communicates a precise description of a part. They are legal documents, so they must be formal and precise. They are drawn using from compasses to drafters to bring precision to the drawings. Ex: Draw the chair with dimensions so that they can manufacture.
- Computer Aided Engineering Drawing is a file that communicates a precise description of a part with all details. Wherein they can be easily edited as per requirements of individual (customized). They are drawn using Computer and CAD software as a tool. Computer-stored files generated by the variety of packages can also check for volume and mass property calculations, finite-element analysis, process planning, computer numerically controlled (CNC) machining or high-resolution displays, in a formal three-dimensional geometric modeling terms.

  Words are not the natural language of engineers. Drawings are their prose, mathematics their grammar and differential equations their poetry.

  –Glegg

Drawing communicates the use of graphical symbols such as points, lines, planes and pictures. It gives the detailed description about any component in a pictorial form. It has its origin about 500 BC when symbols were used to convey the ideas among people. Later orthographic projection was formalized by Gaspard Monge in 1746, French mathematician, the inventor of descriptive geometry. He worked as a drafter in the fortification design office of the school at Mezier for French army officers. His work was kept a military secret for a number of years until he was allowed to publish in 1795. Stone cutters were the first to adopt his methods. Later carpenters and other trades abandoned their old methods for orthographic projection.

Technical Graphics, also called as Engineering Drawing is a graphics language. It cannot be spoken or read out like many languages having phonetics and script. The knowledge of the language of graphics communications will influence the way of thinking. Normally, human thoughts are interlinked with the language they know. Image of imagining, having third eye in the human brain is the language of Technical Graphics or Engineering Drawing. The engineering problems can be more clearly visualized and can help to find solutions with greater ease. A designer has to imagine about many features of an object that cannot be communicated by verbal/written description. The designs are thought in the mind of designer in terms of 'visual images'. They can be reviewed and modified before they are finalized. The designer translates the mental picture into a drawing or model that will produce a similar picture in the mind of every one who sees the drawing.

Technical Graphics or Engineering Drawing, the language of engineers and technologists also has been devised according to certain rules. As an engineering drawing displays the information on shape, size and other details with graphic symbols, it conveys the same ideas to every trained person. Irrespective of language barriers, the drawing can be effectively used in any country and universally. Thus, "the engineering drawing is the worldly language of engineers". Hence, all engineers should know the Engineering Drawing.

OBJECTIVES IN DRAWING

Accuracy: The drawings are not useful to the maximum extent if they are not accurate.

Speed: "Convert Time into Money" in industry. There is no place for the slow technician, or engineer. Speed is not attained in a hurry; it should be with intelligent and continuous work. It comes with practice.

Legibility: Drawing is a means of communication to others, and that it should be clear and legible to serve its purpose. Care should be taken especially in dimensioning and lettering.

Neatness: If a drawing is to be acceptable it should be clean and neat because even small dust particle can act as smallest entity as point.

DRAWING INSTRUMENTS

The accuracy and speed of the Engineering Drawing is aided by tools. The conventional tools used to make engineering drawing have evolved over years to develop geometry. Conventional tools are devices used in making engineering drawings. It includes drawing straight lines, inclined lines, making arcs and circles, to increase speed with which drawings are made. The tools and accessories typically used are:

(a) Wood and Mechanical Pencils (2H, H, HB, B, 2B, etc.)
(b) T-square or Mini-drafter, 45° and 30°/60° set squares (triangles)
(c) Compass and dividers
(d) Protractor
(e) Eraser
(f) Scales set (metric)
(g) Irregular curve (French curves)
(h) Drawing sheets (A1/A2/A3/A4 size)
(i) Drawing Clips
(j) Drawing Board, etc.

COMPUTER AIDED DRAWING TOOLS

Conventional tools can be useful for sketching and rough layout. The use of computers in every phase of engineering, design, drawing, analysis is well known. The integration of computers into the manufacturing industry from design to marketing, is changing the methods used in the technical education and training of technicians, designers and engineers.

A computer system consists of hardware and software. The various pieces of physical equipment that comprises a computer system are known as hardware. The programs, instructions that permit computer system to operate are classified as software. Computer software is categorized as either application programs or operating system (OS) programs. Operating system programs are set of instructions that control the operation of computer and peripheral devices. This type of program may also provide support for activities and programs such as input/output (I/O) control, editing, storage, assigning drives for I/O, in addition to providing support for standard system commands and networking. Some typically used hardware is explained below.

Central Processing Unit

Most of the central processing units (CPU) use Pentium chips. They are available with random access memory (RAM) ranging from 512 mega bytes (MB) to a few giga bytes (GB). A byte consists of eight bits. Bit is acronym for binary digit which can have on or off. Clock speed plays an important role in the computational speed. Higher the clock speed higher the computational and processing speed.

Hard Disk

Hard disk is an internal storage device. It stores the programs, drawings, documents and other data inside the computer. Hard disks up to 120 GB capacity are available with PC based CAD systems.

Display Devices

The most obvious component of a CAD system is the video display screen or monitor. It is familiar piece of equipment because it looks like a TV screen. The most common forms of monitors are vector stroke and raster scan displays. The resolution of the display depends upon the picture (pix) and elements (el). The greater the number of pixel on the screen provides higher the resolution. Low resolution screens may produce lines that have a jagged look which can be seen predominantly in inclined lines or curves.

Color and Monochrome

The color monitor is similar to a color TV set. A pixel on color screen is actually composed of three primary colors, red, green, and blue (RGB). In monochrome monitors grey level can be controlled by the intensity of pixel values. Monochrome screens are available in a variety of single display colors such as green, amber, blue, black on white, and red. The size of the viewing area or screen (14″ 15″, 17″, 19″, or 21″) is measured diagonally across the screen. For CAD systems large size monitors with high resolutions are recommended.

Input Devices

The alphanumeric keyboard is a well known input device. A CAD system may use one or a combination of input devices to create images on the display screen. The main function of the input devices is to specify points and line, usually done by controlling the position of a set of cursor cross hairs on the screen. The input devices are also used for the selection of menu items and manipulate parts of the constructed image on the screen. The some main input devices are:

(a) **Tablet or Digitizer:** The tablet is a flat surface over which 'a stylus' or 'hand cursor' is moved. The position of the hand cursor or stylus is available to the computer.

(b) **Mouse:** Mouse is a hand held device with rollers on its base. Mouse has several push buttons which can be used to input commands or other information. Mouse requires only a small table area to use and is inexpensive to manufacture. Hence, it became a very popular input device.

(c) **Scanners:** A scanner is an input device used for converting an existing paper drawing made by traditional tools to CAD drawing.

(d) **Keyboard:** The keyboard is a device used to input alphanumeric data. It can also be used to select CAD menu and control the cursor movement with arrow keys on a key board. It is more cumbersome to use keyboard as an input device.

Output Devices

Printers and plotters are main output devices in a CAD system. Printers usually provide hard copies of text as well as graphics. Laser or inkjet printers are used for printing of drawings up to A0 size. Pen plotters are two types, viz. flat-bed and drum. In the flat-bed plotter, the paper is stationary and the pen holding mechanism can move in two axes.

Software

A computer program that provides specific instructions to enable a computer to do a certain task is called software. When CADD software is purchased from a manufacturer, it is known as application program or application software. This specialized software provides service for a specific endeavor such as mechanical drawing, piping layout, solid modeling, structural, and architectural drawing.

Data Storage Devices

All the data is kept in random access memory (RAM) when a job is processed in a computer. This data will be lost when the computer is turned off, hence it should be saved or stored, before the power is off. Data storage devices provide a place to save information permanently for later use. When the drawing is completed or the operator wanted to stop the work, the drawing and all the associated data must be saved before the program is exited or computer is shut off. Otherwise all accumulated data from that work session will be lost. The storage medium for the computer drafting system is hard disk. Another form of disk is compact disk (CD) drive. The CDs are removable and store the data up to 700 MB. Rewritable compact disks CD-RW permit to over write the data on an already recorded disk.

The third form is floppy disk drive. It is simple, and removable flexible plastic disks (floppies) are used in this device. Existing data can be erased and new data copied or new data over written on existing data any number of times. The other form is Memory stick (pen drive) and external Hard Disk can also be used.

CAD Software

The computer programs designed for specific tasks in response to user's requirements are called application software. It is time consuming, tedious, and expensive to develop application programs and hence it is considered advantageous to buy existing software. Some of the CAD software used for drafting and design are:

Software	Developer
THINK3	
Auto CAD	
Pro/Engineer	
CATIA	
Unigraphics	
Solidworks	
Solidedge	
CADAM	

Media

Media are the surfaces upon which the graphical information is communicated. The media used for engineering drawing are different types or grades of paper, such as tracing paper, vellum, and polyester film. Tracing paper is a thin translucent paper widely used for general purpose. Vellum is a tracing paper chemically treated to improve translucency. Polyester film (trade name Mylar) is transparent, waterproof, and difficult to tear. Mylar is an excellent drawing surface. It can be used for lead pencil or ink drawings and leaves no traces of eraser.

Special papers have been developed for CAD plotters. For example, plotter paper for fiber-tipped pens has a smooth or glossy surface to enhance line definition and minimize skipping.

BIS CONVENTIONS FOR LETTERING AND DIMENSIONS

Standards like Bureau of Indian Standards (BIS), International Standards Organization (ISO), etc., are used in engineering drawing practice. SP46:2003 gives the consolidated list of BIS and ISO codes for engineering drawing practice.

Two types of lettering formats in both upper and lower case are used. Type A in this type of lettering the height of letter is divided into 14 equal parts. Type B in this type of lettering the height of letter is divided into 10 equal parts.

LETTERING AND DIMENSIONING WITH CAD

Lettering is called text when using a CAD system. The TEXT or FONT command is one of that can be found in a section of the menu labeled text or text attributes. The first decision regarding the text is to determine its height, width, and slant angle. Most CAD systems maintain default text size that is used if the operator chooses not to change it. Location can be identified using a pointing input device. After deciding the location, text can be keyed in. Another method is type the text and it appears on the screen with the crosshairs at the point of location previously specified. Then the text can be dragged to the desired location, and placed in the position by pressing a button on the keyboard or mouse.

Dimensioning is called distance between, distance, angular dimension, and smart dimension when using a CAD system. The command is executed by selecting the icon and click on the geometry to get the dimensions. Even the arrow head/slash/dot/eee as per requirement is taken care using CAD system very systematically as per standards.

SELECTION OF DRAWING SHEET SIZE AND SCALE

The drawing sheet size and the scale for the drawing an object can be systematically selected as per the requirement. The standard drawing sheet sizes used are A_4 (841 × 1189) as shown below. The commonly used drawing scales are enlarged (2 : 1, 5 : 1, 10 : 1, 20 : 1, 50 : 1), full size (1 : 1) and reduced (1 : 2, 1 : 5, 1 : 10, 1 : 100).

Designation	Dimensions (mm)
A0	841 × 1189
A1	594 × 841
A2	420 × 594
A3	297 × 420
A4	210 × 297

Selection of Sizes

The original drawing should be made on the smallest sheet permitting the necessary clarity and resolution. Drawings may be used with their longer sides positioned either horizontally as shown in Fig. 1.1 or vertically as shown in Fig 1.2. General features of a drawing sheet with border, edge, grid reference, title block is shown in Fig 1.3.

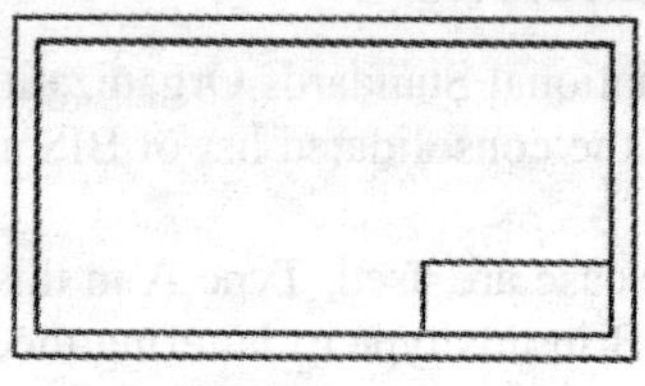

Fig. 1.1 Horizontal Sheet

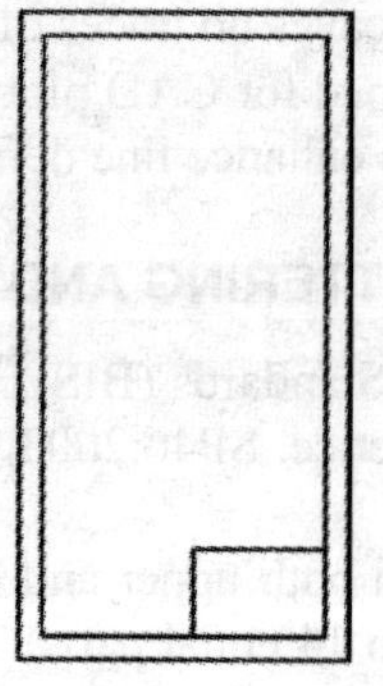

Fig. 1.2 Vertical Sheet

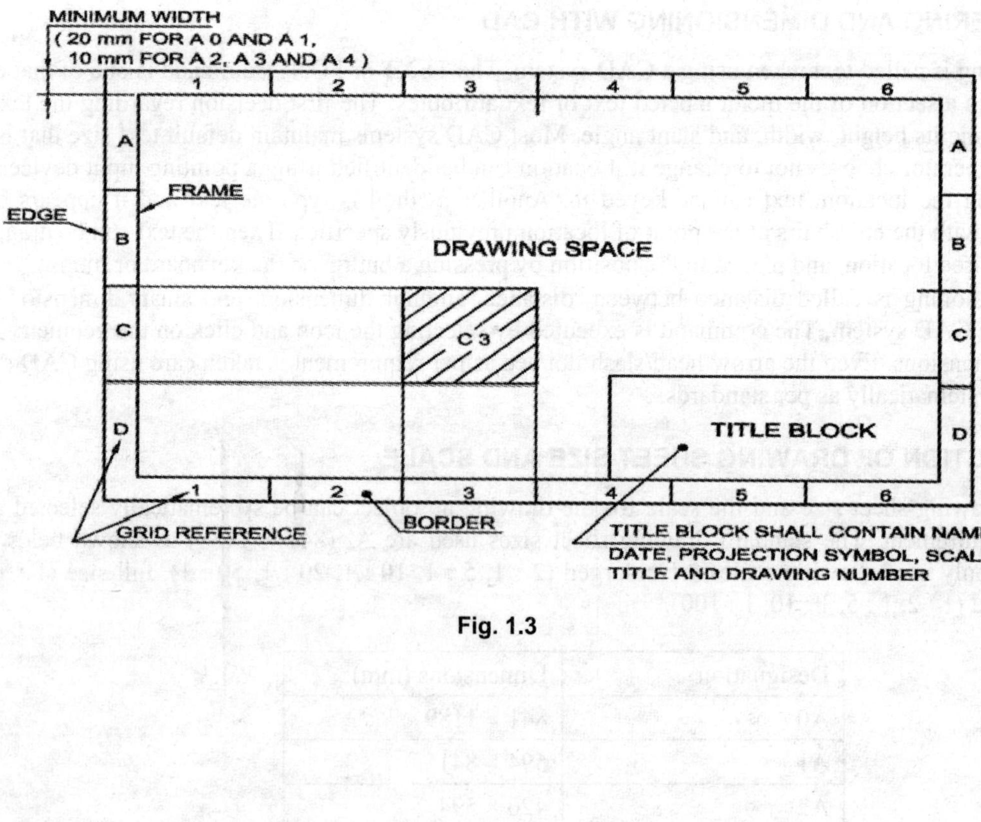

Fig. 1.3

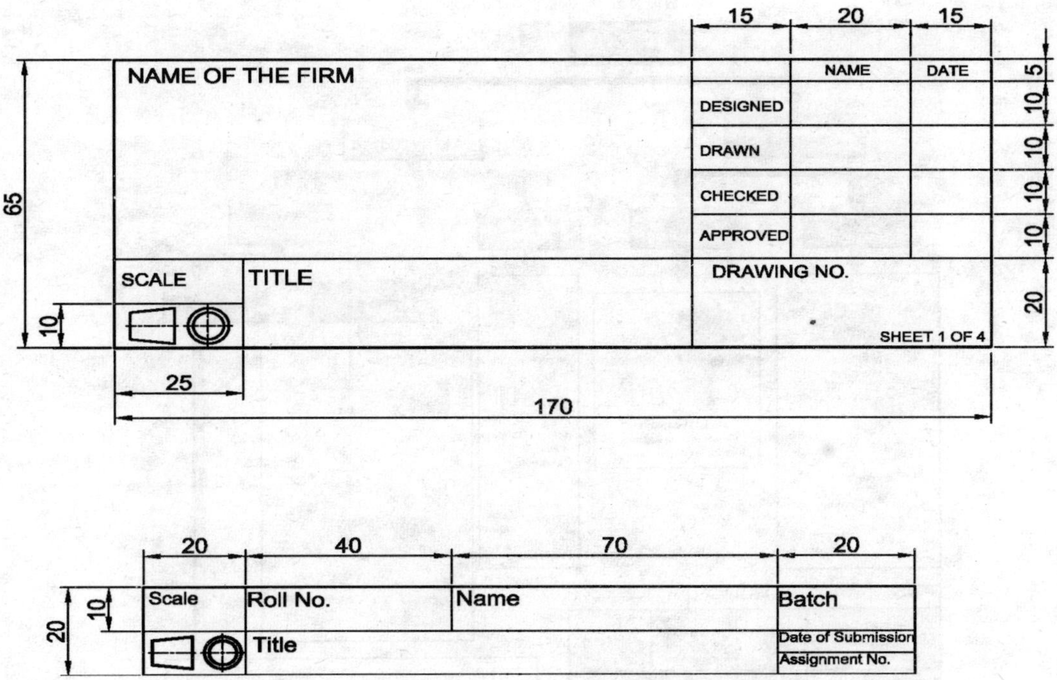

Fig. 1.4 General Features of Drawing Sheet

Title Block

The title block should be within the drawing space located at the bottom right hand corner. The direction of viewing of the title block should correspond in general with that of the drawing. Title block should preferably consist of one or more adjoining rectangles. These may be sub-divided into boxes for the insertion of specific information such as:

(i) Name of the firm
(ii) Title of the drawing
(iii) Drawing number
(iv) Scale
(v) Projection symbol (first angle or third angle)
(vi) Drawing number

Initials of staff designed, drawn, and approved. Title blocks used are shown in Figure 1.4.

Engineering Graphics are prepared to show the shape and size of the product/object to be manufactured or constructed. Shape is described by projection and size is described by the dimensions. All objects are in three dimensions (3D) whereas the picture plane or projection planes are in two dimensions (2D). The 3D objects are represented in a 2D plane by means of projections.

Projection is a process of causing an image by rays of light taken in a particular direction from an object to a picture plane. The imaginary ray of light between the object and the projection plane is called line of sight or projector. The projection methods are categorized as shown on next page.

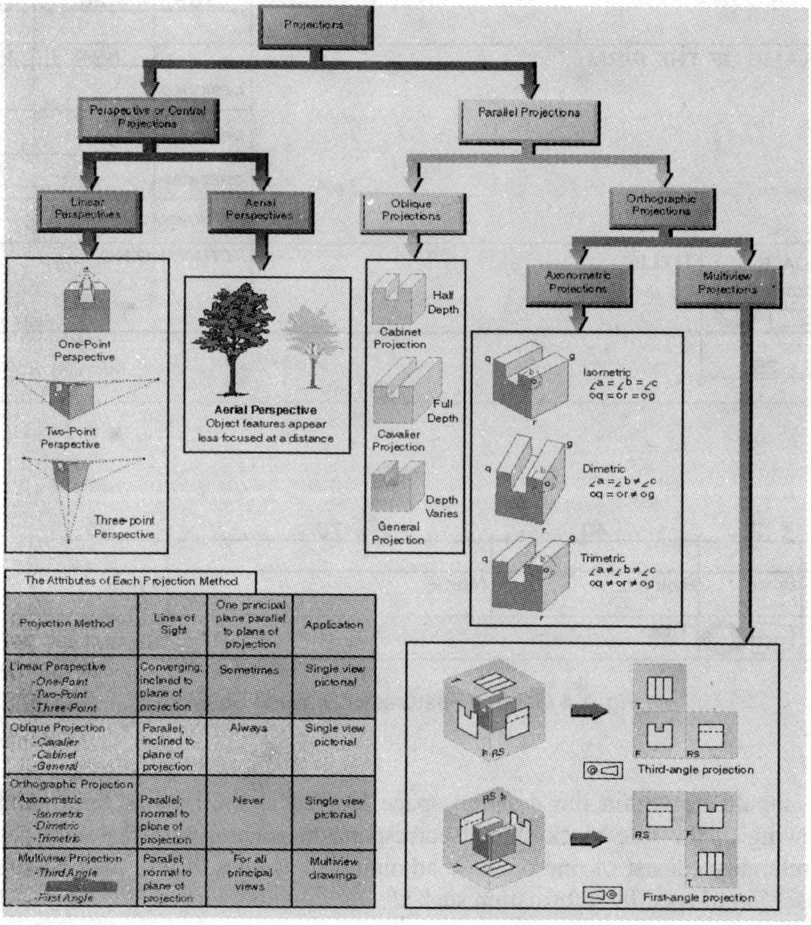

The Attributes of Each Projection Method

Projection Method	Lines of Sight	One principal plane parallel to plane of projection	Application
Linear Perspective -One-Point -Two-Point -Three-Point	Converging; inclined to plane of projection	Sometimes	Single view pictorial
Oblique Projection -Cavalier -Cabinet -General	Parallel; inclined to plane of projection	Always	Single view pictorial
Orthographic Projection Axonometric -Isometric -Dimetric -Trimetric	Parallel; normal to plane of projection	Never	Single view pictorial
Multiview Projection -Third Angle -First Angle	Parallel; normal to plane of projection	For all principal views	Multiview drawings

First Angle Projection

An arrangement of vertical, horizontal, and profile planes and quadrants used to draw first angle projections is shown below. Front view is projected onto the vertical plane, top view onto the horizontal plane, and side view onto the profile plane.

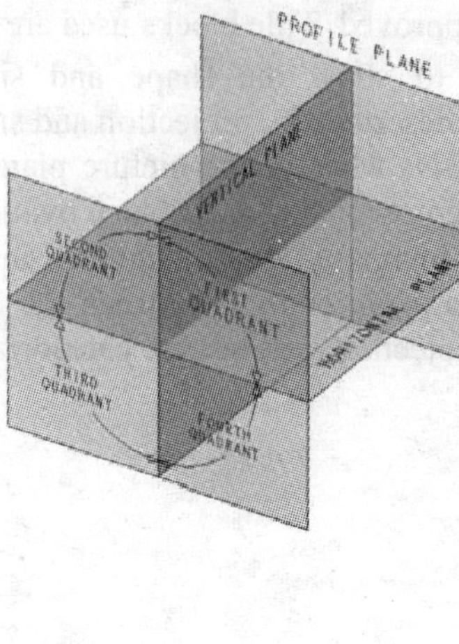

Multiview Projection

It consists of a set of two or more orthographic views of an object taken from different directions which are mutually perpendicular. These views are arranged relative to each other in a particular way. Each of these views shows the shape of the object for a particular view direction. Multiple views collectively describe the object completely and exactly. Hence multiview projections are used in engineering to describe the true shape of any object.

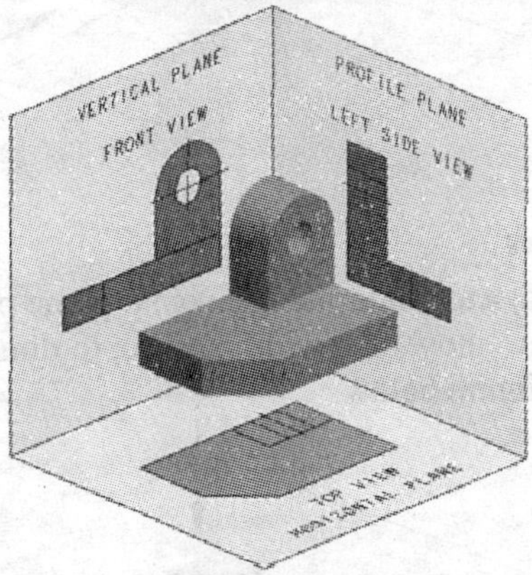

Orthographic Projection

In orthographic projection, the projectors are parallel and perpendicular to the plane of projection. Orthographic projections on mutually perpendicular projection planes will fully describe the object in its shape and size. Hence, all design and manufacturing drawings are made with orthographic projections.

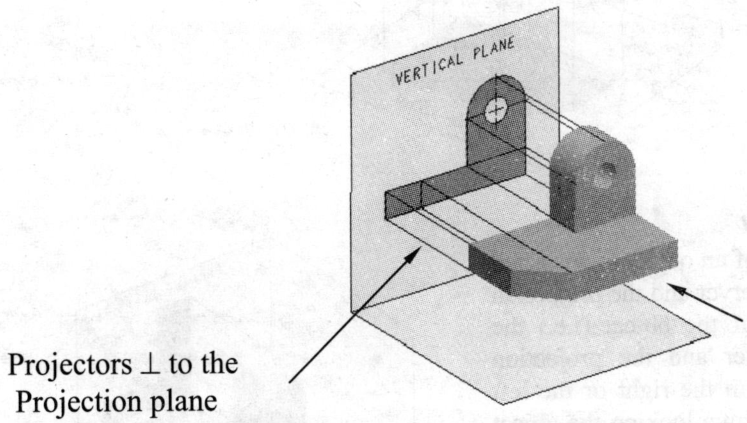

Vertical Plane and Front Elevation

A view looking from the front is projected onto the vertical plane. This view is called front view or front elevation and shows the width and height dimensions. A vertical plane of projection which is behind the object in relation to the observer is shown in figure below.

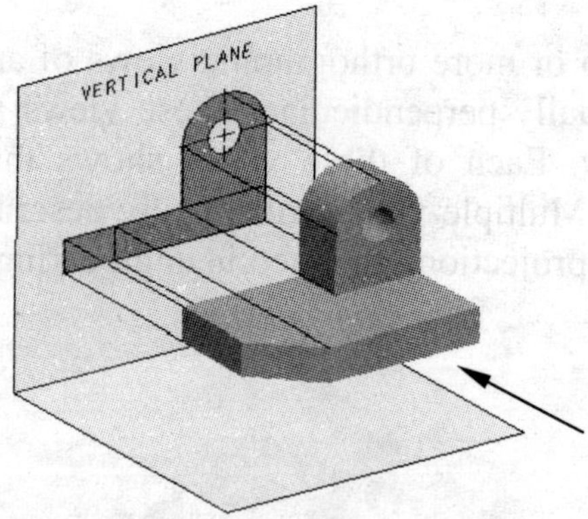

Horizontal Plane and Top View

A view looking from the top is projected onto the horizontal plane placed below the object. This view is called top view or plan. Top view shows the width and depth dimensions of an object. A horizontal plane with a top view is shown in figure below.

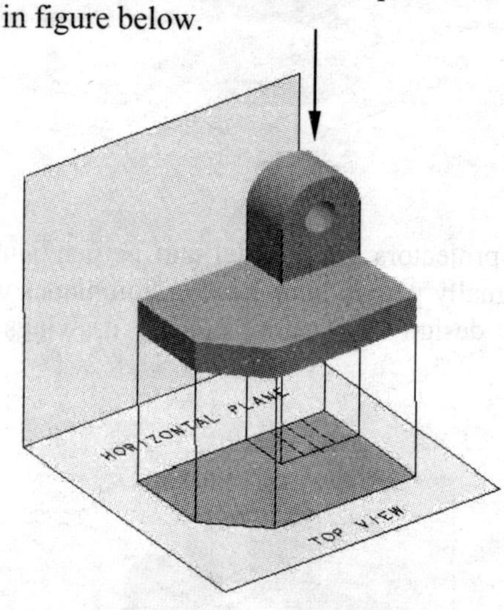

Profile Plane and End View

A view looking from the side of an object is projected onto the profile plane. The observer and the projection plane are on different sides of the object (i.e.) the object is between the observer and the projection plane. The viewing can be from the right or the left side of the object. The view drawn looking the object from the right is called right side view or right end elevation. The view looking the object from the left is called left side view or left end elevation. Side view of an object shows the depth and height dimensions. A profile plane with a left side view is shown in figure below.

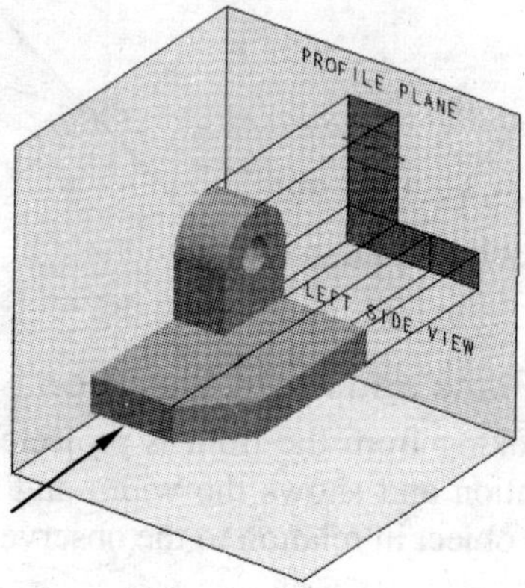

Projection in First Angle

An object placed in the first quadrant. The vertical plane is behind the object, horizontal plane below the object, and profile plane to right of the object. The views with the corresponding planes are shown in figure. The top view is seen below the elevation and left side view is seen on the right of front view. This is the arrangement of views in the first angle projection.

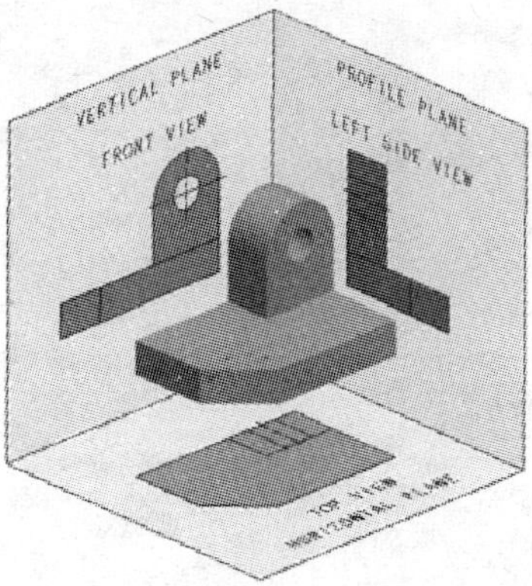

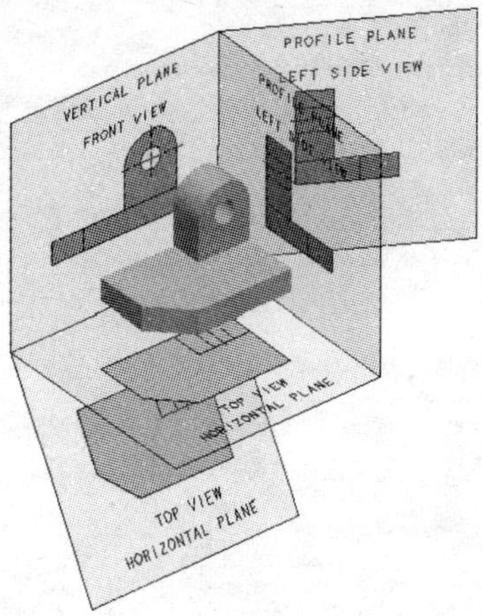

Projection in Third Angle

An object placed in the third quadrant. The vertical plane is in front of the object, horizontal plane above the object and profile plane to the left of the object. The views with corresponding planes are shown in figure. Top view is above the front view and left side view is to the left of the front view. This is the arrangement of the views in third angle projection.

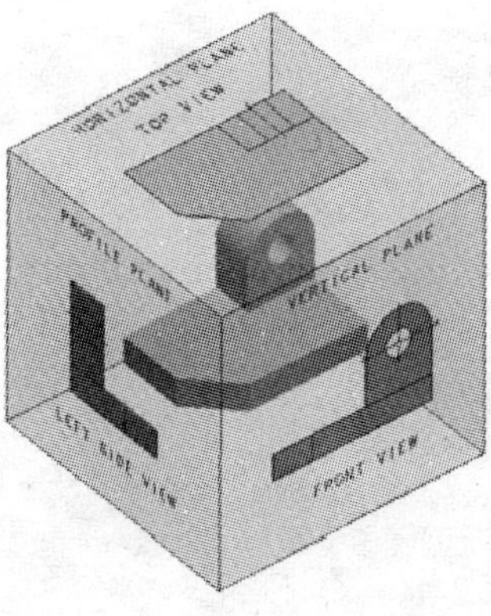

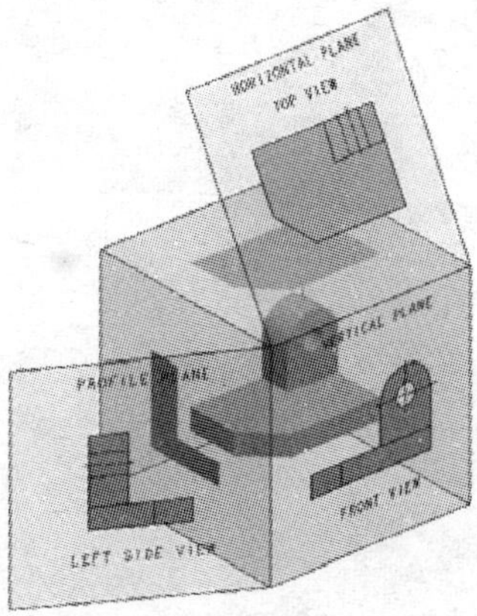

■■■

2

ORTHOGRAPHIC PROJECTIONS OF POINTS

INTRODUCTION

- A point usually represented by a dot. It is dimensionless geometrical entity which has position but no magnitude. Whereas in computer aided engineering drawing the point has dimension but it is not considered or neglected. A point is obtained wherever two straight or curved lines intersect each other.
- Projection of points in various quadrants is the basis for projection of lines, projection of planes and projection of solids.
- In a conventional coordinate system, the position of a point in space is denoted by its three coordinates i.e., x, y and z.
- In engineering drawing two planes (horizontal plane and vertical plane) are used to present a point and sometimes one more plane (profile plane).
- The position of point can be as shown below; these are the only nine positions in projection of points.

When	VP	HP	quadrant
Point is	Infront	Above	I
Point is	Behind	Above	II
Point is	Behind	Below	III
Point is	Infront	Below	IV
Point is	Infront	In or on	I or IV
Point is	In or on	Above	I or II
Point is	Behind	In or on	II or III
Point is	In or on	Below	III or IV
Point is	In or on	In or on	I, II, III or IV

System of Notation

1. The actual points in space are denoted by capital letters A, B, C etc.
2. The front view (FV) of a points are denoted by their corresponding lower case letters with dashes as a′, b′, c′, etc.
3. The top view (TV) of a points are denoted by their corresponding lower case letters without dashes as a, b, c etc.
4. The side view (SV) of a points are denoted by their corresponding lower case letters with double dashes as a″, b″, c″ etc.
5. Projectors are always drawn as continuous thin lines.
6. Points with Dot.

In Computer Aided Engineering Graphics for projection of points following commands are used other than evoking software, opening file, saving file and giving print command. Using these minimum nine commands any type of projection of point problem can be solved they are as follows:

1. Select tool Command.
2. Point command.
3. Poly-line command.
4. Two point line command.
5. Parallel line command.
6. Bisector command.
7. Smart dimension command.
8. Line width command.
9. Insert text command.

PROBLEM 2.1

A point P is 30 mm in front of VP, 40 mm above HP and 50 mm from RPP. Draw its projections.

SOLUTION

Manual Method

(a) Draw the XY line. Mark VP above it and HP below it.
(b) Mark a point 40 mm above XY line. This is the front view of P. Name it as a p′.
(c) Draw a vertical projector downwards through p′ measure a distance of 30 mm below XY line. This is the top view of P. Name it as p.
(d) Draw a reference line X_1Y_1 perpendicular to XY at a distance of 50 mm from the projector, which intersects at O.
(e) Draw a line passing through O inclined at 45° in HP.
(f) Draw a horizontal projector through P until it meets 45° line, from there draw a vertical projector upwards above XY line.
(g) Draw a horizontal projector through P′. which gives lefts side view. Name as P″.

Computer Aided Drafting Procedure

1. Open the **SOFTWARE**. Click on the **DRAWING** in the open dialog box and say **OK**.

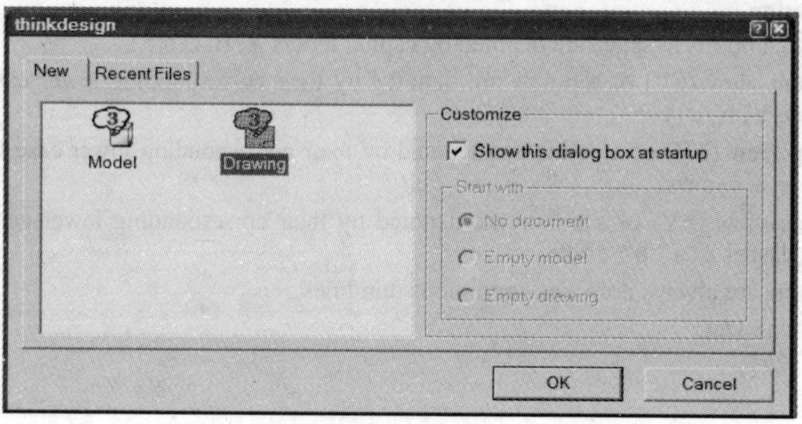

2. To set up the sheet of required size (Ex: A4) by selecting **TOOLS** from Main Menu Bar and click on **OPTIONS/PROPERTIES**. Select document properties in dialog box appeared and then select drawing in selection panel. Select the required size say A4, and click **OK**.

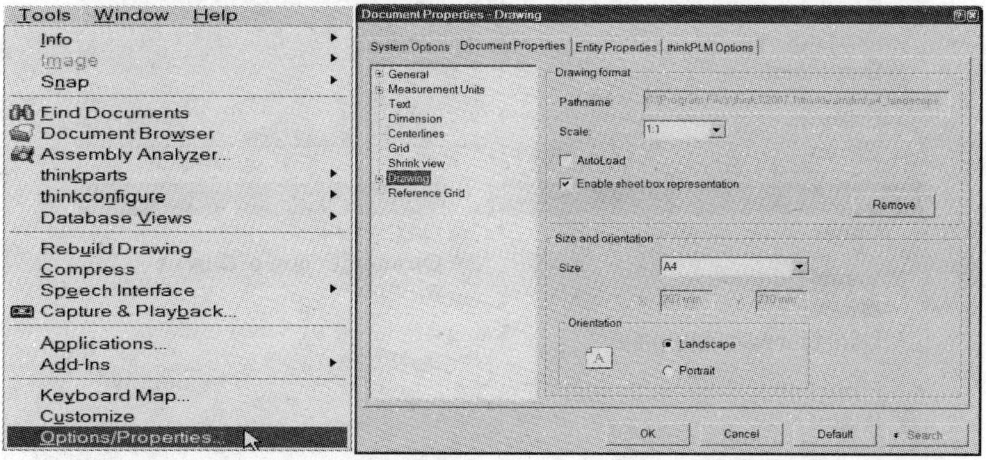

3. Draw the line by using **POLYLINE**  command from drafting tool bar.

4. Make Annotation X, Y, VP, and HP to the line drawn by using **INSERT TEXT** Command  from drafting tool bar, just by typing X, Y, VP and HP in Text Box and insert these in the required position by left click of the mouse, as shown below.

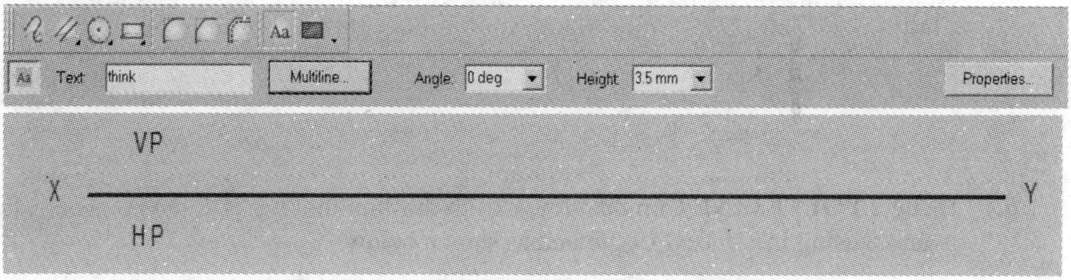

5. As per the problem, 40 mm above the HP we see in VP and 30 mm in front of VP we see in HP. Let us mark p′and p above and below XY line using the **POINT** Command  by selecting Tools → Points → Absolute/Delta. Once Absolute/Delta is selected we get selection list. In mode select relative point, let the option be Cartesian. Now select the reference point on line anywhere required and substitute X = 0, Y = 40 in mini dialog box. Next substitute X = 0 and Y = –30 in mini dialog box or X = 0 and Y = –70 from the created point.

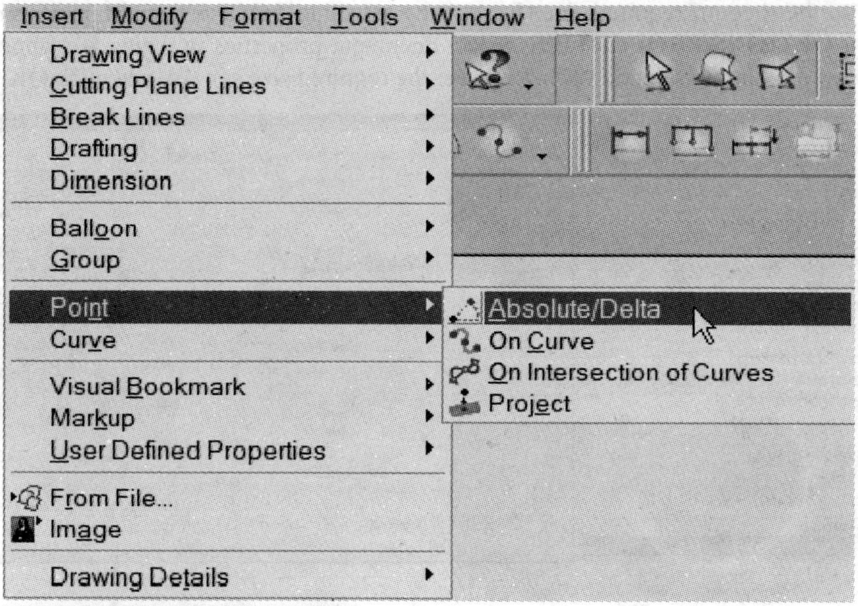

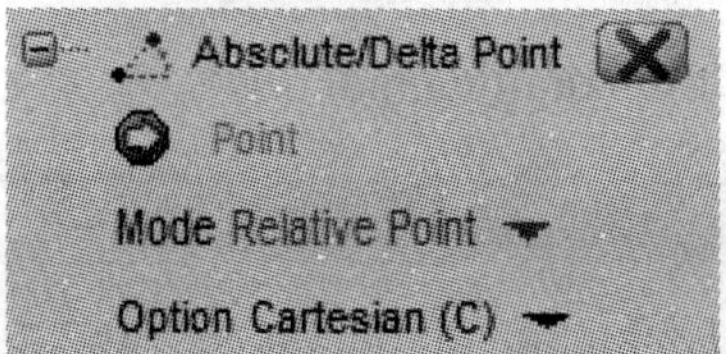

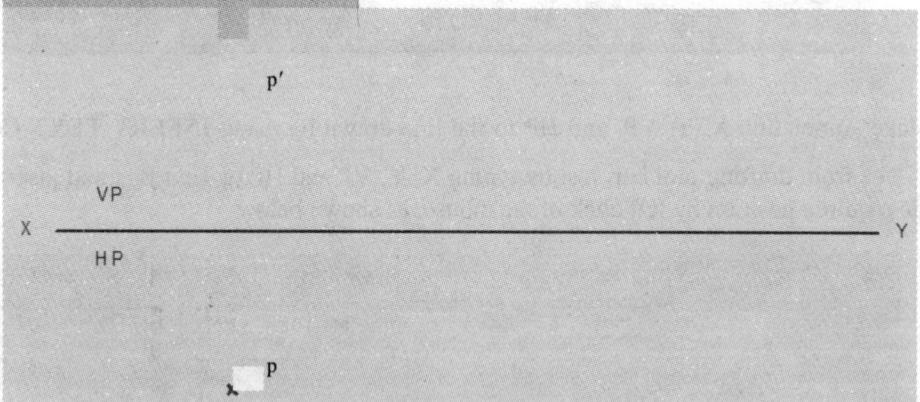

6. Using **2 POINT LINE** Command  from drafting tool bar join the points created and mark p′ and p using Insert Text Command as shown below.

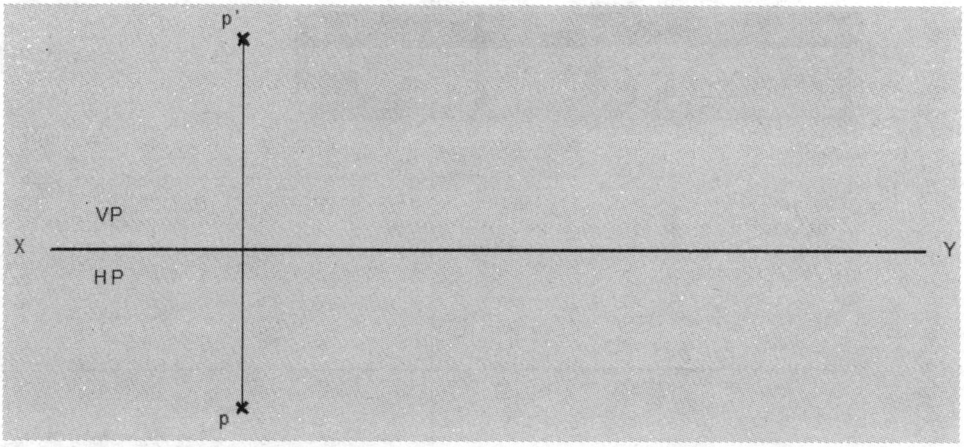

7. Draw the X_1Y_1 line perpendicular to XY line drawn at a distance of 50 mm from the projection line respectively to intersection between VP and RPP at O, using **PARALLEL LINE** Command  in Drafting tool bar by selecting the projection line and substitute 50 mm in the distance mini dialog box.

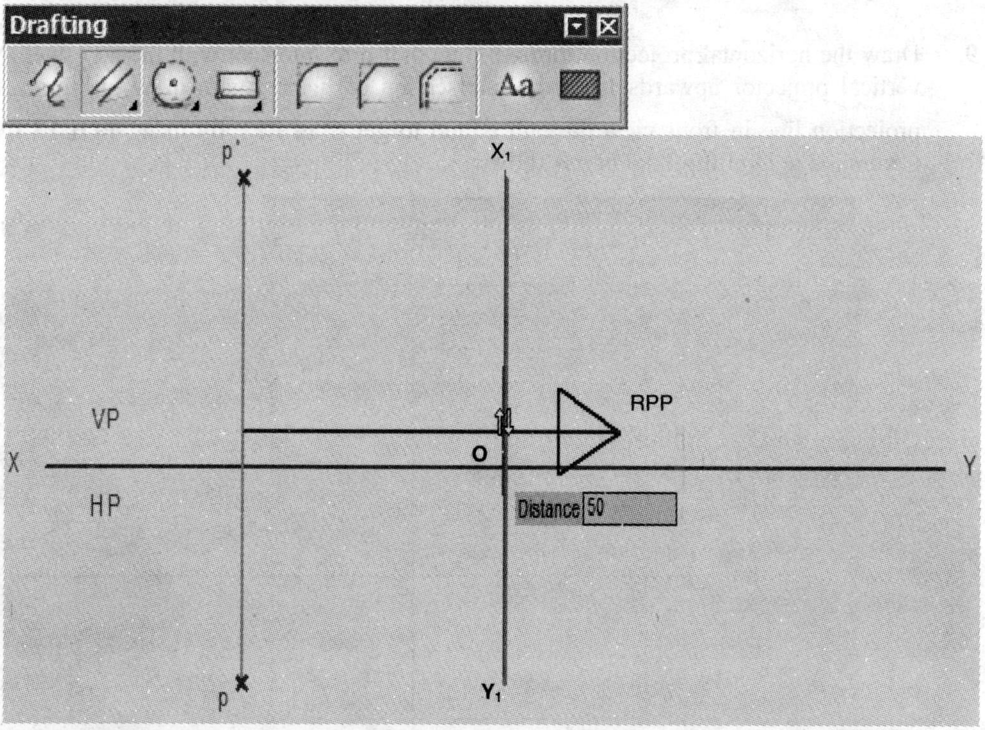

8. To draw the side view draw 45° line through the point O using **BISECTOR**  command in Drafting tool bar by selecting XY and X_1Y_1 line and substitute to required dimension in distance mini dialog box.

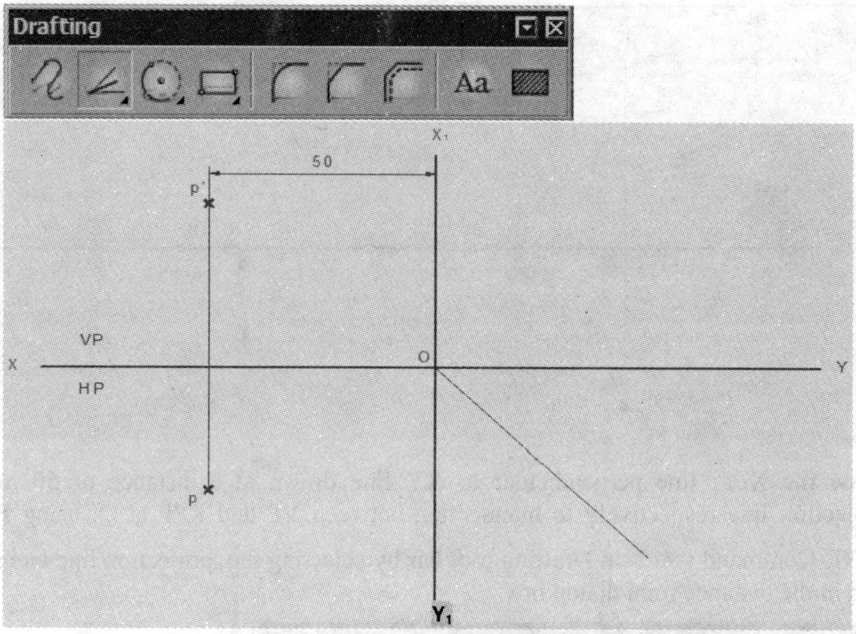

9. Draw the horizontal projection through the point p to intersect with the 45° line. Now draw vertical projector upwards from the intersection of lines. Again draw one more horizontal projection line in front view through p′ and to get p″ in RPP by using **POLYLINE** Command in Drafting Tool bar as shown.

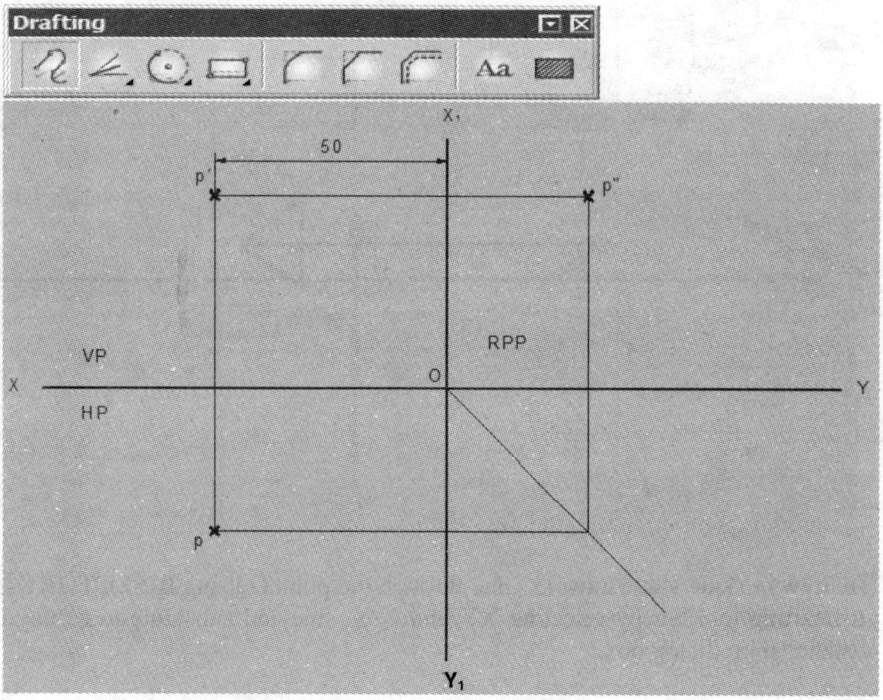

10. Using **SMART DIMENSION** Command 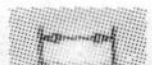 in drawing tool bar dimension the drawing as shown.

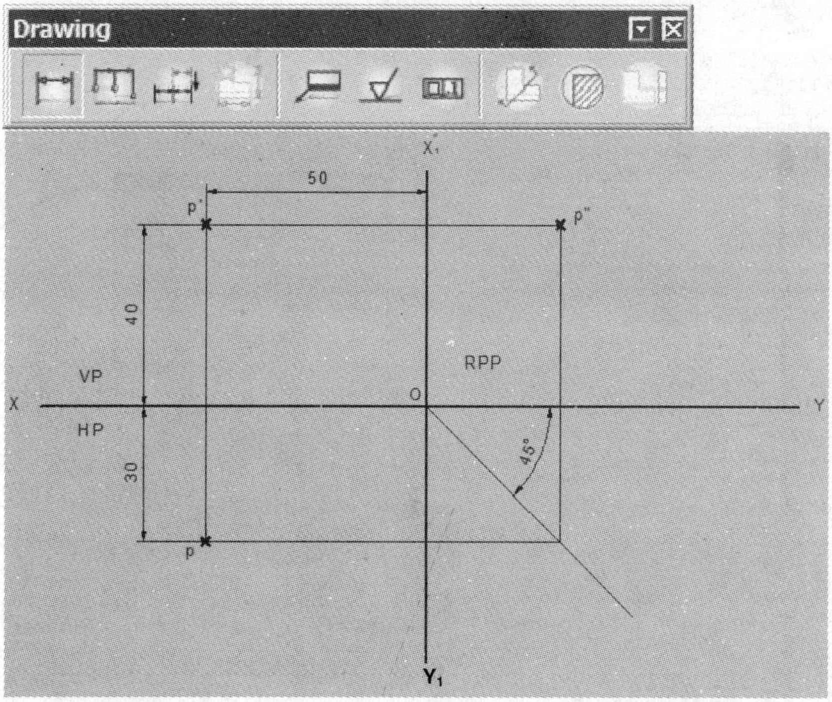

11. To make drawing as a standard drawing change the thickness of the lines by using **LINE WIDTH**  command from status bar. Select the projection lines and 45° line, then assign to line width 1 and Select the XY & X_1Y_1 line assign to line width 2.

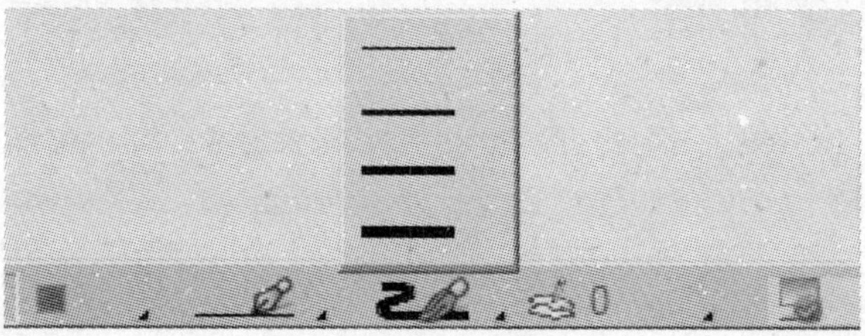

12. To get a Hard Copy of the standard drawing select print from file menu bar. Print dialog window will appear select page and change width to Entities and select the activated button  now substitute width 1 as 0.05 mm, width 2 as 0.15 mm, width 3 as 0 mm and width 4 as 2 mm and say **OK.** Select print to get a hard copy and finally save the file. The required standard drawing is as shown below.

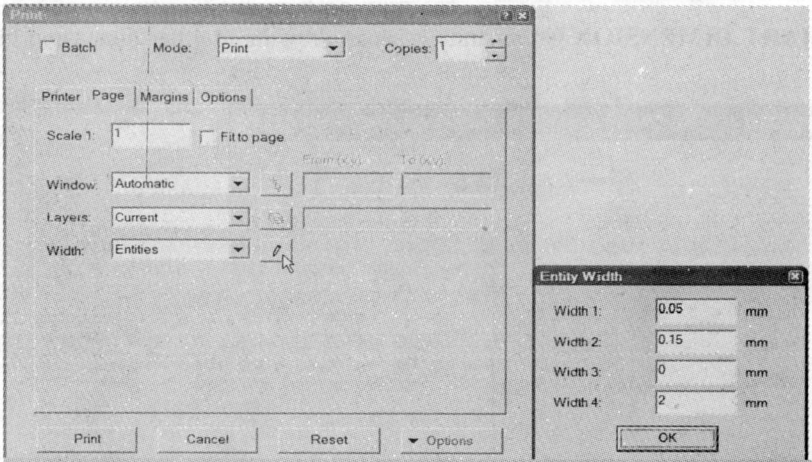

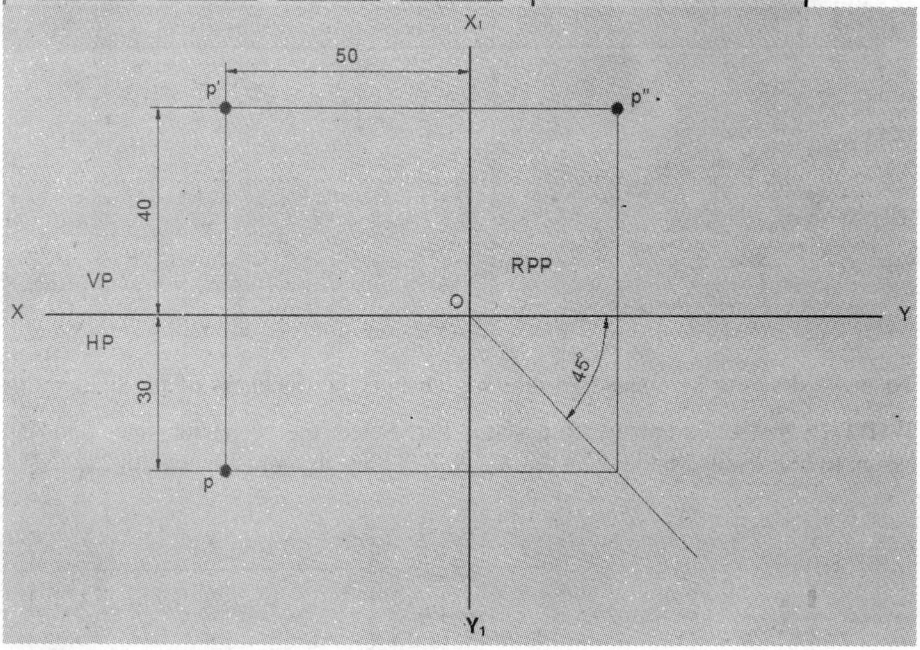

PROBLEM 2.2

The point p is 45 mm above HP, 60 mm behind VP and 30 mm from RPP. Draw the three principle views of the point.

SOLUTION

Manual Method

(a) Draw the XY line. Mark VP and HP above it.

(b) Mark a point 45 mm above XY line. This is the front view of p. Name it as a p′.

(c) Draw a vertical projector through p, measure a distance of 60 mm above XY line. This is the top view of p. Name it as p.

(d) Draw a reference line X_1Y_1 perpendicular to XY at a distance of 30 mm from the projector, which intersects at O.

(e) Draw a line passing through O inclined at 45° in HP.

(f) Draw a horizontal projector through p until it meets 45° line, from there draw a vertical projector downwards.

(g) Draw a horizontal projector through p′ which gives left side view. Name as p″.

Computer Aided Drafting Procedure

1. Open the **SOFTWARE**. Click on the **DRAWING** in the open dialog box and say **OK**.

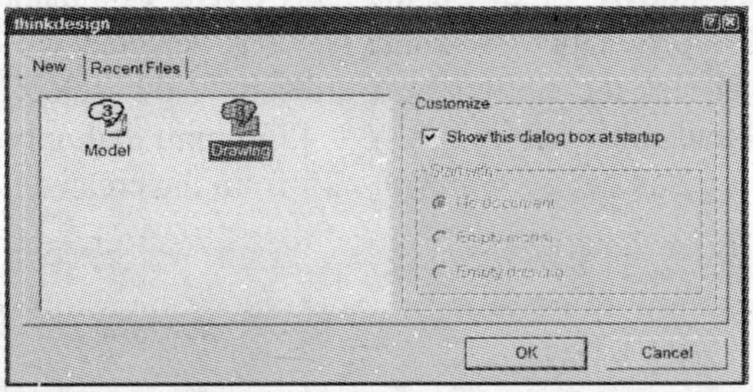

2. To set up the sheet of required size (Ex: A4) by selecting **TOOLS** from Main Menu Bar and click on **OPTIONS/PROPERTIES**. Select document properties in dialog box appeared and then select drawing in selection panel. Select the required size say A4, and click **OK**.

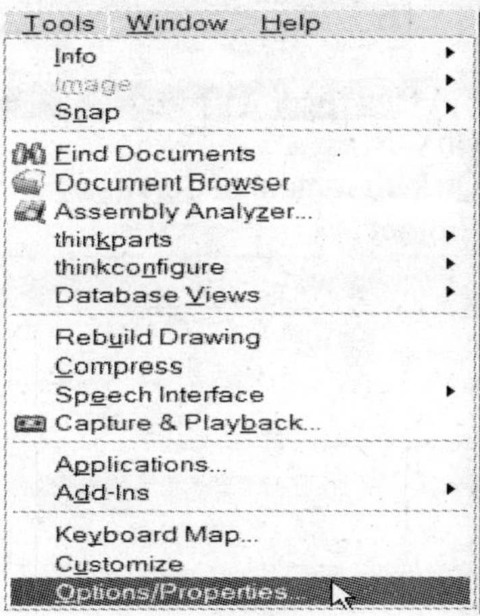

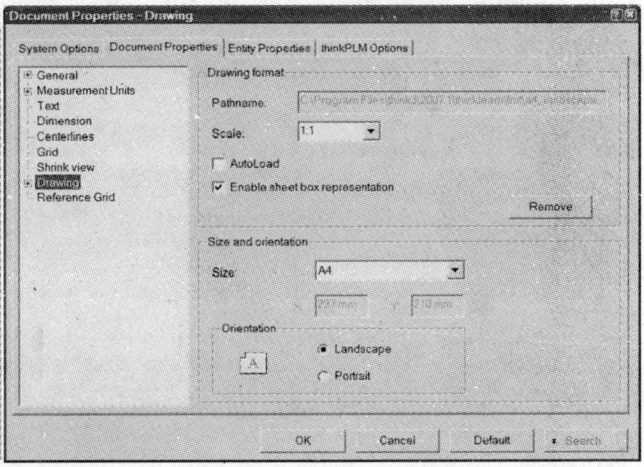

3. Draw the line by using **POLYLINE**  command from drafting tool bar.

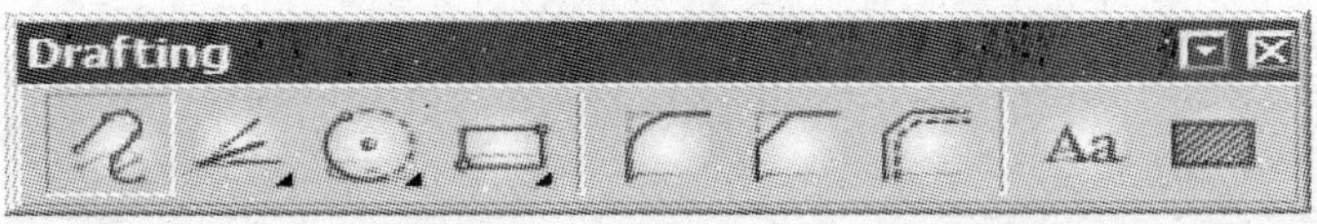

4. Make Annotation X, Y, VP, and HP to the line drawn by using **INSERT TEXT** Command 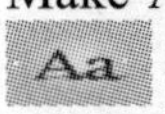 from drafting tool bar, just by typing X, Y, VP and HP in Text Box and insert these in the required position by left click of the mouse, as shown below.

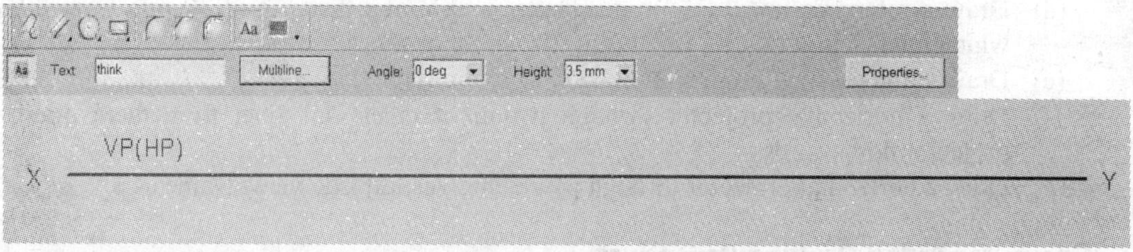

5. As per the problem, 45 mm above the HP we see in VP and 60 mm behind VP we see in HP. Let us mark p′ and p above XY line using the **POINT** Command  by selecting Tools→ Points → Absolute/Delta. Once Absolute/Delta is selected we get selection list. In mode select relative point, let the option be Cartesian. Now select the reference point on line anywhere required and substitute X = 0, Y = 45 in mini dialog box. Next substitute X = 0 and Y = 60 in mini dialog box or X = 0 and Y = 15 from the created point.

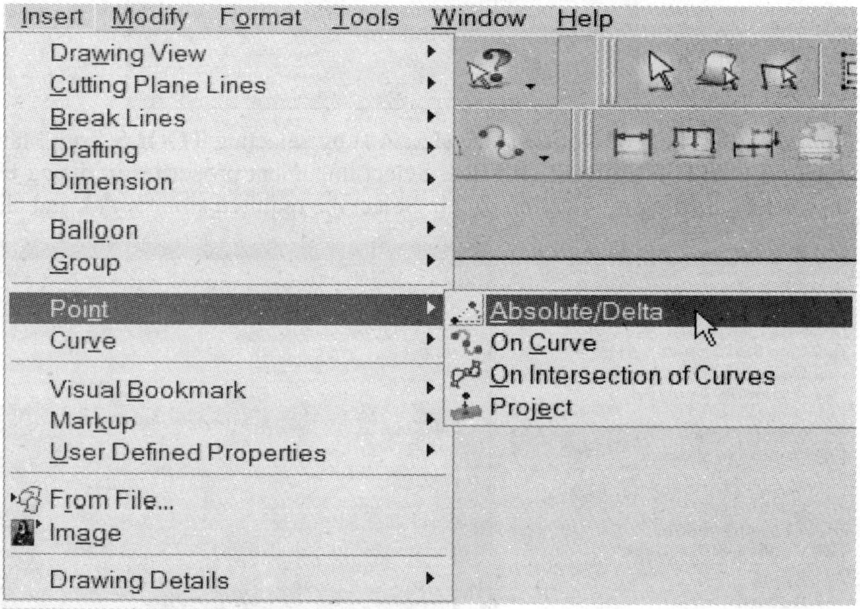

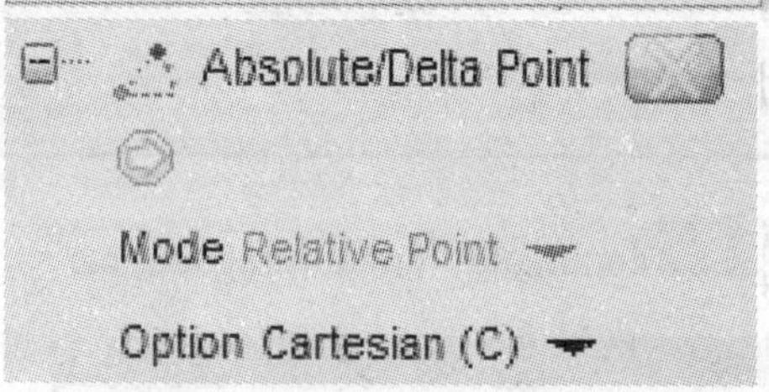

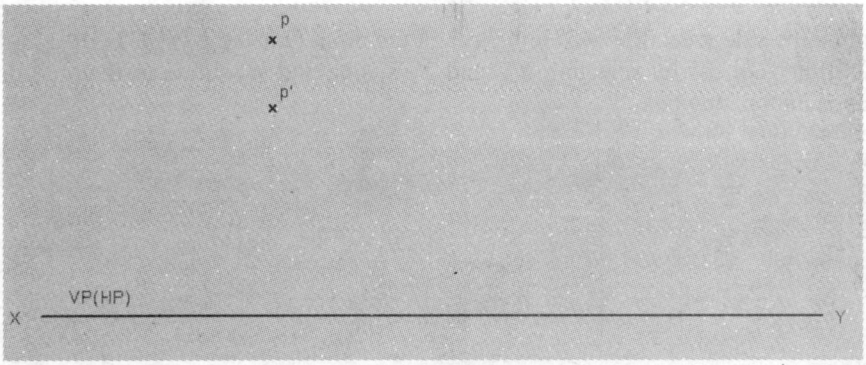

6. Using **2 POINT LINE** Command  from drafting tool bar join the points created and mark p′ and p using Insert Text Command as shown below.

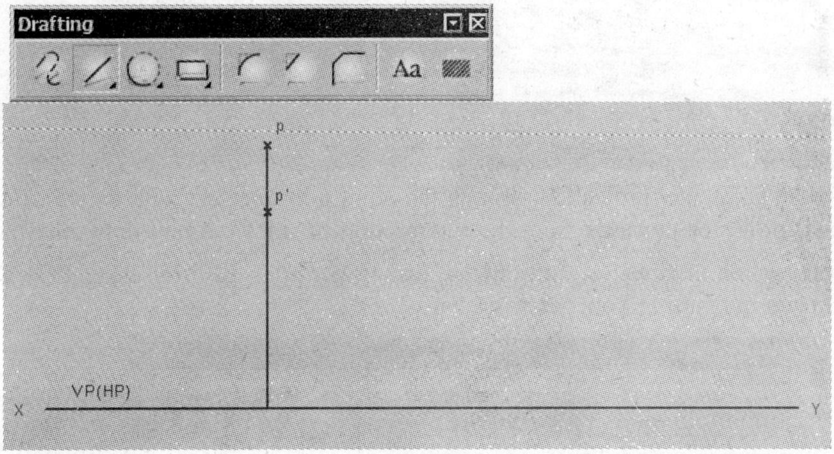

7. Draw the X_1Y_1 line perpendicular to XY line drawn at a distance of 30mm from the projection line representing the intersection between VP and RPP at O, using **PARALLEL LINE** command 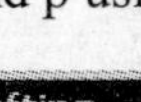 in Drafting tool bar by selecting the projection line and substitute 30 mm in the distance mini dialog box.

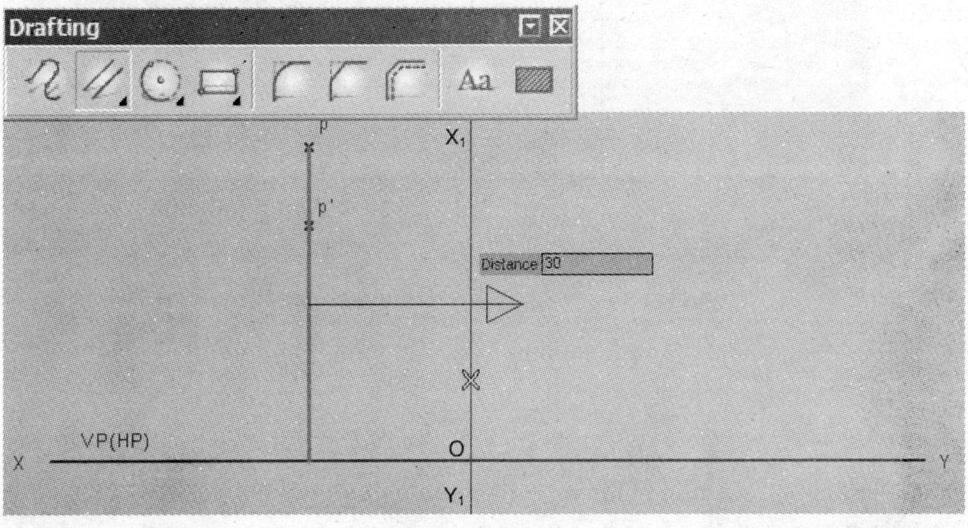

8. To draw the side view draw 45° line through the point O using **BISECTOR** command in Drafting tool bar by selecting XY and X_1Y_1 line and substitute to required dimension in distance mini dialog box.

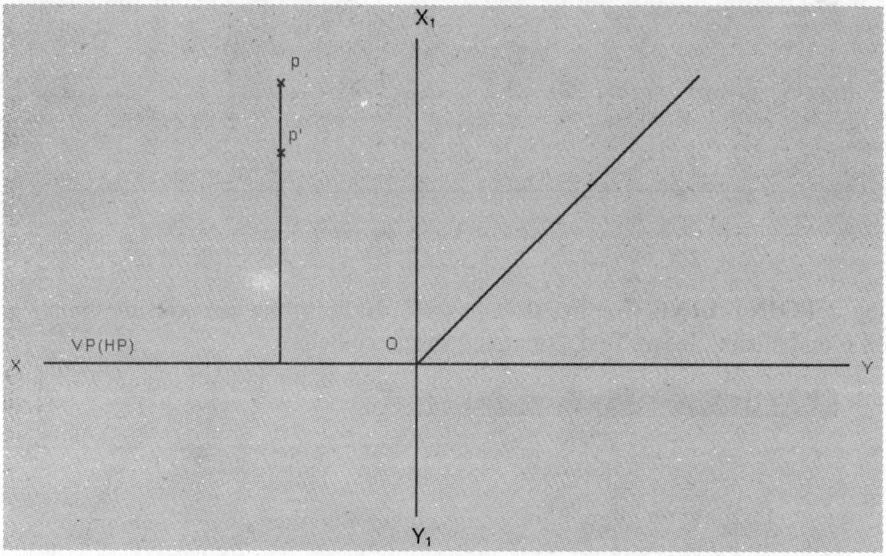

9. Draw the horizontal projection through the point p to intersect with the 45° line. Now draw vertical projector upwards from the intersection of lines. Again draw one more horizontal projection line in front view through p′ and to get p″ in RPP by using **POLYLINE** Command in Drafting Tool bar as shown.

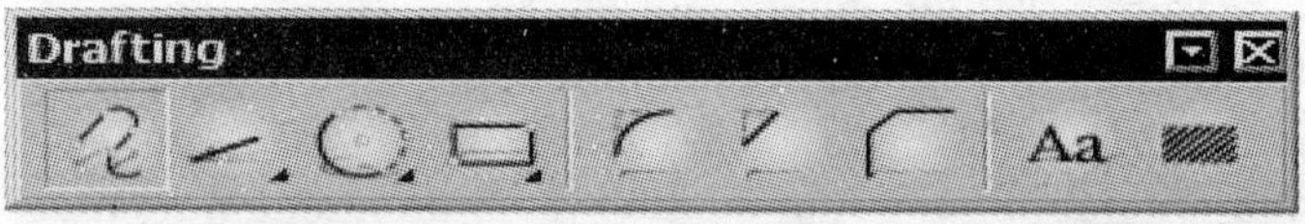

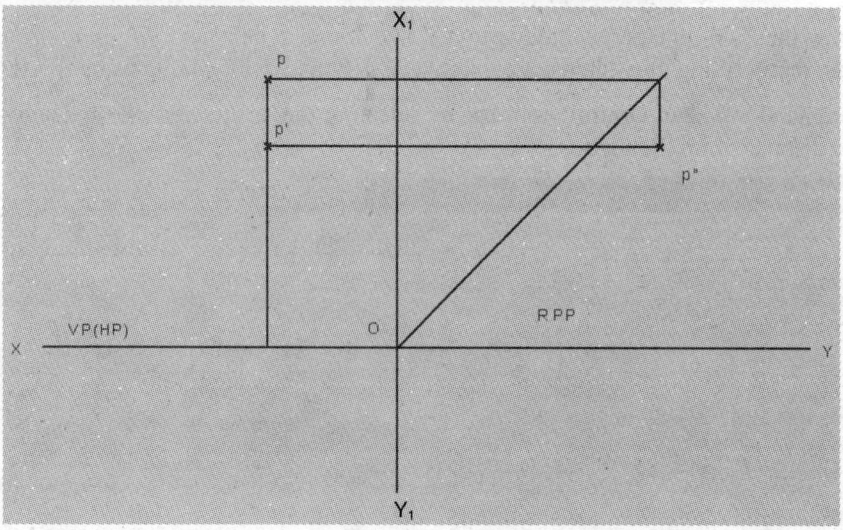

10. **USING SMART DIMENSION** Command in drawing tool bar dimension the drawing as shown.

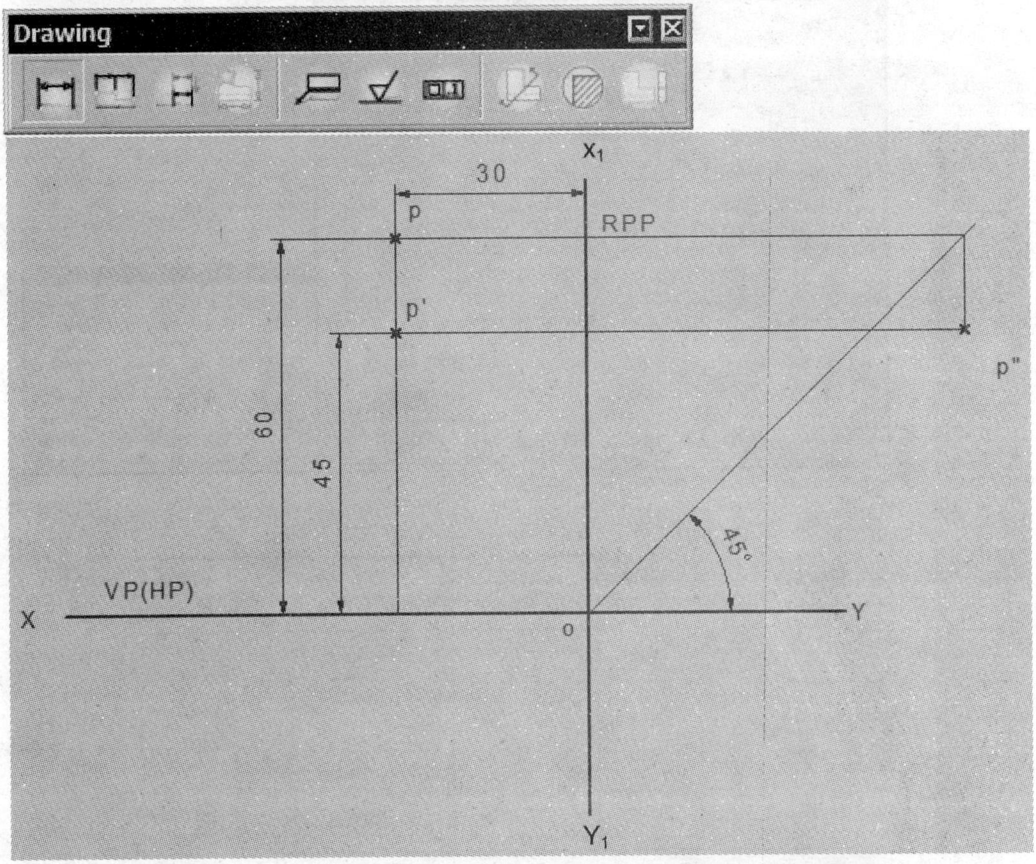

11. To make drawing as a standard drawing change the thickness of the lines by using **LINE WIDTH** command from status bar. Select the projection lines and 45° line then assign to line width 1 and Select the XY & X_1Y_1 line assign to line width 2.

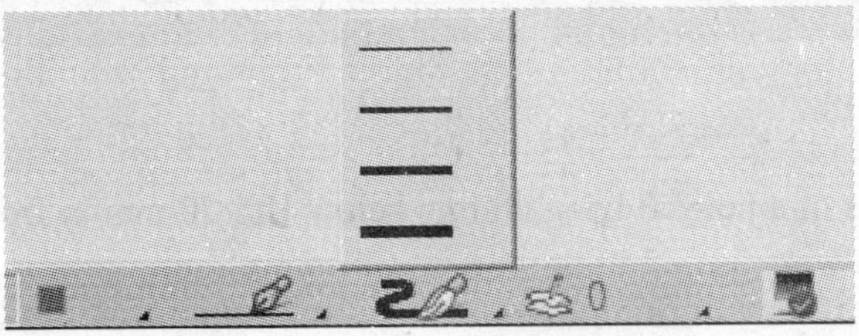

12. To get a Hard Copy of the standard drawing select print from file menu bar. Print dialog window will appear select page and change width to Entities and select the activated button now substitute width 1 as 0.05 mm, width 2 as 0.15 mm, width 3 as 0 mm and width 4

as 2 mm and say **OK.** Select print to get a hard copy and finally save the file. The required standard drawing is as shown below.

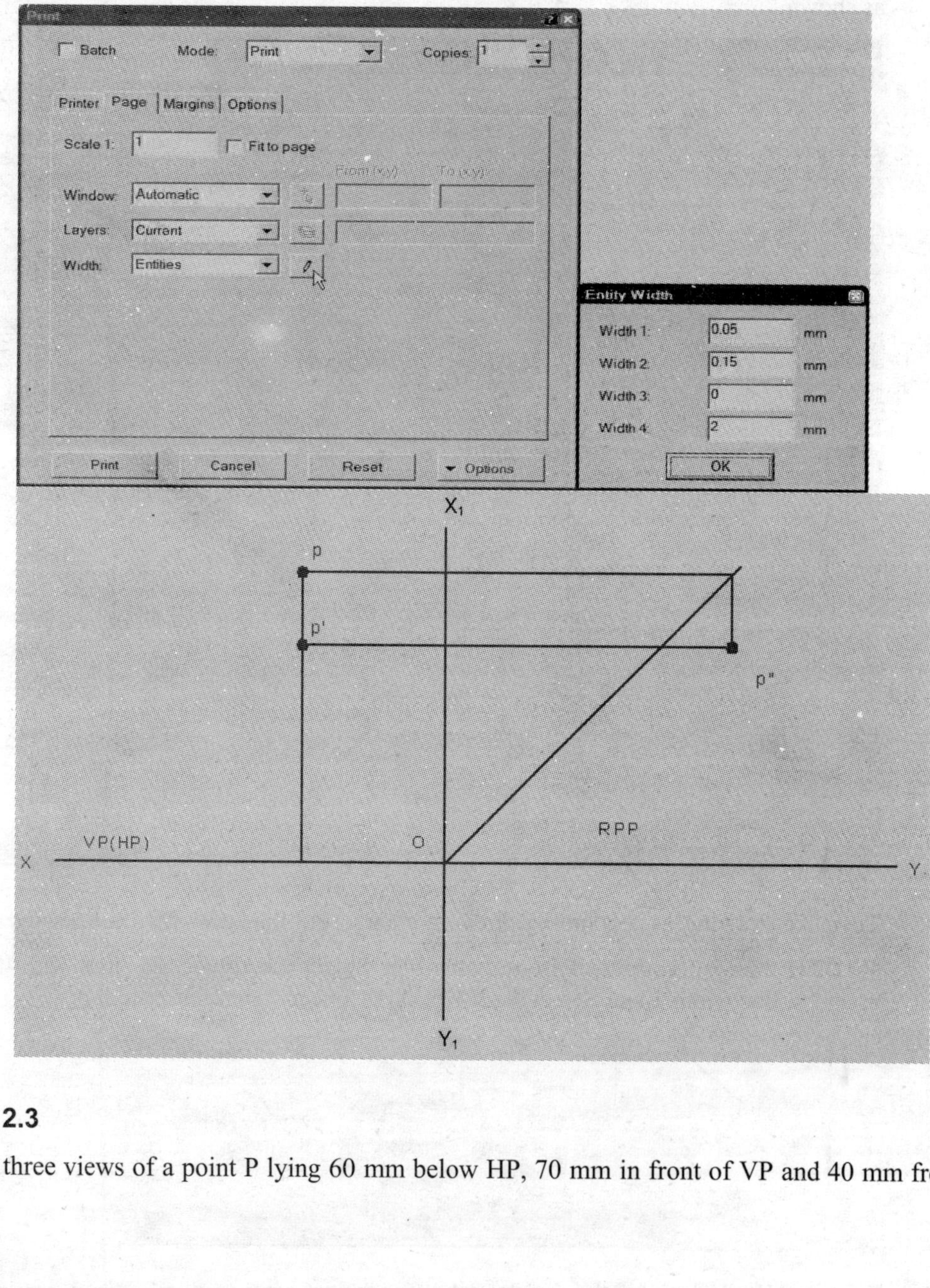

PROBLEM 2.3

Draw all the three views of a point P lying 60 mm below HP, 70 mm in front of VP and 40 mm from the RPP.

SOLUTION

Manual Method

(a) Draw the XY line. Mark HP and VP below it.

(b) Mark a point 60 mm below XY line. This is the front view of p. Name it as a p′.

(c) Draw a vertical projector downwards through p, measure a distance of 70 mm below XY line. This is the top view of p. Name it as p.

(d) Draw a reference line X_1Y_1 perpendicular to XY at a distance of 40 mm from the projector, which intersects at O.

(e) Draw a line passing through O inclined at 45° in HP.

(f) Draw a horizontal projector through p until it meets 45° line, from there draw a vertical projector upwards above XY line.

(g) Draw a horizontal projector through p' which gives left side view. Name as p″.

Computer Aided Drafting Procedure

1. Open the **SOFTWARE**. Click on the **DRAWING** in the open dialog box and say **OK**.

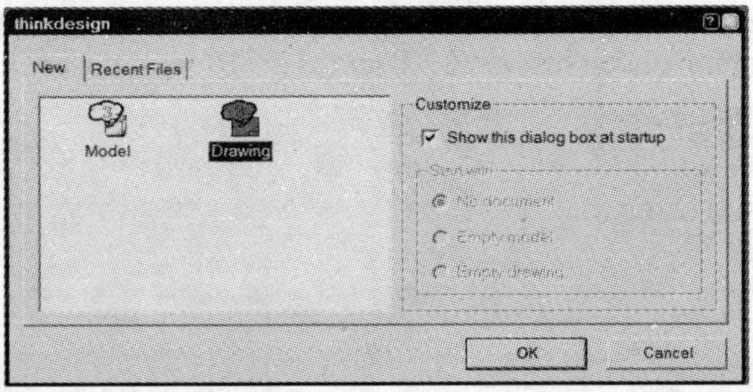

2. To set up the sheet of required size (Ex: A4) by selecting **TOOLS** from Main Menu Bar and click on **OPTIONS/PROPERTIES**. Select document properties in dialog box appeared and then select drawing in selection panel. Select the required size say A4, and click **OK**.

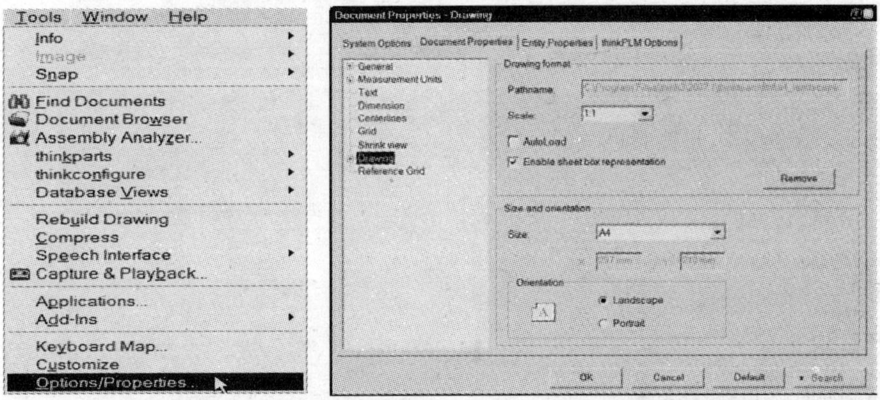

3. Draw the line by using **POLYLINE**  command from drafting tool bar.

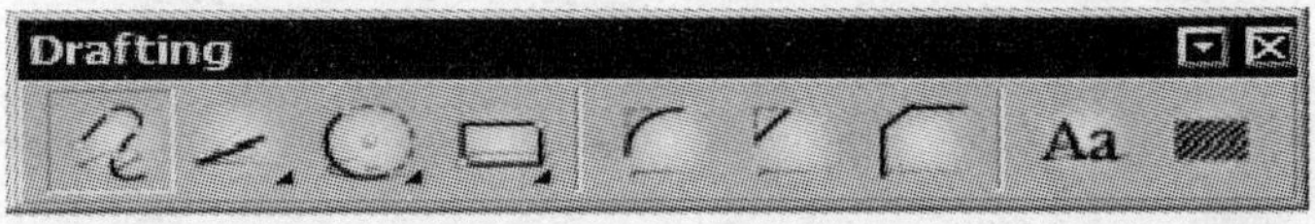

4. Make Annotation X, Y, VP, and HP to the line drawn by using **INSERT TEXT** Command  from drafting tool bar, just by typing X, Y, VP and HP in Text Box and insert these in the required position by left click of the mouse, as shown below.

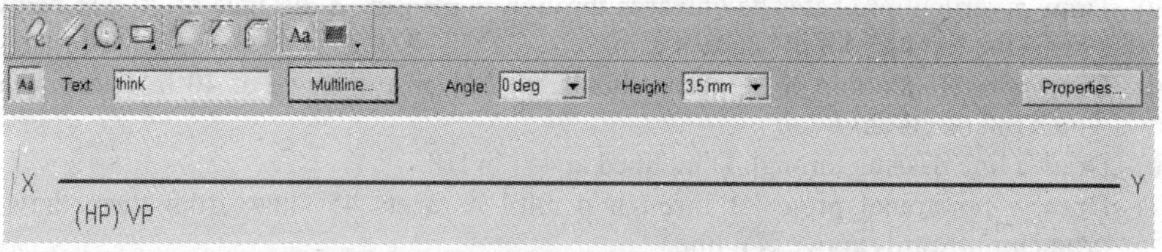

5. As per the problem, 60 mm below the HP we see in VP and 70 mm in front of VP we see in HP. Let us mark p′ and p below XY line using the **POINT** Command  by selecting Tools→ Points→Absolute/Delta. Once Absolute/Delta is selected we get selection list. In mode select relative point, let the option be Cartesian. Now select the reference point on line anywhere required and substitute X = 0, Y = –60 in mini dialog box. Next substitute X = 0 and Y = –70 in mini dialog box or X = 0 and Y = –10 from the created point.

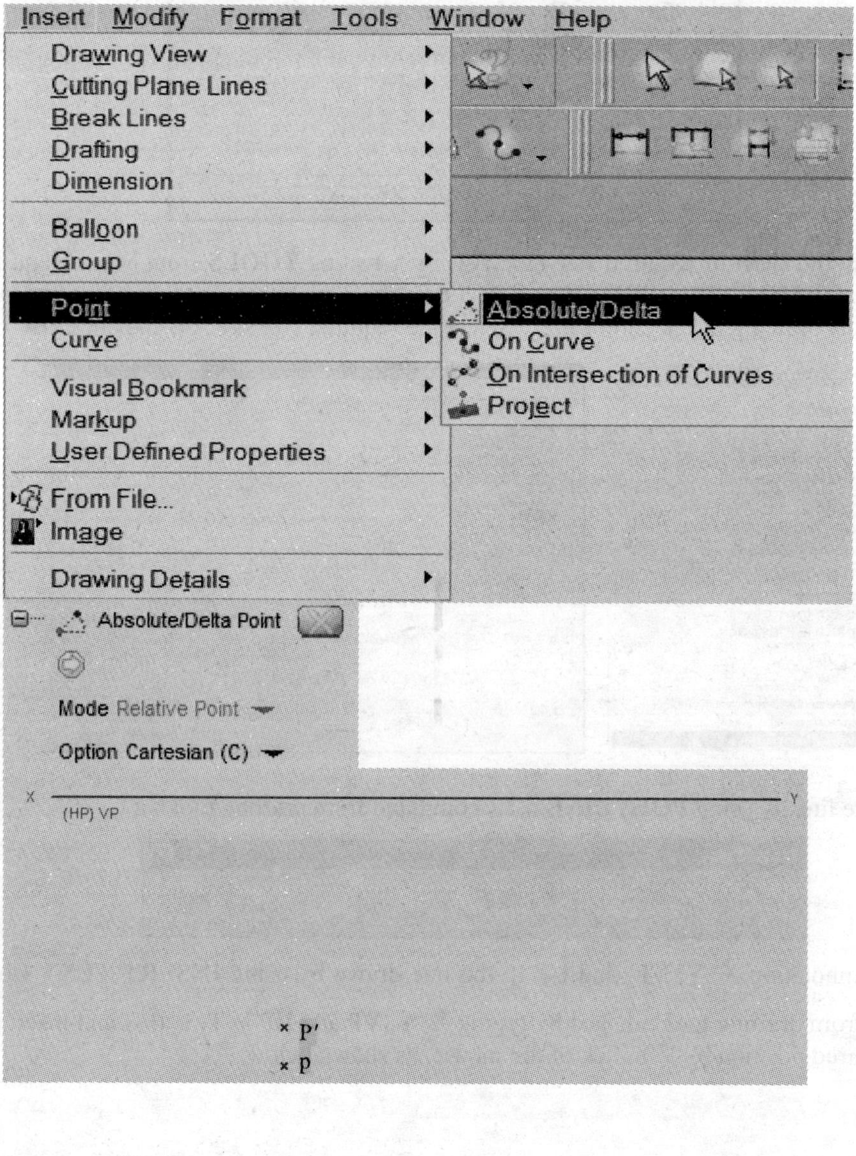

6. Using **2 POINT LINE** Command  from drafting tool bar join the points created and mark p′ and p using Insert Text Command as shown below.

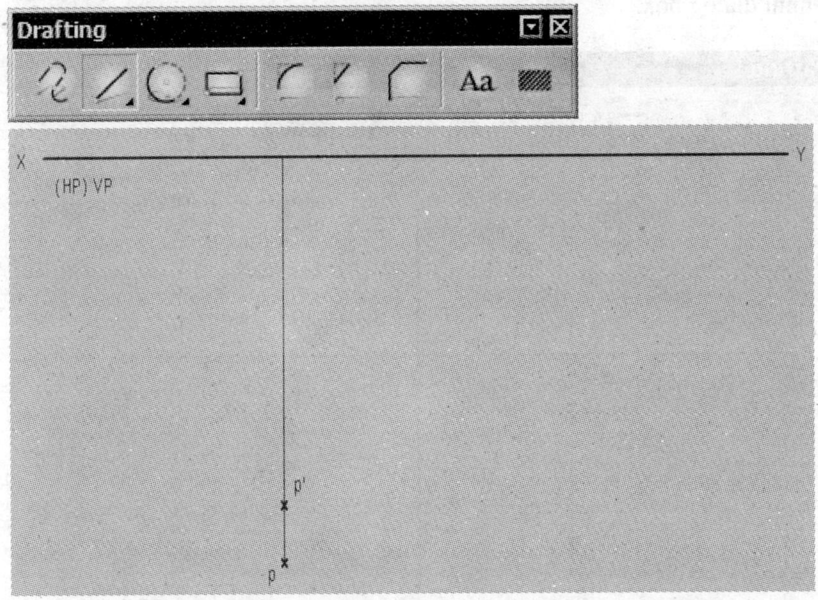

7. Draw the X_1Y_1 line perpendicular to XY line drawn at a distance of 40 mm from the projection line representing the intersection between VP and RPP at O, using **PARALLEL LINE** Command  in Drafting tool bar by selecting the projection line and substitute 40 mm in the distance mini dialog box.

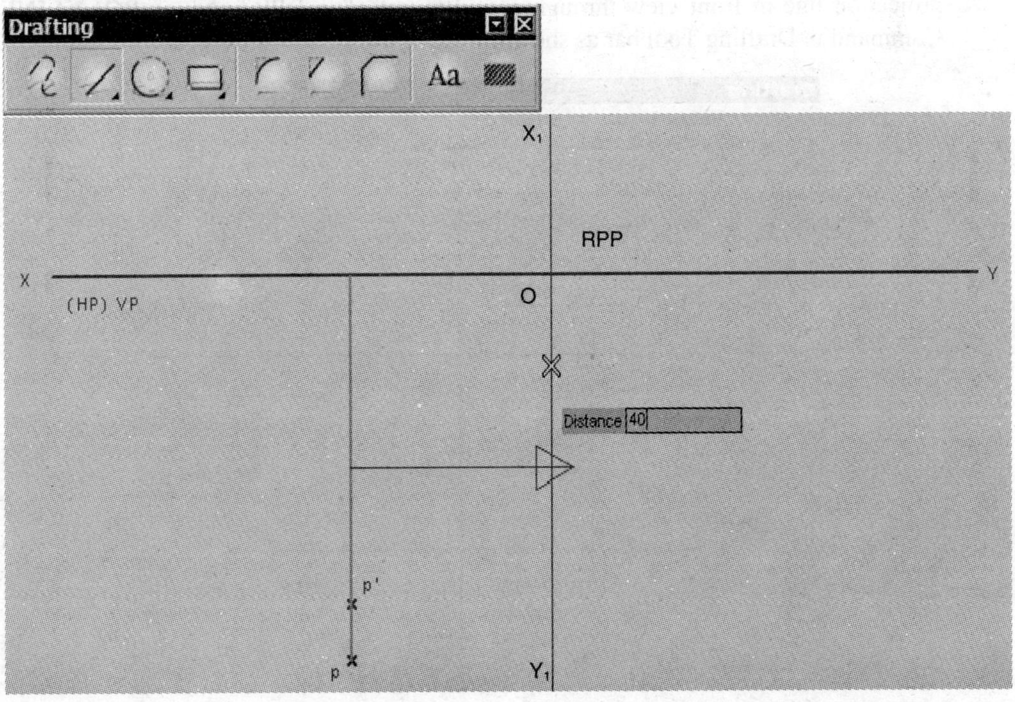

8. To draw the side view draw 45° line through the point O using **BISECTOR**  command in Drafting tool bar by selecting XY and X_1Y_1 line and substitute to required dimension in distance mini dialog box.

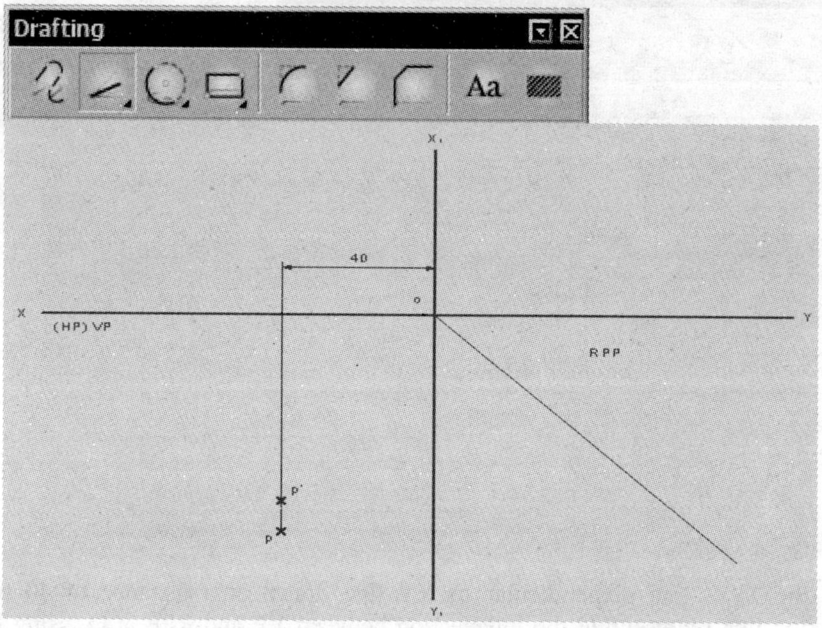

9. Draw the horizontal projection through the point p to intersect with the 45° line. Now draw vertical projector upwards from the intersection of lines. Again draw one more horizontal projection line in front view through p′ and to get p″ in RPP by using **POLYLINE**  Command in Drafting Tool bar as shown.

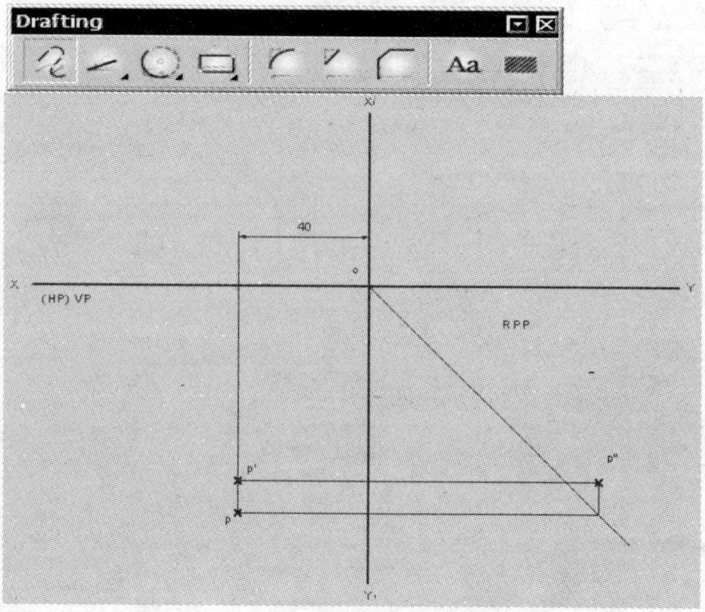

10. Using **SMART DIMENSION** Command  in drawing tool bar dimension the drawing as shown.

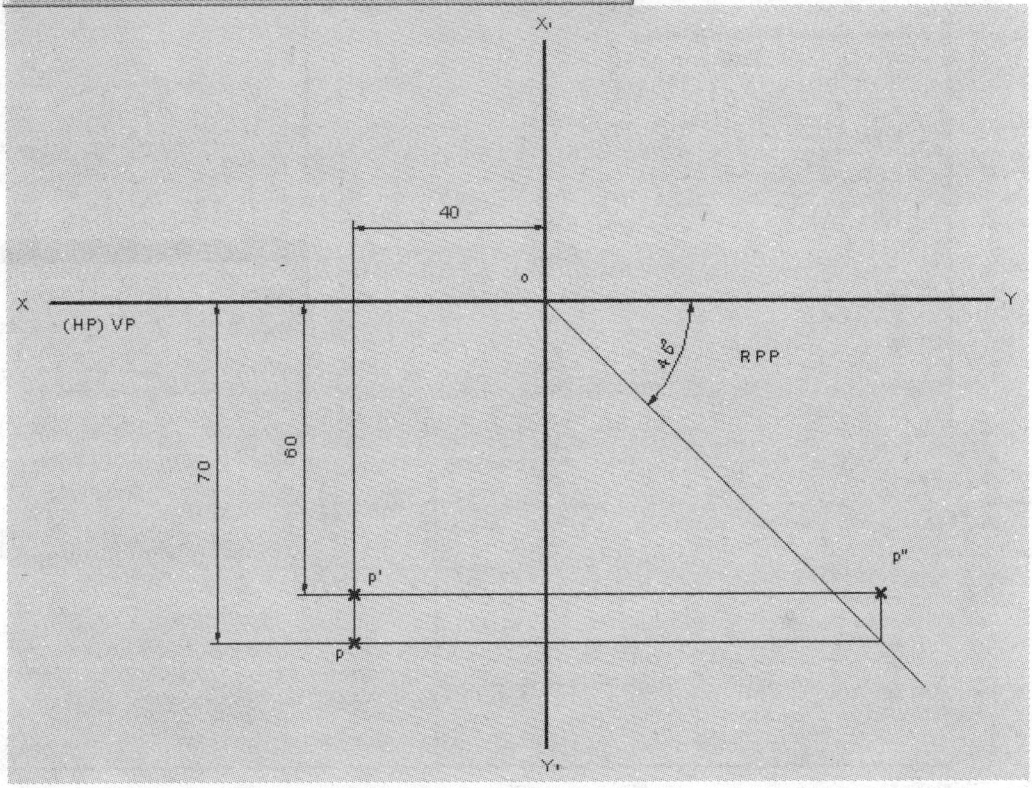

11. To make drawing as a standard drawing change the thickness of the lines by using **LINE WIDTH**  command from status bar. Select the projection lines and 45° line then assign to line width 1 and Select the XY & X_1Y_1 line assign to line width 2.

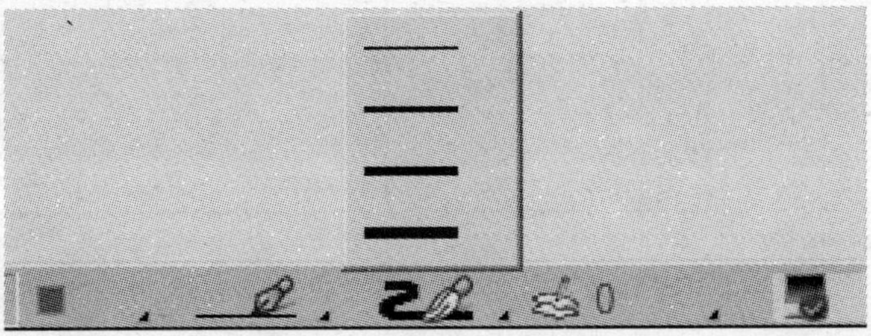

12. To get a Hard Copy of the standard drawing select print from file menu bar. Print dialog window will appear select page and change width to Entities and select the activated button now substitute width 1 as 0.05 mm, width 2 as 0.15 mm, width 3 as 0 mm and width 4 as 2 mm and say **OK.** Select print to get a hard copy and finally save the file. The required standard drawing is as shown below.

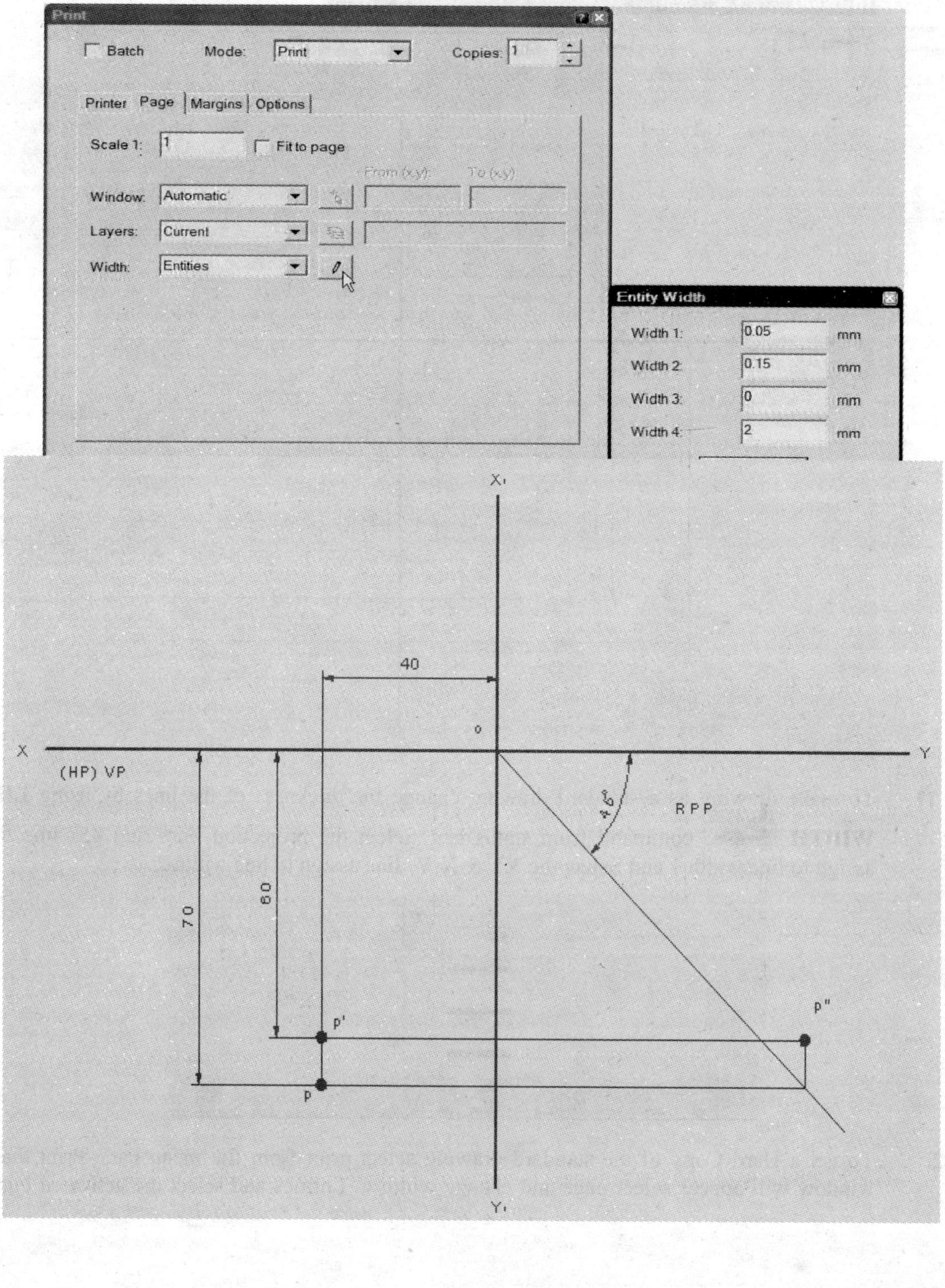

PROBLEM 2.4

A point is 35 mm below HP, 20 mm behind VP and 25 mm behind RPP. Draw its projections.

SOLUTION

Manual Method

(a) Draw the XY line. Mark VP below and HP above it.

(b) Mark a point 35 mm below XY line. This is the front view of P. Name it as a p′.

(c) Draw a vertical projector upwards through p, measure a distance of 20 mm above XY line. This is the top view of p. name it as p.

(d) Draw a reference line X_1Y_1 perpendicular to XY at a distance of 25 mm from the projector, which intersects at O.

(e) Draw a line passing through O inclined at 45° in HP.

(f) Draw a horizontal projector through p until it meets 45° line, from there draw a vertical projector downwards below XY line.

(g) Draw a horizontal projector through p′ which gives left side view. Name as p″.

Computer Aided Drafting Procedure

1. Open the **SOFTWARE**. Click on the **DRAWING** in the open dialog box and say **OK**.

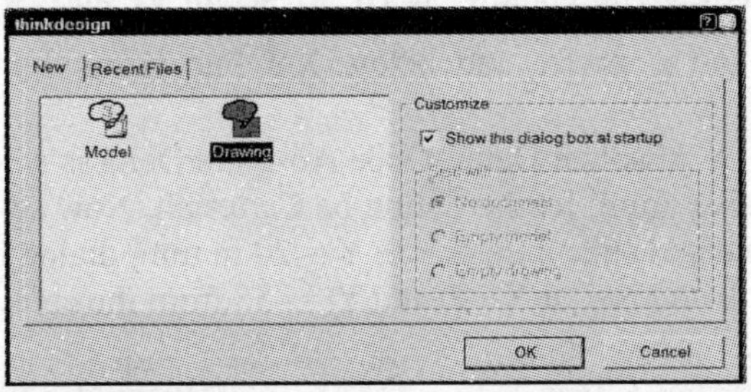

2. To set up the sheet of required size (Ex: A4) by selecting **TOOLS** from Main Menu Bar and click on **OPTIONS/PROPERTIES**. Select document properties in dialog box appeared and then select drawing in selection panel. Select the required size say A4, and click **OK**.

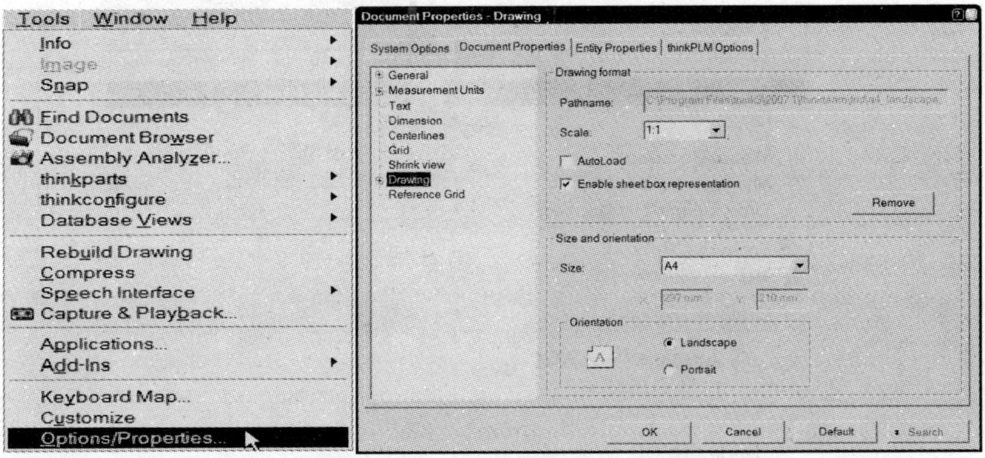

3. Draw the line by using **POLYLINE**  command from drafting tool bar.

4. Make Annotation X, Y, VP, and HP to the line drawn by using **INSERT TEXT** Command  from drafting tool bar, just by typing X, Y, VP and HP in Text Box and insert these in the required position by left click of the mouse, as shown below.

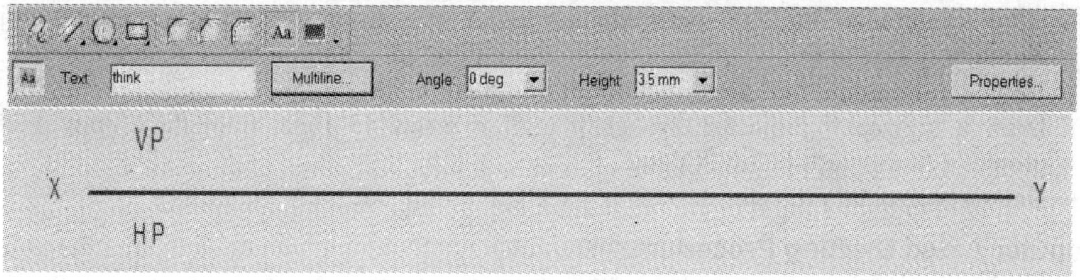

5. As per the problem, 35 mm below the HP we see in VP and 20 mm behind VP we see in HP.

Let us mark a and a′ above and below XY line using the **POINT** Command  by selecting
Tools → Points → Absolute/Delta. Once Absolute/Delta is selected we get selection list. In mode select relative point, let the option be Cartesian. Now select the reference point on line anywhere required and substitute X = 0, Y = 20 in mini dialog box. Next substitute X = 0 and Y = –35 in mini dialog box or X = 0 and Y = –55 from the created point.

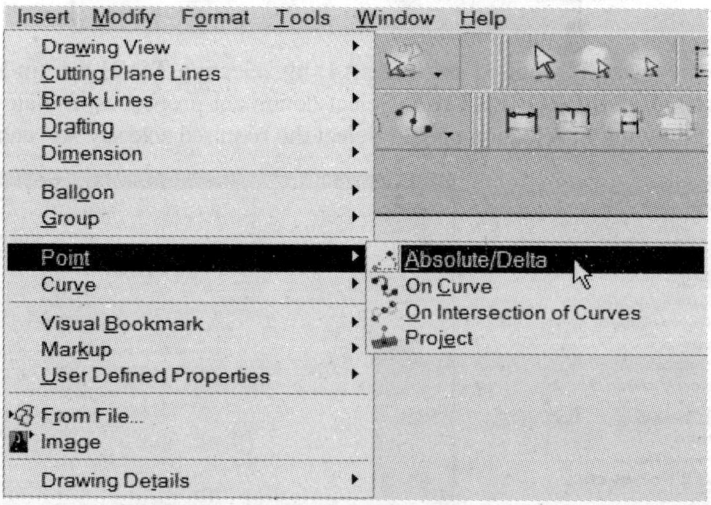

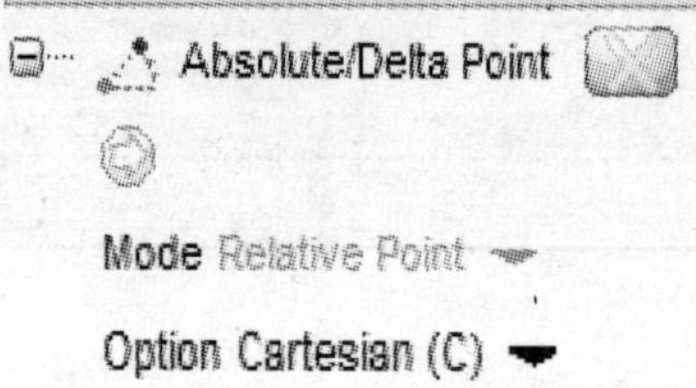

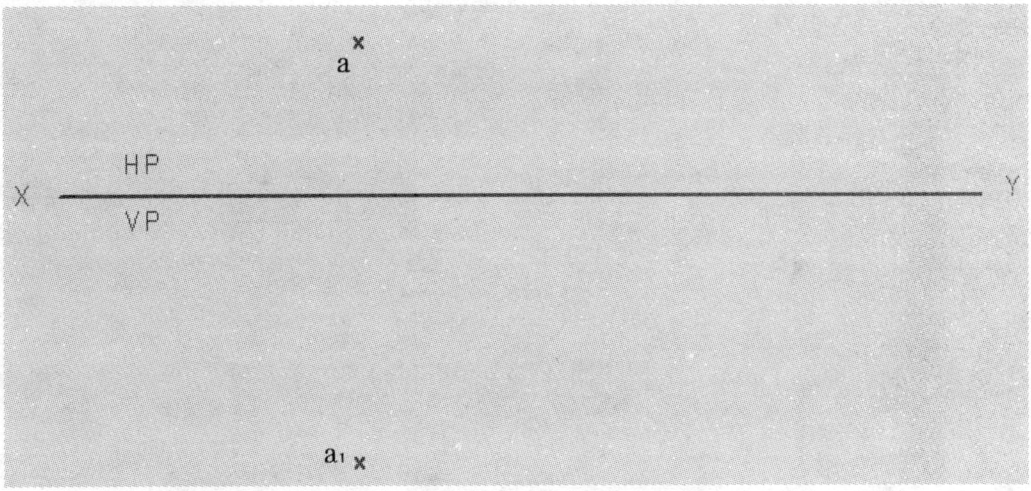

6. Using **2 POINT LINE** Command  from drafting tool bar join the points created and mark a′ and a using Insert Text Command as shown below.

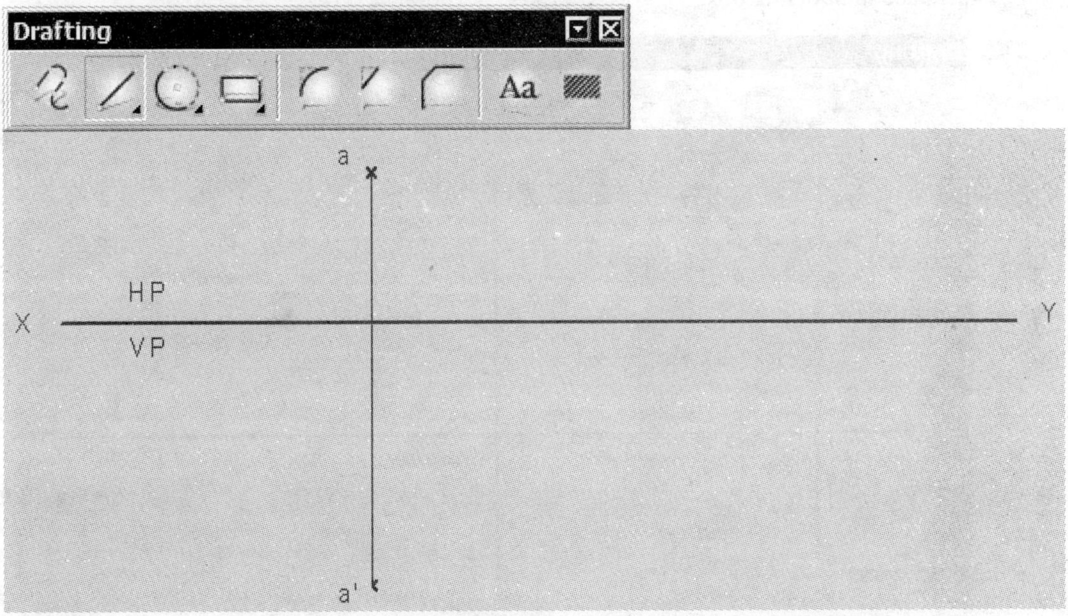

7. Draw the X_1Y_1 line perpendicular to XY line drawn at a distance of 25 mm from the projection line representing the intersection between VP and RPP at O, using **PARALLEL LINE** Command  in Drafting tool bar by selecting the projection line and substitute 25 mm in the distance mini dialog box.

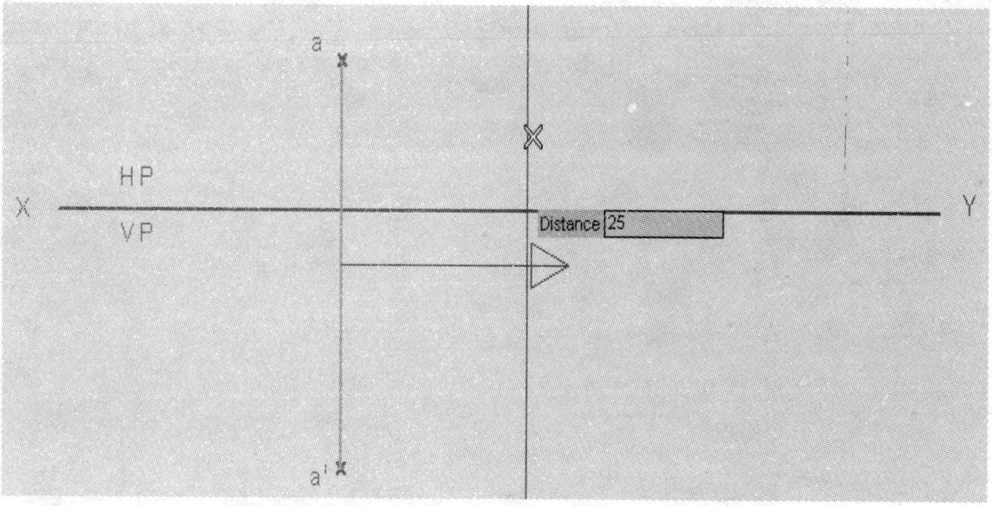

8. To draw the side view draw 45° line through the point O using **BISECTOR** 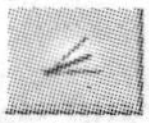 command in Drafting tool bar by selecting XY and X_1Y_1 line and substitute to required dimension in distance mini dialog box.

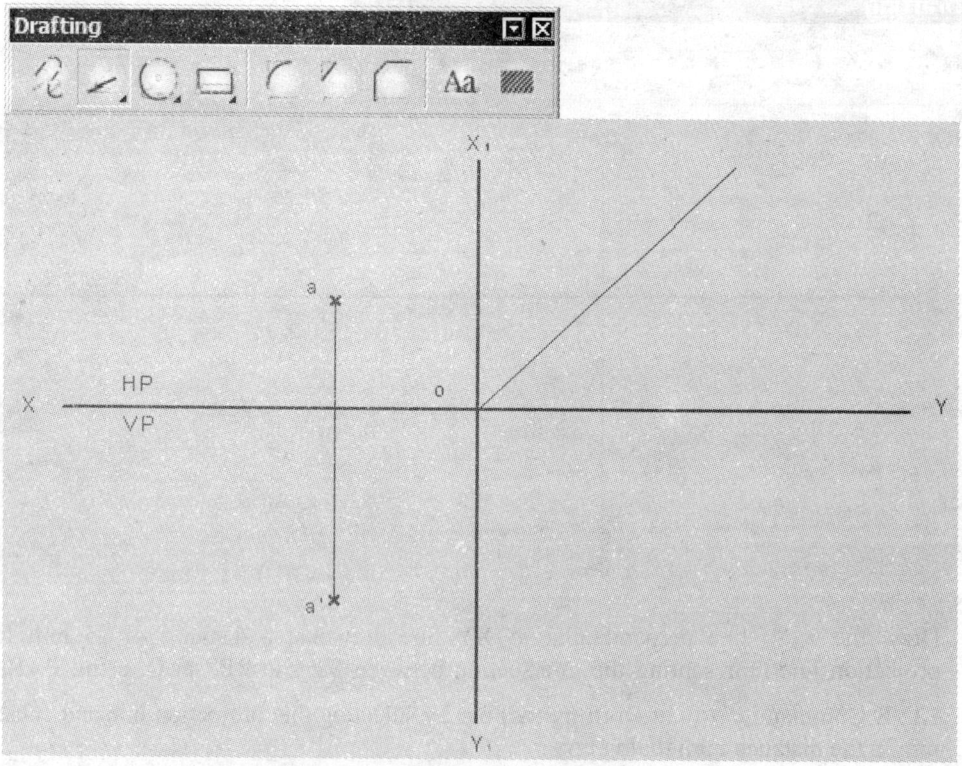

9. Draw the horizontal projection through the point a to intersect with the 45° line. Now draw vertical projector downwards from the intersection of lines. Again draw one more horizontal

projection line in front view through a′ and to get a″ in RPP by using **POLYLINE** Command in Drafting Tool bar as shown.

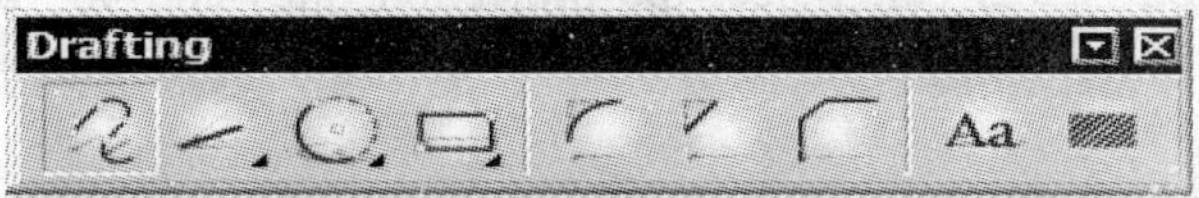

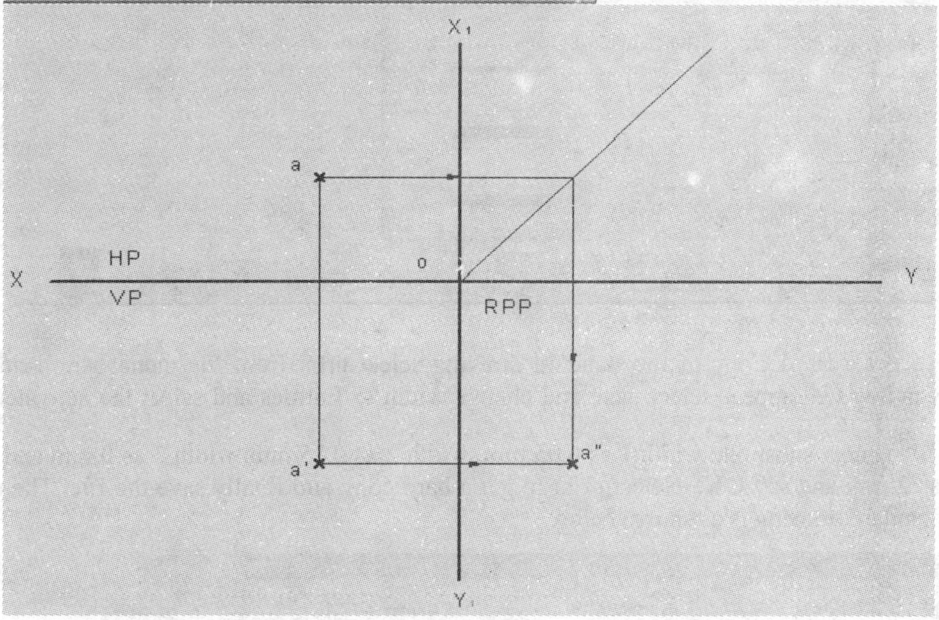

10. Using **SMART DIMENSION** Command in drawing tool bar dimension the drawing as shown.

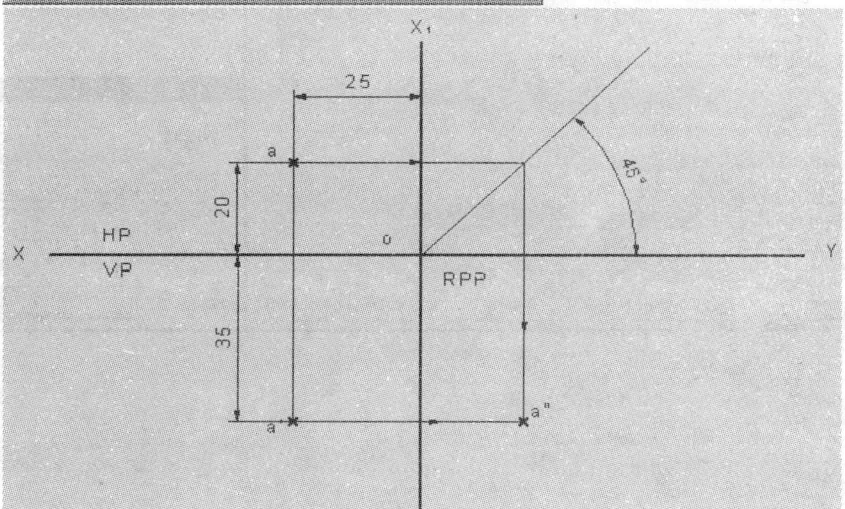

11. To make drawing as a standard drawing change the thickness of the lines by using **LINE WIDTH**  command from status bar. Select the projection lines and 45° line then assign to line width 1 and Select the XY & X_1Y_1 line assign to line width 2.

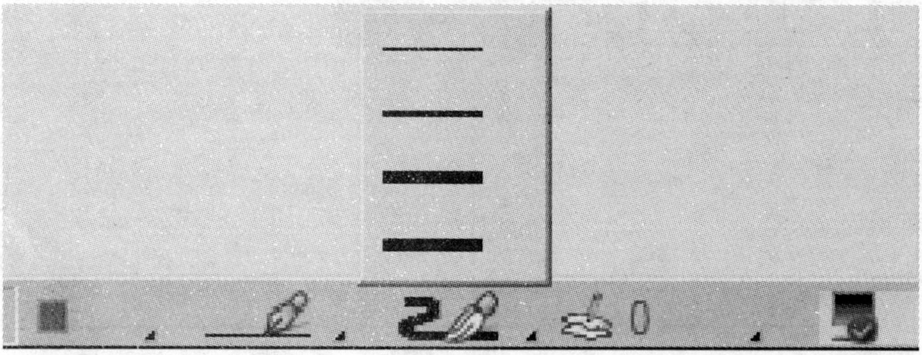

To get a Hard Copy of the standard drawing select print from file menu bar. Print dialog window will appear select page and change width to Entities and select the activated button  now substitute width 1 as 0.05 mm, width 2 as 0.15 mm, width 3 as 0 mm and width 4 as 2 mm and say **OK.** Select print to get a hard copy and finally save the file. The required standard drawing is as shown below.

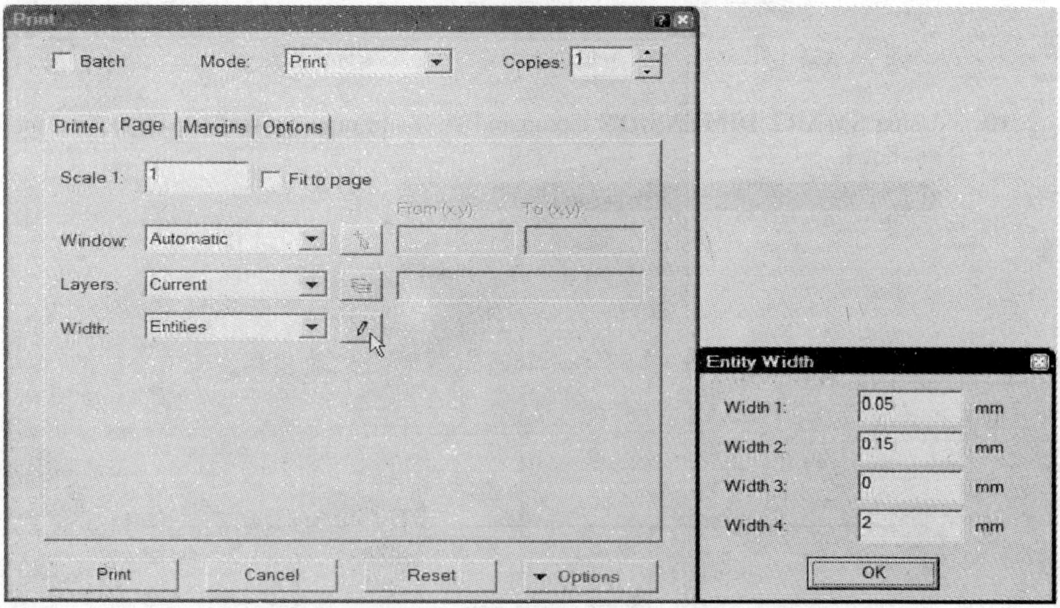

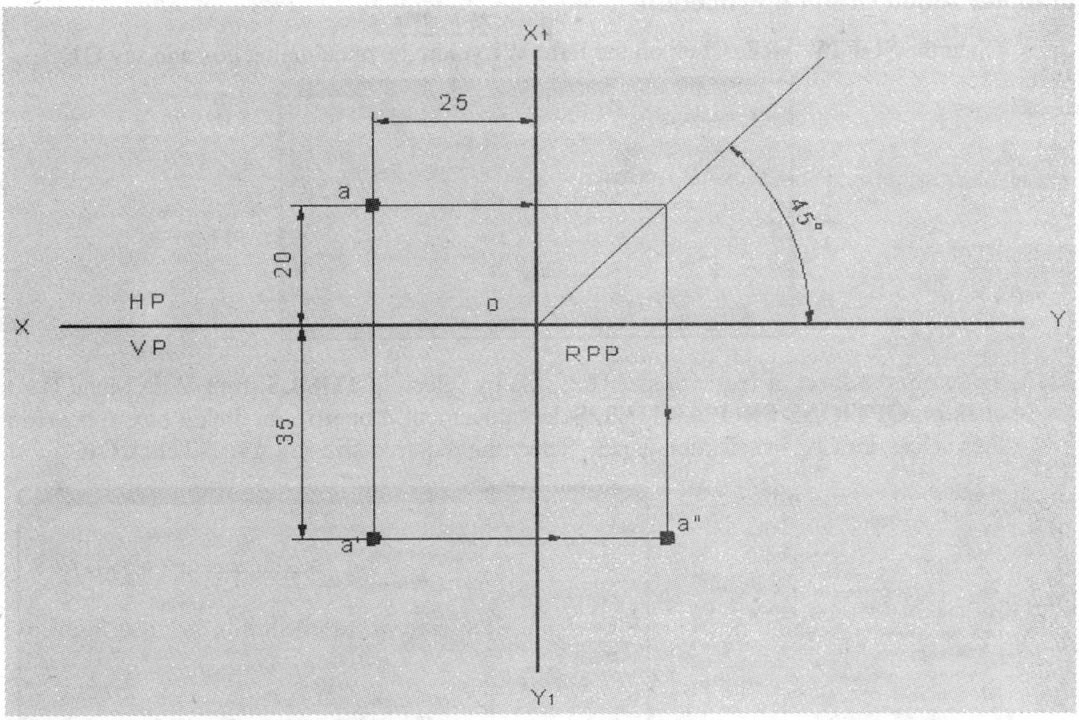

PROBLEM 2.5

A point M is 30 mm in front of VP and 20 mm above HP, another point N is 15 mm behind VP and 25 mm below HP. The horizontal distance between the points parallel to XY line is 50 mm. Draw the projections of the points M and N and join their front and top views. Draw the right side view of the point N only.

SOLUTION

Manual Method

(a) Draw the XY line.

(b) Mark a point 20mm above XY line. This is the front view of m. Name it as m′.

(c) Draw a vertical projector downwards through m, measure a distance of 30 mm below XY line. This is the top view of M. Name it as m.

(d) Similarly mark a point 15 mm above XY line. Such it is 50 mm from the point M. This is the top view of N. Name it as n.

(e) Draw a vertical projector downwards through n, measure a distance of 25 mm below XY line. This is the front view of N. Name it as n′.

(f) Draw a reference line X_1Y_1 perpendicular to XY at any distance from the projector of n and n′, which intersects at O.

(g) Draw a line passing through O inclined at 45° in HP.

(h) Draw a horizontal projector through n until it meets 45° line, from there draw a vertical projector downwards below XY line.

(i) Draw a horizontal projector through n′. Which gives lefts side view. Name as n″.

Computer Aided Drafting Procedure

1. Open the **SOFTWARE**. Click on the **DRAWING** in the open dialog box and say **OK**.

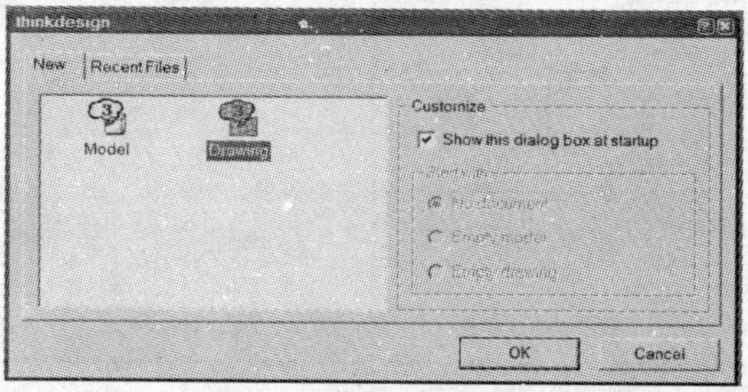

2. To set up the sheet of required size (Ex: A4) by selecting **TOOLS** from Main Menu Bar and click on **OPTIONS/PROPERTIES**. Select document properties in dialog box appeared and then select drawing in selection panel. Select the required size say A4, and click **OK**.

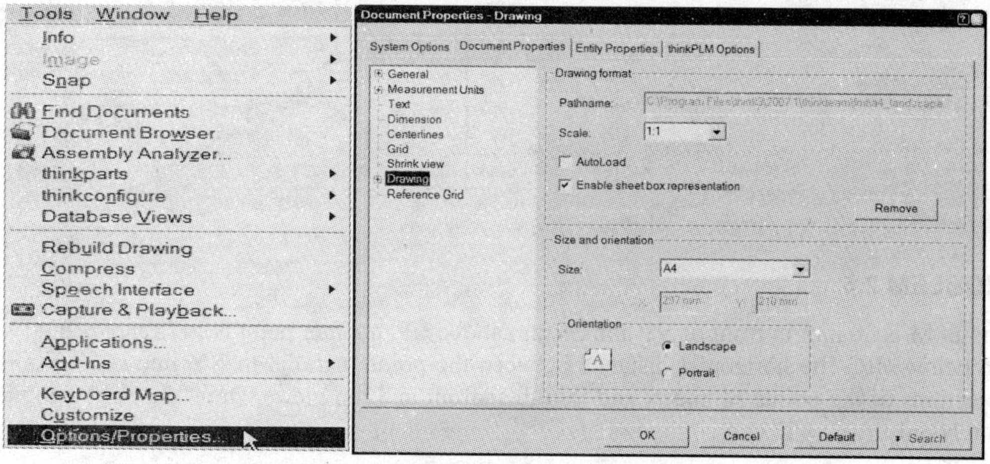

3. Draw the line by using **POLYLINE**  command from drafting tool bar.

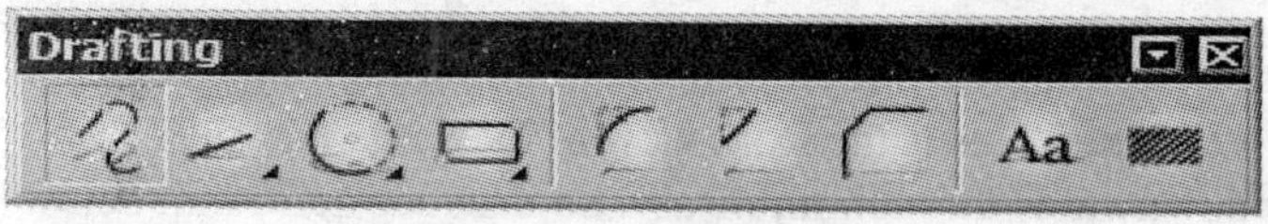

4. Make Annotation X, Y, VP, and HP to the line drawn by using **INSERT TEXT** Command  from drafting tool bar, just by typing X, Y, VP and HP in Text Box and insert these in the required position by left click of the mouse, as shown below.

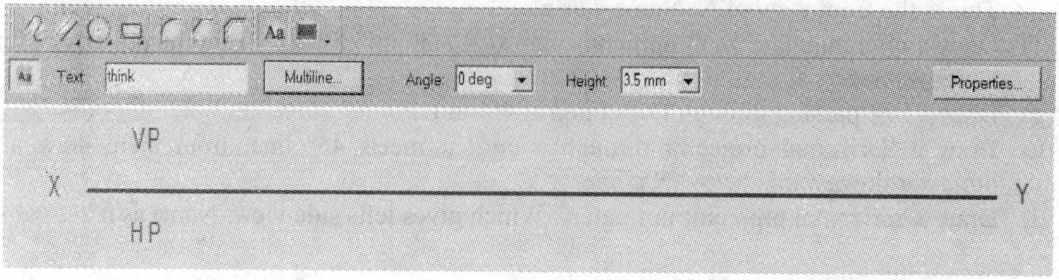

5. As per the problem, point M is 30 mm infront of VP we see in HP and 20 mm above HP we see in VP another point N is 15 mm behind VP we see in HP and 25 mm below HP we see in VP. Let us mark m′ and m above and below XY line using the **POINT** Command  by selecting Tools → Points → Absolute/Delta. Once Absolute/Delta is selected we get selection list. In mode select relative point, let the option be Cartesian. Now select the reference point on line anywhere required and substitute X = 0, Y = 20 in mini dialog box. Next substitute X = 0 and Y = –30 in mini dialog box or X = 0 and Y = –50 from the created point.

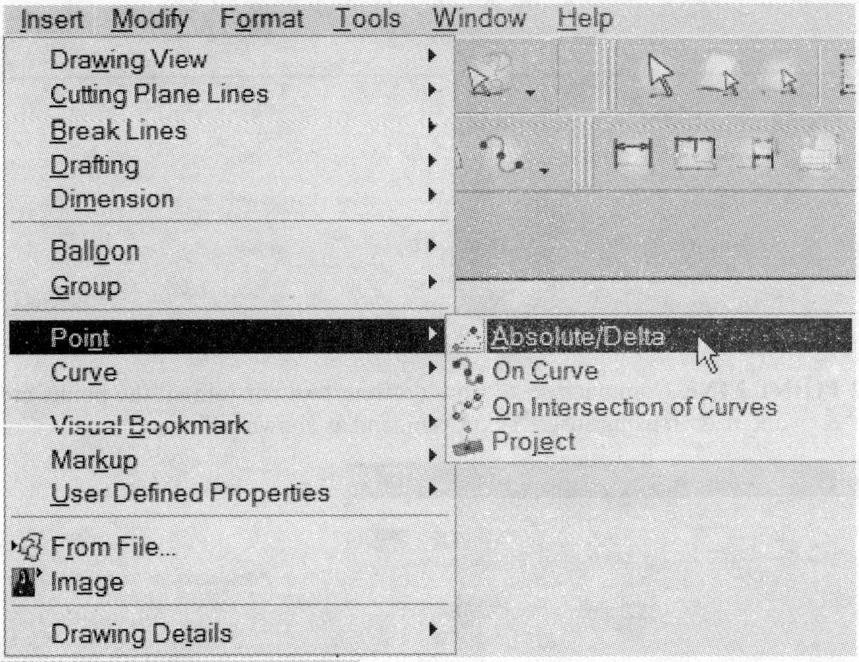

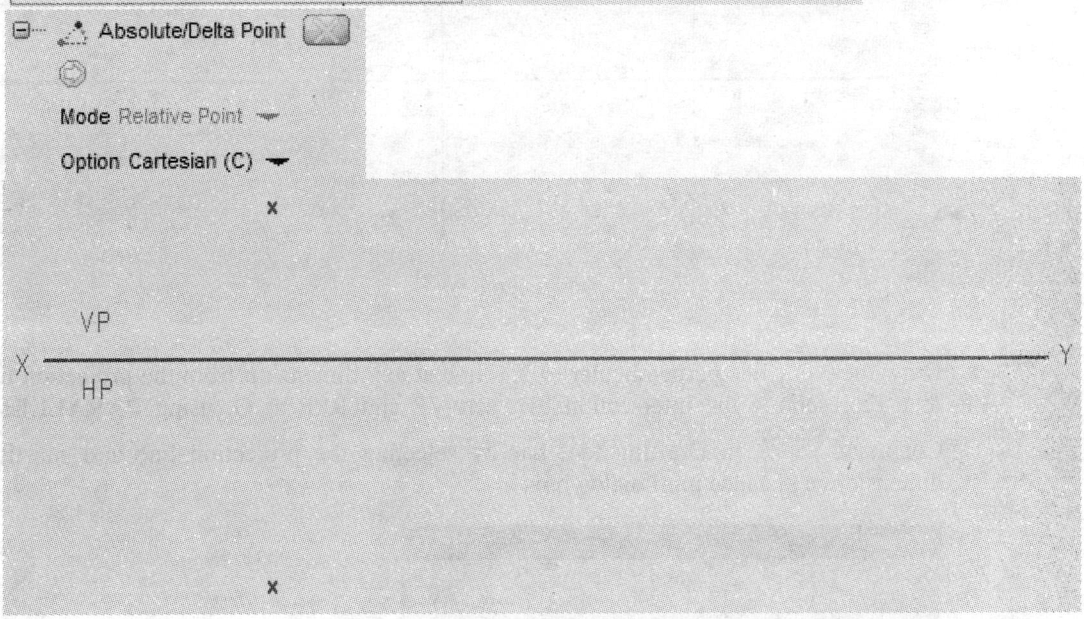

6. Let us mark n and n′ above and below XY line using the **POINT** Command  by selecting Tools→Points→Absolute/Delta. Once Absolute/Delta is selected we get selection list. In mode select relative point, let the option be Cartesian. Now select the reference point on line anywhere required and substitute X = 50, Y = 15 in mini dialog box. Next substitute X = 50 and Y = –25 in mini dialog box or X = 50 and Y = –40 from the created point. (by selecting X = 50 mm the point N will be exactly 50 mm from the point M)

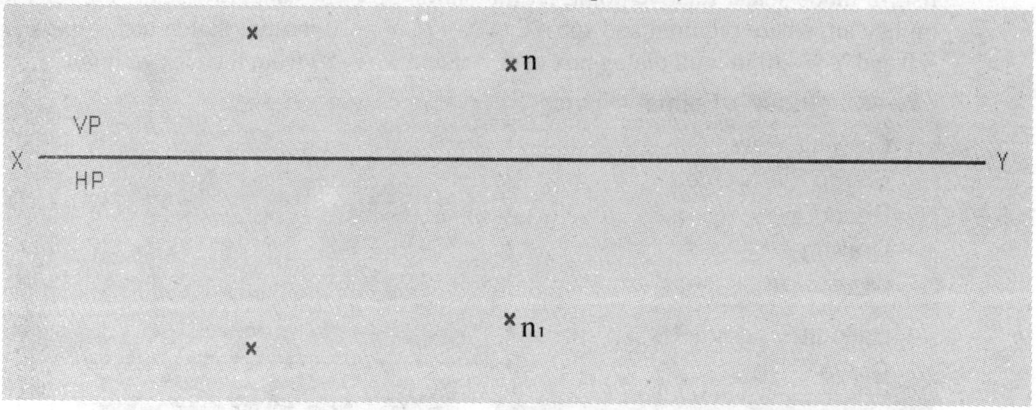

7. Using **2 POINT LINE** Command  from drafting tool bar join all the points created and mark m' & m and n′ & n using Insert Text Command as shown below.

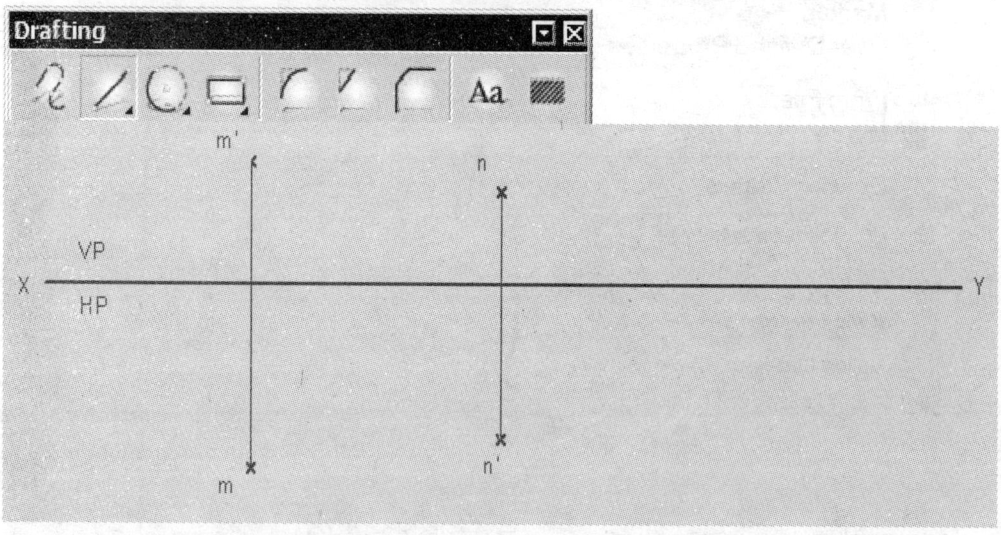

8. Draw the X_1Y_1 line perpendicular to XY line at any dimension from the projection line of n′ & n representing the intersection between VP and RPP at O, using **PARALLEL LINE** Command  in Drafting tool bar by selecting the projection line and substitute any dimension in distance mini dialog box.

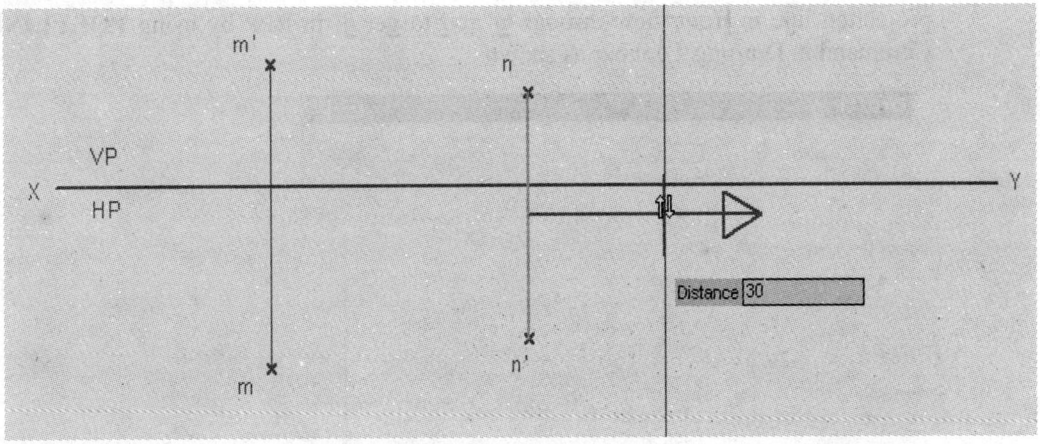

9. To draw the side view draw 45° line through the point O using **BISECTOR**  command in Drafting tool bar by selecting XY and X_1Y_1 line and substitute to required dimension in distance mini dialog box.

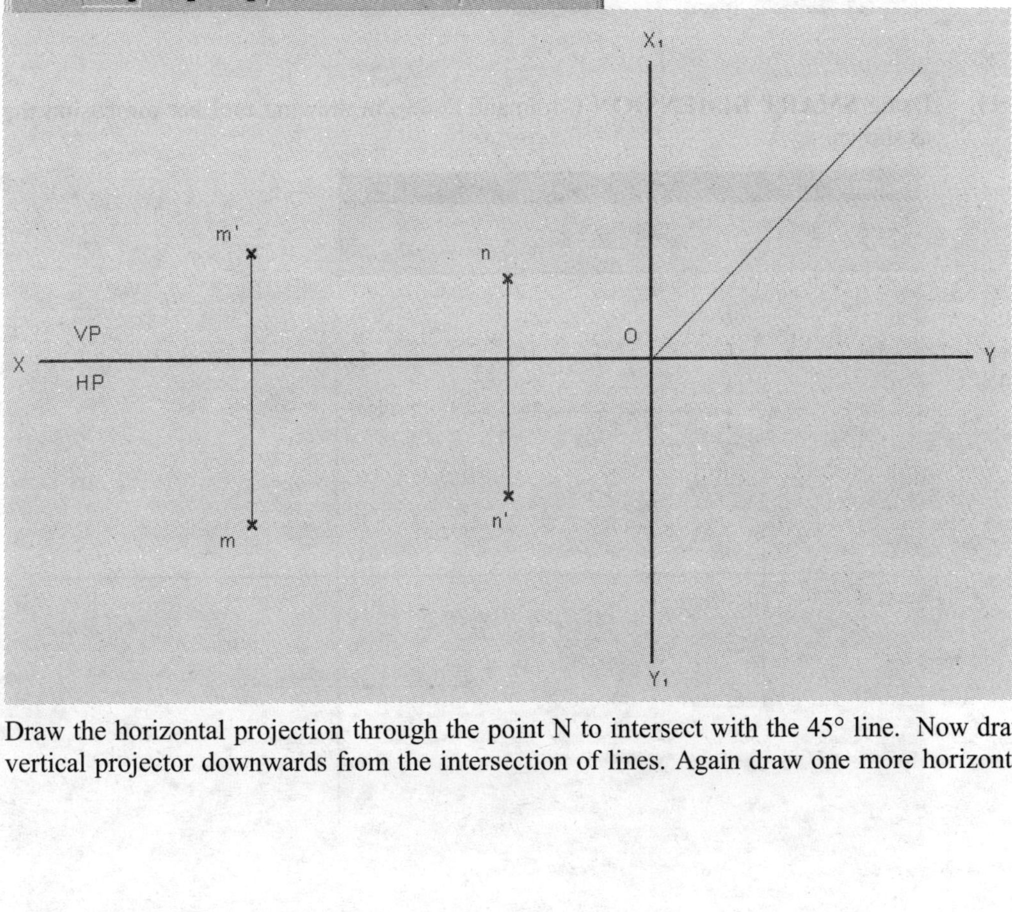

10. Draw the horizontal projection through the point N to intersect with the 45° line. Now draw vertical projector downwards from the intersection of lines. Again draw one more horizontal

projection line in front view through n′ and to get n″ in RPP by using **POLYLINE** Command in Drafting Tool bar as shown.

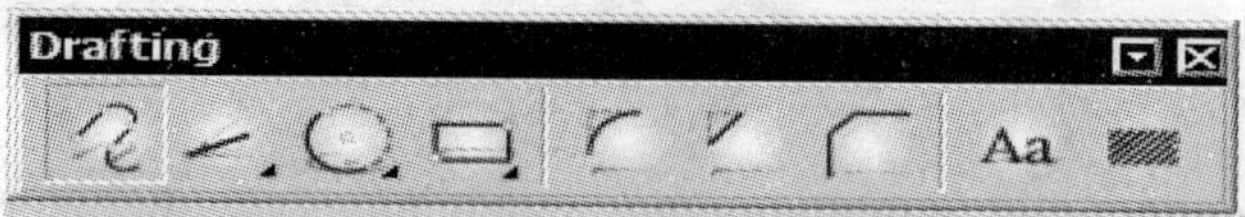

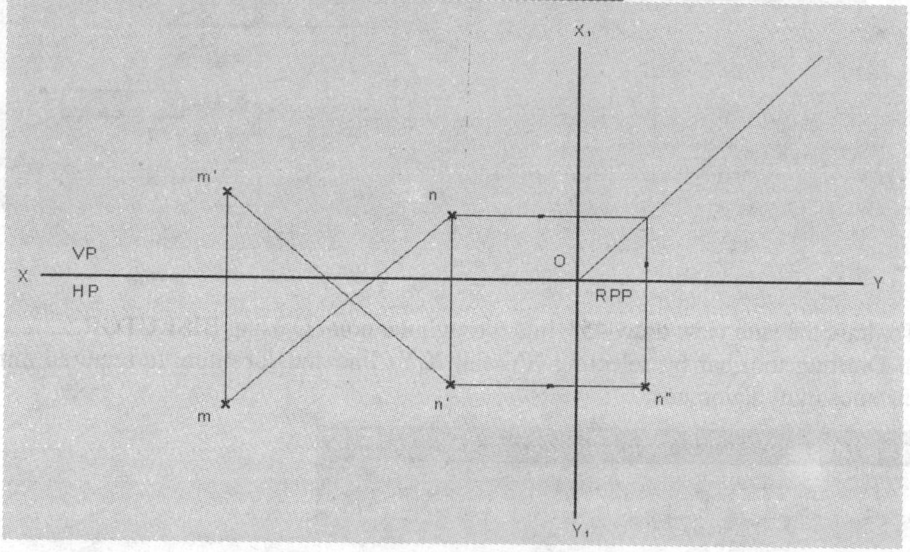

11. Using **SMART DIMENSION** Command in drawing tool bar dimension the drawing as shown.

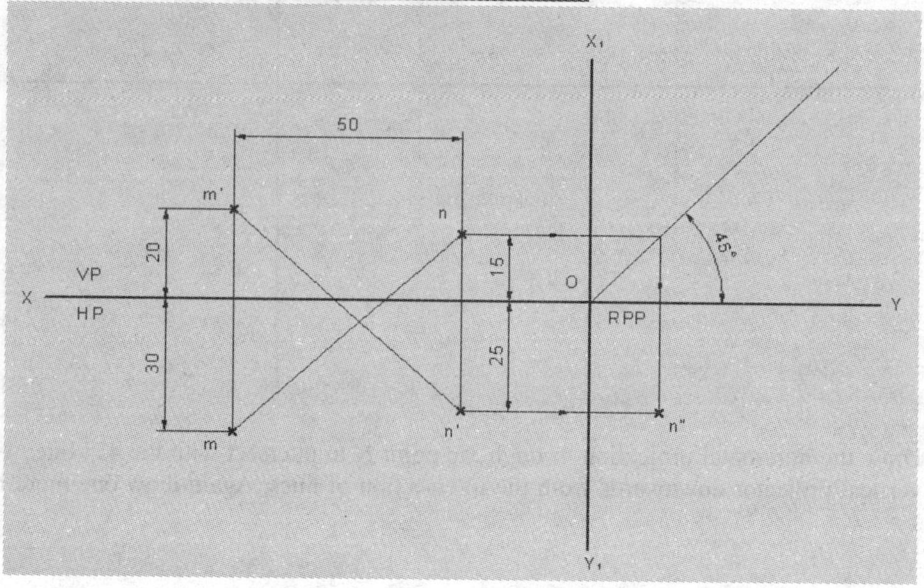

12. To make drawing as a standard drawing change the thickness of the lines by using **LINE WIDTH**  command from status bar. Select the projection lines and 45° line then assign to line width 1 and Select the XY & X_1Y_1 line assign to line width 2.

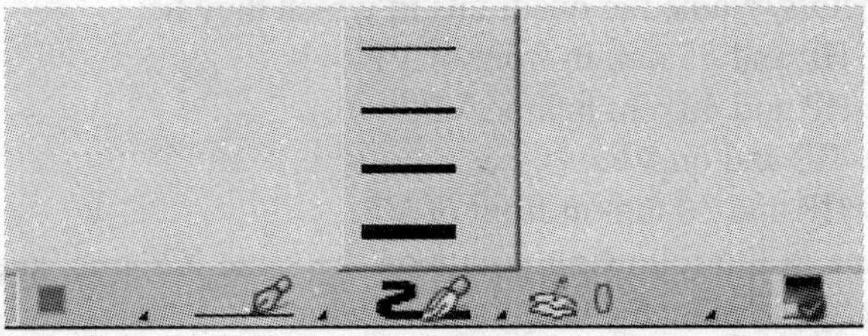

13. To get a Hard Copy of the standard drawing select print from file menu bar. Print dialog window will appear select page and change width to Entities and select the activated button  now substitute width 1 as 0.05 mm, width 2 as 0.15 mm, width 3 as 0 mm and width 4 as 2 mm and say **OK.** Select print to get a hard copy and finally save the file. The required standard drawing is shown below.

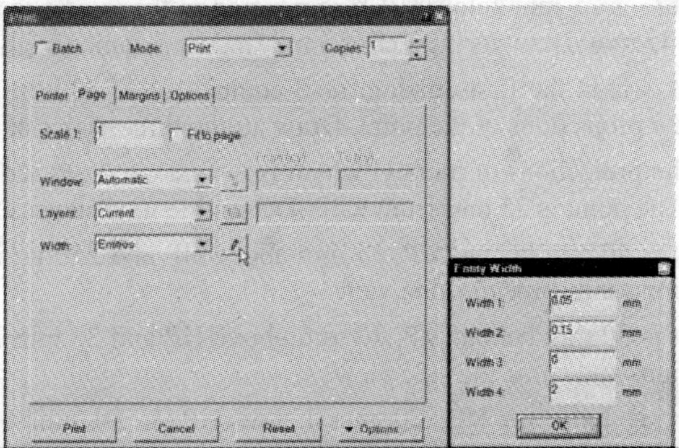

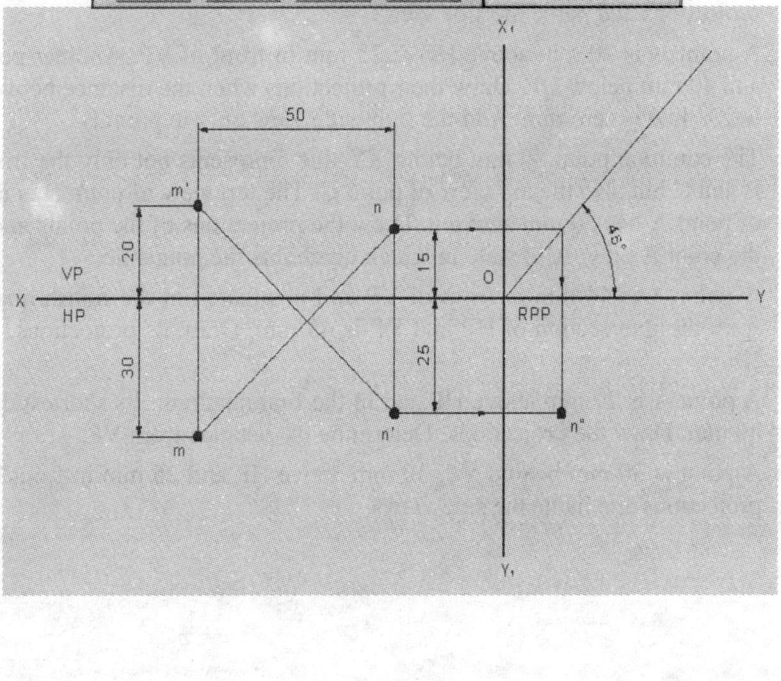

EXERCISE PROBLEMS

1. Draw the projections of the following points on the same XY line, keeping convenient distance between each projectors. Name the quadrants in which they lie.
   A — 30 mm above HP and 35 mm in front of VP.
   B — 35 mm above HP and 40 mm behind VP.
   C — 40 mm above HP and on VP.
   D — 35 mm below HP and 30 mm in front of VP.
2. Draw the projections of the following points on the same XY line, keeping convenient distance between each projectors. Name the Quadrants in which they lie.
   E — 30 mm below HP and 25 mm behind VP.
   F — 35 mm below HP and 30 mm in front of VP.
   G — On HP and 30 mm in front of VP.
   H — On HP and 35 mm behind VP.
3. Draw all the three views of a point P lying 60 mm below HP, 70 mm infront of VP and 40 mm from the RPP. Also state the quadrant in which it lies.
4. A point G is 25 mm below HP & is situated in the third quadrant. Its shortest distance from XY line is 45 mm. Draw its projections and find its distance from VP.
5. A point S is in the first quadrant and equidistant of 50 mm from all the three principal planes. Draw the projections of the point. Draw all the three views of the point.
6. Draw the projections of point G which is in first quadrant such that it is equidistant from HP, VP & PP. The point is 25 mm from RPP. Determine its distances from HP&VP.
7. A point is 40 mm behind VP, 15 mm above HP and 25 mm in front/behind/from LPP. Draw its projections and name the side view.
8. A point is 30 mm behind VP, 30 mm above HP and 25 mm in front/behind/from LPP. Draw its projections and name the side view.
9. A point is lying on VP, 20 mm below HP & 30 mm behind/infront/from LPP. Draw its projections and name the side view.
10. A point A is 20 mm above HP & 25 mm in front of VP. Another point B is 25 mm behind VP and 40 mm below HP. Draw their projections when the distance between their projectors parallel to XY line is zero mm. Add the right side view only to point B.
11. The common point 40 mm below XY line represents not only the front views of three points A, B and C but also the top view of point C. The top view of point B is ies on XY line and top view of point A lies 50 mm above it. Draw the projections of the points and add the right side view to the point A only. Also state in which quadrants the points lie.
12. A point A is 40 mm in front of VP and is situated in the fourth quadrant. Its shortest distance from the intersection of HP and VP is 45 mm. Draw its projections. Also find its distance from HP.
13. A point A is 20 mm above HP and in the first quadrant. Its shortest distance from the XY line is 40 mm. Draw the projections. Determine its distance from VP.
14. A point is 30 mm behind VP, 30 mm above HP and 25 mm in front/behind/from RPP. Draw its projections and name the side views.

15. A point is lying on VP, 10 mm below HP & 30 mm behind / in front / from LPP. Draw its projections and name the side view.

16. Draw the projections of the following points on the same XY line, keeping convenient distance between the projectors. Also state the quadrants in which they lie.

A — 30 mm below HP and 25 mm behind VP.

B — 35 mm below HP and 30 mm in front of VP.

C — on HP and 30 mm in front of VP.

D — on HP and 35 mm behind of VP.

17. Point P is on HP and 35 mm in front of VP. Another Point Q is on VP and below HP. The line joining their front views makes an angle of 30° to XY line, while the line joining their top views makes an angle of 45° with XY line. Find the distance of the point Q from HP.

18. A point P is 25 mm above HP & 20 mm in front of VP. Another point Q is on HP and 30 mm behind VP. The distance between their projectors measured parallel to the line of intersection of VP and HP is 50 mm. Find the distance between the top views of points P and Q.

19. A point A is on HP & 30 mm in front of VP. Another point B is 20 mm below HP and 20 mm in front of VP. The distance between their projectors measured parallel to XY line is 50 mm. Find the distance between the front views of the points A & B.

20. A point P is on HP and 30 mm in front of VP. Another point Q is on VP and 40 mm above HP. The distance between their projectors parallel to XY line is 50 mm. Find the distance between their front and top views of the points P and Q.

■■■

3

ORTHOGRAPHIC PROJECTIONS OF LINES

INTRODUCTION

A straight line is the shortest distance between two any points. It has only length but no thickness but for thickness 2H, H, HB B 2B etc pencils were used. Whereas in computer aided engineering graphics the line has length and thickness. A line represents the locus of a point moving along a fixed path. A line consists of a number of points; its projections are drawn by joining the projection of its extreme (end) points. Hence, the projections of a straight line may be drawn by joining the respective projections of its ends, which are points.

The position of a straight line may have different orientations in space.

As per first angle projection, it may be parallel, perpendicular or inclined to either or both the reference planes (horizontal or vertical planes).

Positions of straight lines

1. Line parallel to both the reference planes (HP & VP)
   (a) Line away from both HP and VP.
   (b) Line in HP and away from VP.
   (c) Line in VP and above HP.
   (d) Line on both HP and VP.
2. Line perpendicular to either of reference planes (HP or VP)
   (a) Line perpendicular to HP and away from VP.
   (b) Line perpendicular to HP and on VP.
   (c) Line perpendicular to VP and above HP.
   (d) Line perpendicular to VP and on HP.
3. Line inclined to HP and parallel to VP
   (a) Line inclined to HP, parallel to VP and away from VP.
   (b) Line ınclined to HP, parallel to VP and in VP.
4. Line inclined to VP and parallel to HP
   (a) Line inclined to VP, parallel to HP and away from HP.
   (b) Line inclined to VP, parallel to HP and in HP.
5. Line inclined to both HP and VP
   (a) One end of line in HP and the other end away from VP.
   (b) One end of line in VP and the other end away from HP.
   (c) One end above HP and the other end away from VP.
   (d) One end away from VP and the other end above HP.
   (e) One end in HP and VP and other end away from HP and VP.
   (f) Both ends on HP and VP.
6. Line parallel to profile plane (PP)
   (a) Line parallel to PP and on HP.
   (b) Line parallel to PP and above HP.
   (c) Line parallel to PP and in VP

(d) Line parallel to PP and away from VP.
(e) Line parallel to PP and inclined to HP.
(f) Line parallel to PP and inclined to VP.
(g) Line parallel to PP and inclined to HP and VP.

System of Notation

1. The actual line in space is denoted by capital letters A and B, or C and D etc.
2. The front view (FV) of a line is denoted by their corresponding lower letters with dashes as a′ and b′, c′ and d′ etc.
3. The top view (TV) of a line is denoted by their corresponding lower case letters without dashes as a and b, c and d etc.
4. The side view (SV) of a line are denoted by their corresponding lower case letters with double dashes as a" and b″, c″ and d″ etc.
5. Projectors are always drawn as continuous thin lines.
6. Line with specific thickness for a particular type of line.
7. In Computer Aided Engineering Graphics for projection of line following commands are used other than evoking software, opening file, saving file and giving print command. Using these minimum 10 commands any type of projection of line problem can be solved they are as follows:

1. Select Tool Command.
2. Point command.
3. Poly-Line command.
4. Two Point Line command.
5. Parallel line command.
6. Center Circle command
7. Bisector command.
8. Smart Dimension command.
9. Line Width command.
10. Insert Text command.

PROBLEM 3.1

A line AB 80 mm long has its end A 20 mm above the HP and 30 mm in front of VP. It is inclined at 30° to HP and 45° to VP. Draw the projections of the line.

SOLUTION

Manual Method

(a) Draw the XY line. Mark VP above it and HP below it.
(b) Mark a′ 20mm above XY line. Project from a′ below XY line of 30 mm to get a.
(c) Draw $a'b_1'$ line at an angle of 30° and length equal to 80 mm (given).
(d) Draw ab_2 line at an angle of 45° and length equal to 80 mm (given).
(e) From b_1' project vertically downward to get b_1 on locus a, similarly from b_2 project vertically upward to get b_2' on locus a′.
(f) With a as center and ab_1 as radius, draw an arc until it cuts the locus of b in top view to get b.
(g) With a′ as center and $a'b_2'$ as radius, draw an arc until it cuts the locus of b′ in front view to get b′.
(h) Join ab and a′b′ to the top and front view of the line.

Computer Aided Drafting Procedure

1. Open the SOFTWARE. Click on the DRAWING in the open dialog box and say OK.

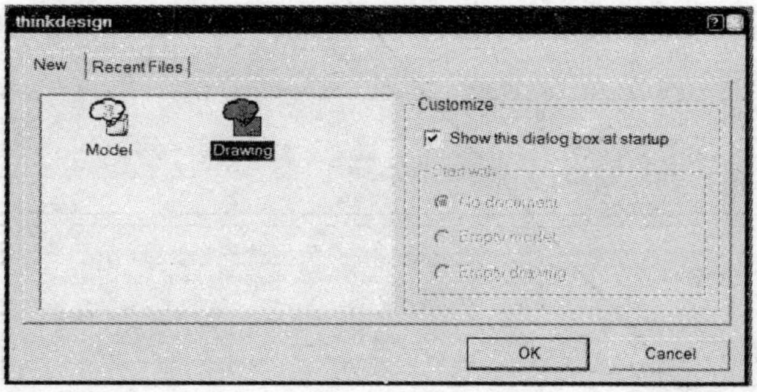

2. To set up the sheet of required size (Ex: A4) by selecting TOOLS from Main Menu Bar and click on OPTIONS/PROPERTIES. Select document properties in dialog box appeared and then select drawing in selection panel. Select the required size say A4, and click OK.

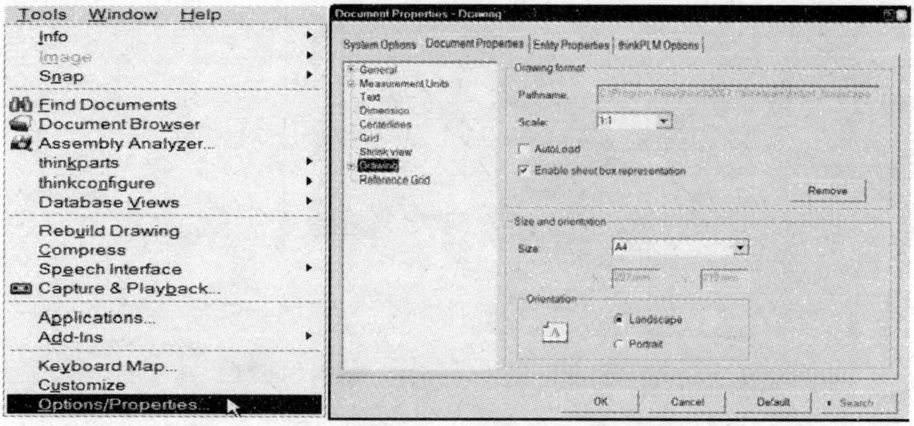

3. Draw the line by using POLYLINE  command from drafting tool bar.

4. Make Annotation X, Y, VP, and HP to the line drawn by using INSERT TEXT Command  from drafting tool bar, just by typing X, Y, VP and HP in Text Box and insert these in the required position by left click of the mouse, as shown below.

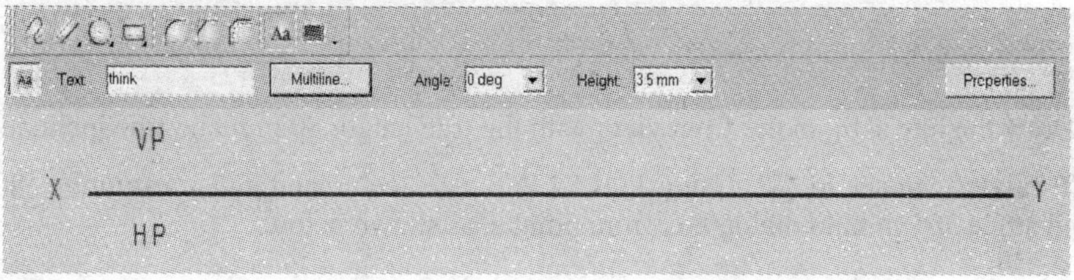

5. As per the problem, one end A is 20 mm above HP and 30 mm in front of VP. Let us mark point a′ and a above and below XY Line. Using the POINT Command  and mark annotations a′and a using INSERT TEXT Command  as shown below.

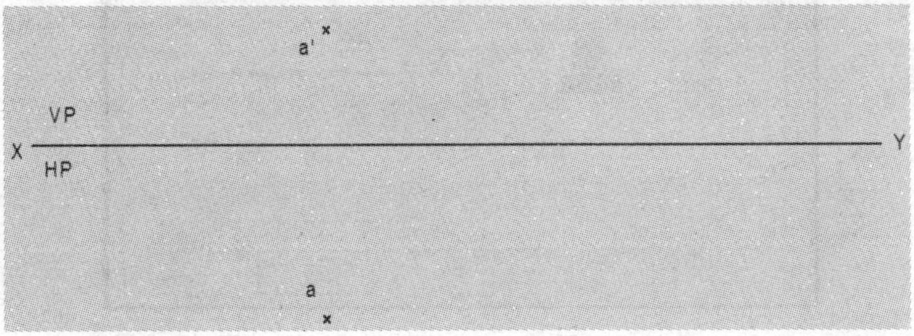

6. Using 2 POINT LINE Command 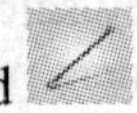 join a′ and a. Using POLYLINE  command draw the locus from a′ and a, to change the line type of locus drawn. Select locus and assign to line type 4 in the status bar as shown.

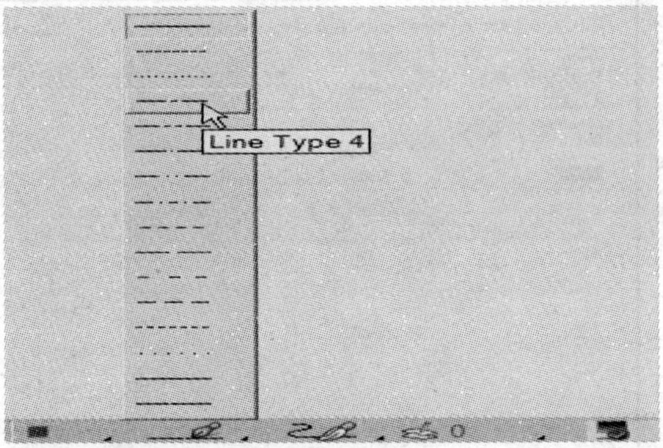

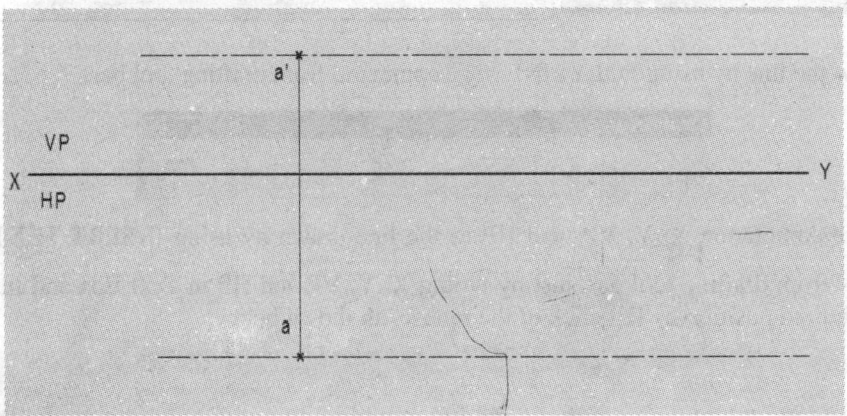

7. Draw the line $a'b_1'$ in the front view with the true length 80 mm and true inclination of 30° to HP (given) we see in VP. Using POLYLINE  command and substituting 80 mm length and angle 30° in mini dialog box from point a′ as shown below.

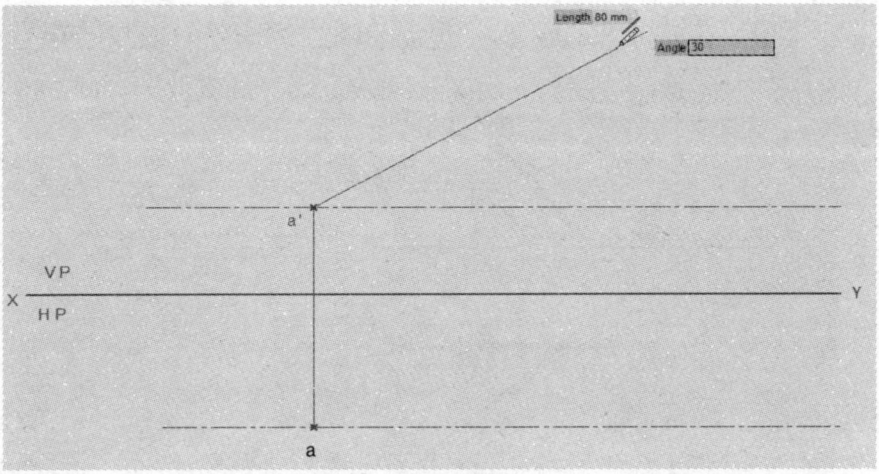

8. Draw the line ab_2 in the top view with the true length 80 mm and true inclination of 45° to HP (given) we see in VP. Using POLYLINE  command and substituting 80 mm length and angle –45° in mini dialog box from point a as shown below.

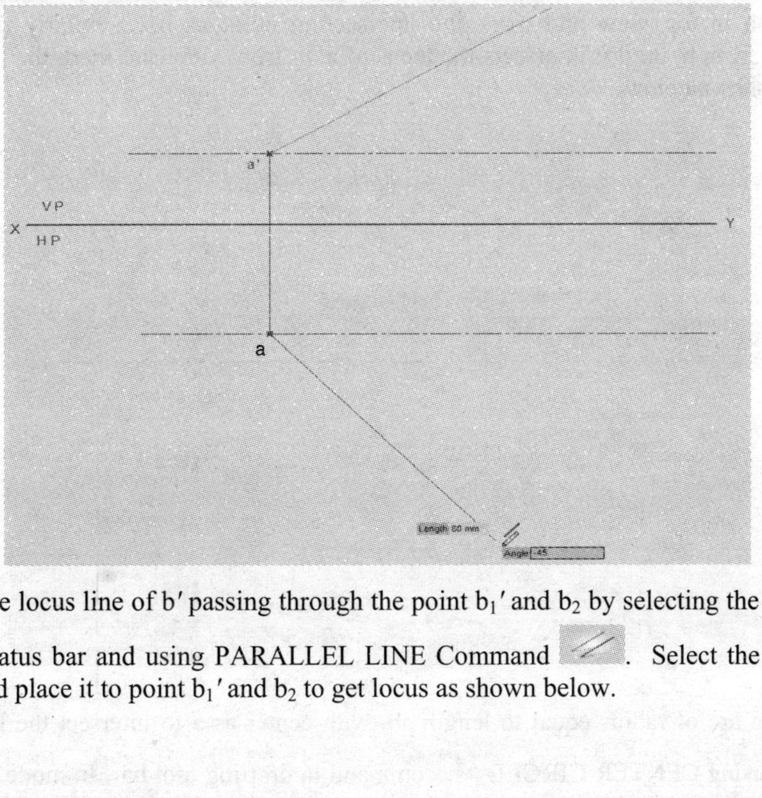

9. Draw the locus line of b′ passing through the point b_1' and b_2 by selecting the line to line type 4 from status bar and using PARALLEL LINE Command . Select the locus a already drawn and place it to point b_1' and b_2 to get locus as shown below.

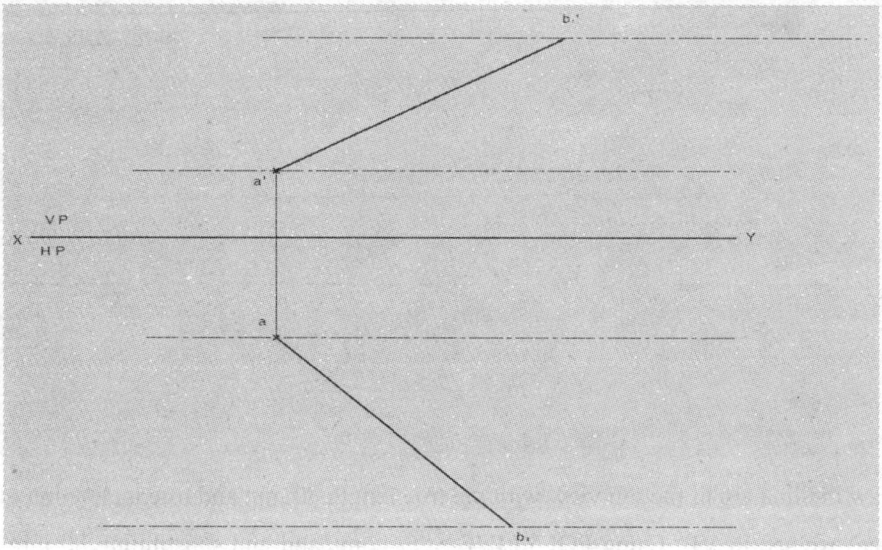

10. Using POLYLINE  command draw downward projector from b_1' until it intersects the locus of a in top view and mark the intersection point as b1. Similarly draw the upward projector from b_2 until it intersects the locus of a′ in front view and mark the intersection point as b_2' as shown below.

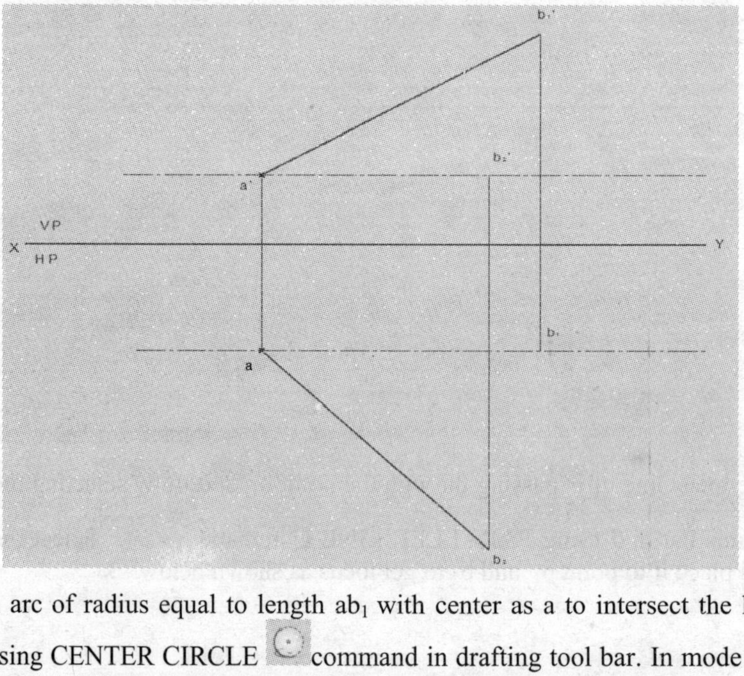

11. Draw an arc of radius equal to length ab_1 with center as a to intersect the locus of b in top view by using CENTER CIRCLE 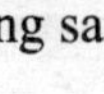 command in drafting tool bar. In mode option select arc to get point b. Similarly, draw an arc of radius equal to length $a'b_2'$ with center as a′ to intersect the locus of b′ in front view by using same commands to get point b′ as shown below.

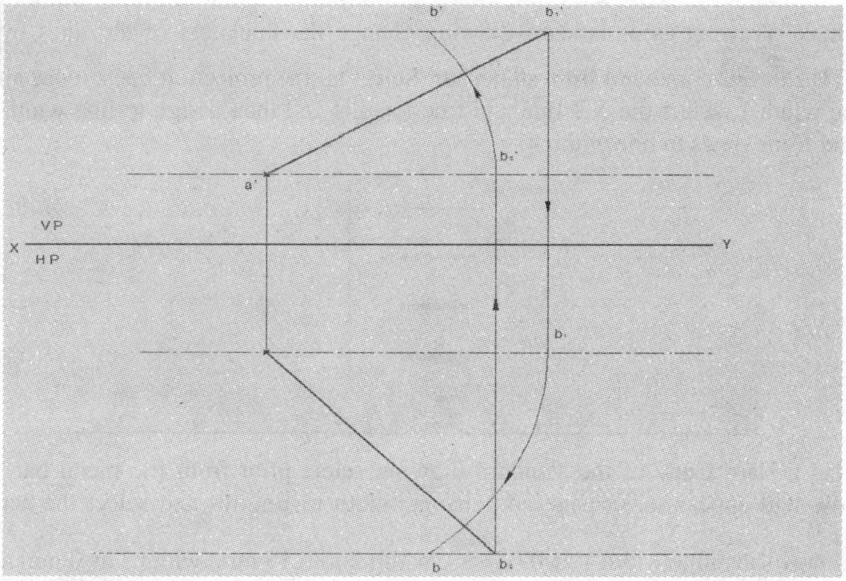

12. Using POLYLINE command join a'b' and ab to get front and top views of the line AB.

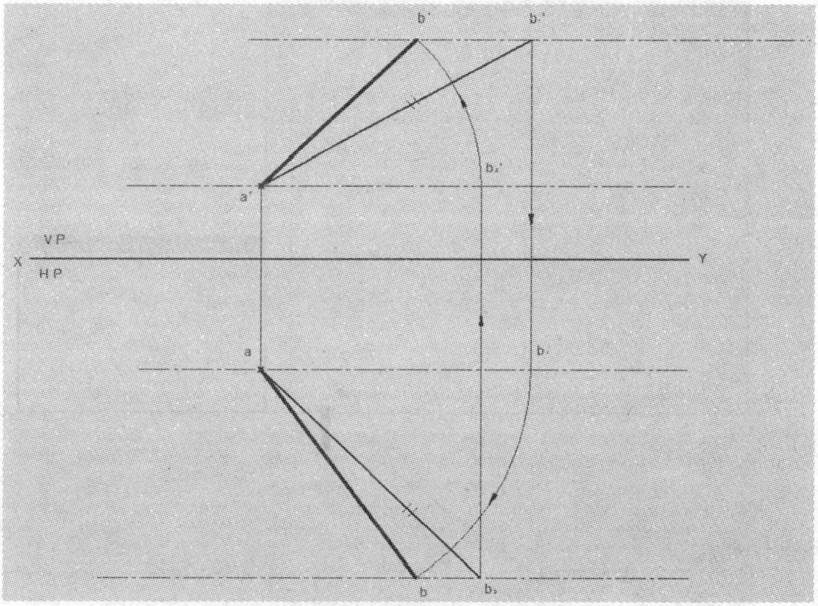

13. Using SMART DIMENSION Command in drawing tool bar dimension the drawing as shown.

14. To make drawing as a standard drawing change the thickness of the lines by using LINE WIDTH  command from status bar. Select all the projection lines, locus and then assign to line width 1, select the XY line and true lengths and then assign to line width 2 and assign top and from views to line width 4.

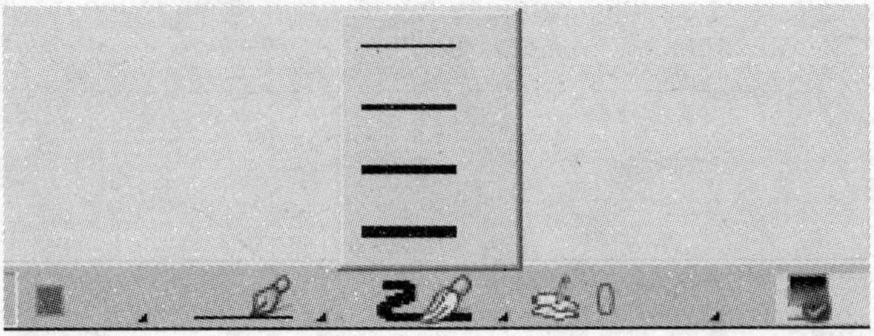

15. To get a Hard Copy of the standard drawing select print from file menu bar. Print dialog window will appear select page and change width to Entities and select the activated button  now substitute width 1 as 0.05 mm, width 2 as 0.15 mm, width 3 as 0 mm and width 4 as 0.5 mm and say OK. Select print to get a hard copy and finally save the file. The required standard drawing is as shown below.

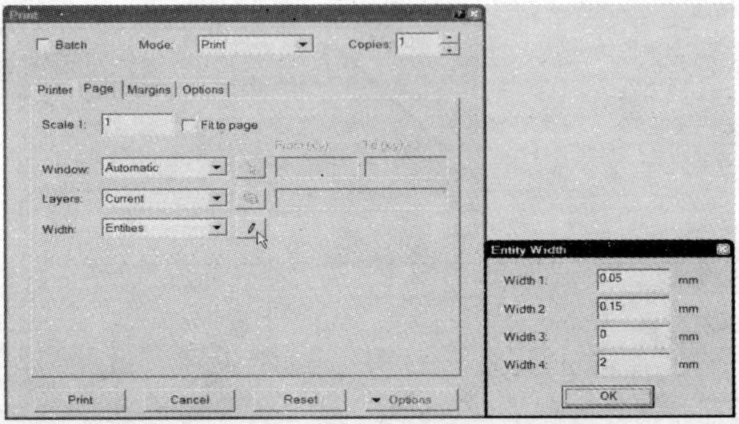

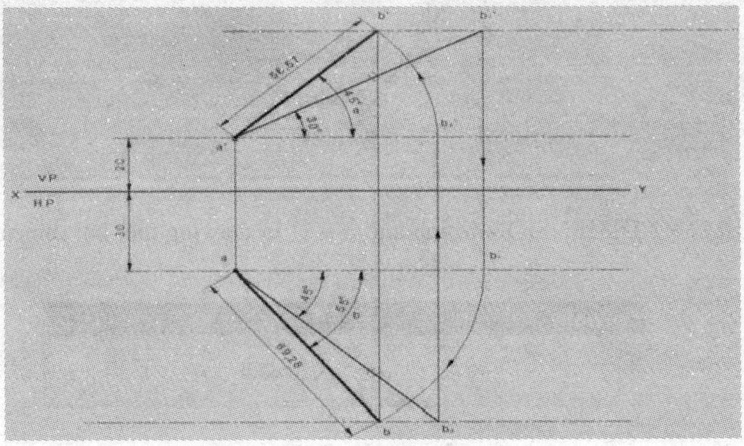

PROBLEM 3.2

The top view PQ of a straight line is 70 mm and makes an angle of 60° with XY line. The end Q is 10 mm in front of VP and 30 mm above the HP. The difference between the distances of p and q above the HP is 45 mm. Draw the projections. Find its true length and true inclinations with HP and VP.

SOLUTION

Manual Method

(a) Draw the XY line. Mark VP above and HP below it.
(b) Mark q′ 30 mm above XY line. Project from q′ below XY line of 10 mm to get q.
(c) Draw qp line at an angle of 60° and length equal to 70 mm (given).
(d) Draw locus line at a distance of 45 mm above XY line (given).
(e) Project from p to meet locus in front view to get p′. Join q′p′.
(f) With q as center and qp as radius, draw an arc until it cuts the locus of p in top view to get p_1. From p_1 project upwards to meet locus of p in front view to get p_1'.
(g) With q′ as center and q′p′ as radius, draw an arc until it cuts the locus of b′ in front view to get p_2'. From p_2' project downwards to meet locus of p in top view to get p_2.
(h) Join qp_1' and $q'p_2'$ to the true length of line. Measure length and angle with HP and VP.

Computer Aided Drafting Procedure

1. Open the SOFTWARE. Click on the DRAWING in the open dialog box and say OK.

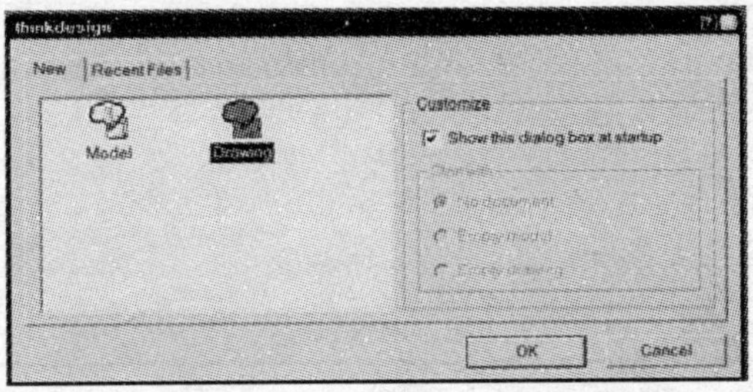

2. To set up the sheet of required size (Ex: A4) by selecting TOOLS from Main Menu Bar and click on OPTIONS/PROPERTIES. Select document properties in dialog box appeared and then select drawing in selection panel. Select the required size say A4, and click OK.

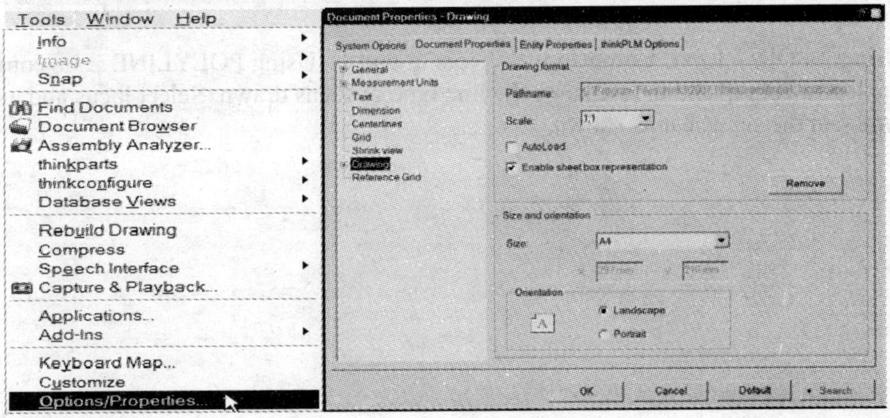

3. Draw the line by using POLYLINE command from drafting tool bar.

4. Make Annotation X, Y, VP, and HP to the line drawn by using INSERT TEXT Command from drafting tool bar, just by typing X, Y, VP and HP in Text Box and insert these in the required position by left click of the mouse, as shown below.

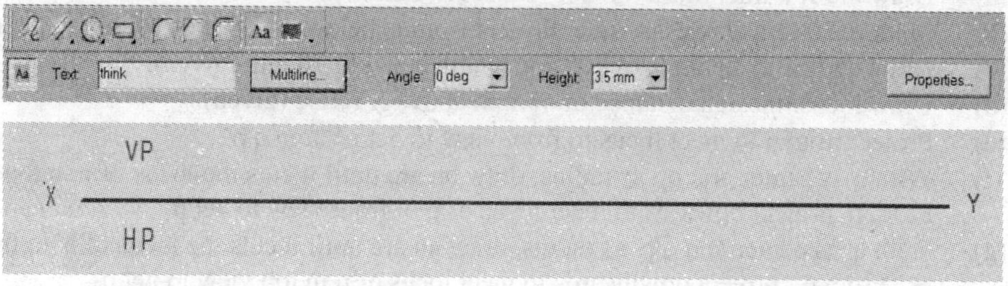

5. As per the problem, one end q is 30 mm above HP and 10 mm in front of VP. Let us mark point q′ and q above and below XY Line. Using the POINT Command and mark annotations q′ and q using INSERT TEXT Command as shown below.

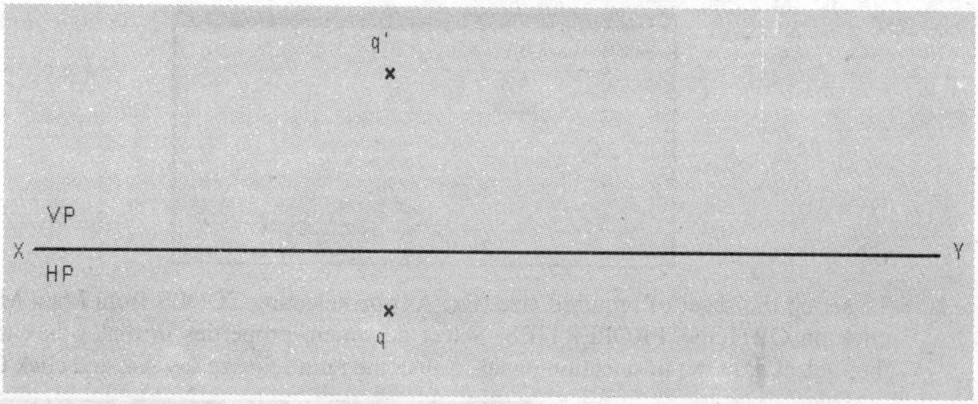

6. Using 2 POINT LINE Command join q′ and q. Using POLYLINE command draw the locus from q′ and q, to change the line type of locus drawn. Select locus and assign to line type 4 in the status bar as shown.

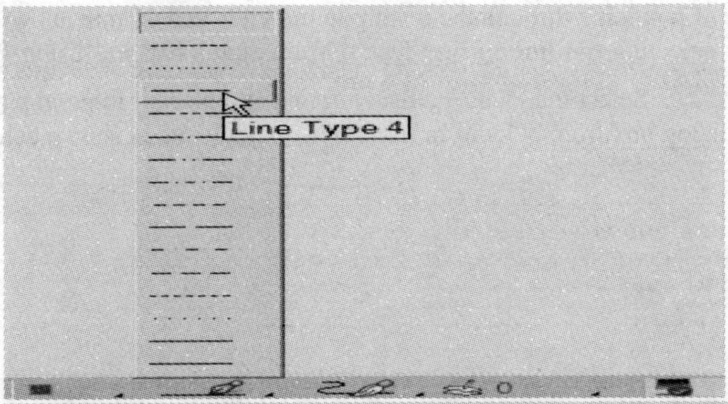

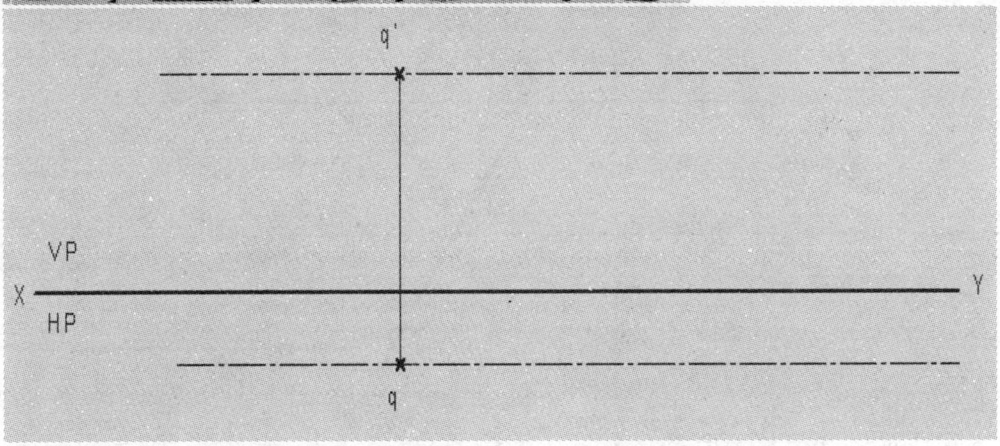

7. Draw the line qp in the top view with the length of 70 mm and inclination of 60° in HP. Using POLYLINE  command and substituting 70 mm length and angle –60° in mini dialog box from point q as shown below.

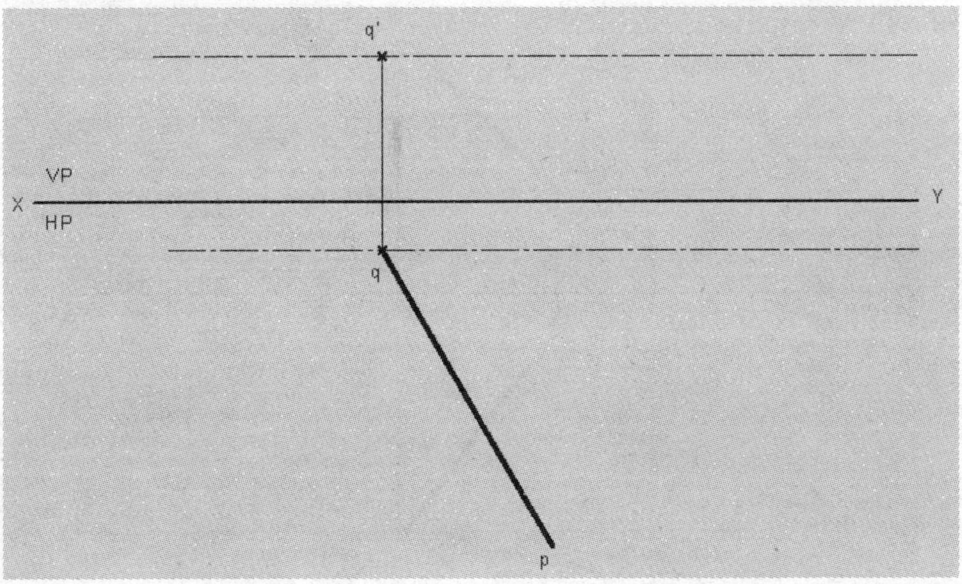

8. Draw the locus line of p passing through the point p in top view and 45 mm above the locus of q in front view by selecting the line to line type 4 from status bar and using PARALLEL LINE Command . Select the locus q already drawn and place it to point p and enter 45 mm offset in mini dialog box from q′ locus in front view to get locus as shown below.

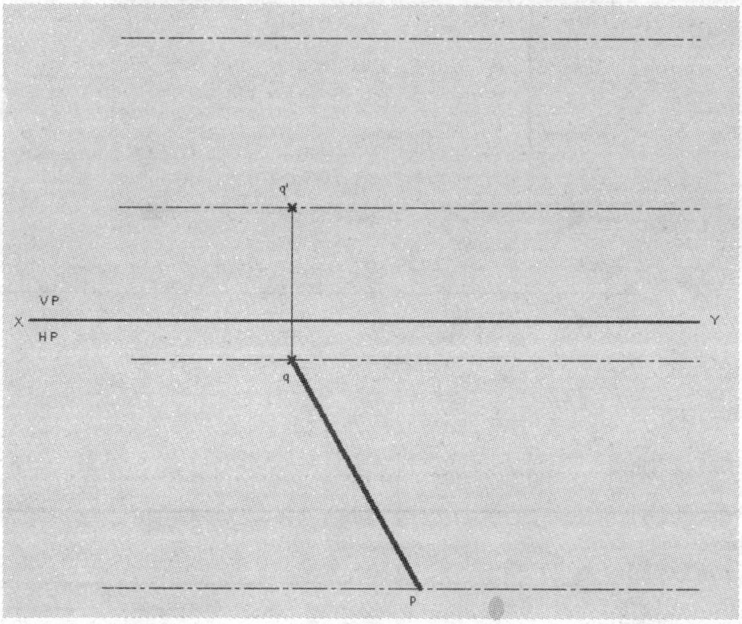

9. Using POLYLINE  command draw upward projector from p until it intersects the locus of p′ in front view and mark the intersection point as p′. Using 2 POINT LINE Command  join p′ and q′ to get the front view of the line.

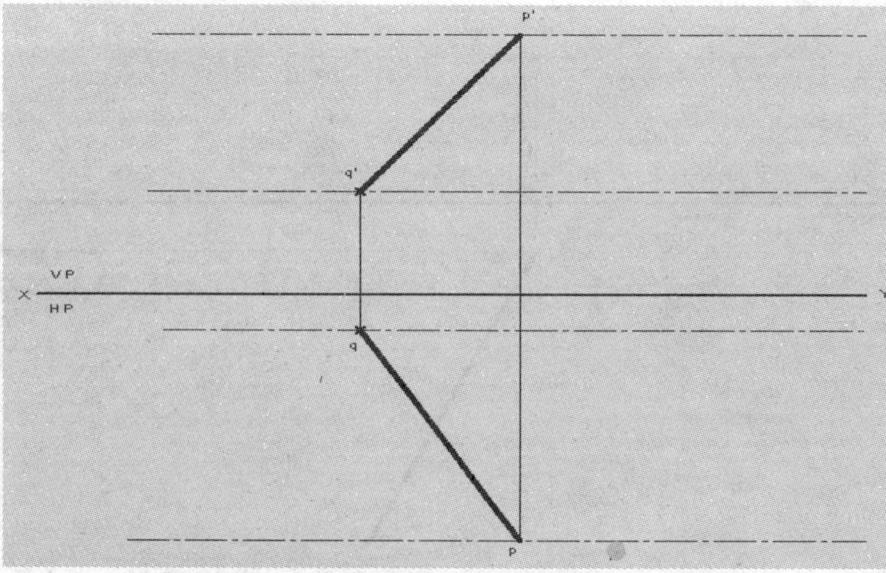

10. Draw an arc of radius equal to length $q'p'$ with center as q' to intersect the locus of q' in front view by using CENTER CIRCLE  command in drafting tool bar. In mode option select arc to get point p_2'. Similarly draw an arc of radius equal to length qp with center as q to intersect the locus of q in top view by using same commands to get point p_1 as shown below.

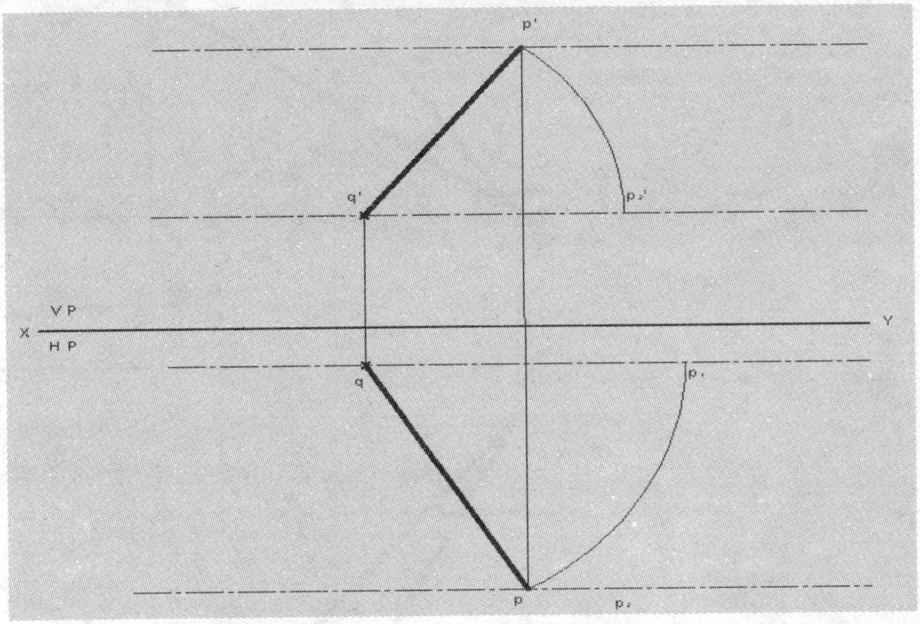

11. Using POLYLINE  command draw downward projector from p_2' until it intersects with the locus of p in top view to get p_2. Similarly draw upward projector from p_1 until it intersects with the locus of p' in front view to get p_1' using same commands as shown below.

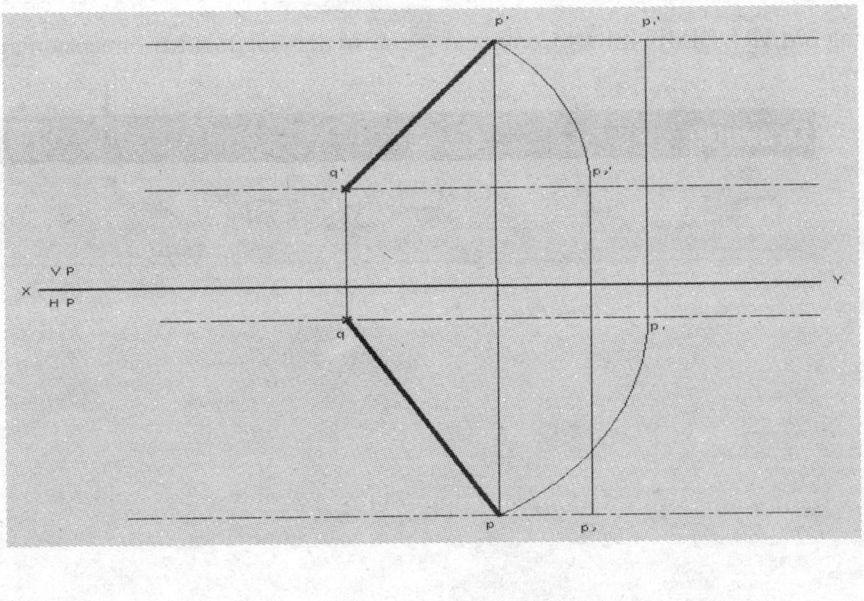

12. Using 2 POINT LINE Command  join p_1' and q' to get the true length of the line. Similarly join p_2 and q to get the true length of the line as shown below.

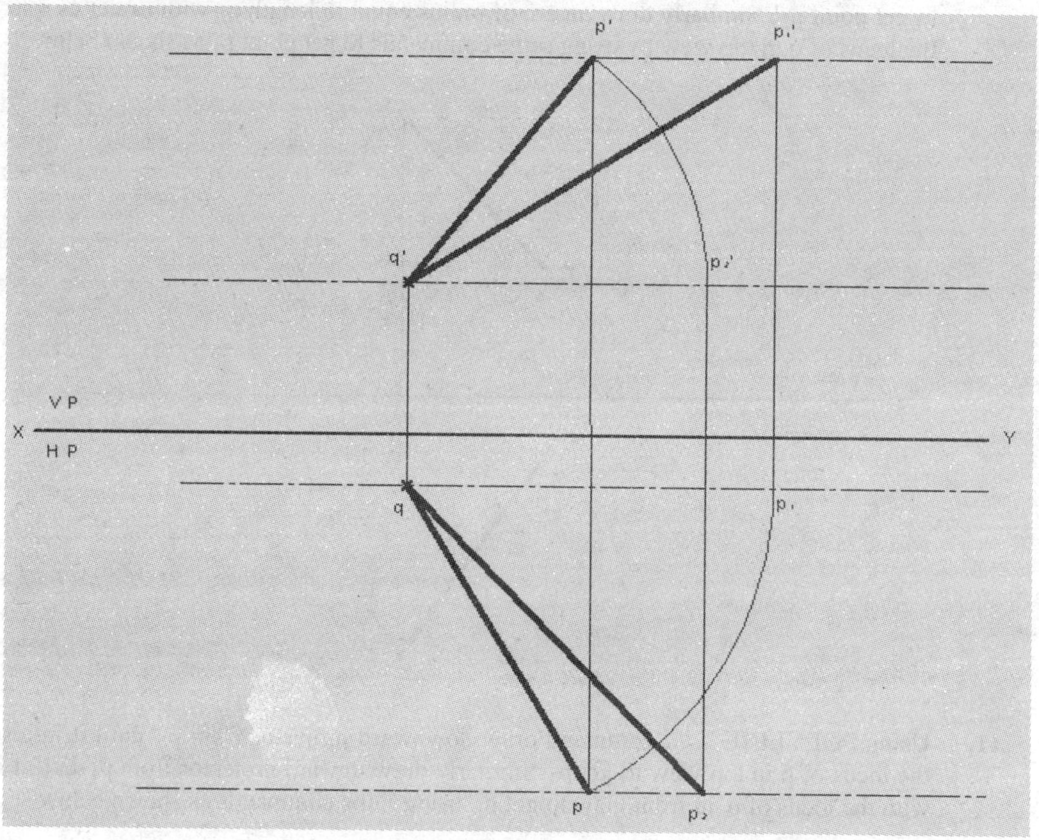

13. Using SMART DIMENSION Command 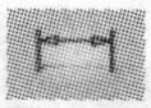 in drawing tool bar dimension the drawing as shown.

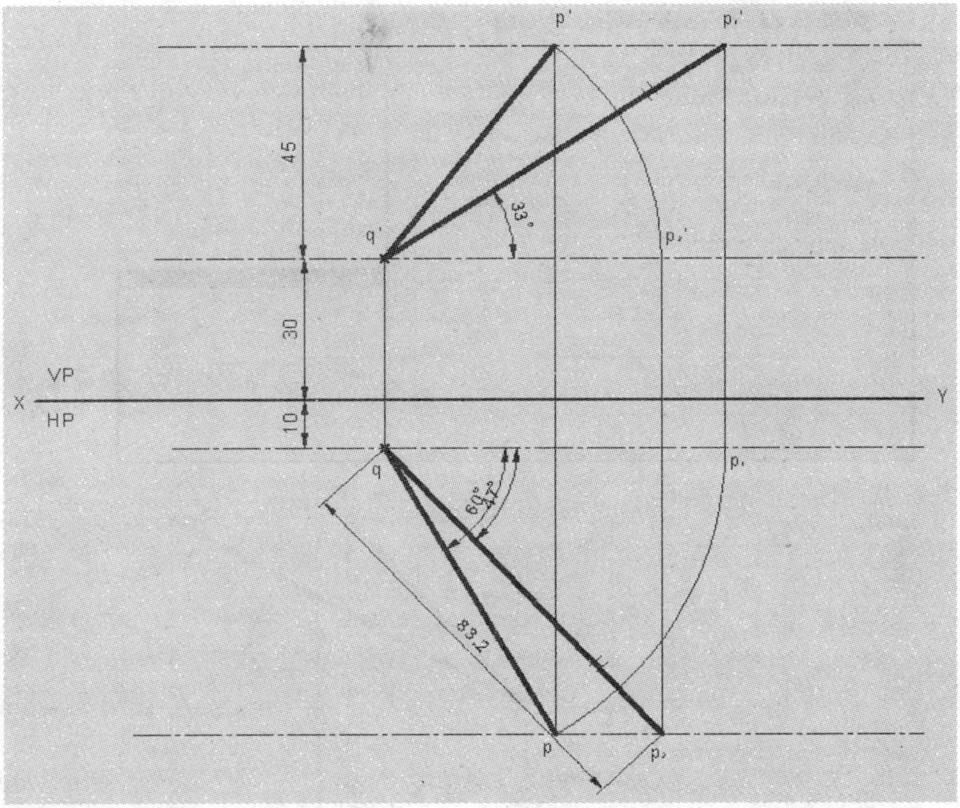

14. To make drawing as a standard drawing change the thickness of the lines by using LINE WIDTH 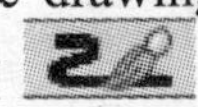 command from status bar. Select all the projection lines, locus and then assign to line width 1, select the XY line and true lengths and then assign to line width 2 and assign top and from views to line width 4.

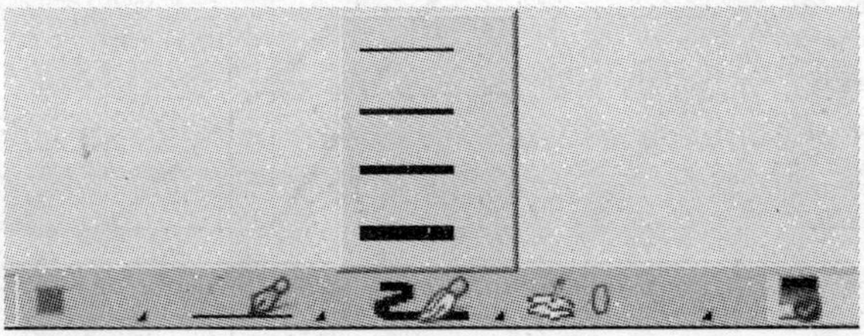

15. To get a Hard Copy of the standard drawing select print from file menu bar. Print dialog window will appear select page and change width to Entities and select the activated button 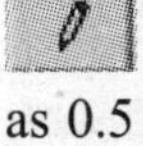 now substitute width 1 as 0.05 mm, width 2 as 0.15 mm, width 3 as 0 mm and width 4 as 0.5 mm and say OK. Select print to get a hard copy and finally save the file. The required standard drawing is as shown below.

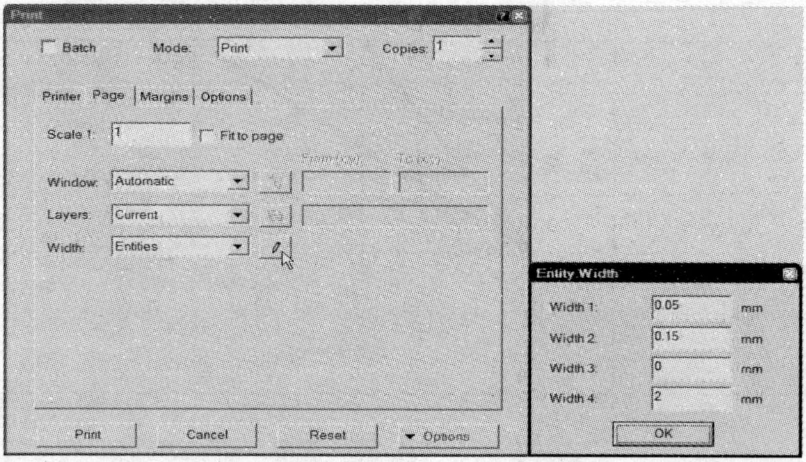

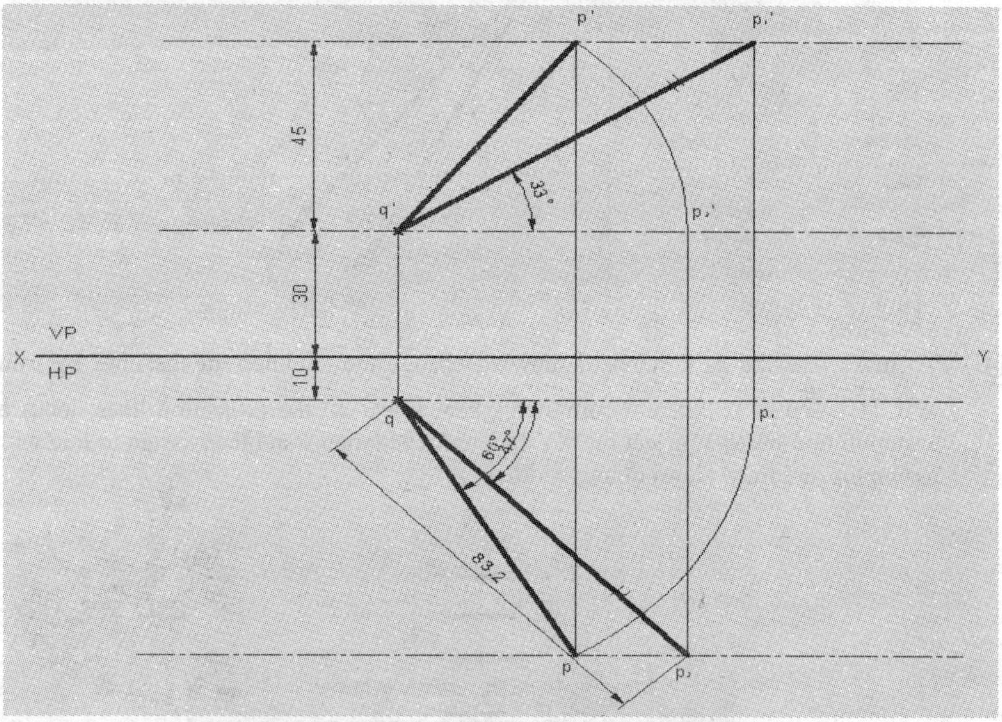

PROBLEM 3.3

A line PQ 85 mm long has its end P 10 mm above the HP and 15 mm in front of the VP. The top view and front view of line PQ are 75 mm and 80 mm respectively. Draw its projections also determine the true and apparent inclinations of the line.

SOLUTION

Manual Method

(a) Draw the XY line. Mark VP above and HP below it.

(b) Mark p′ 10 mm above XY line. Project from p′ below XY line of 15 mm to get p.

(c) Draw an arc arbitrarily from p and p′ of radius 85 mm (given).

(d) Draw an arc from p and p′ of radius 75 mm and 80 mm to cut locus of p and p′ (given).

(e) Draw projector from q_2' and q_1 to intersect the true length arcs to get pq_2' and pq_1.

(f) Extend an arc from p and p′ of radius 75 mm and 80 mm to cut locus of p and p′ to get q and q′.

(g) Join pq and p′q′ to the top and front view of the line. Measure the angles.

Computer Aided Drafting Procedure

1. Open the SOFTWARE. Click on the DRAWING in the open dialog box and say OK.

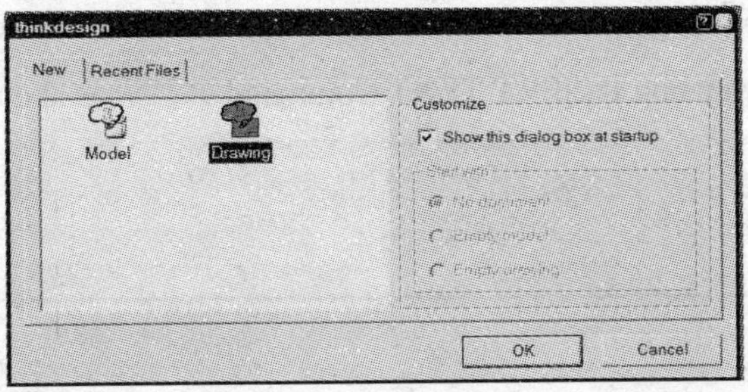

2. To set up the sheet of required size (Ex: A4) by selecting TOOLS from Main Menu Bar and click on OPTIONS/PROPERTIES. Select document properties in dialog box appeared and then select drawing in selection panel. Select the required size say A4, and click OK.

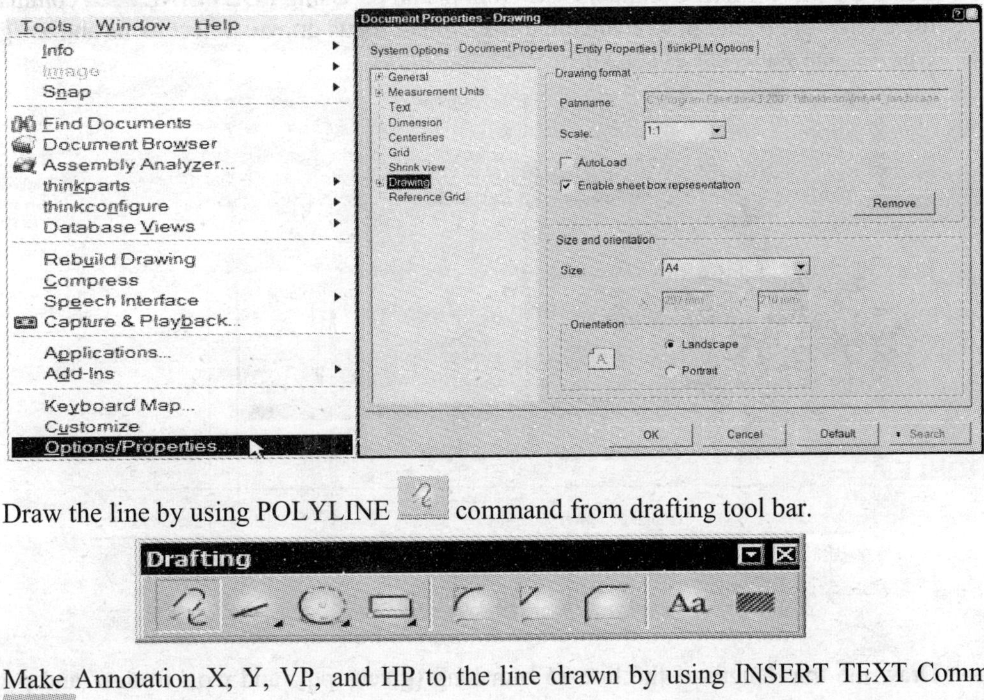

3. Draw the line by using POLYLINE 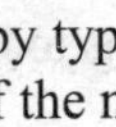 command from drafting tool bar.

4. Make Annotation X, Y, VP, and HP to the line drawn by using INSERT TEXT Command from drafting tool bar, just by typing X, Y, VP and HP in Text Box and insert these in the required position by left click of the mouse, as shown on next page.

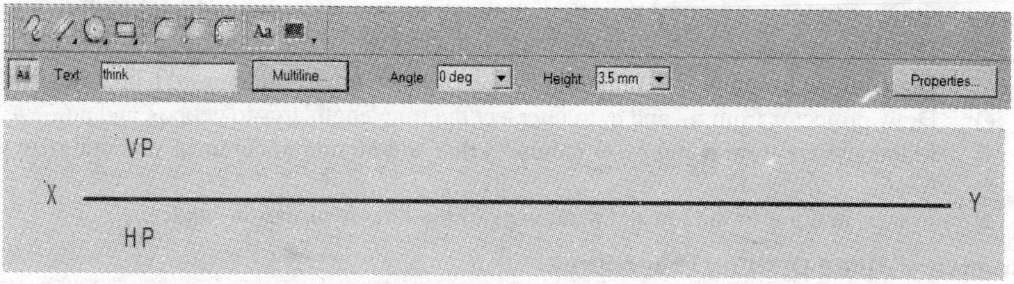

5. As per the problem, one end p is 10 mm above HP and 15 mm in front of VP. Let us mark point p′ and p above and below XY Line. Using the POINT Command and mark annotations p′ and p using INSERT TEXT Command as shown below.

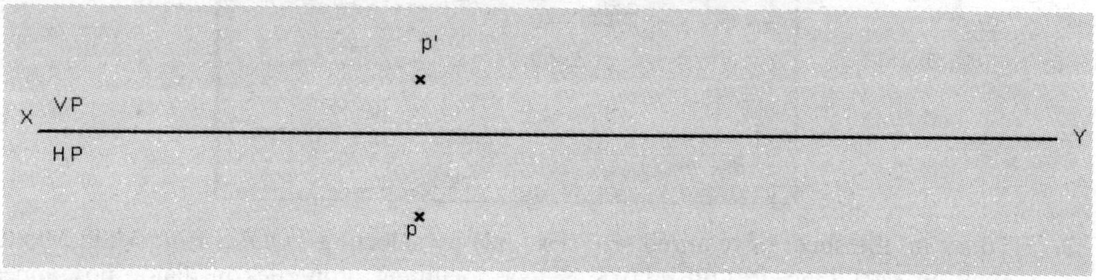

6. Using 2 POINT LINE Command join p′ and p. Using POLYLINE command draw the locus from p′ and p, to change the line type of locus drawn. Select locus and assign to line type 4 in the status bar as shown.

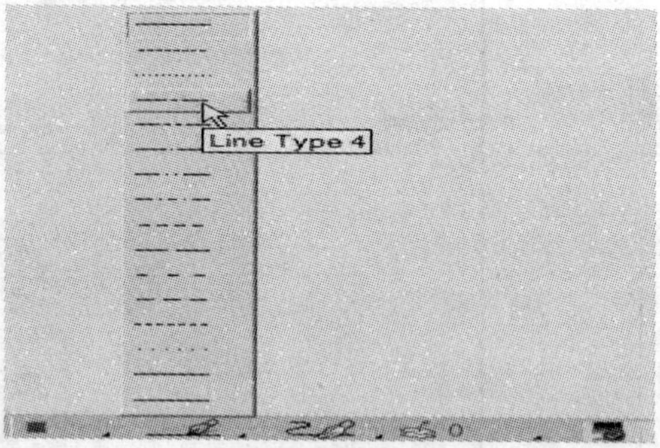

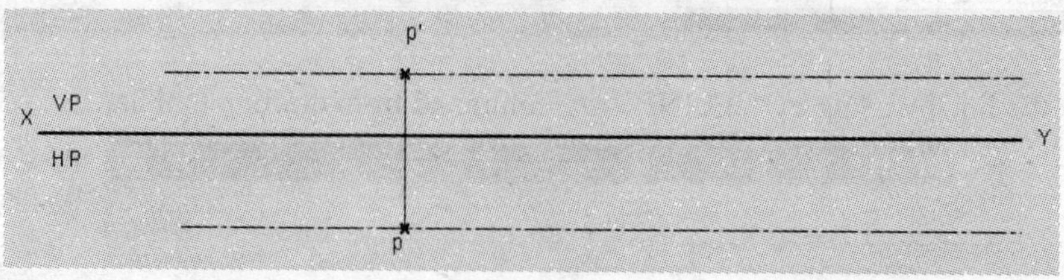

7. Draw the true length of the line 85 mm long (given) pq_2 and $p'q_1'$ from p′ and p by using CENTER CIRCLE command in drafting tool bar. In mode option select arc to get arc approximately.

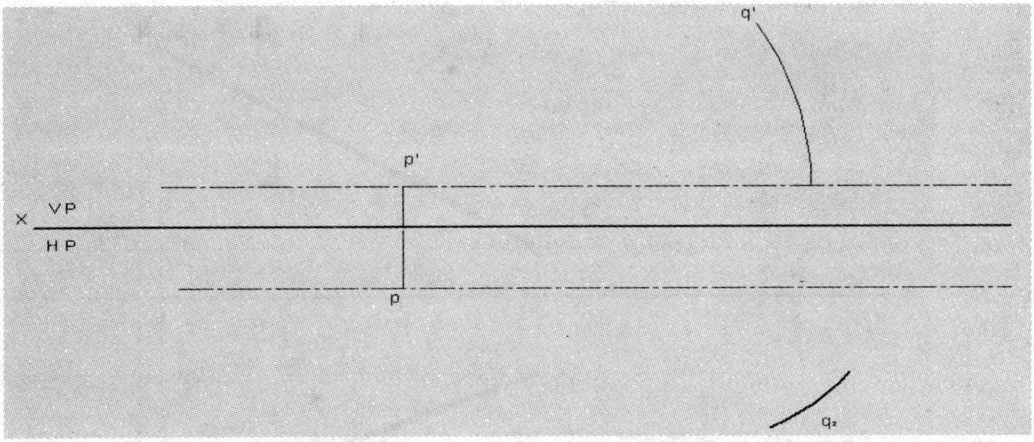

8. Draw the arc to intersect the locus of p and p′ from top and front views of the line 75 mm and 85 mm long (given) p′q′ and pq from p′ and p by using CENTER CIRCLE 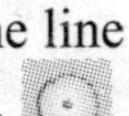 command in drafting tool bar. In mode option select arc, to cut the locus draw an arc to get q_2' and q_1.

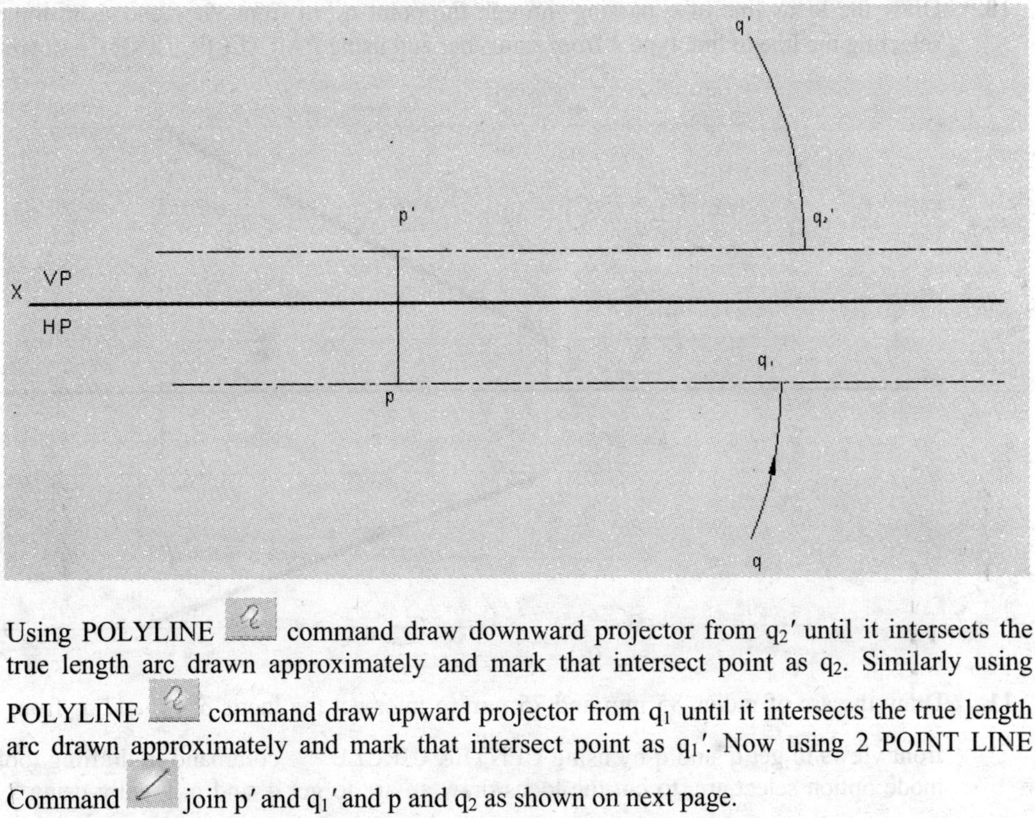

9. Using POLYLINE command draw downward projector from q_2' until it intersects the true length arc drawn approximately and mark that intersect point as q_2. Similarly using POLYLINE command draw upward projector from q_1 until it intersects the true length arc drawn approximately and mark that intersect point as q_1'. Now using 2 POINT LINE Command join p′ and q_1' and p and q_2 as shown on next page.

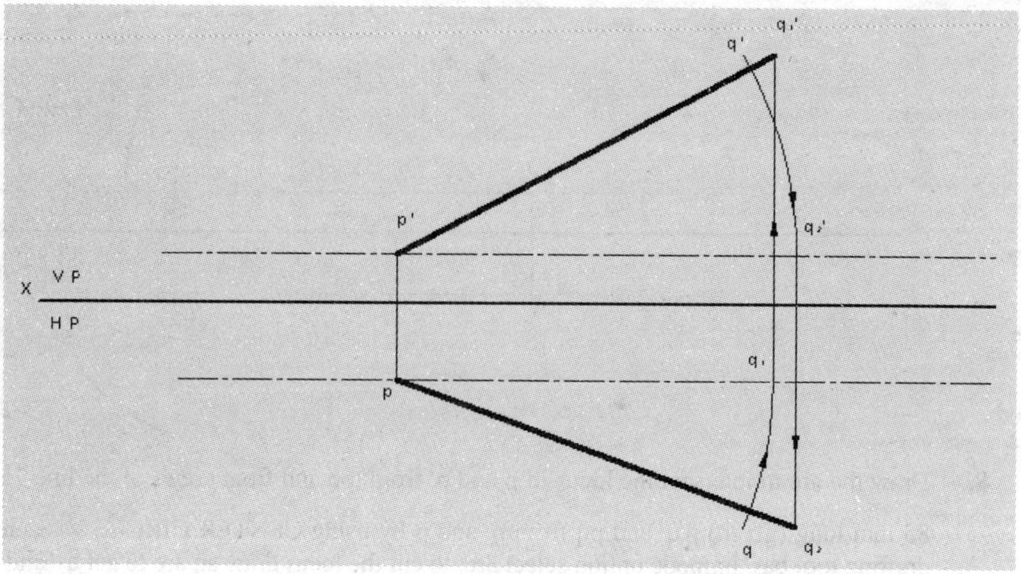

10. Draw the locus line of q passing through the point q_1' in front view and q_2 in top view by selecting the line to line type 4 from status bar and using PARALLEL LINE Command .

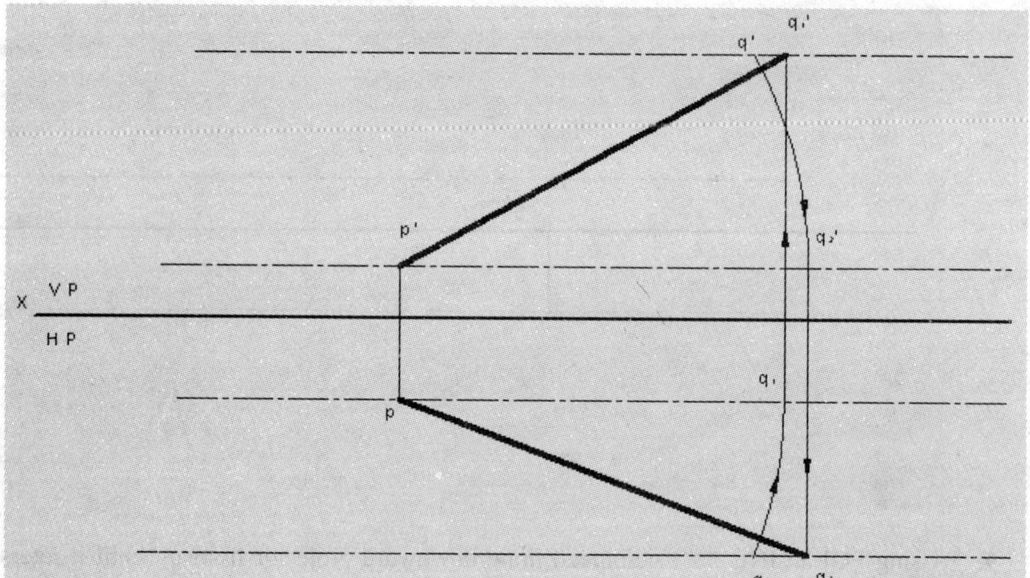

11. Draw the arc of radius 85 mm and 75 mm to intersect the locus of q_2' and q_1 from top and front views to get q′ and q by using CENTER CIRCLE command in drafting tool bar. In mode option select arc, to cut the locus draw an arc to get q′ and q. Finally using 2 POINT LINE Command join p′q′ and pq to get top and front views of the line PQ.

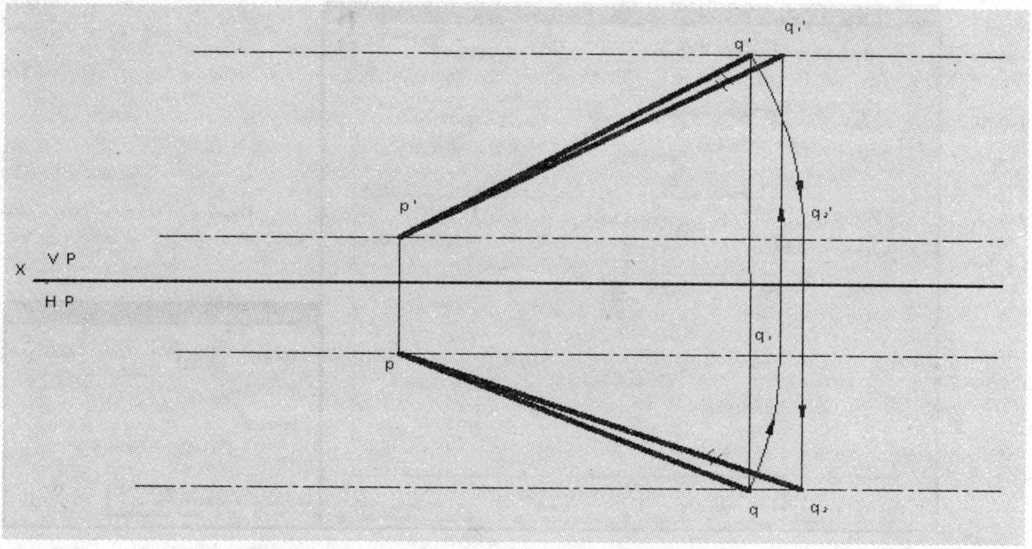

12. Using SMART DIMENSION Command  in drawing tool bar dimension the drawing as shown.

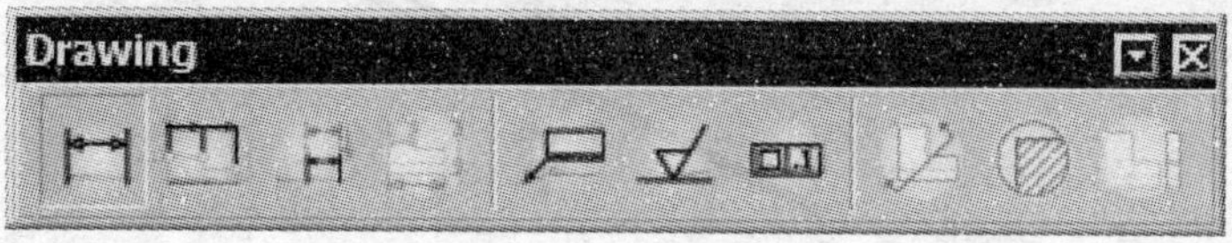

13. To make drawing as a standard drawing change the thickness of the lines by using LINE WIDTH  command from status bar. Select all the projection lines, locus and then assign to line width 1, select the XY line and true lengths and then assign to line width 2 and assign top and from views to line width 4.

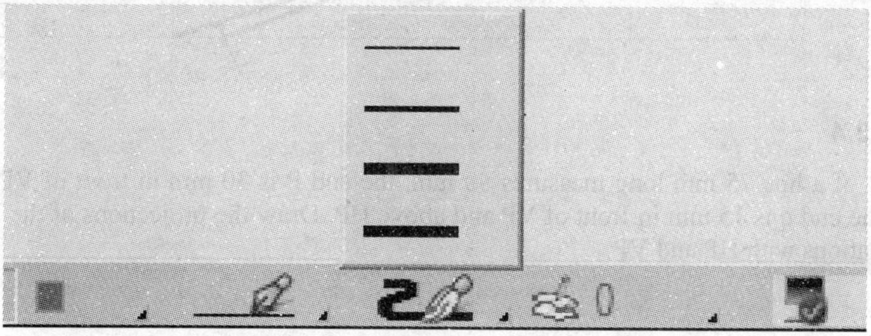

14. To get a Hard Copy of the standard drawing select print from file menu bar. Print dialog window will appear select page and change width to Entities and select the activated button  now substitute width 1 as 0.05 mm, width 2 as 0.15 mm, width 3 as 0 mm and width 4 as 0.5 mm and say OK. Select print to get a hard copy and finally save the file.

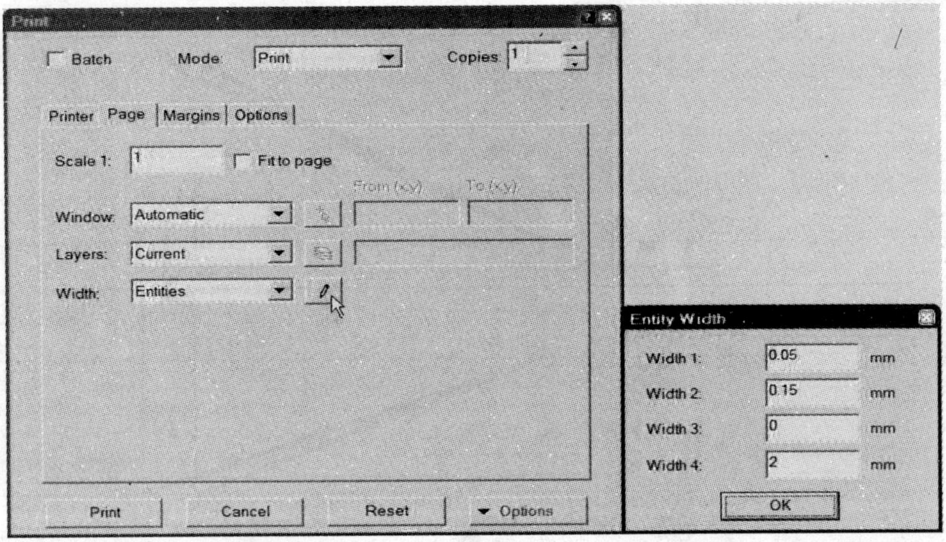

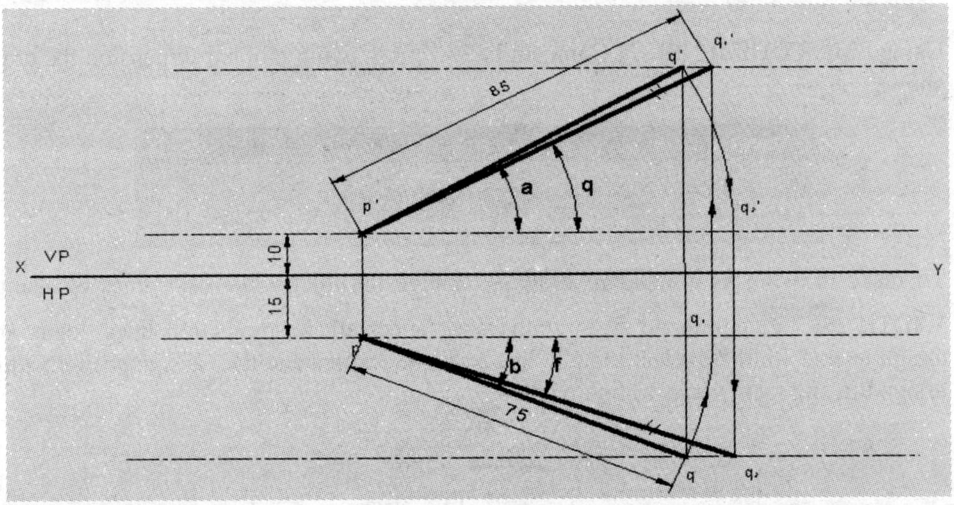

PROBLEM 3.4

The top view of a line 75 mm long measures 50 mm. the end P is 30 mm in front of VP and 15 mm above HP. The end q is 15 mm in front of VP and above HP. Draw the projections of the line and find its true inclinations with HP and VP.

SOLUTION

Manual Method

(a) Draw the XY line. Mark VP above it and HP below it.

(b) Mark p′ 15 mm above XY line. Project from p′ below XY line of 30 mm to get p.

(c) Mark q 15 mm below XY line (given).

(d) With p as center draw, an arc of radius 50 mm to cut the locus of p and q in top view, to get q. Join pq and q_1. From q and q_1 project upwards.

(e) With p as center draw an arc of radius 75 mm to cut the locus, to get q_2, join pq_2.

(f) From q_2 project upwards to meet the locus at q_2'. With pq_2' as radius, draw an arc with p' as center to get q'. Join $p'q'$ and $p'q_1'$.

(g) Measure the angles with HP and VP.

Computer Aided Drafting Procedure

1. Open the SOFTWARE. Click on the DRAWING in the open dialog box and say OK.

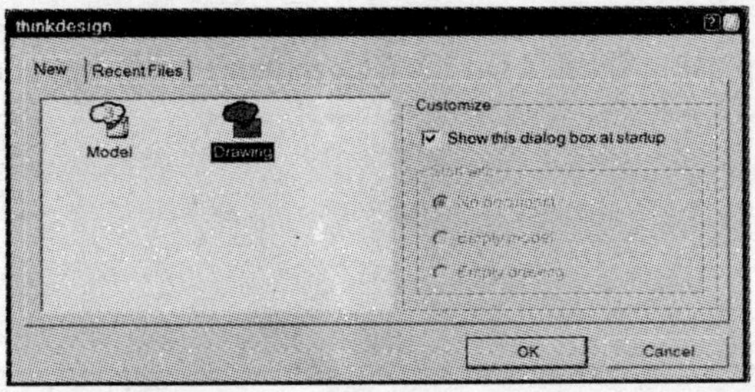

2. To set up the sheet of required size (Ex: A4) by selecting TOOLS from Main Menu Bar and click on OPTIONS/PROPERTIES. Select document properties in dialog box appeared and then select drawing in selection panel. Select the required size say A4, and click OK.

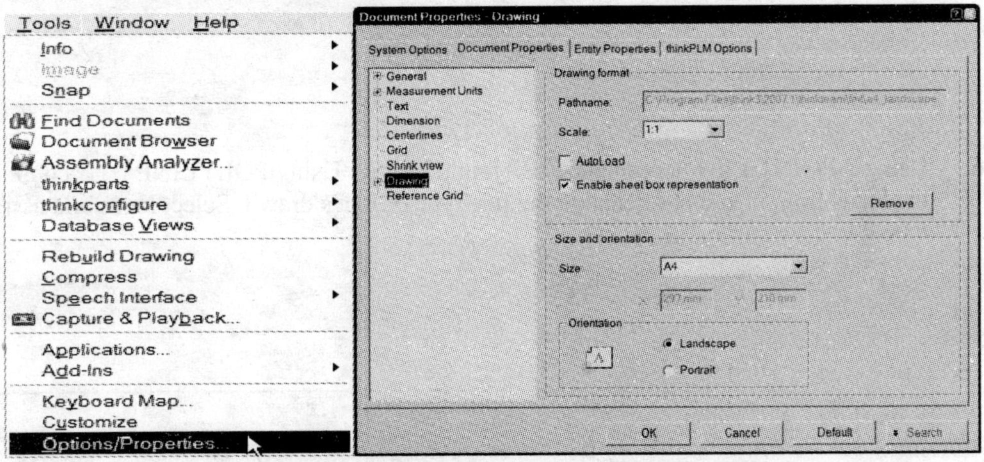

3. Draw the line by using POLYLINE  command from drafting tool bar.

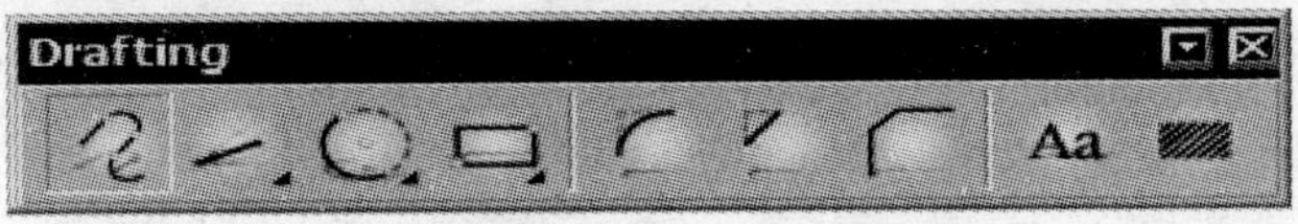

4. Make Annotation X, Y, VP, and HP to the line drawn by using INSERT TEXT Command 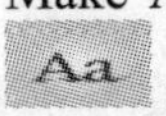

from drafting tool bar, just by typing X, Y, VP and HP in Text Box and insert these in the required position by left click of the mouse, as shown below.

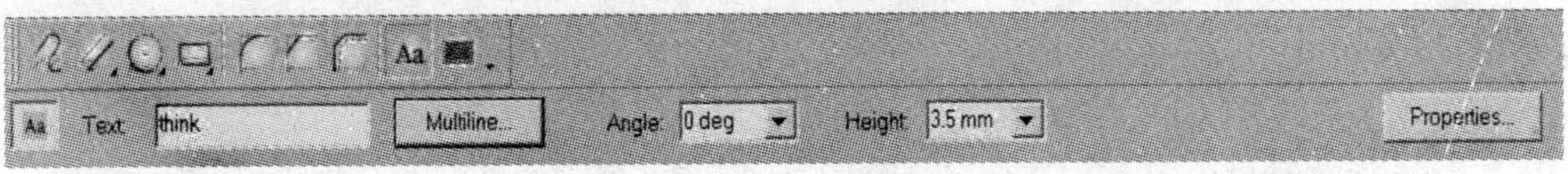

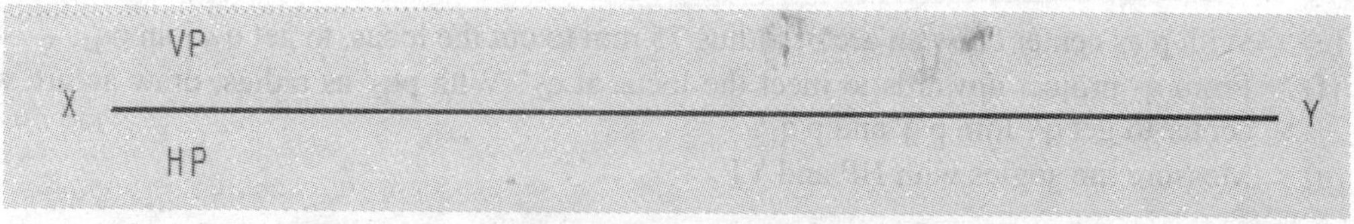

5. As per the problem, one end P is 15 mm above HP and 30 mm infront of VP. Let us mark point p′ and p above and below XY Line. Using the POINT Command 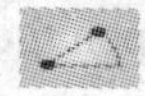 and mark annotations p′and p using INSERT TEXT Command 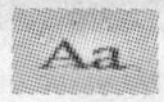 as shown below.

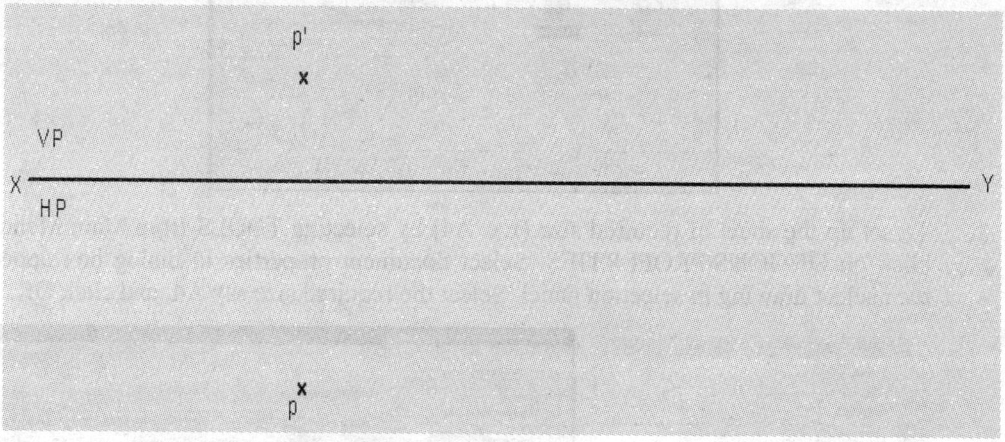

6. Using 2 POINT LINE Command  join p′ and p. Using POLYLINE  command draw the locus from p′ and p, to change the line type of locus drawn. Select locus and assign to line type 4 in the status bar as shown.

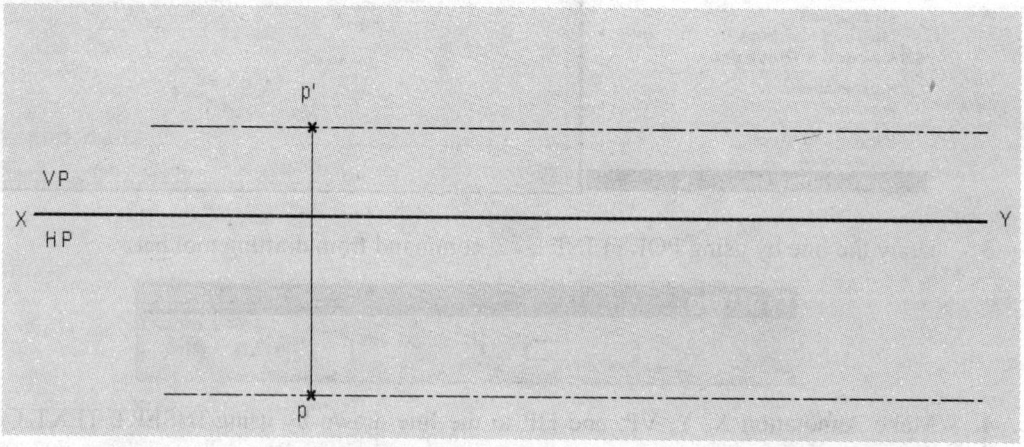

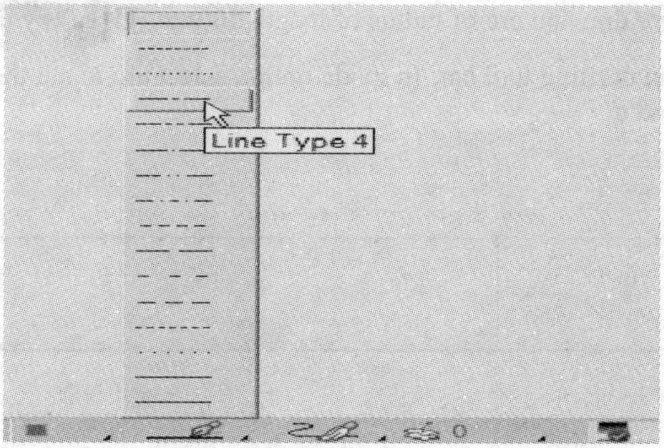

7. Another point Q is 15 mm infront of VP, hence draw the locus for Q. Draw line parallel to XY line using POLYLINE command 15 mm from XY line in HP, to change the line type of locus drawn. Select locus and assign to line type 4 in the status bar as shown.

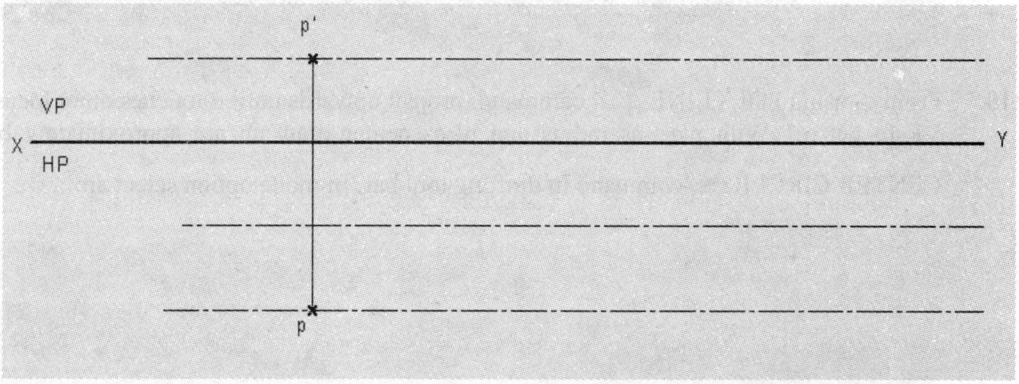

8. Draw the true length of the line 75 mm long (given) pq_2 by using CENTER CIRCLE command in drafting tool bar. In mode option select arc to get arc approximately, so that it can cut the locus from q drawn to get q_2.

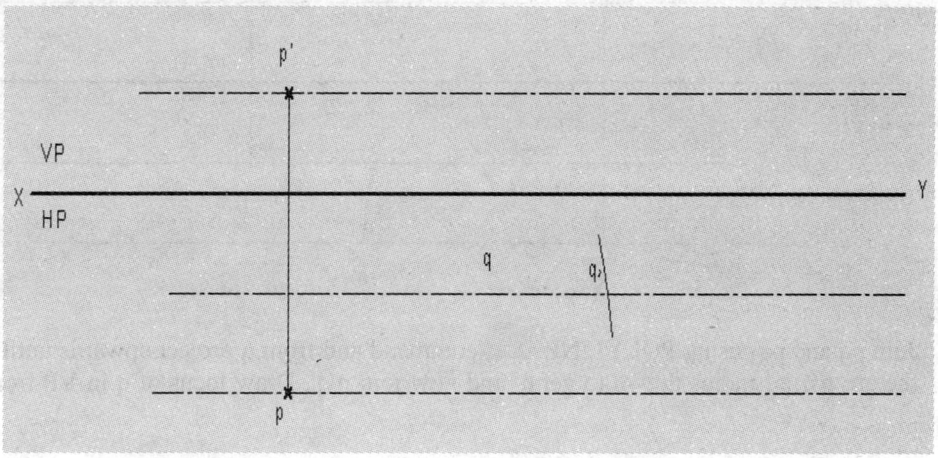

9. From p as center draw an arc of radius of length 50 mm (given) by using CENTER CIRCLE command in drafting tool bar. In mode option select arc to cut the locus of p and q in top view to get q and q_1.

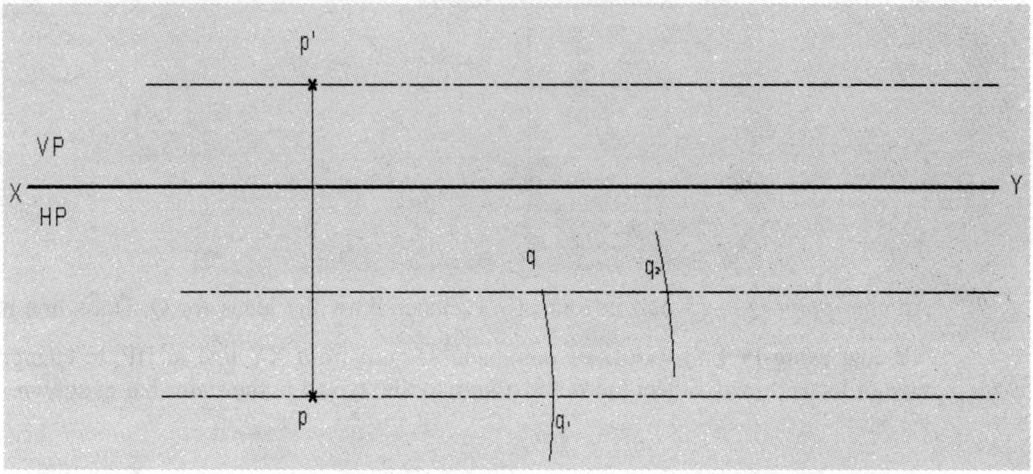

10. From q_2 using POLYLINE command, project upwards until it touches other locus of P in VP to get q_2'. With $p'q_2'$ as radius and p' as center draw an arc approximately by using CENTER CIRCLE command in drafting tool bar. In mode option select arc.

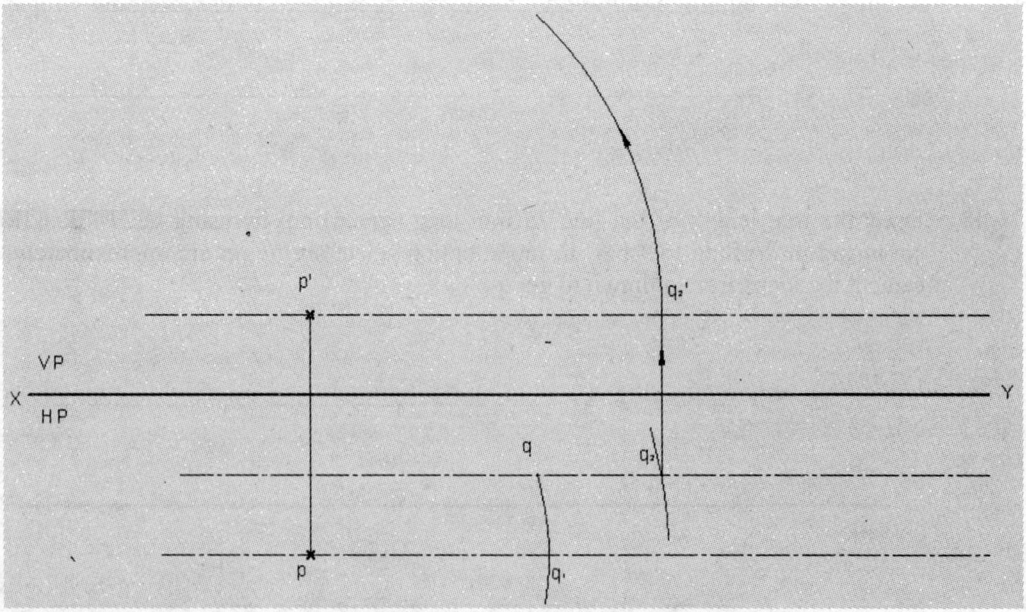

11. Join pq and pq_2 using POLYLINE command and from q project upwards until it touches the arc $p'q_2'$of radius drawn to get q' and now join $p'q'$. Draw locus of q in VP from point q'

using POLYLINE command, to change the line type of locus drawn. Select locus and assign to line type 4 in the status bar as shown.

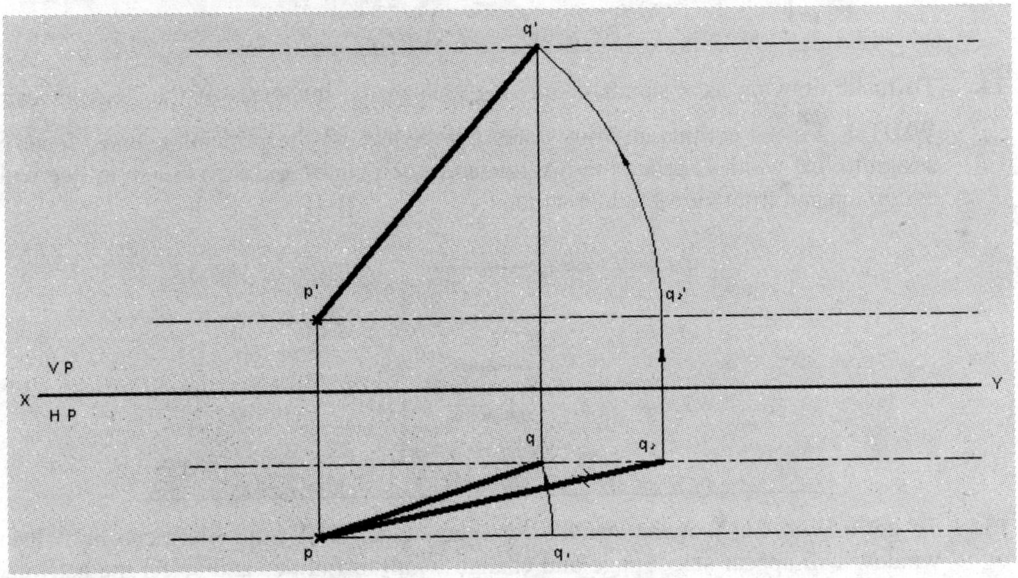

12. From q_1 using POLYLINE command, project upwards until it touches other locus of p in VP to get q_1'. Join $p'q_1'$.

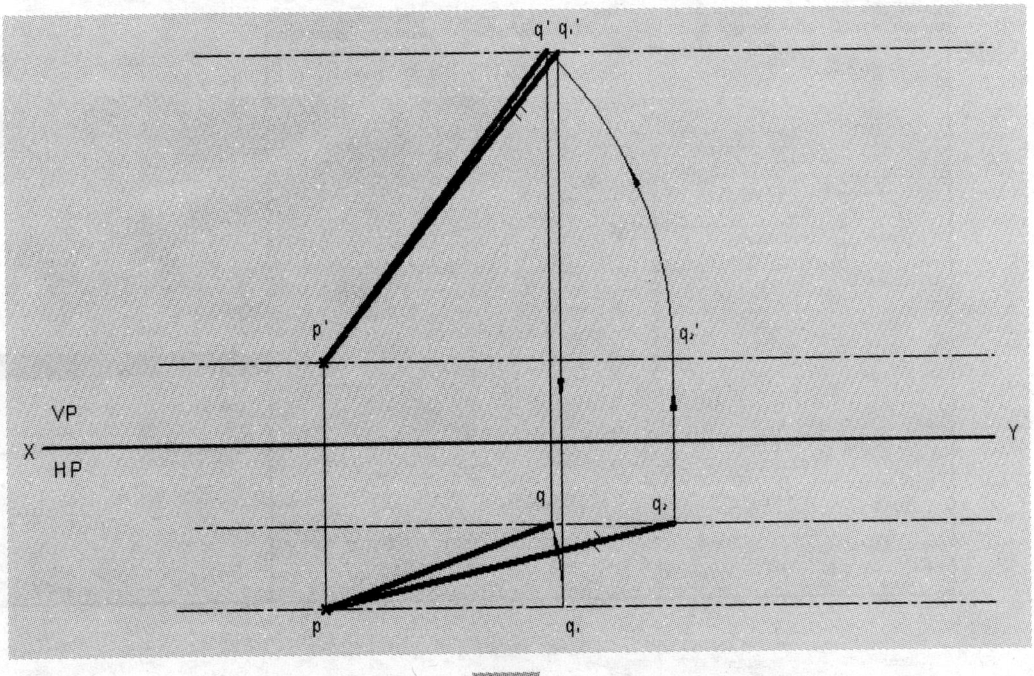

13. Using SMART DIMENSION Command in drawing tool bar dimension the drawing as shown.

14. To make drawing as a standard drawing change the thickness of the lines by using LINE WIDTH  command from status bar. Select all the projection lines, locus and then assign to line width 1, select the XY line and true lengths and then assign to line width 2 and assign top and from views to line width 4.

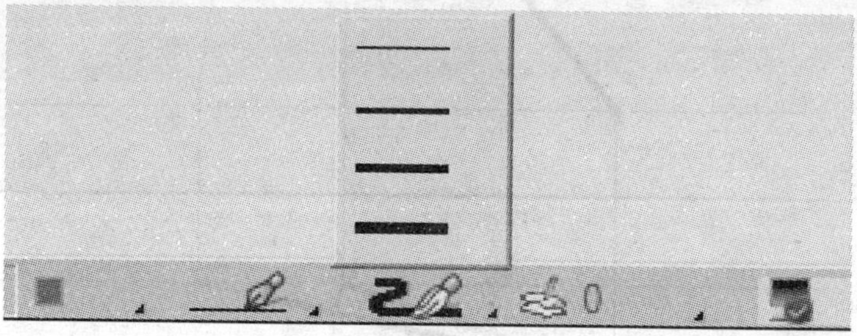

15. To get a Hard Copy of the standard drawing select print from file menu bar. Print dialog window will appear select page and change width to Entities and select the activated button  now substitute width 1 as 0.05 mm, width 2 as 0.15 mm, width 3 as 0 mm and width 4 as 0.5 mm and say OK. Select print to get a hard copy and finally save the file.

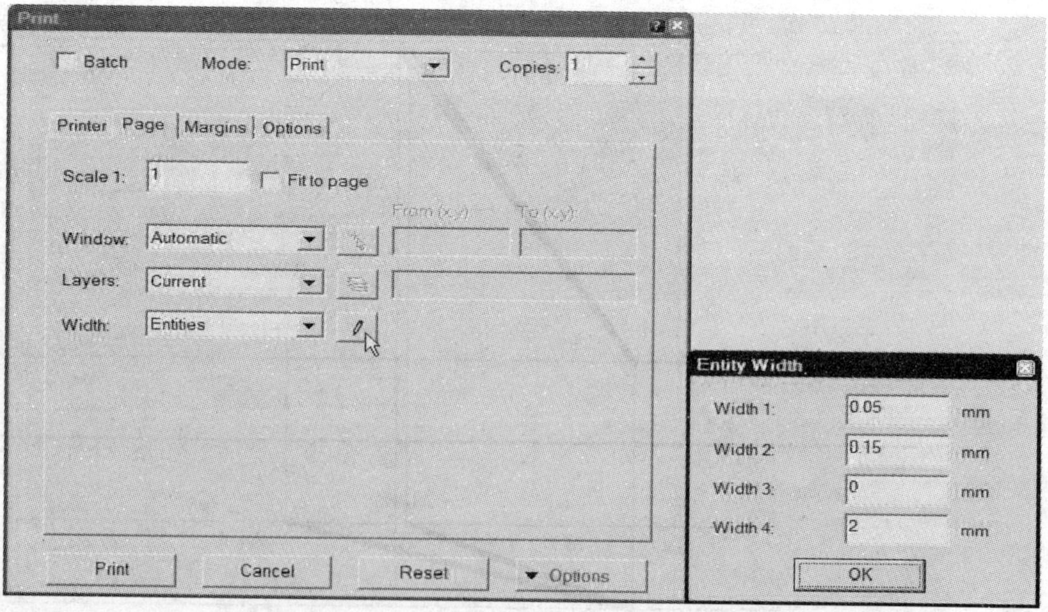

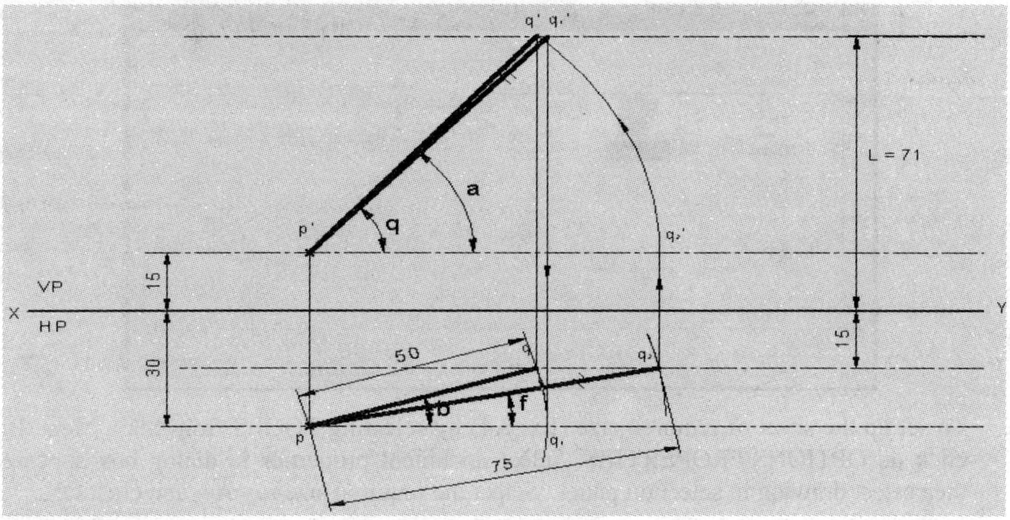

PROBLEM 3.5

The point B of a line AB is on the horizontal plane, ab, the top view of the line makes an angle of 30º with XY line, ab being 80 mm. The point A is on the vertical plane and 50 mm above the horizontal plane. Draw the top and front views of the line and obtain the true length of the line. Also find the inclinations of the line with the two planes.

SOLUTION

Manual Method

(a) Draw the XY line. Mark VP above it and HP below it.

(b) Mark a′ 20mm above XY line. Project from a′ below XY line of 30 mm to get a.

(c) Draw a′b_1′ line at an angle of 30° and length equal to 80 mm (given).

(d) Draw ab_2 line at an angle of 45° and length equal to 80 mm (given).

(e) From b_1′ project vertically downward to get b_1 on locus a, similarly from b_2 project vertically upward to get b_2′ on locus a′.

(f) With a as center and ab_1 as radius, draw an arc until it cuts the locus of b in top view to get b.

(g) With a′ as center and a′b_2′ as radius, draw an arc until it cuts the locus of b′ in front view to get b′.

(h) Join ab and a′b′ to the top and front view of the line.

Computer Aided Drafting Procedure

1. Open the SOFTWARE. Click on the DRAWING in the open dialog box and say OK.

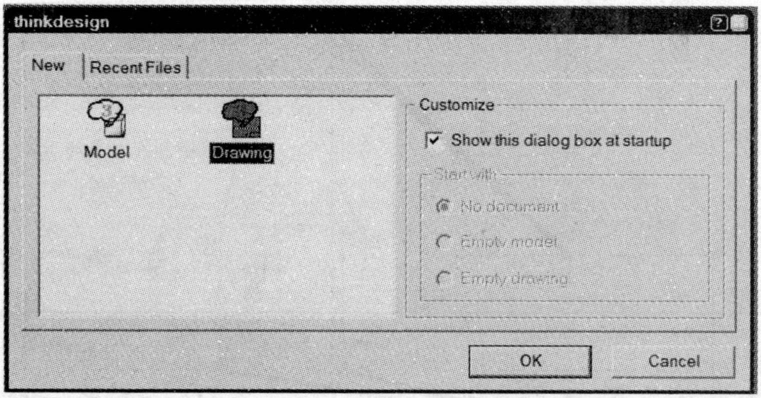

2. To set up the sheet of required size (Ex: A4) by selecting TOOLS from Main Menu Bar and click on OPTIONS/PROPERTIES. Select document properties in dialog box appeared and then select drawing in selection panel. Select the required size say A4, and click OK.

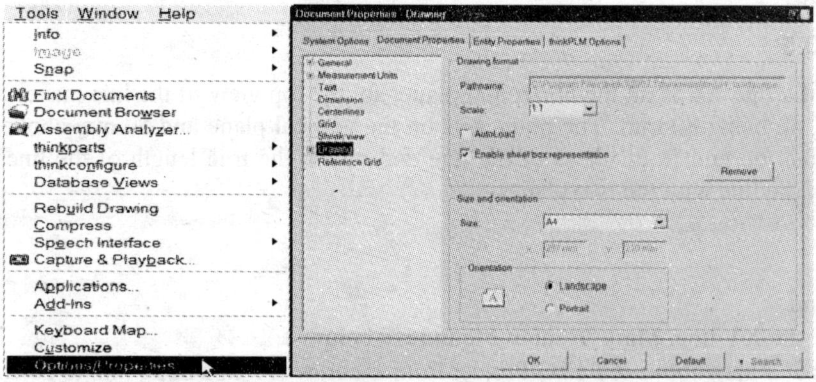

3. Draw the line by using POLYLINE  command from drafting tool bar.

4. Make Annotation X, Y, VP, and HP to the line drawn by using INSERT TEXT Command 

from drafting tool bar, just by typing X, Y, VP and HP in Text Box and insert these in the required position by left click of the mouse, as shown below.

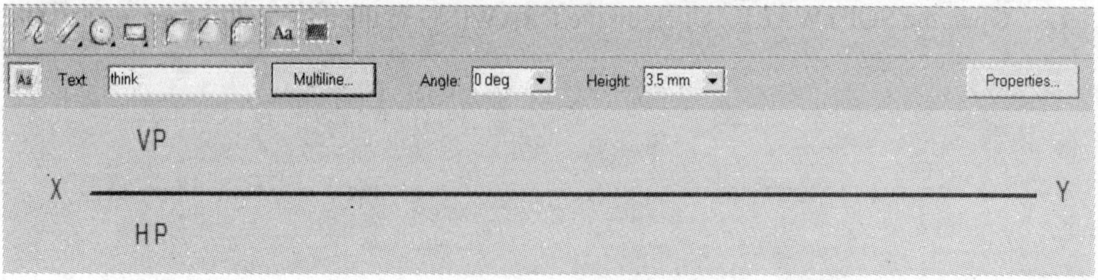

5. As per the problem, one end A is on XY line and 50 mm above HP. Let us mark point a′ and a above and on XY Line respectively. Using the POINT Command and mark annotations a′ and a using INSERT TEXT Command as shown below.

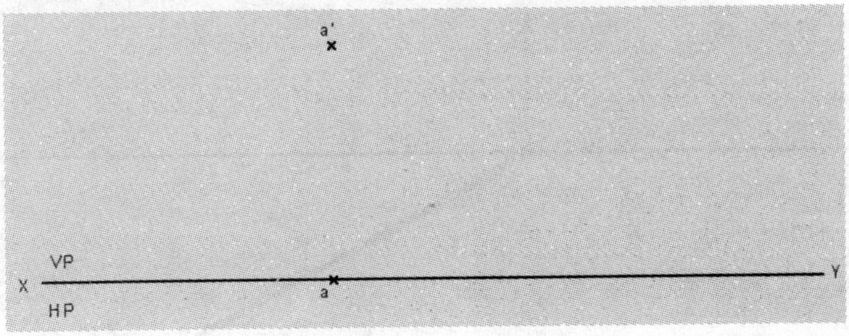

6. Using 2 POINT LINE Command join a′ and a. Using POLYLINE command draw the locus from a′, to change the line type of locus drawn. Select locus and assign to line type 4 in the status bar as shown.

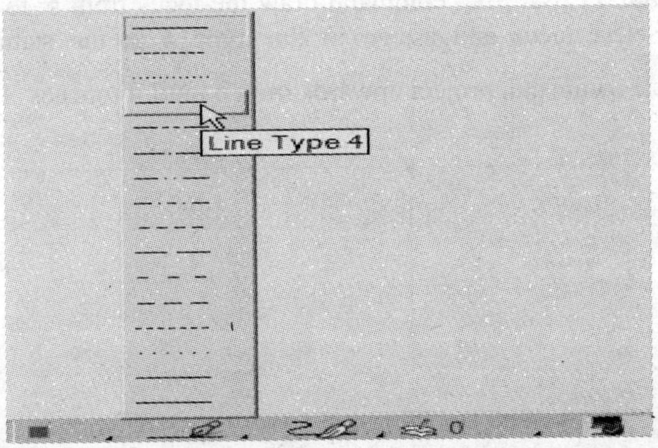

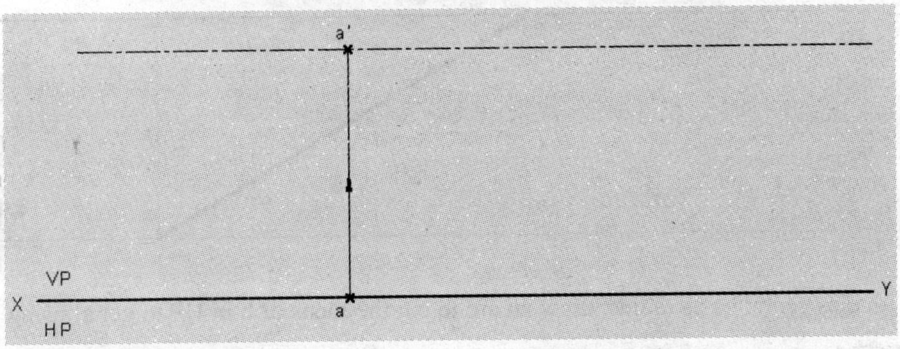

7. Another point q is not known, but top view (80 mm) and angle (30°) is being given, hence draw the line from point a using POLYLINE command and enter length as 80 mm and angle as 30 in mini dialog box as shown. To get top view ab.

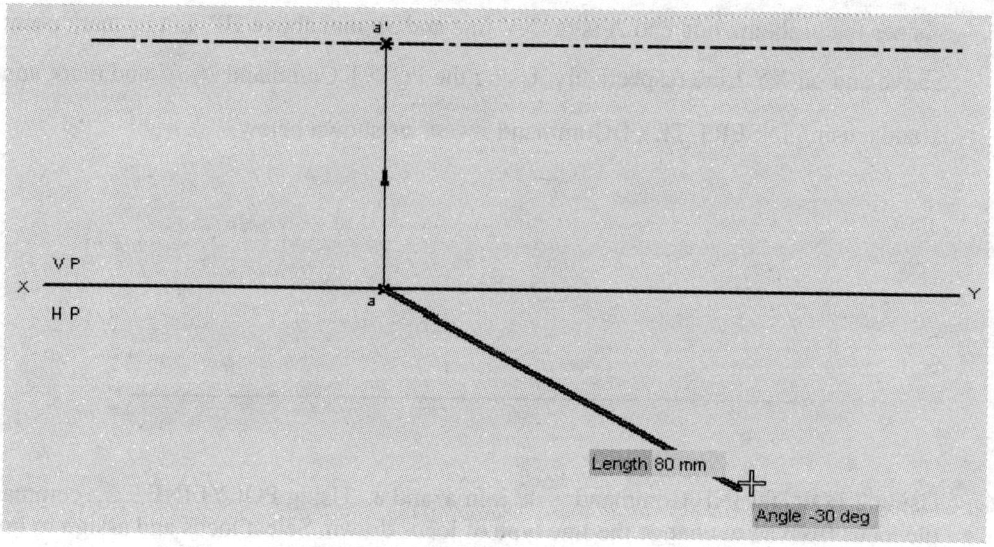

8. From b using POLYLINE  command draw the locus from b, to change the line type of locus drawn. Select locus and assign to line type 4 in the status bar and using same POLYLINE  command, project upwards from b until it touches XY line to get b′.

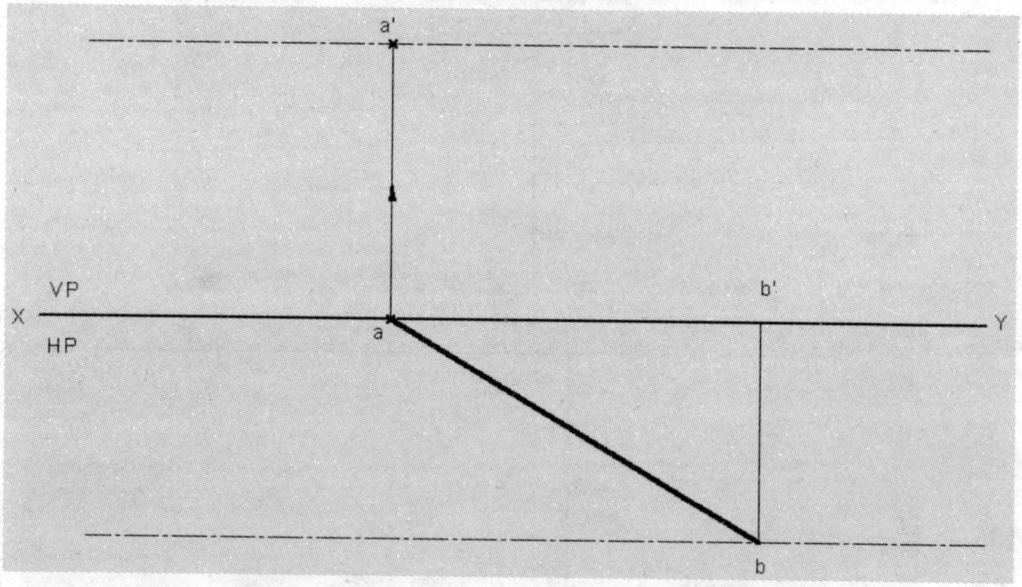

9. With b as center ba as radius, draw an arc to cut the locus of b in HP to get a_1 using CENTER CIRCLE  command in drafting tool bar. In mode option select arc to get arc approximately.

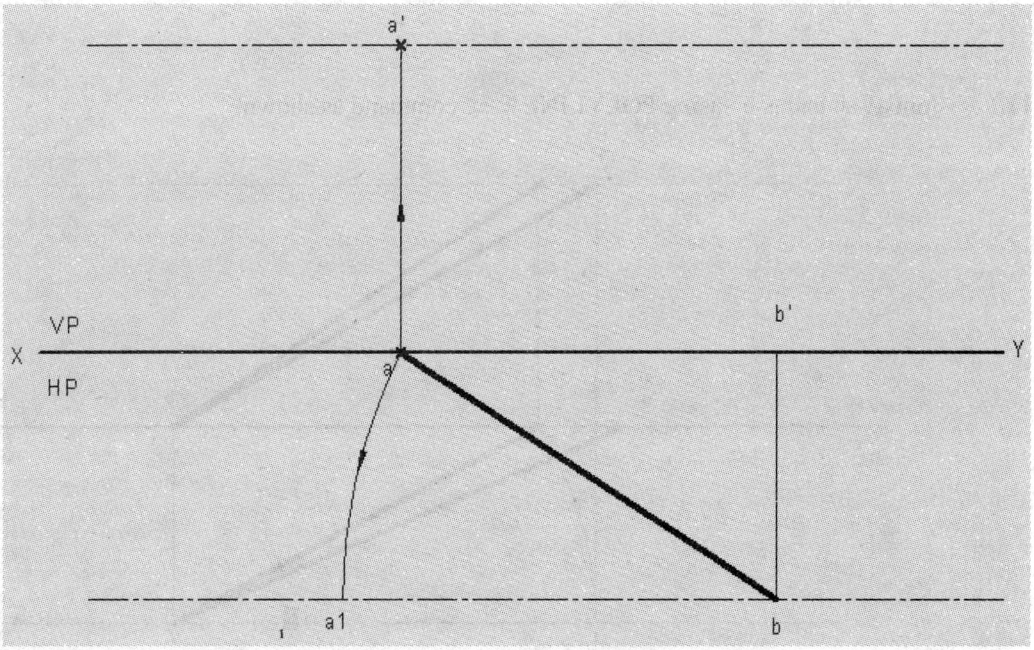

10. From a_1 using POLYLINE command, project upwards until it touches other locus of a′ in VP to get a_1'. Join a_1' and b′.

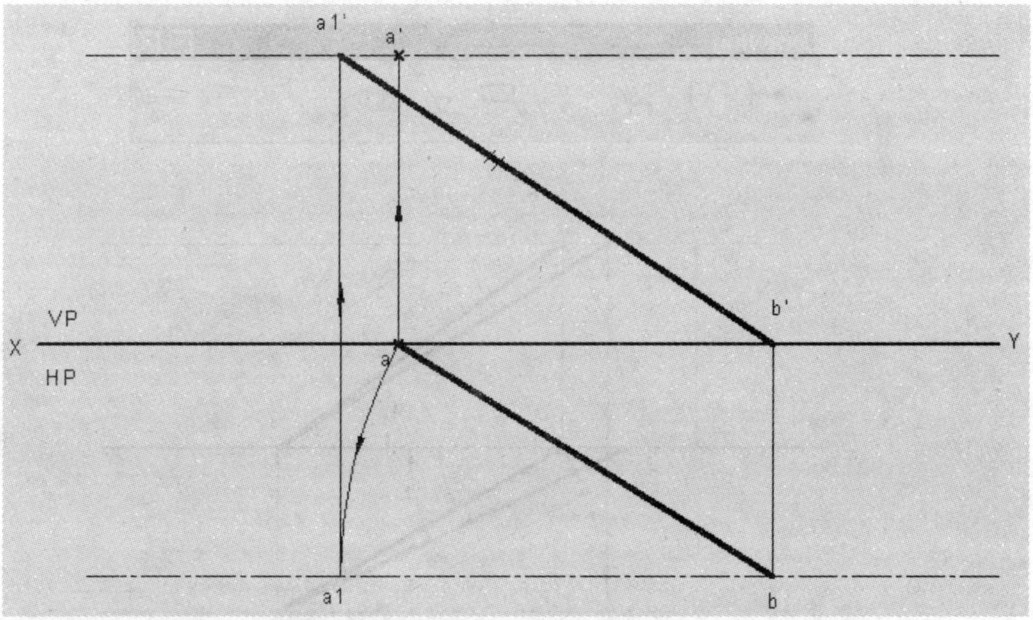

11. Join a′, ab and a′b′ using POLYLINE command as shown.

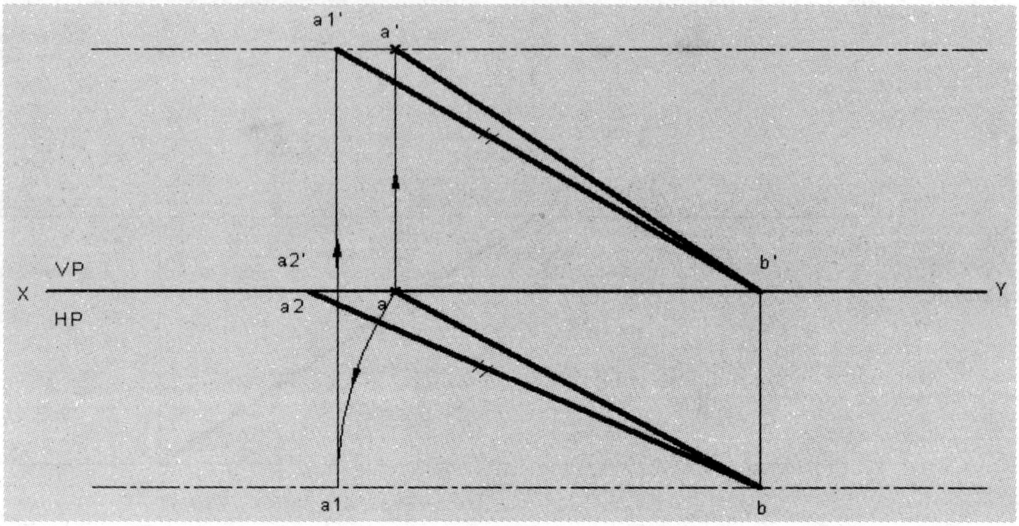

12. Using SMART DIMENSION Command in drawing tool bar dimension the drawing as shown.

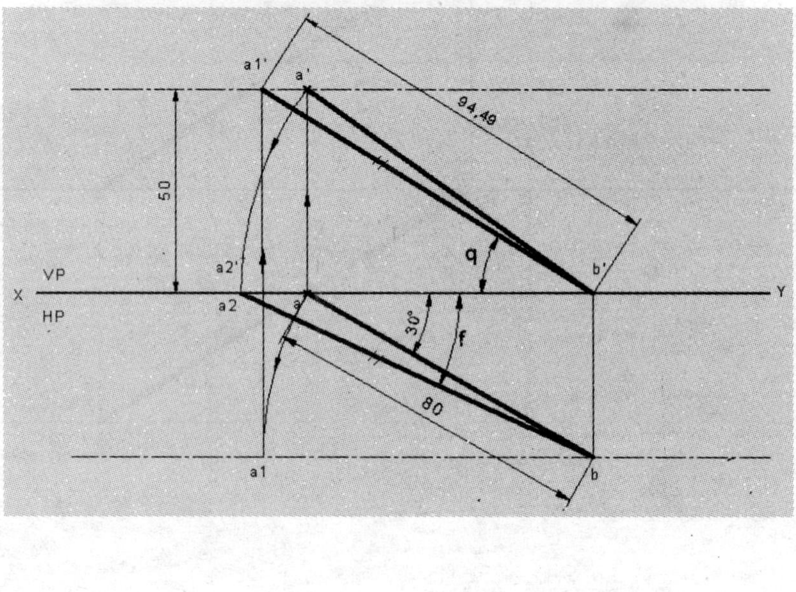

13. To make drawing as a standard drawing change the thickness of the lines by using LINE WIDTH  command from status bar. Select all the projection lines, locus and then assign to line width 1, select the XY line and true lengths and then assign to line width 2 and assign top and from views to line width 4.

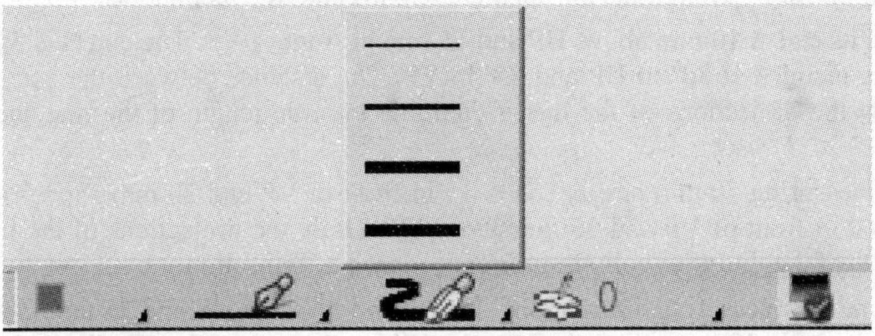

14. To get a Hard Copy of the standard drawing select print from file menu bar. Print dialog window will appear select page and change width to Entities and select the activated button  now substitute width 1 as 0.05 mm, width 2 as 0.15 mm, width 3 as 0 mm and width 4 as 0.5 mm and say OK. Select print to get a hard copy and finally save the file.

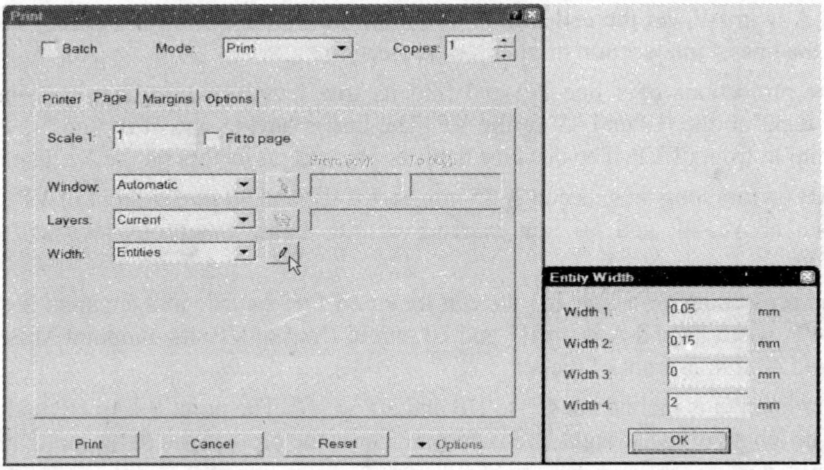

EXERCISE PROBLEMS

1. A line AB 80 mm long is inclined to HP at 30º and inclined to VP at 45º. The end A touches both HP & VP. Draw front and top views of line and determine their lengths. Also measure the perpendicular distance of end B from both HP and VP.

2. The front view of a 90 mm long line which is inclined at 45º to the XY line, measures 65 mm. End A is 15 mm above the XY line and is in VP. Draw the projections of the line and find its inclinations with HP and VP.

3. The top view of a line AB, 80 mm long measures 65 mm and the length of the front view is 50 mm. The end A is on HP and 15 mm infront of VP. Draw the projections
4. Line AB has its end A 20 mm above the HP and 15 mm infront of the VP. The other end B is 60 mm above the HP and 45 mm in front of VP. The distance between end projectors is 70 mm. Draw its projections. Determine the apparent lengths and true inclinations.
5. A line has its end A 10 mm above HP and 15 mm in front of VP. The end B is 55 mm above HP and line is inclined at 30° to HP and 35° to VP. The distance between the end projectors is 50 mm. Draw the projections of the line. Determine the true length of the line and its inclination with VP.
6. Line AB measuring 70 mm has its end A 15 in front of VP and 20 mm above HP and the other end B is 60 in front of VP and 50 mm above HP. Draw the projections of the line and find the inclinations of the line with both the reference planes of projection.
7. Straight line AB measuring 80 mm long has the end A in the HP and 25 mm in front of the VP. Its mid point M is 25 mm above the HP and 40 mm in front of the VP. Draw the projections of the line and determine the inclination of the line with HP and VP.
8. Line has one end 30 mm in front of VP and 15 mm above HP and the other end is 15 mm in front of VP and is above HP. Length of the line is 60 mm. Top view of the line is 40 mm long. Draw the two views of the line and obtain the inclination of the line with HP and VP.
9. Draw the projections of a straight line AB, 100 mm long, inclined at 45° to HP and 30° to VP. The end A is in HP and the end B is in VP. Find the shortest distance between the straight line AB and the line of intersection of planes of projection.
10. Draw the projections of a line PQ and find its true length and inclinations when the line is inclined at 30° to the HP and 45° to the VP. The line is having one of its ends 15 mm above HP and 20 mm in front of VP. The distance between the end projectors on the XY line is 60 mm.
11. A line AB 65 mm long, has its end A 25 mm above HP and 30 mm in front of VP. The other end is 45 mm above HP and 50 mm in front of VP. Draw the projections and determine its inclinations.
12. Draw the projections of a line AB 90 mm long and find its true and apparent inclinations with HP and VP, when its end A is on HP and 20 mm in front of VP. Its midpoint M is 20 mm above the HP and 40 mm in front of the VP.
13. A straight line PQ is inclined at 45° to HP and 30° to VP. The point P is in HP and the point Q is in VP. The length of the straight line is 65 mm. Draw the projections of the straight line AB.
14. The profile view of a line PQ 80 mm long, makes an angle of 30° with the XY line. Draw the top and front views of the line, when the length of the profile view is 50 mm. The point P of the line is 15 mm above HP and 60 mm in front of VP. The point Q of the line is close to VP.
15. A straight line AB measuring 80 mm long has the end A in the HP and 25 mm infront of the VP. Its mid point M is 25 mm above HP and 40 mm infront of the VP. Draw the views of the line and determine the inclination of the line with HP and VP. And also find distance between end projector.
16. The end A of a line AB is in HP and 25 mm in front of VP. The end B is in VP and 50mm above HP. The distance between the end projectors when measured parallel to the line of intersection of HP & VP is 65 mm. Draw the projections of the line AB and determine its true length and true inclinations with HP & VP.

17. The top view of a line PQ is 70 mm and front view is 60 mm long. The end Q is nearer to both HP and VP than the end P and is 15 above HP and 20 mm in front of VP. Draw the projections of the line if the distance between the end projectors is 50 mm.

18. A line MN 90 mm long has a point P on it which divides the line in the ratio 2:1, *i.e.* MP : PN = 2:1. This point P is 50 mm above HP and 60 mm in front of VP. The line is inclined at 35° to HP and 40° to VP. Draw the projections of the line. Find the distance between end projectors and the position of the ends of the line with HP and VP.

19. A straight line PQ inclined at 40° to VP has pq = 60 mm and front view = 50 mm. The end P is both in HP and VP, and 40 mm to the right of left profile plane.

(a) Draw the projections of the straight line PQ.

(b) Find the true length and true inclination with HP.

(c) Draw the profile view of the straight line.

(d) Find the position of the end Q with HP and VP.

20. The front view of the line PQ 80 mm long measures 50 mm and it is inclined to XY (reference line) at 50°. One end of the line P is 20 mm above the HP and 25 mm in front of the VP. Draw the front view and top view of the line and find the inclinations of the line with HP and VP.

■■■

4

ORTHOGRAPHIC PROJECTIONS OF PLANES

INTRODUCTION

- A plane has only two dimension, length and breadth. It has zero thickness. For practical purposes, a flat face of an object can be treated as a plane. A plane which has limited extend is called as lamina. A simple plane can be located with help of three non-collinear points. A plane may be of any shape, such as triangular, square, pentagonal, hexagonal, circular etc.
- Planes may be divided into two types: (a) regular planes (b) irregular planes.
- The position of a plane may have different orientations in space.
- As per first angle projection, it may be parallel, perpendicular or inclined to either or both the reference planes (horizontal or vertical planes).
- Positions of plane
  1. Plane parallel and perpendicular to reference planes (HP & VP)
     (a) Plane parallel to HP and perpendicular to VP.
     (b) Plane parallel to VP and perpendicular to HP.
  2. Plane perpendicular and inclined to reference planes (HP & VP)
     (a) Plane perpendicular to HP and inclined to VP.
     (b) Plane perpendicular to VP and inclined to HP.
  3. Plane perpendicular to both HP & VP.
  4. Plane inclined to both HP & VP
     (a) Inclination to HP and VP is not equal to 90°.
     (b) Inclination to HP and VP is equal to 90°.

System of Notation

1. The actual plane in space is denoted by capital letters A , B, C and D etc.
2. The front view (FV) of a plane is denoted by their corresponding lower case letters with dashes as a′, b′, c′ and d′ etc.
3. The top view (TV) of a plane is denoted by their corresponding lower case letters without dashes as a, b, c and d etc.
4. The side view (SV) of a plane are denoted by their corresponding lower case letters with double dashes as a″, b″, c″ and d″ etc.
5. Projectors are always drawn as continuous thin lines.
6. Line with specific thickness for a particular type of line.

In Computer Aided Engineering Graphics for projection of plane following commands are used other than evoking software, opening file, saving file and giving print command. Using these minimum12 commands any type of projection of line problem can be solved they are as follows:

1. Select tool Command.
2. Point command.
3. Poly-Line command.

4. Two Point Line command.
5. Parallel line command.
6. Center Circle command
7. Bisector command.
8. Smart Dimension command.
9. Line Width command.
10. Insert Text command.
11. Move Copy command.
12. Rectangle command.

PROBLEM 4.1

An equilateral triangular lamina of 25 mm side lies with one of its edges on HP such that the surface of the lamina is inclined to HP at 60º. The edge on which it rests is inclined to VP at 60º. Draw the projections.

SOLUTION

Manual Method

(a) Draw the XY line. Mark VP and HP above and below it.
(b) Draw an equilateral triangle below XY line. Name the vertices as a b and c.
(c) Project the front view on the XY line. Name the intersection end as a′ b′ and c′.
(d) Redraw the front view at an angle of 60° to XY line, with a′ b′ on XY line.
(e) Draw vertical projectors from a′ b′ and c′. Draw horizontal projectors from first stage top view intersect vertical projectors at a b and c to get second stage top view.
(f) Draw a line inclined at 60° to XY line and redraw the second stage top view, such that one of its edges rests on 60° line drawn, to get third stage top view.
(g) Project vertically upwards from third stage top view. Draw horizontal projectors from second stage front view to intersect vertical projectors to get final front view.
(h) Mark annotations correctly and dimension necessarily.

Computer Aided Drafting Procedure

1. Open the SOFTWARE. Click on the DRAWING in the open dialog box and say OK.

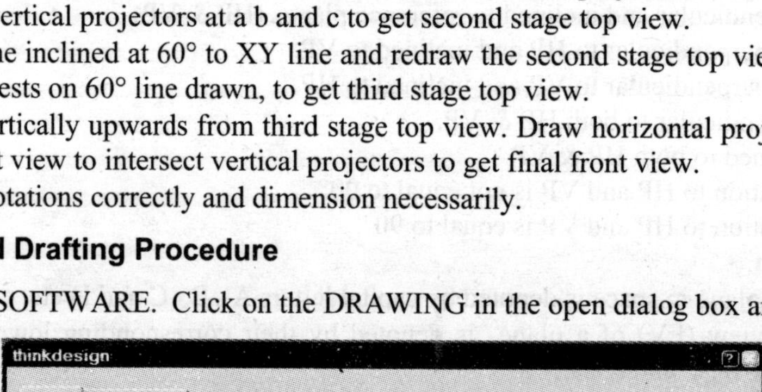

2. To set up the sheet of required size (Ex: A4) by selecting TOOLS from Main Menu Bar and click on OPTIONS/PROPERTIES. Select document properties in dialog box appeared and then select drawing in selection panel. Select the required size say A4, and click OK.

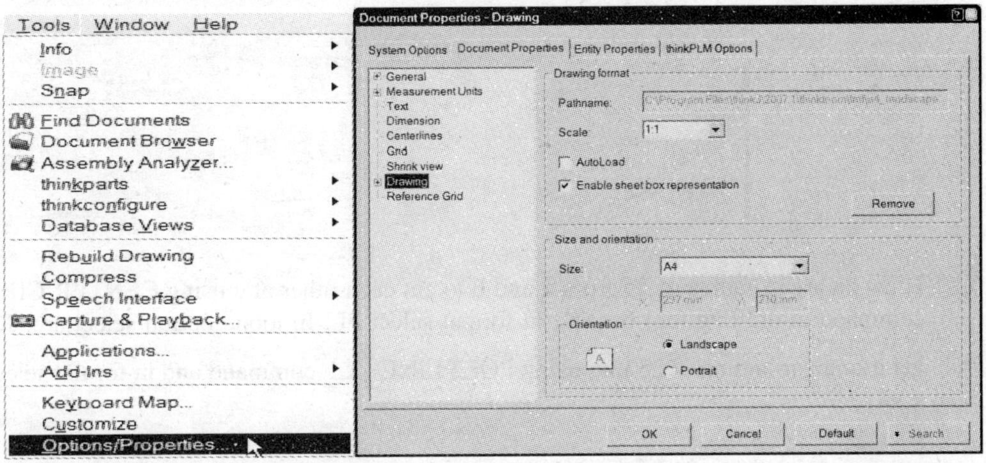

3. To draw XY line, projection lines and top & front view lines. After selecting line command, in format select XY for XY line, PL for projection lines and VL for top and front view lines before drawing these lines.

4. Draw the line by using POLYLINE  command from drafting tool bar and in format select XY.

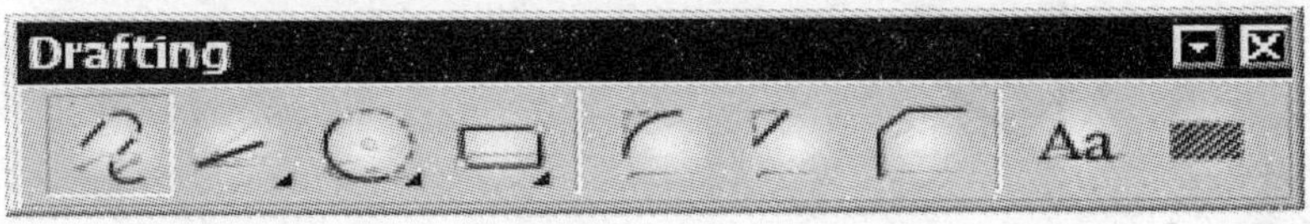

5. Make Annotation X, Y, VP, and HP to the line drawn by using INSERT TEXT Command  from drafting tool bar, just by typing X, Y, VP and HP in Text Box and insert these in the required position by left click of the mouse, as shown below.

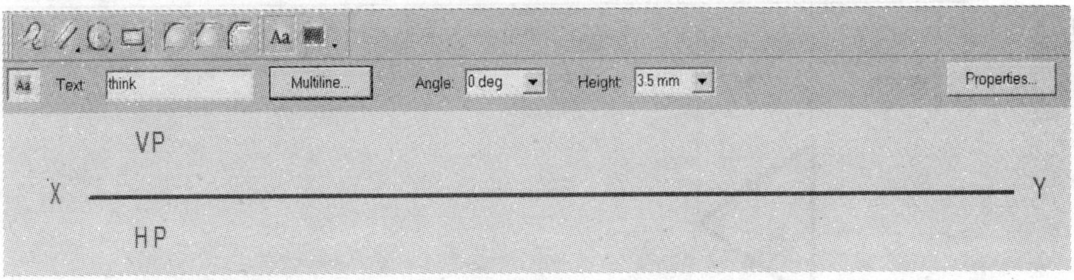

6. As per the problem equilateral triangular lamina of 25mm has to be drawn in HP, hence draw a vertical line of 25 mm using POLYLINE  command and in format select VL and enter length as 25 and angle as –90 in mini dialog box. Mark annotations a and b using INSERT TEXT Command 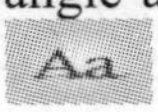 as shown below.

7. Draw an arc of radius of 25 from a and b to cut each other at c using CENTER CIRCLE command in drafting tool bar and in format select PL. In mode option select arc. Join abc to get triangular lamina of 25 mm using POLYLINE command and in format select VL.

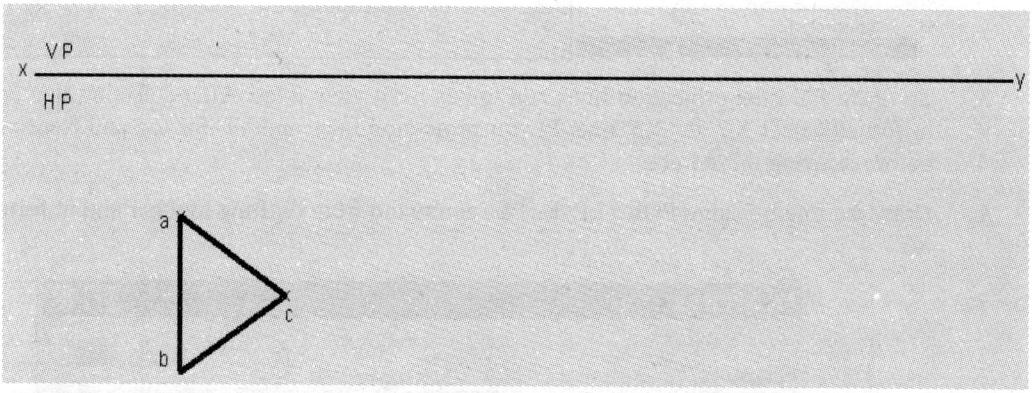

8. Draw the vertical projection upwards from all the corners of triangular lamina in top view until it touches XY line, using POLYLINE command and in format select PL.

9. Draw front view of the triangular lamina using POLYLINE command and in format select VL, mark annotations as (a′) b′ and c′ as shown below.

10. Since the lamina is inclined at 60° to HP. By using POLYLINE  command and in format select VL enter length equal to length of first stage front view and angle as 60 in mini dialog box, mark annotations as (a′) b′ and c′ using INSERT TEXT Command  as shown below.

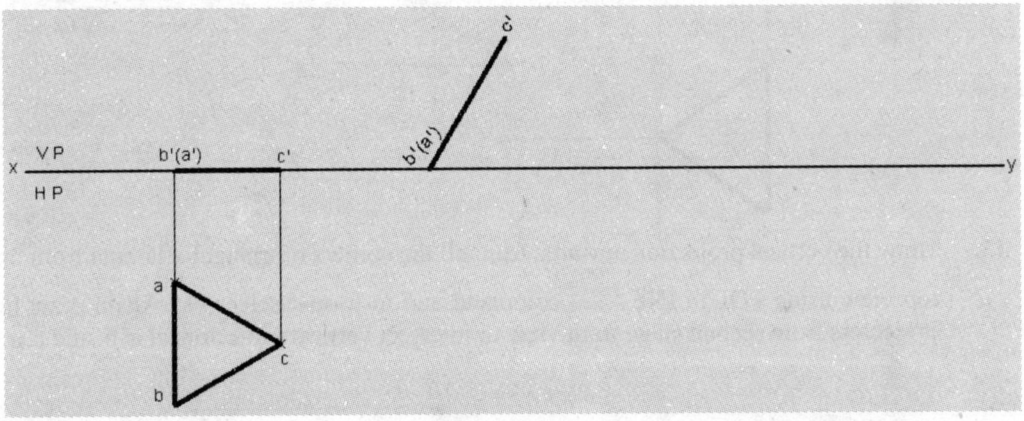

11. Draw vertical projectors downwards from the second front view using POLYLINE  command and in format select PL. Draw horizontal projectors from top view to intersect vertical projectors at a, b and c which forms the second stage top view as shown below.

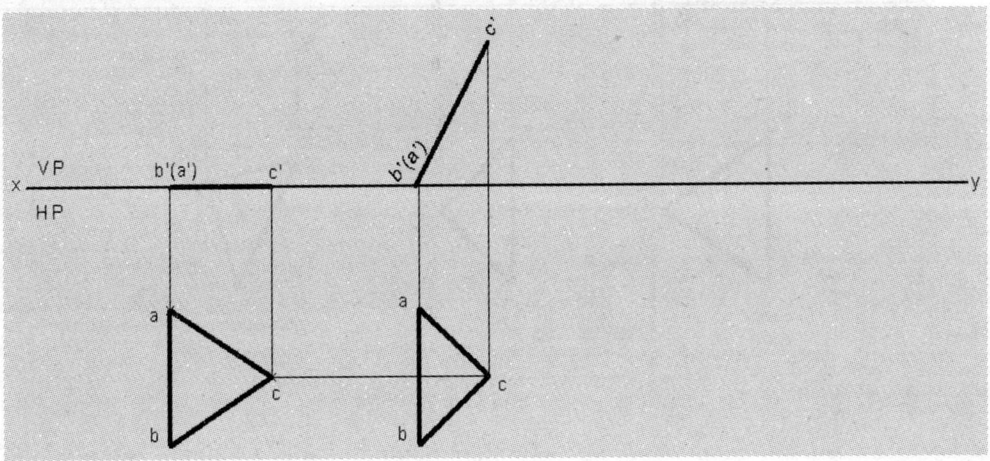

12. Since the edge on which it rests is inclined to VP to 60° Draw a line of 60° in HP using POLYLINE command and in format select PL. From edit menu select MOVE COPY command and then select second stage top view. In selection tree right click on the start point and click reset to select the start point any where on the edge of lamina to shift on to 60° line drawn. Click and drag the lamina on 60° line. Click or drag to rotate and enter angle as 30 in mini dialog box and click on OK in selection tree.

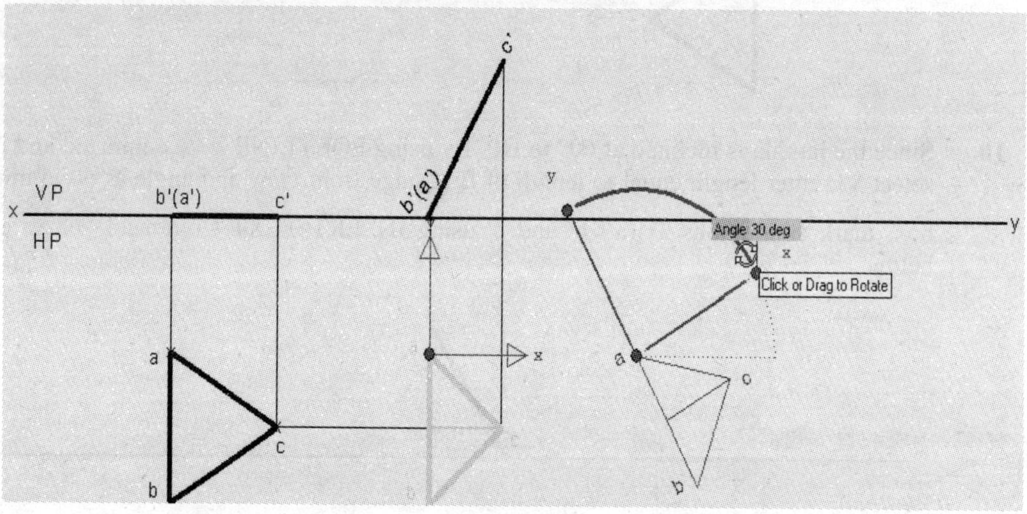

13. Draw the vertical projection upwards from all the corners of triangular lamina from third stage top view using POLYLINE command and in format select PL. Again draw horizontal projectors from second stage front view to intersect vertical projectors at a′ b′ and c′.

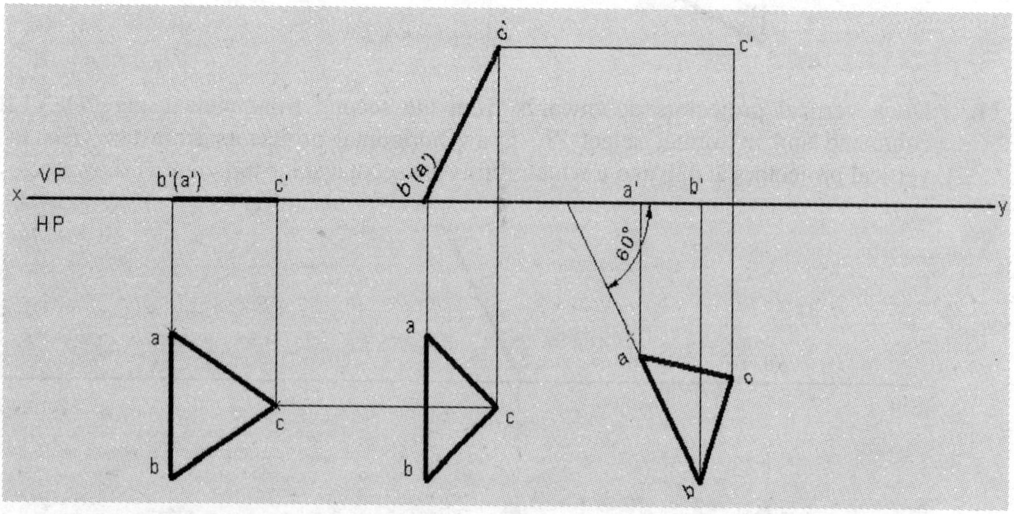

14. Join a′b′ and c′ using 2 POINT LINE Command  and in format select VL.

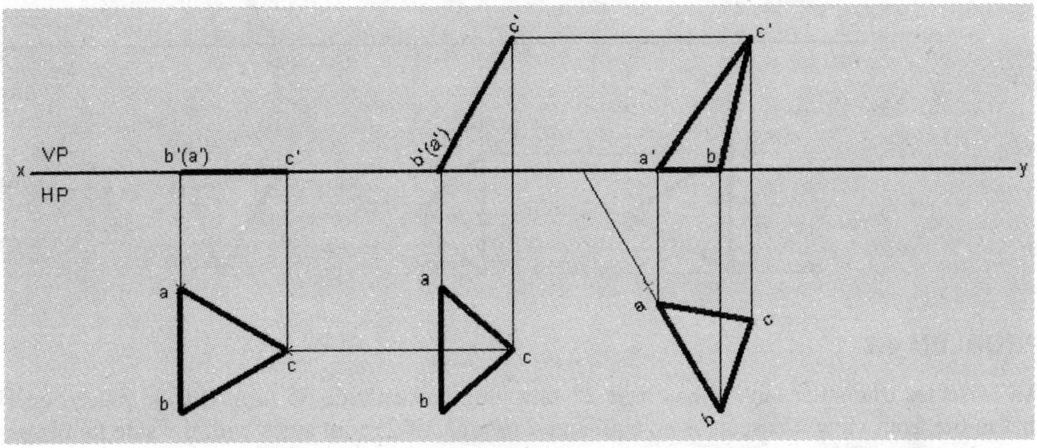

15. Using SMART DIMENSION Command  in drawing tool bar dimension the drawing as shown.

16. To get a Hard Copy of the standard drawing select print from file menu bar. Print dialog window will appear select page and change width to Entities and select the activated button  now substitute width 1 as 0.15 mm, width 2 as 0.05 mm, width 3 as 0.5 mm and say OK. Select print to get a hard copy and finally save the file. The required standard drawing is as shown below.

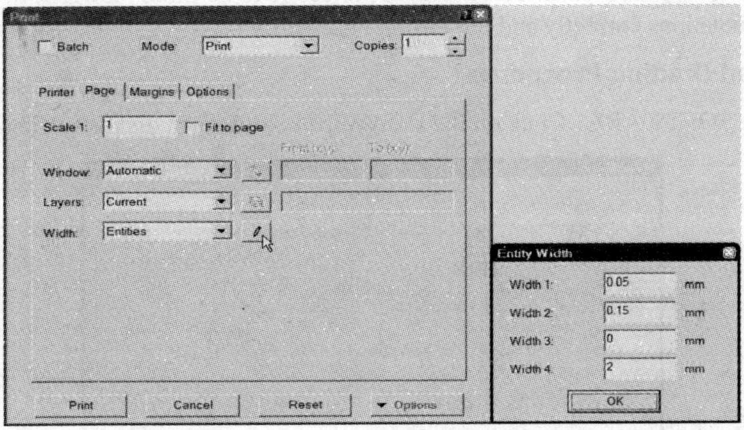

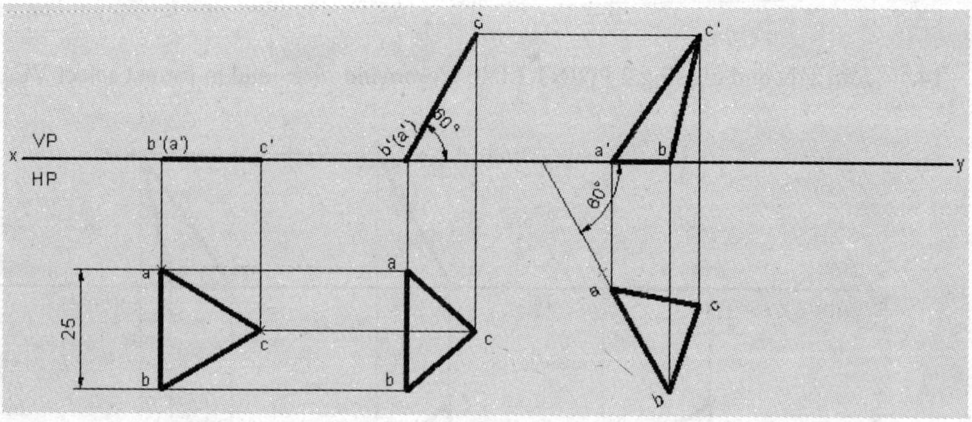

PROBLEM 4.2

An isosceles triangular lamina has base 25 mm long and altitude 35 mm. It is so placed on HP such that in the front view it is seen as an equilateral triangle of 25 mm sides with the side that is parallel to VP is inclined at 45° to HP. Draw its top and front views. Also determine the inclination of the lamina with reference plane.

SOLUTION

Manual Method

(a) Draw the XY line. Mark VP and HP above and below it.

(b) Draw an isosceles triangle above XY line. Name the vertices as a′ b′ and c′.

(c) Project the top view on the XY line. Name the intersection end as a b and c.

(d) Draw an equilateral triangle of side 25 mm (given) above XY line.

(e) Draw vertical projectors from second stage front view. Draw horizontal projectors from first stage top view intersect vertical projectors at a b and c to get second stage top view.

(f) Draw a line inclined at 45° to XY line and redraw the second stage front view, such that edge parallel to VP rests on 45° line drawn, to get third stage front view.

(g) Project vertically downwards from third stage front view. Draw horizontal projectors from second stage top view to intersect vertical projectors to get final top view.

(h) Mark annotations correctly and dimension necessarily.

Computer Aided Drafting Procedure

1. Open the SOFTWARE. Click on the DRAWING in the open dialog box and say OK.

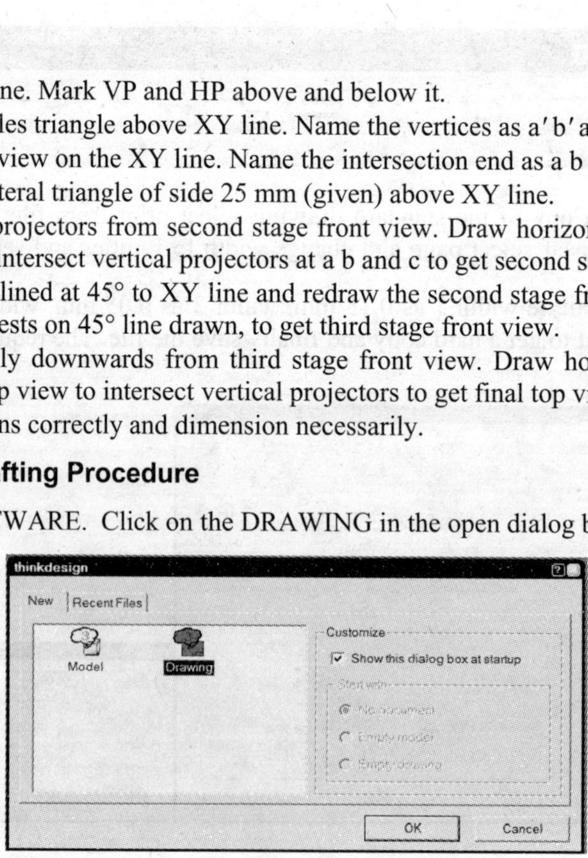

2. To set up the sheet of required size (Ex: A4) by selecting TOOLS from Main Menu Bar and click on OPTIONS/PROPERTIES. Select document properties in dialog box appeared and then select drawing in selection panel. Select the required size say A4, and click OK.

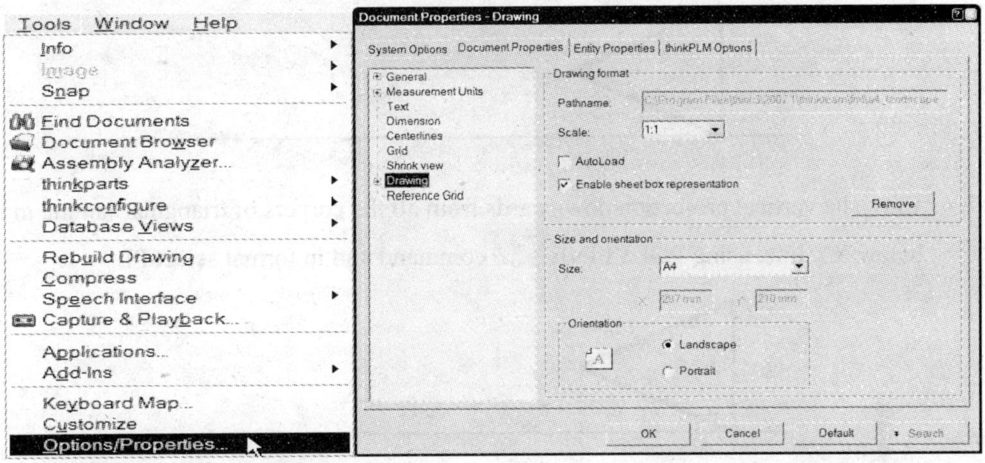

3. To draw XY line, projection lines and top & front view lines. After selecting line command, in format select XY for XY line, PL for projection lines and VL for top and front view lines before drawing these lines.

4. Draw the line by using POLYLINE  command from drafting tool bar and in format select XY.

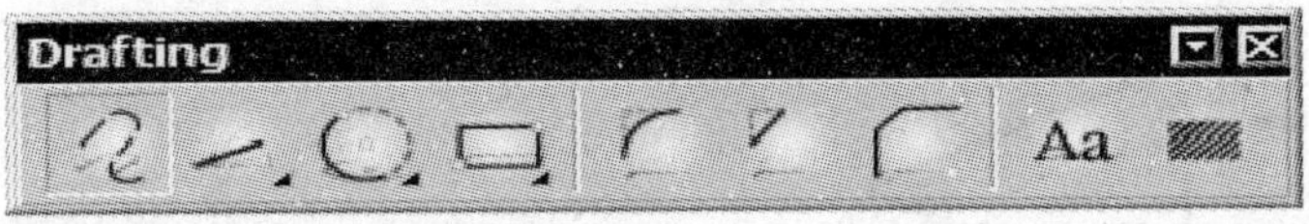

5. Make Annotation X, Y, VP, and HP to the line drawn by using INSERT TEXT Command  from drafting tool bar, just by typing X, Y, VP and HP in Text Box and insert these in the required position by left click of the mouse, as shown below.

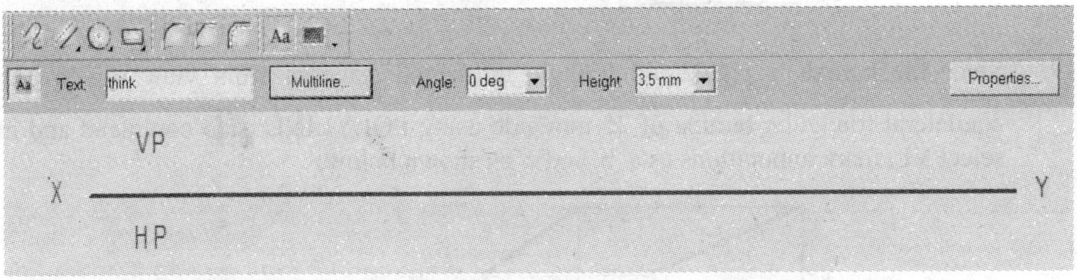

6. As per the problem isosceles triangular lamina of base 25 mm and altitude 35 mm has to be drawn in VP, hence draw a vertical line of 25 mm using POLYLINE  command and in format select VL and enter length as 25 and angle as –90 in mini dialog box. To get another corner of isosceles triangle, draw horizontal line of length 35 mm from mid point of the line drawn. Using 2 POINT LINE Command  and in format select VL join a′ b′ and c′ b′ to get the first stage of the front view. Mark annotations a′ b′ and c′ using INSERT TEXT Command as shown below.

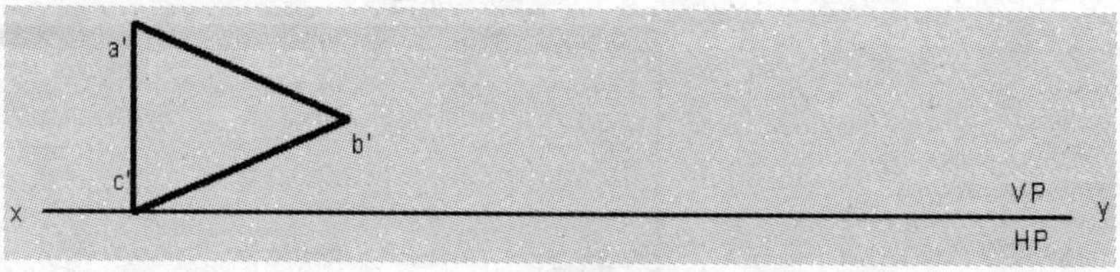

7. Draw the vertical projection downwards from all the corners of triangular lamina in front view below XY line, using POLYLINE command and in format select PL.

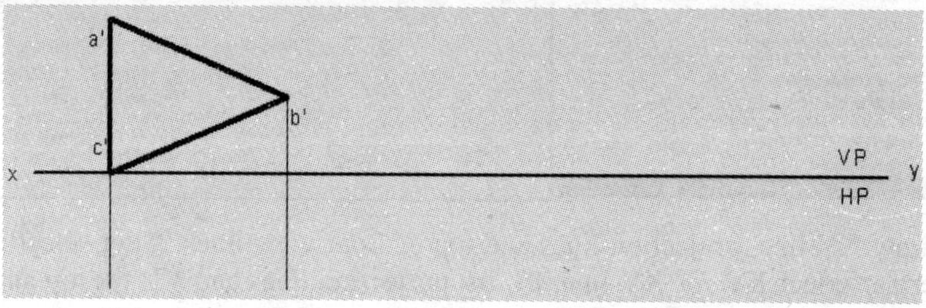

8. Draw top view of the triangular lamina using POLYLINE command and in format select VL, mark annotations as a (c) and b as shown below. Since lamina is perpendicular to HP, hence we see top view as a line.

9. Since the lamina is equilateral triangle in second stage of front view (given). Draw the equilateral triangular lamina of 25 mm side using POLYLINE command and in format select VL, mark annotations as a′ b′ and c′ as shown below.

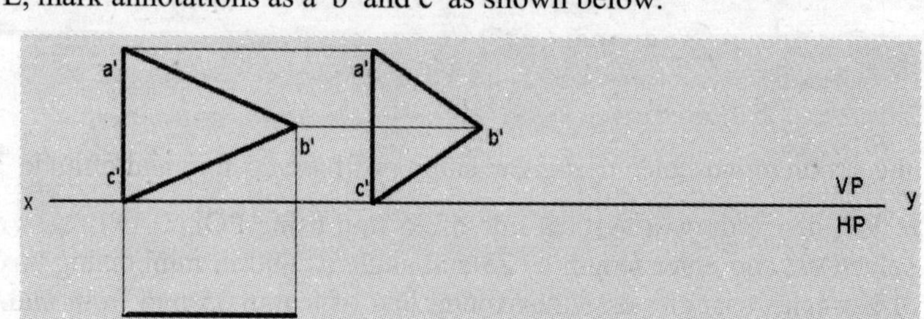

10. Draw vertical projectors downwards from the second front view using POLYLINE command and in format select PL. Draw horizontal projectors from top view to intersect vertical projectors at a, b and c which forms the second stage top view as shown below.

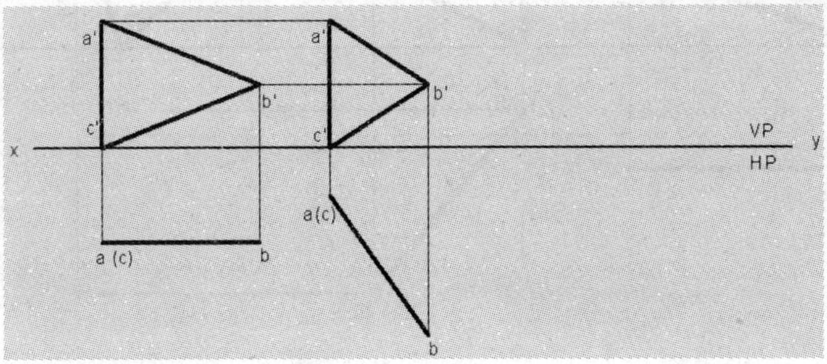

11. Since the edge that is parallel to VP is inclined at 45° to HP. Draw a line of 45° in VP using POLYLINE command and in format select PL. From edit menu select MOVE COPY command and then select second stage front view. In selection tree right click on the start point and click reset to select the start point any where on the edge of lamina to shift on to 45° line drawn. Click and drag the lamina on 45° line. Click or drag to rotate and enter angle as 45 in mini dialog box and click on OK in selection tree. Mark annotations as a′ b′ and c′ as shown below.

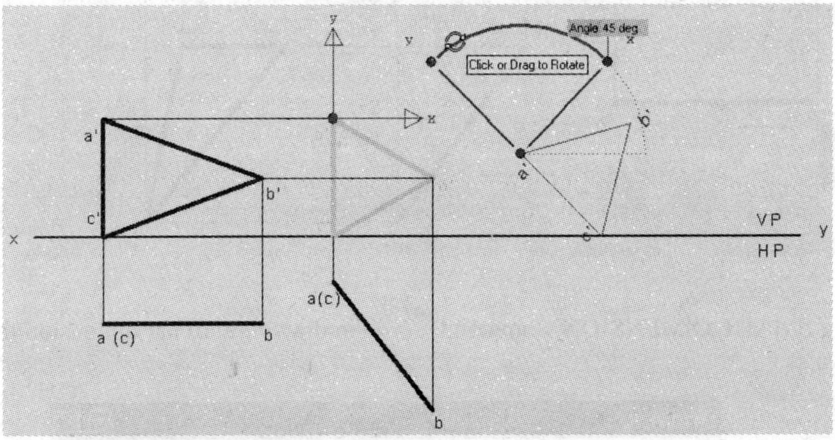

12. Draw the vertical projection downwards from all the corners of triangular lamina from third stage front view using POLYLINE command and in format select PL. Again draw horizontal projectors from second stage top view to intersect vertical projectors at a b and c.

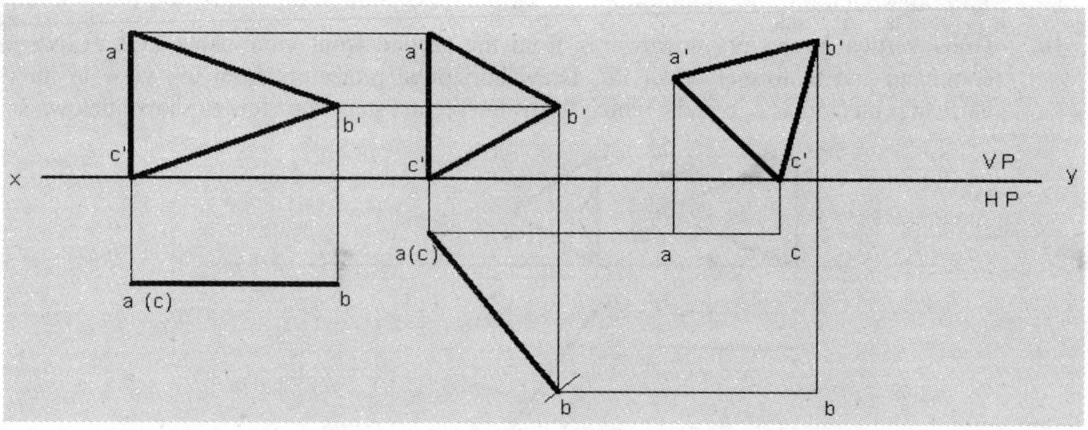

13. Join a b and c using 2 POINT LINE Command  and in format select VL to get the final top view as shown below.

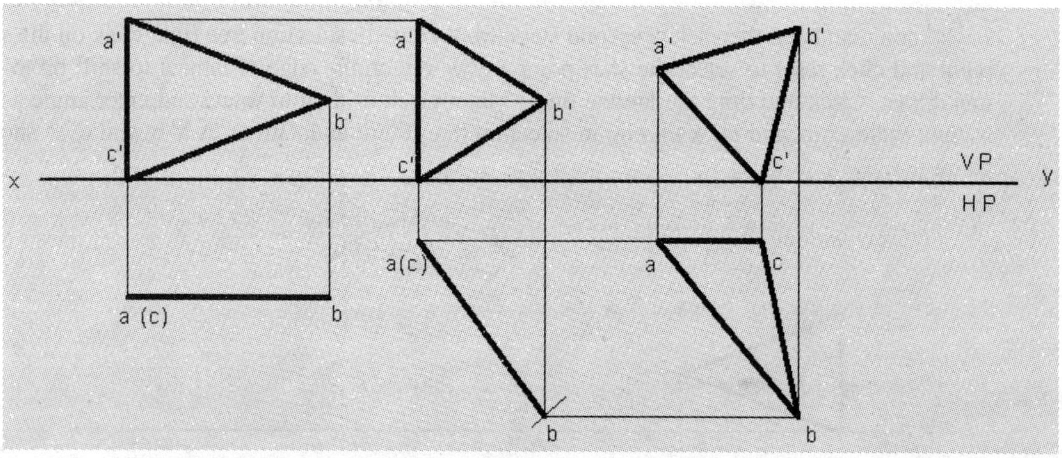

14. Using SMART DIMENSION Command  in drawing tool bar dimension the drawing as shown.

15. To get a Hard Copy of the standard drawing select print from file menu bar. Print dialog window will appear select page and change width to Entities and select the activated button 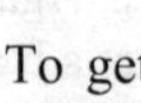 now substitute width 1 as 0.15 mm, width 2 as 0.05 mm, width 3 as 0.5 mm and say OK. Select print to get a hard copy and finally save the file. The required standard drawing is as shown below.

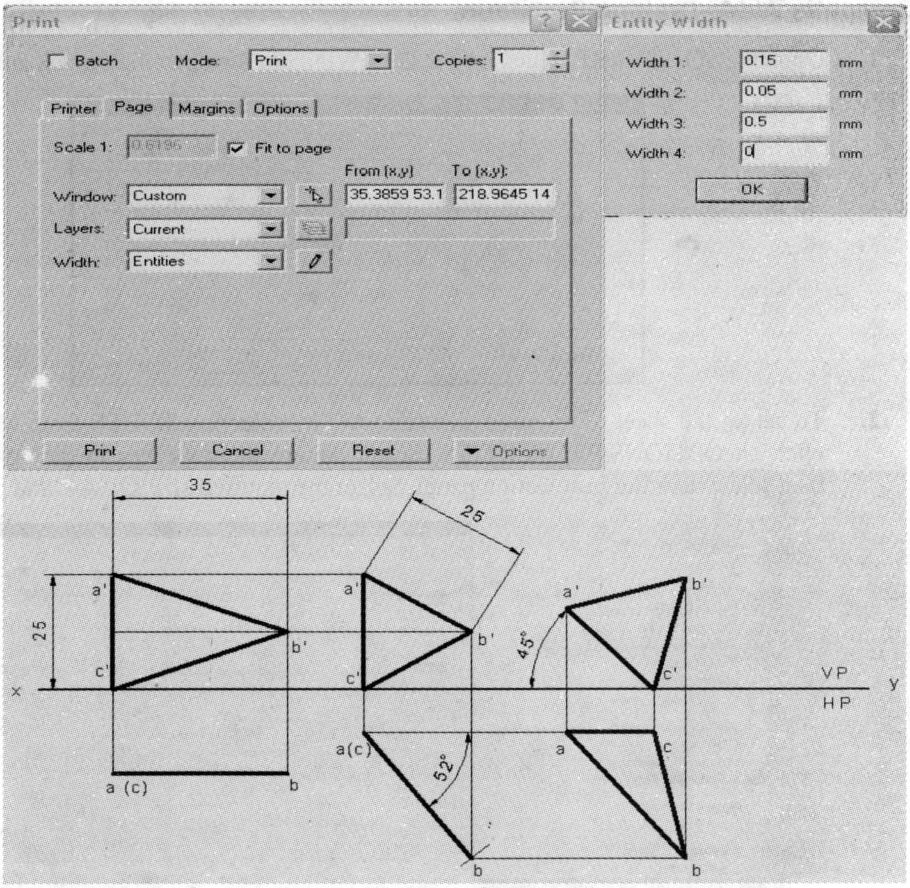

PROBLEM 4.3

A square plate of 40 mm side rests on HP such that one of the diagonals is inclined at 30° to HP and 45° to VP. Draw its projections.

SOLUTION

Manual Method

(a) Draw the XY line. Mark VP and HP above and below it.

(b) Draw square below XY line. Name the vertices as a b c and d.

(c) Project the front view on the XY line. Name the intersection end as a′ b′ c′ and d′.

(d) Redraw the front view at an angle of 30° to XY line, with a′ on XY line.

(e) Draw vertical projectors from a′ b′ c′ and d′. Draw horizontal projectors from first stage top view intersect vertical projectors at a b c and d to get second stage top view.

(f) Draw a line inclined at 45° to XY line and mark a_1c, at a_1 draw a locus. With ac diagonal from second stage top view, draw an arc with c as center and ac as radius to cut locus. Redraw second stage top view such that diagonal match with ac to get third stage top view.

(g) Project vertically upwards from third stage top view. Draw horizontal projectors from second stage front view to intersect vertical projectors to get final front view.

(h) Mark annotations correctly and dimension necessarily.

Computer Aided Drafting Procedure

1. Open the SOFTWARE. Click on the DRAWING in the open dialog box and say OK.

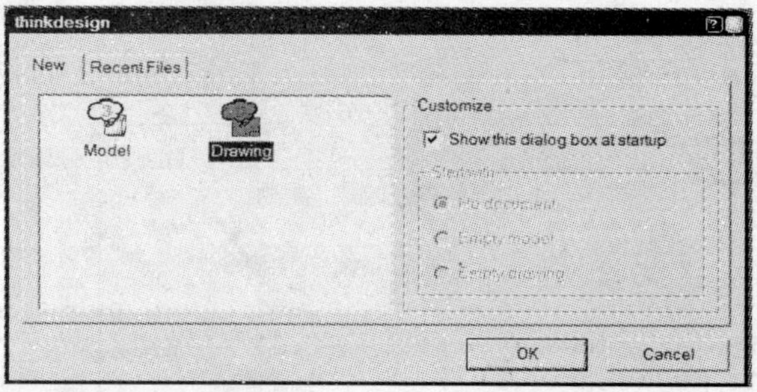

2. To set up the sheet of required size (Ex: A4) by selecting TOOLS from Main Menu Bar and click on OPTIONS/PROPERTIES. Select document properties in dialog box appeared and then select drawing in selection panel. Select the required size say A4, and click OK.

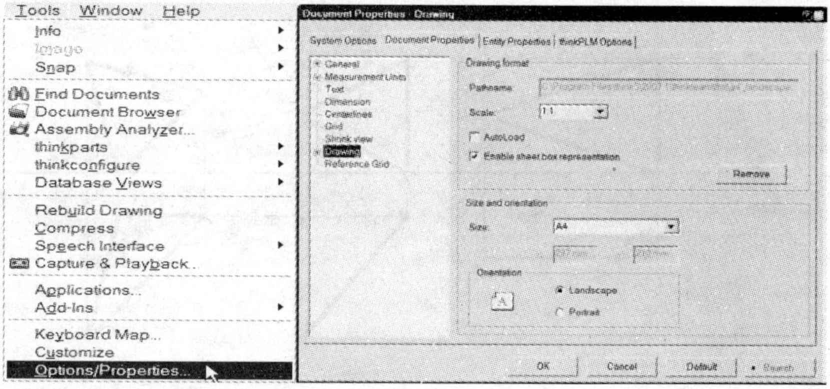

3. To draw XY line, projection lines and top & front view lines. After selecting line command, in format select XY for XY line, PL for projection lines and VL for top and front view lines before drawing these lines.

4. Draw the line by using POLYLINE  command from drafting tool bar and in format select XY.

5. Make Annotation X, Y, VP, and HP to the line drawn by using INSERT TEXT Command  from drafting tool bar, just by typing X, Y, VP and HP in Text Box and insert these in the required position by left click of the mouse, as shown below.

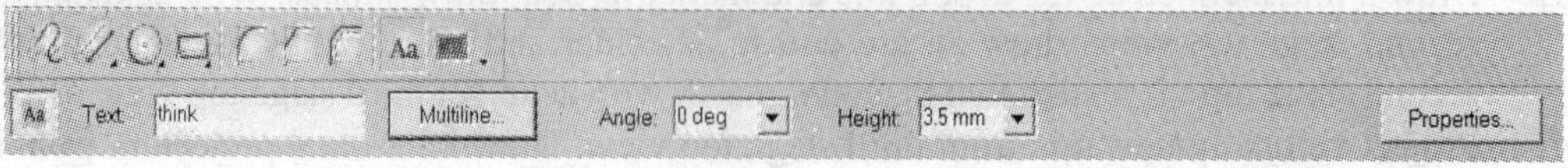

6. As per the problem a square lamina of 40 mm has to be drawn in HP, hence draw a square of 40 mm using REACTANGLE command and in format select VL and in mode as center+sizes in selection tree. Now enter X size = 40, Y size = 40 and angle as 45 in mini dialog box. Mark annotations a b c and d using INSERT TEXT Command as shown below.

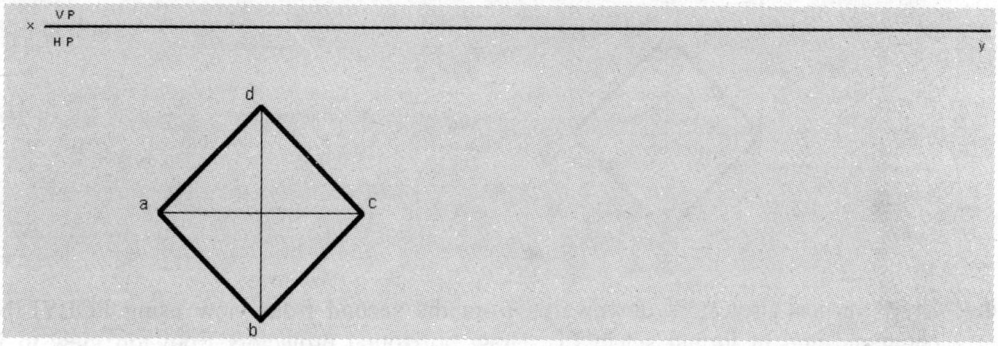

7. Draw the vertical projection upwards from all the corners of square lamina in top view until it touches XY line, using POLYLINE command and in format select PL.

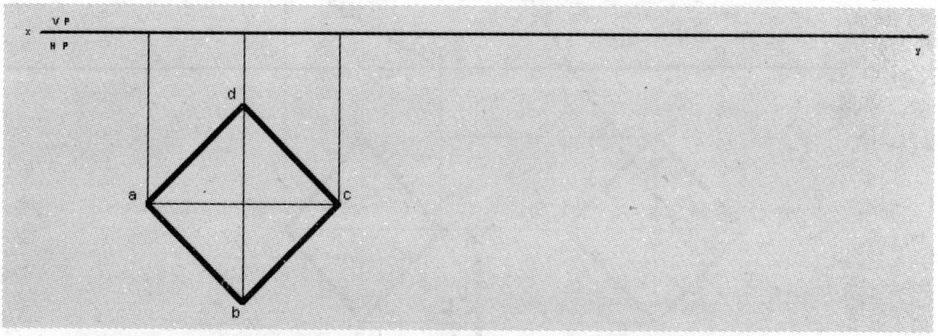

8. Draw front view of the triangular lamina using POLYLINE command and in format select VL, mark annotations as a′ b′ c′ and (d′) as shown below.

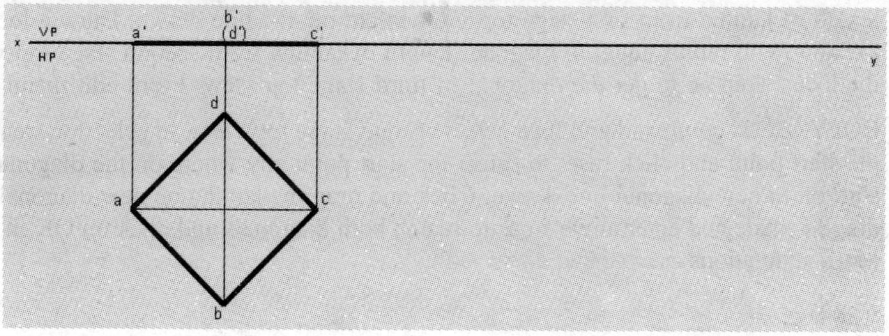

9. Since the diagonal of lamina is inclined at 30° to HP. By using POLYLINE command and in format select VL enter length equal to length of first stage front view and angle as 30 in mini dialog box, mark annotations as a′ b′ (d′) and c′ using INSERT TEXT Command as shown below.

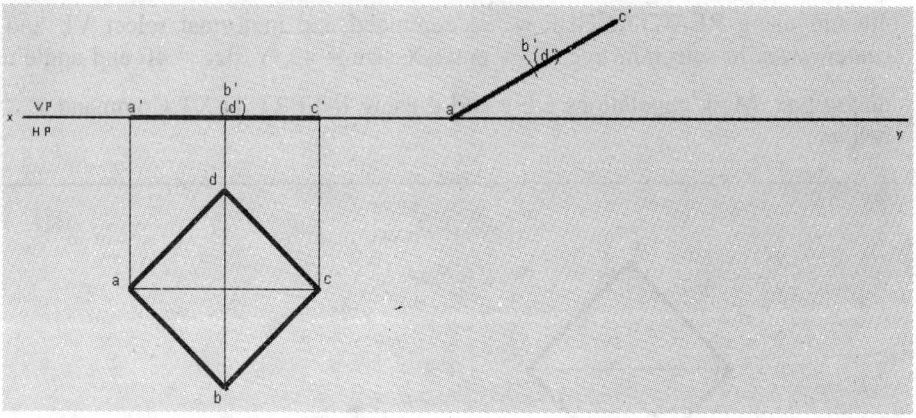

10. Draw vertical projectors downwards from the second front view using POLYLINE command and in format select PL. Draw horizontal projectors from top view to intersect vertical projectors at a, b c and d which forms the second stage top view as shown below.

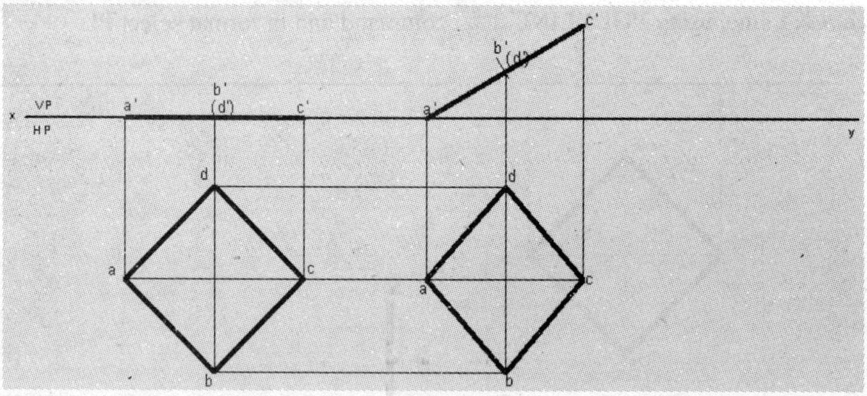

11. Since the diagonal of lamina is inclined to VP at 45°. Draw a line of 45° in HP using POLYLINE command and in format select PL. Draw an arc of radius equal to diagonal length of lamina from first stage top view to cut on 45° line drawn. Draw a locus from point a1, now with radius equal to diagonal length of lamina from second stage top view to cut on the locus. Join ac to get the diagonal of third stage top view. From edit menu select MOVE COPY command and then select second stage top view. In selection tree right click on the start point and click reset to select the start point any where on the diagonal of lamina to shift on to new diagonal line drawn. Click and drag the lamina on new diagonal line. Click or drag to rotate and enter angle so as to match both diagonals and click on OK in sèlection tree. Mark annotations as a b c and d.

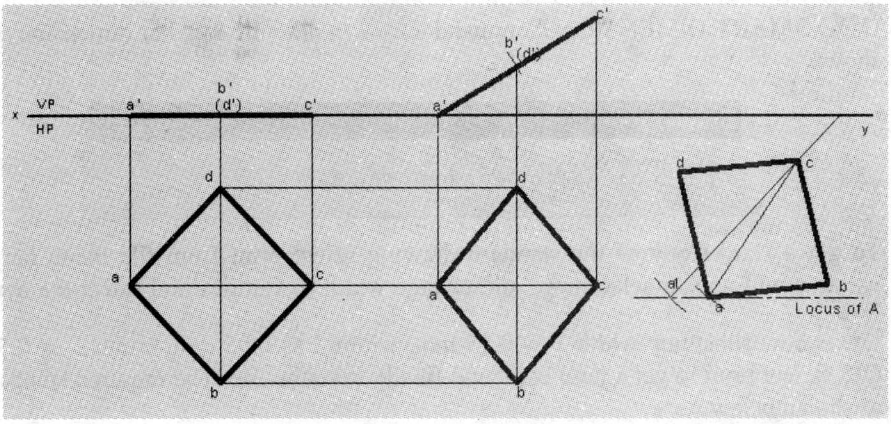

12. Draw the vertical projection upwards from all the corners of square lamina from third stage top view using POLYLINE command and in format select PL. Again draw horizontal projectors from second stage front view to intersect vertical projectors at a′b′c′ and d′.

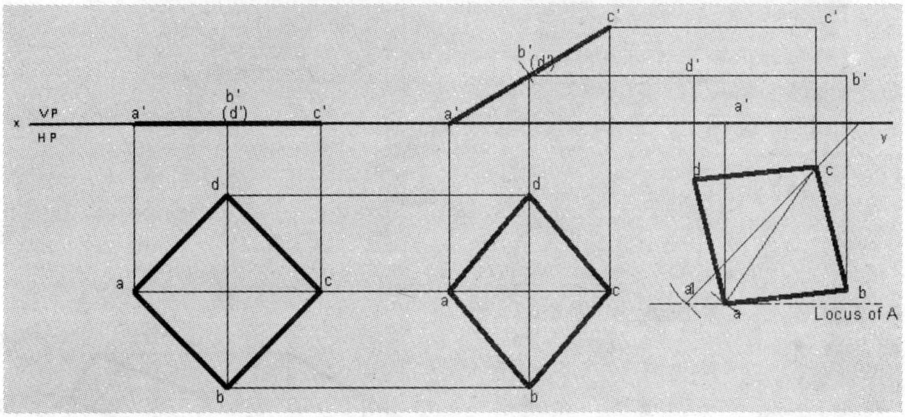

13. Join a′b′c′ and d′ using 2 POINT LINE Command and in format select VL.

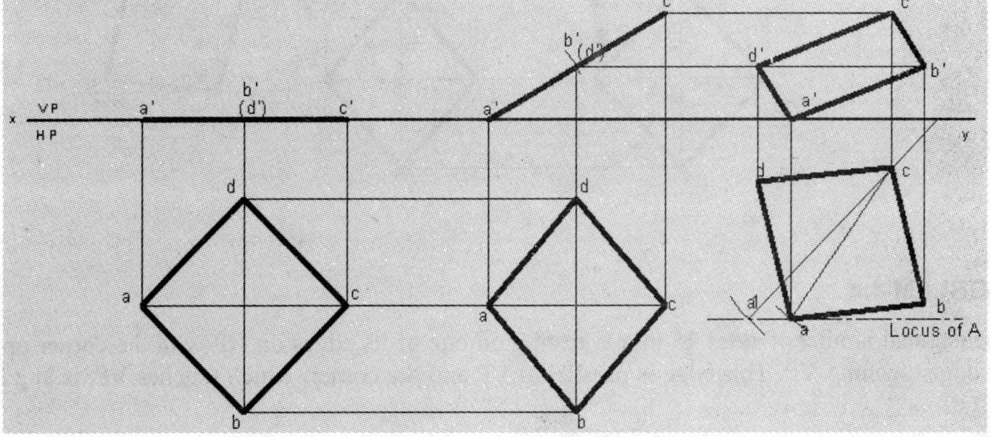

14. Using SMART DIMENSION Command  in drawing tool bar dimension the drawing as shown.

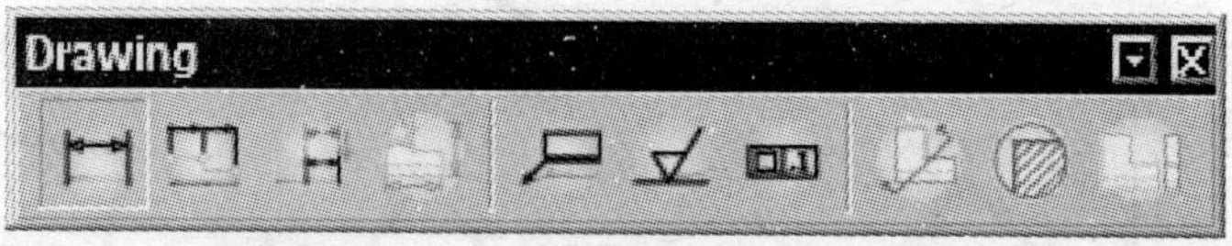

15. To get a Hard Copy of the standard drawing select print from file menu bar. Print dialog window will appear select page and change width to Entities and select the activated button  now substitute width 1 as 0.15 mm, width 2 as 0.05 mm, width 3 as 0.5 mm and say OK. Select print to get a hard copy and finally save the file. The required standard drawing is as shown below.

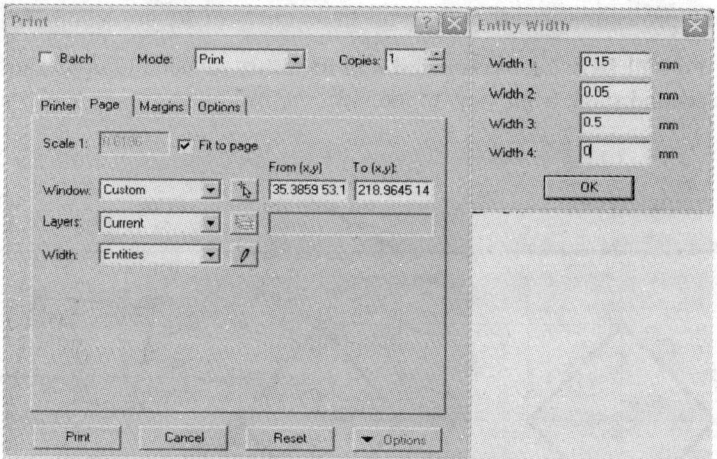

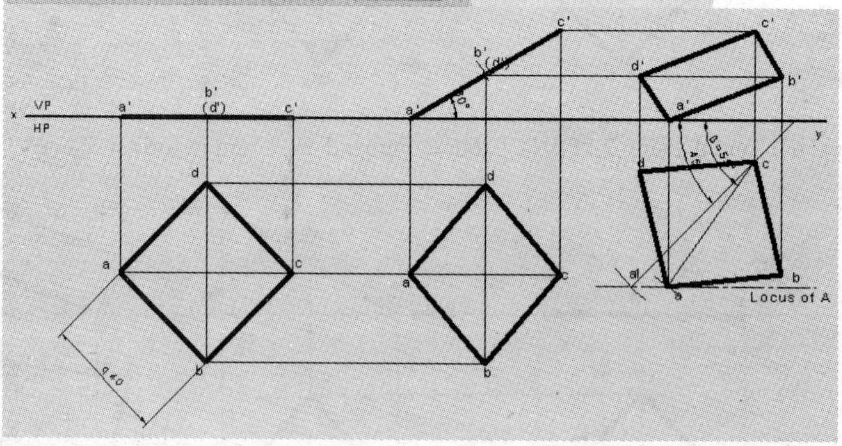

PROBLEM 4.4

A pentagonal lamina of sides 25 mm is resting on one of its edges on HP with the corner opposite to that edge touching VP. This edge is parallel to VP and the corner, which touches VP, is at a height of

15 mm above HP. Draw the projections of the lamina and determine the inclinations of the lamina with HP and VP and the distance at which the parallel edge lies from VP.

SOLUTION

Manual Method

(a) Draw the XY line. Mark VP and HP above and below it.

(b) Draw the pentagon of side 25 mm below XY line. Name the vertices as a b c etc.

(c) Project the front view on the XY line. Name the intersection end as a′ b′ c′ etc.

(d) Redraw the front view at a height equal to 15 mm (given) from XY line, with a′ e′ on XY line.

(e) Draw vertical projectors from a′ b′ c′ etc. Draw horizontal projectors from first stage top view intersect vertical projectors at a b c etc, to get second stage top view.

(f) Redraw second stage top view, such that corner c touches XY line, to get third stage top view.

(g) Project vertically upwards from third stage top view. Draw horizontal projectors from second stage front view to intersect vertical projectors to get final front view.

(h) Mark annotations correctly and dimension necessarily.

Computer Aided Drafting Procedure

1. Open the SOFTWARE. Click on the DRAWING in the open dialog box and say OK.

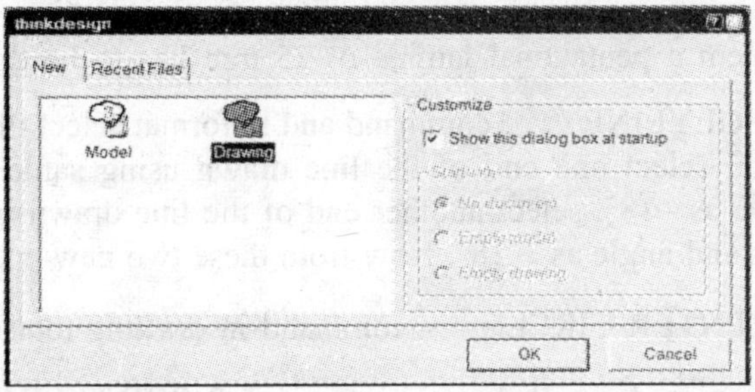

2. To set up the sheet of required size (Ex: A4) by selecting TOOLS from Main Menu Bar and click on OPTIONS/PROPERTIES. Select document properties in dialog box appeared and then select drawing in selection panel. Select the required size say A4, and click OK.

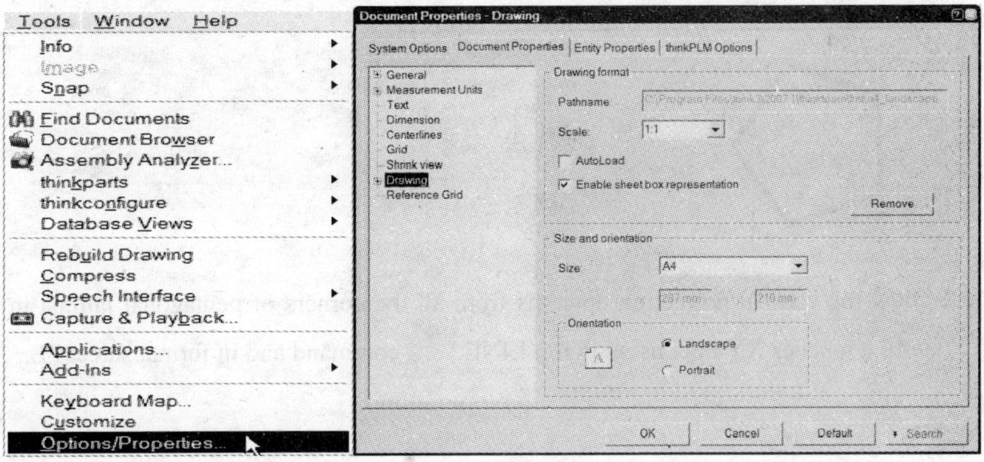

3. To draw XY line, projection lines and top & front view lines. After selecting line command, in format select XY for XY line, PL for projection lines and VL for top and front view lines before drawing these lines.

4. Draw the line by using POLYLINE  command from drafting tool bar and in format select XY.

5. Make Annotation X, Y, VP, and HP to the line drawn by using INSERT TEXT Command  from drafting tool bar, just by typing X, Y, VP and HP in Text Box and insert these in the required position by left click of the mouse, as shown below.

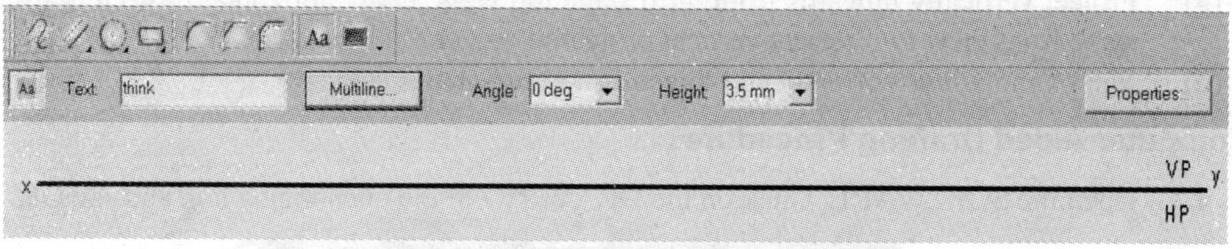

6. As per the problem a pentagonal lamina of 25 mm has to be drawn in HP, hence draw a pentagon using POLYLINE  command and in format select PL. First draw a vertical line of length 25 mm, select one end of the line drawn using same command enter length as 25 mm and angle as –18°, select another end of the line drawn using same command enter length as 25 mm and angle as + 18°. Now from these two new ends draw an arc of radius of 25 mm using CENTER CIRCLE  command in drafting tool bar. In mode option select arc, to get final point. Join all these points using 2 POINT LINE Command  and in format select VL. Mark annotations a b c d and e using INSERT TEXT Command 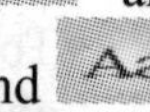 as shown below.

7. Draw the vertical projection upwards from all the corners of pentagonal lamina in top view until it touches XY line, using POLYLINE 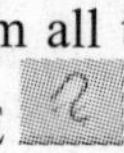 command and in format select PL.

8. Draw front view of the pentagonal lamina using POLYLINE command and in format select VL, mark annotations as a′ (e′) b′ (d′) and c′ as shown below.

9. Since height of second stage front view given (15 mm). Draw a locus parallel to XY line at a height of 15 mm above XY line using POLYLINE command and in format select PL. Now with length equal to length of first stage front view, draw an arc to cut the locus drawn. Join and mark annotations as a′ (e′) b′ (d′) and c′ using INSERT TEXT Command as shown below.

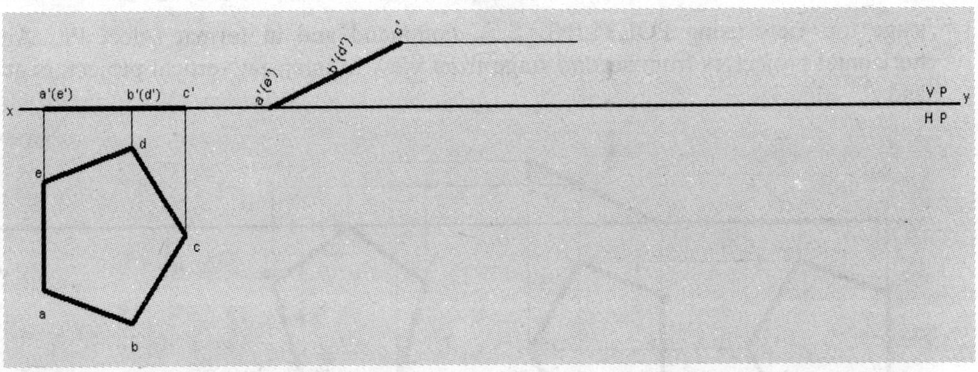

10. Draw vertical projectors downwards from the second stage front view using POLYLINE command and in format select PL. Draw horizontal projectors from top view to intersect vertical projectors at a b c d and e which forms the second stage top view as shown below.

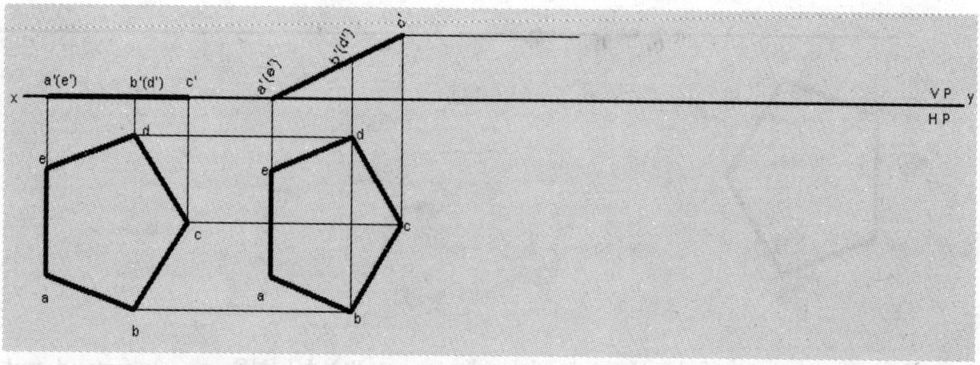

11. Since the edge is parallel to VP and the corner, which touches VP. From edit menu select MOVE COPY  command and then select second stage top view. In selection tree right click on the start point and click reset to select the start point as c. Click and drag the lamina on XY line. Click or drag to rotate and enter angle 90 so to get final top view and click on OK in selection tree. Mark annotations as a b c d and e.

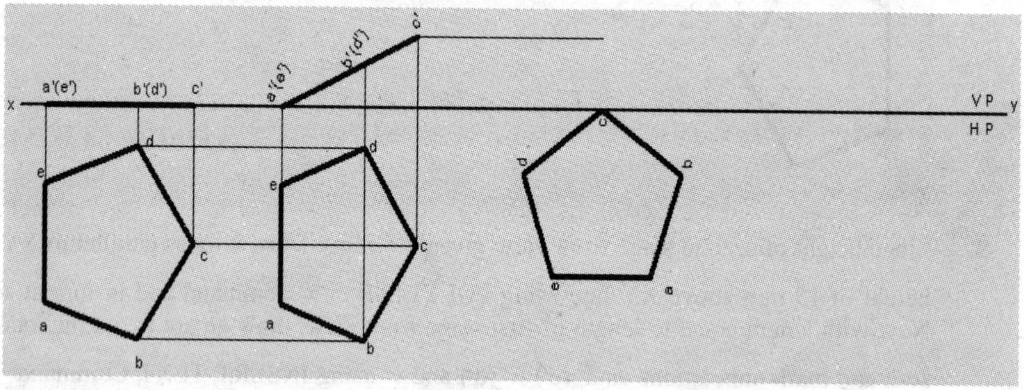

12. Draw the vertical projection upwards from all the corners of pentagonal lamina from third stage top view using POLYLINE  command and in format select PL. Again draw horizontal projectors from second stage front view to intersect vertical projectors at a′ b′ c′ d′ and e'.

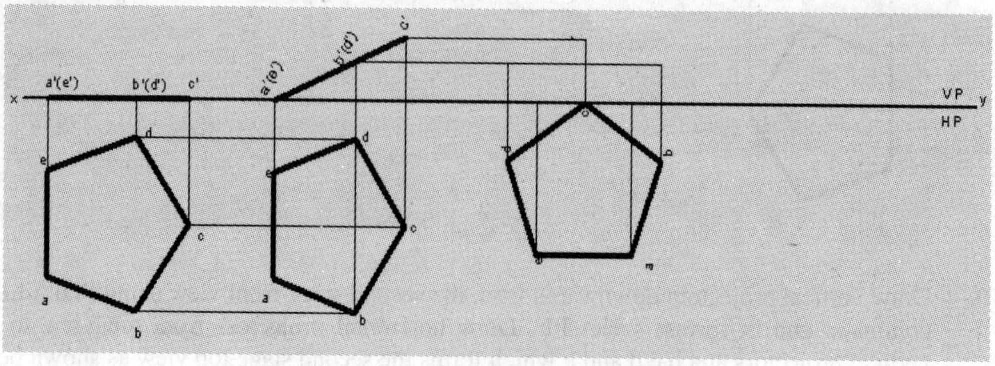

13. Join a′ b′ c′ d′ and e′ using 2 POINT LINE Command  and in format select VL.

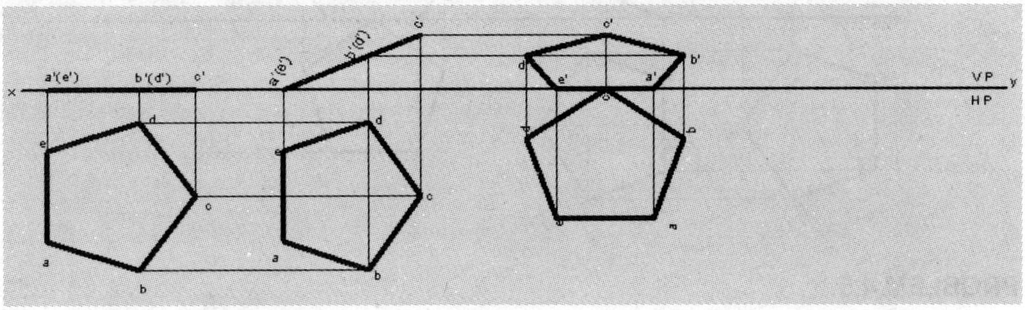

14. Using SMART DIMENSION Command  in drawing tool bar dimension the drawing as shown.

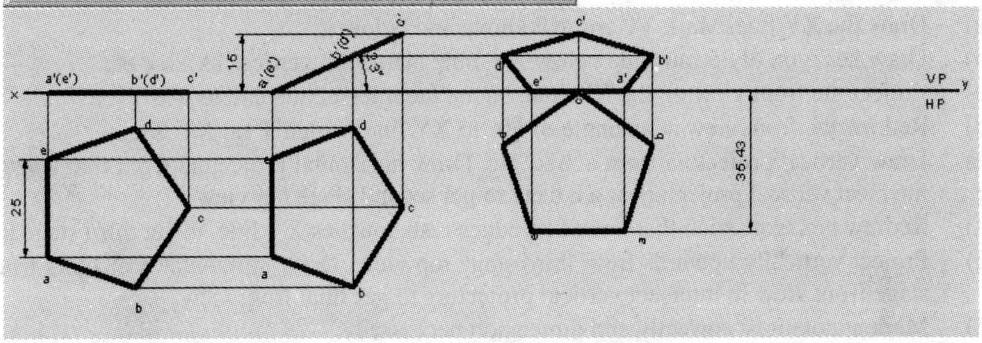

15. To get a Hard Copy of the standard drawing select print from file menu bar. Print dialog window will appear select page and change width to Entities and select the activated button  now substitute width 1 as 0.15 mm, width 2 as 0.05 mm, width 3 as 0.5 mm and say OK. Select print to get a hard copy and finally save the file. The required standard drawing is as shown below.

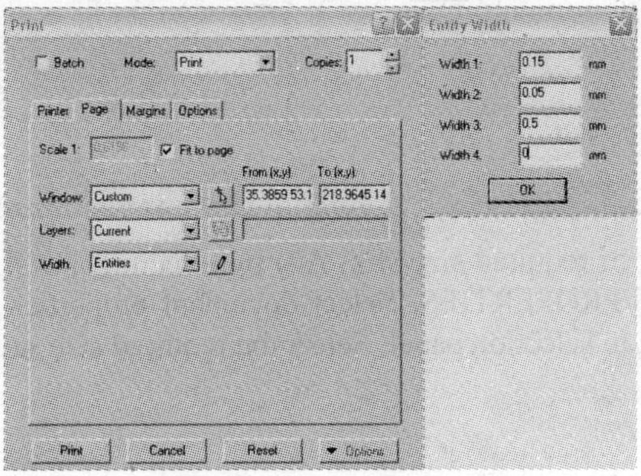

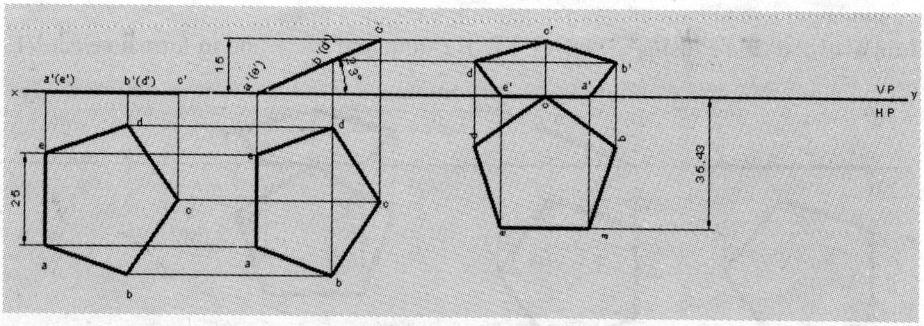

PROBLEM 4.5

A regular hexagonal lamina of sides 25 mm is lying in such a way that one of its sides on HP while the side opposite to the side on which it rests is on VP. If the lamina makes 60º to HP, Draw the projections of the lamina.

SOLUTION

Manual Method

(a) Draw the XY line. Mark VP and HP above and below it.
(b) Draw hexagon of 25 mm side below XY line. Name the vertices as a b c etc.
(c) Project the front view on the XY line. Name the intersection end as a′b′c′etc.
(d) Redraw the front view at an angle of 60° to XY line, with a′f′ on XY line.
(e) Draw vertical projectors from a′b′c′etc. Draw horizontal projectors from first stage top view intersect vertical projectors at a b c etc to get second stage top view.
(f) Redraw hexagon, such that one of its edges rests touches XY line, to get third stage top view.
(g) Project vertically upwards from third stage top view. Draw horizontal projectors from second stage front view to intersect vertical projectors to get final front view.
(h) Mark annotations correctly and dimension necessarily.

Computer Aided Drafting Procedure

1. Open the SOFTWARE. Click on the DRAWING in the open dialog box and say OK.

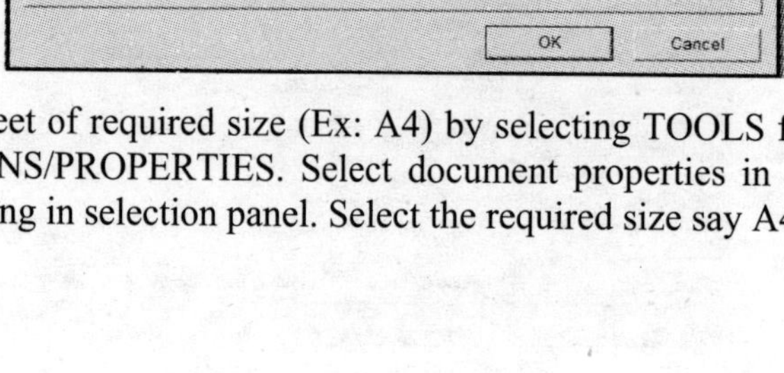

2. To set up the sheet of required size (Ex: A4) by selecting TOOLS from Main Menu Bar and click on OPTIONS/PROPERTIES. Select document properties in dialog box appeared and then select drawing in selection panel. Select the required size say A4, and click OK.

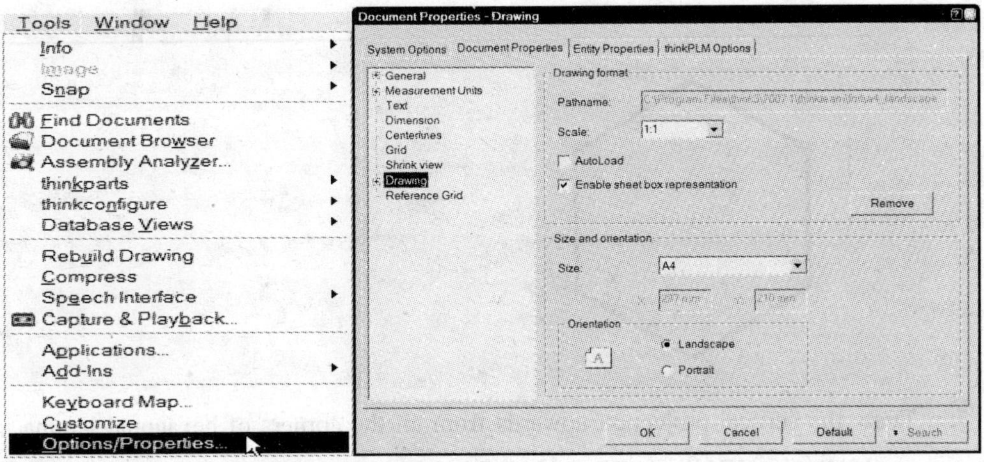

3. To draw XY line, projection lines and top & front view lines. After selecting line command, in format select XY for XY line, PL for projection lines and VL for top and front view lines before drawing these lines.

4. Draw the line by using POLYLINE  command from drafting tool bar and in format select XY.

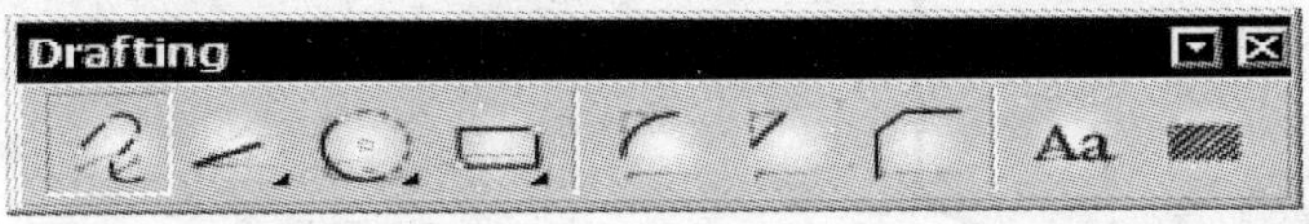

5. Make Annotation X, Y, VP, and HP to the line drawn by using INSERT TEXT Command  from drafting tool bar, just by typing X, Y, VP and HP in Text Box and insert these in the required position by left click of the mouse, as shown below.

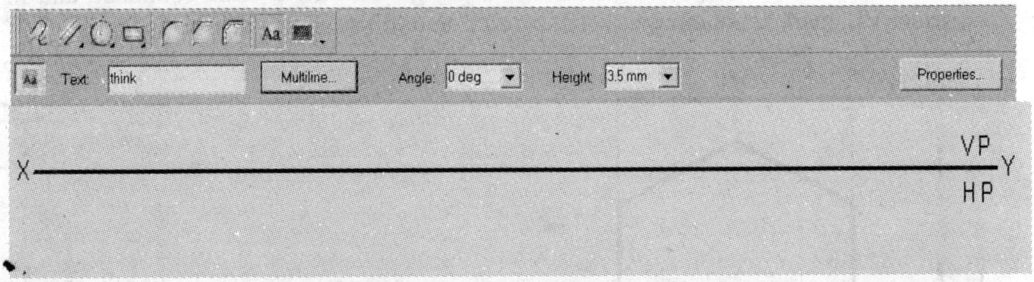

6. As per the problem hexagonal lamina of 25 mm has to be drawn in HP, hence draw a hexagon of 25 mm using POLYGON  command and in format select VL and enter edges as 6, radius as 25 and angle as 90 in mini dialog box. Mark annotations a b c d e and f using INSERT TEXT Command  as shown below.

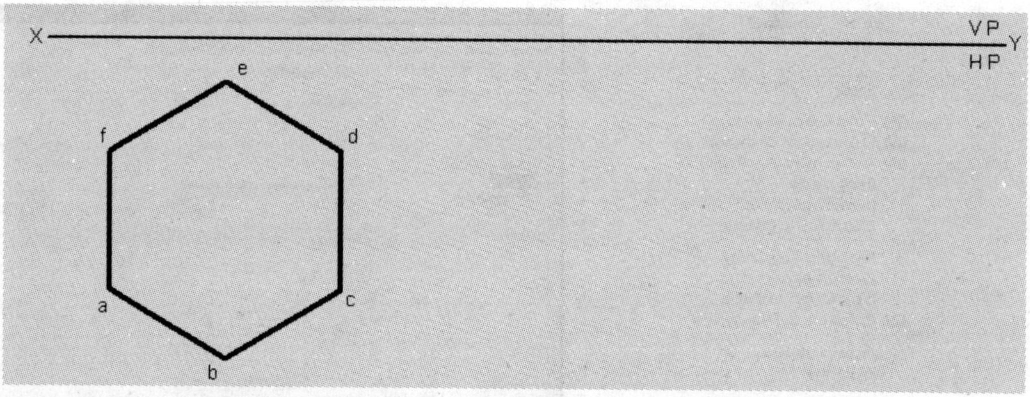

7. Draw the vertical projection upwards from all the corners of hexagonal lamina in top view until it touches XY line, using POLYLINE command and in format select PL.

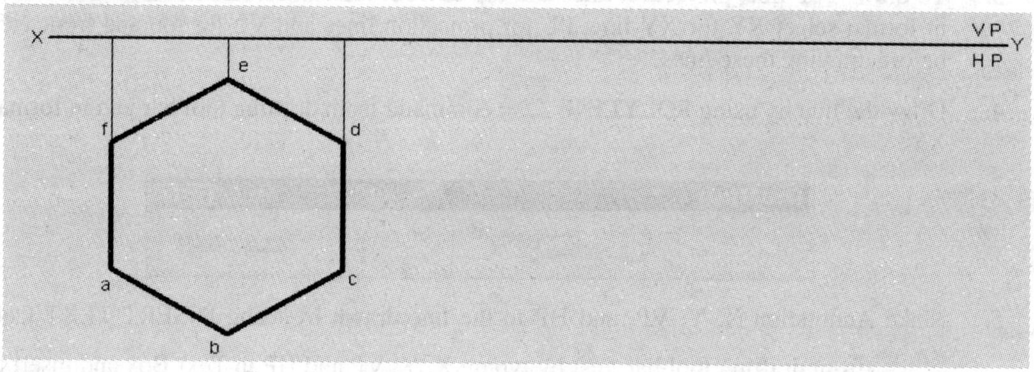

8. Draw front view of the hexagonal lamina using POLYLINE command and in format select VL, mark annotations as a′ (f′) b′ (e′) c′ and (d′) as shown below.

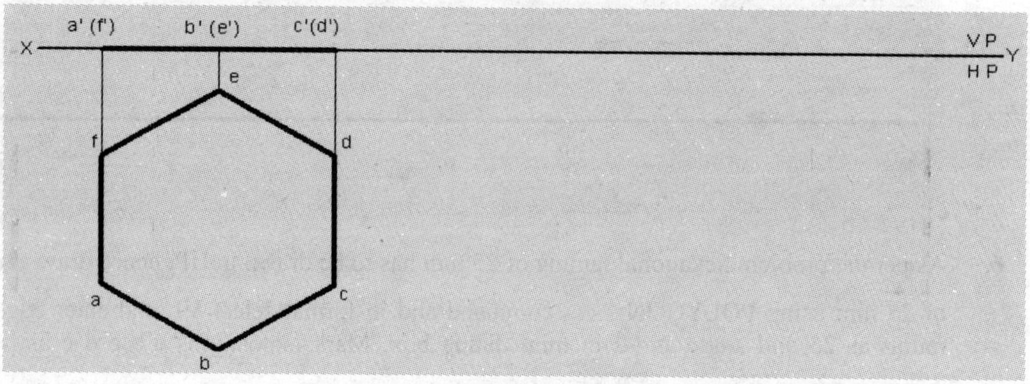

9. Since the lamina is inclined at 60° to HP. By using POLYLINE command and in format select VL enter length equal to length of first stage front view and angle as 60 in mini dialog box, mark annotations as a′ (f′) b′ (e′) c′ and (d′) using INSERT TEXT Command 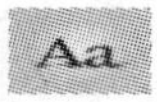 as shown below to get second stage of front view.

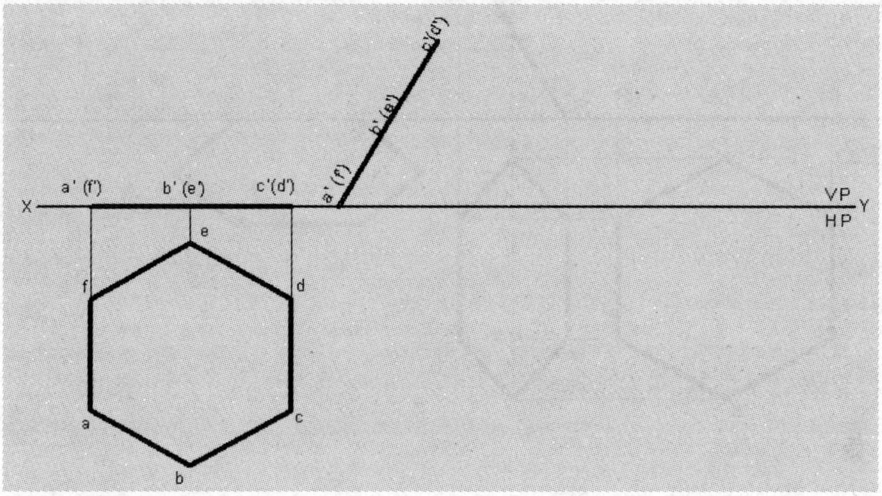

10. Draw vertical projectors downwards from the second stage front view using POLYLINE  command and in format select PL. Draw horizontal projectors from top view to intersect vertical projectors at a b c d e and f which forms the second stage top view as shown below.

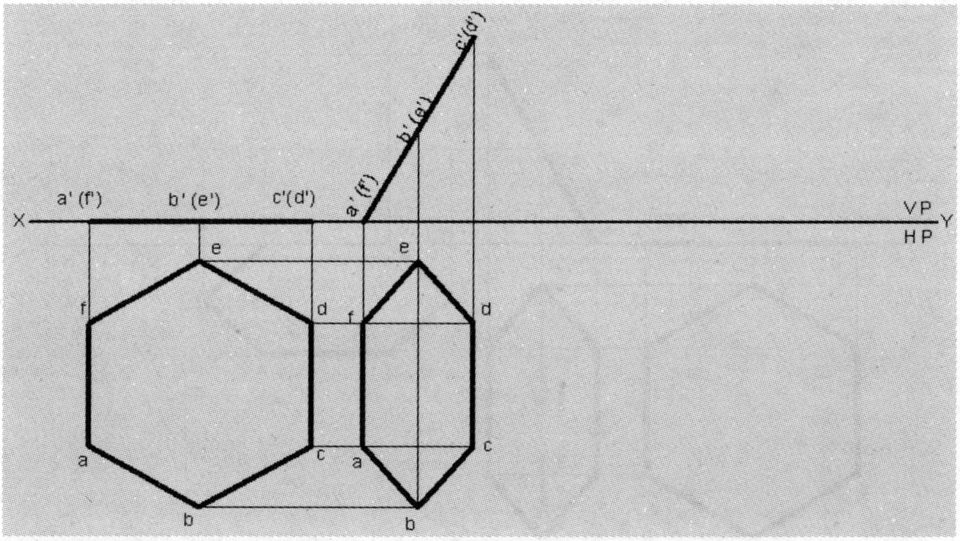

11. Since the one edge is on HP and the opposite edge is on VP. From edit menu select MOVE COPY 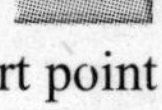 command and then select second stage top view. In selection tree right click on the start point and click reset to select the start point any where on the edge of lamina to shift on to XY line. Click and drag the lamina on XY line. Click or drag to rotate and enter angle as 90 in mini dialog box and click on OK in selection tree.

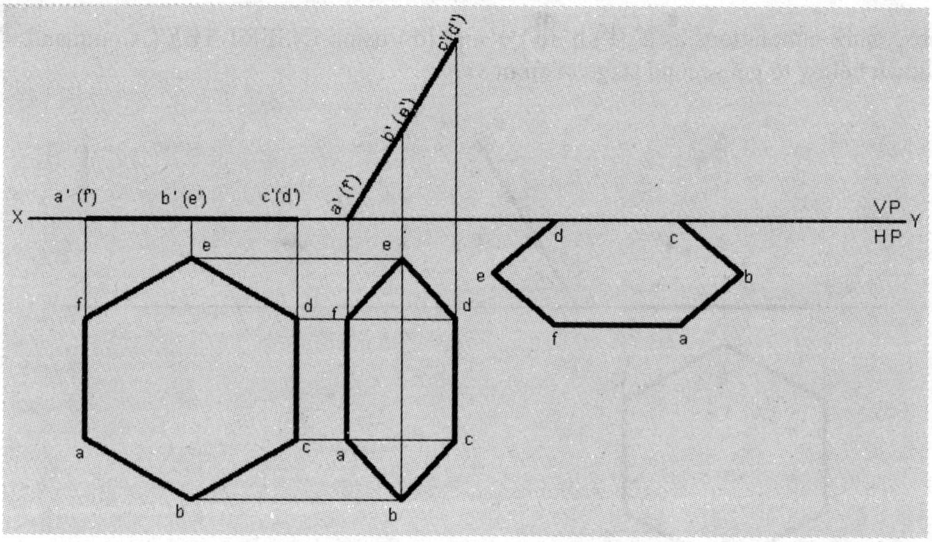

12. Draw the vertical projection upwards from all the corners of hexagonal lamina from third stage top view using POLYLINE  command and in format select PL. Again draw horizontal projectors from second stage front view to intersect vertical projectors at a′ b′ c′ d′ e′ and f′.

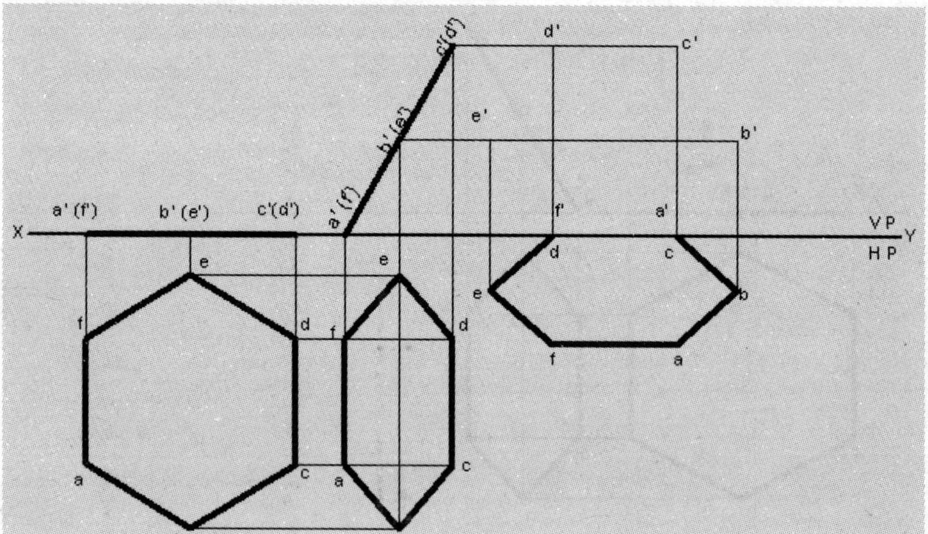

13. Join a′ b′ c′ d′ e′ and f′ using 2 POINT LINE Command  and in format select VL.

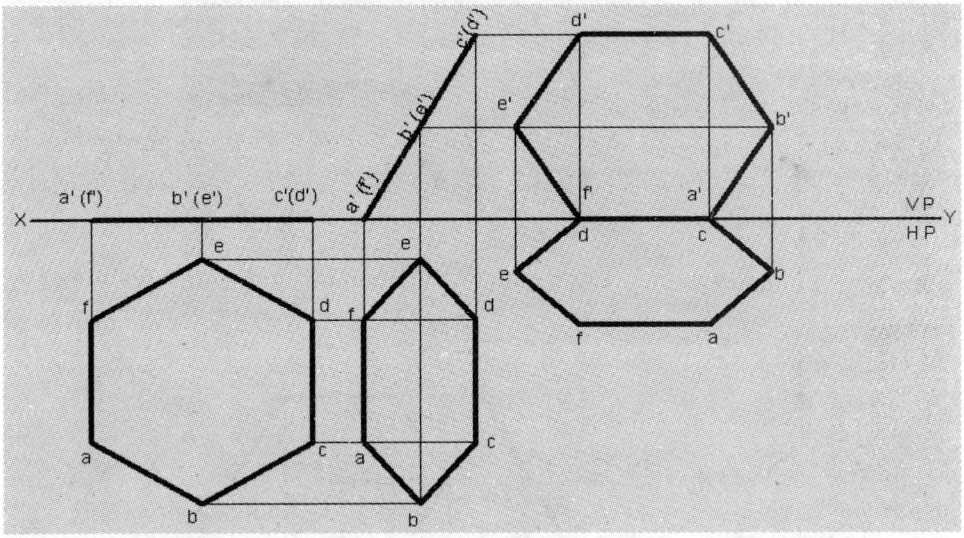

14. Using SMART DIMENSION Command 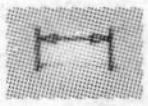 in drawing tool bar dimension the drawing as shown.

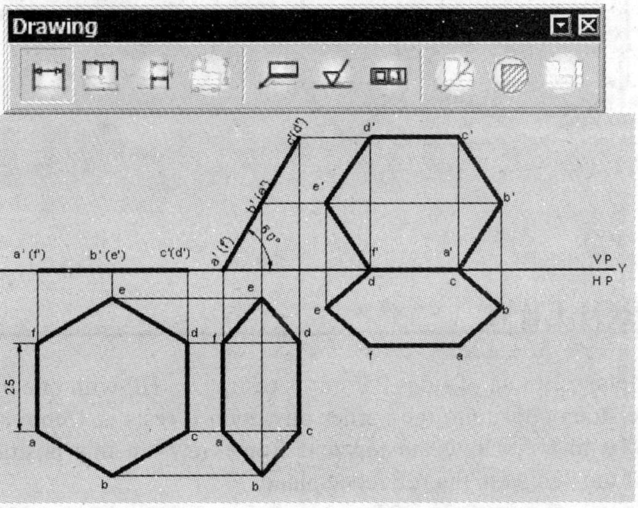

15. To get a Hard Copy of the standard drawing select print from file menu bar. Print dialog window will appear select page and change width to Entities and select the activated button  now substitute width 1 as 0.15 mm, width 2 as 0.05 mm, width 3 as 0.5 mm and say OK. Select print to get a hard copy and finally save the file. The required standard drawing is as shown below.

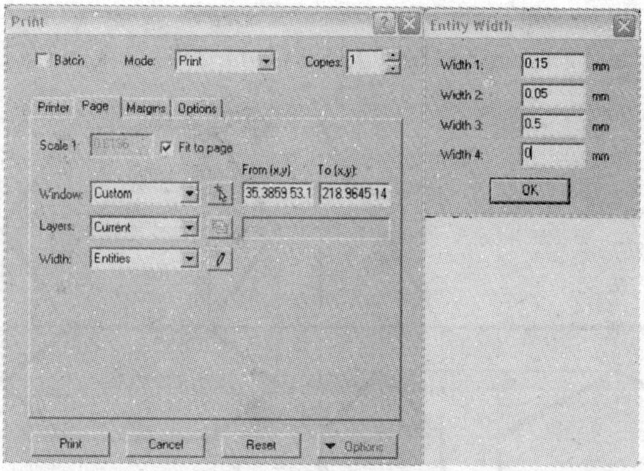

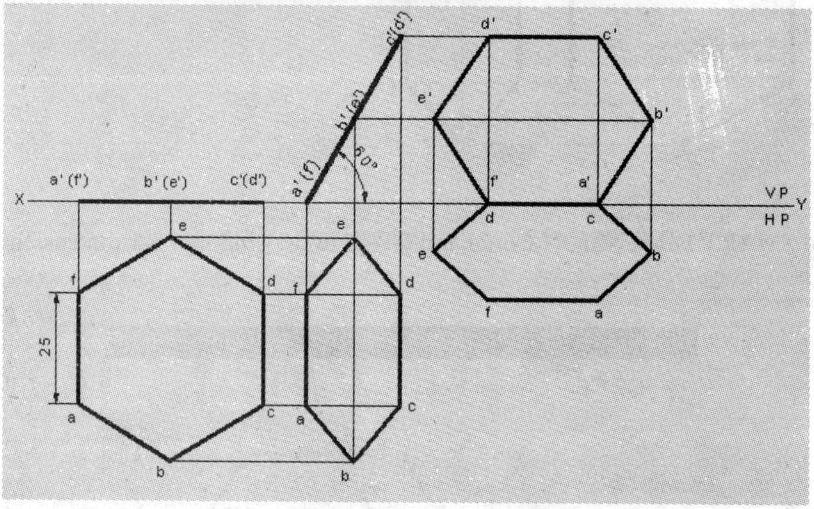

EXERCISE PROBLEM

1. A triangular plane lamina of sides 25 mm is resting on HP with one of its corners touching it, such that the side opposite to the corner on which it rests is 15mm above HP and makes an angle of 30° with VP. Draw the top and front views in this position. Also determine the inclination of the lamina to the reference plane.
2. A triangular plane figure of sides 25 mm is resting on HP with one of its corners, such that the surface of the lamina makes an angle of 60° with HP. If the side opposite to the corner on which the lamina rests makes an angle of 30° with VP, draw the top and front views in this position.
3. A square lamina of 40 mm side rests on one of its sides on HP. The lamina makes 30° to HP and the side on which it rests makes 45° to VP. Draw its projections.

4. The top view of a square lamia of side 30 mm is a rectangle of sides 30 mm × 20 mm with the longer side of the rectangle being parallel to both HP and VP. Draw the top and front views of the square lamina. What is the inclination of the surface of the lamina with HP and VP?
5. The top view of a square lamia of side 30 mm is a rectangle of sides 30 mm × 20 mm with the longer side of the rectangle being parallel to both HP and VP. Draw the top and front views of the square lamina. What is the inclination of the surface of the lamina with HP and VP?
6. The front view of a rectangular lamina of sides 30 mm × 20 mm is a square of 20mm side. Draw the projections and determine the inclinations of the surface of the lamina with HP and VP.
7. A pentagonal lamina of edges 25 mm is resting on HP with one of its sides such that the surface makes an angle of 60° with HP. The edge on which it rests is inclined at 45° to VP. Draw its projections
8. A pentagonal lamina of edges 25 mm is resting on HP with one of its corners such that the plane surface makes an angle of 60° with HP. The two of the edges containing the corner on which the lamia rests make equal inclinations with HP. When the edge opposite to this corner makes an angle of 45° with VP and nearer to the observer, draw the top and front views of the plane lamina in this position.
9. A pentagonal lamina having edges 25 mm is placed on one of its corners on HP such that the perpendicular bisector of the edge passing through the corner on which the lamina rests is inclined at 30° to HP and 45° VP. Draw the top and front views of the lamina.
10. Draw the top and front views of a hexagonal lamina of 30 mm sides having two of its edges parallel to both vertical and horizontal planes and one of its edges is 10mm from each of the planes of projection. The surface of the lamina is inclined at an angle of 60° to the HP.
11. A regular hexagonal lamina of side 30 mm is lying in such a way that one of its sides touches both the reference planes. If the side opposite to the side on which it rests is 45 mm above HP, draw the projections of the lamina.
12. A hexagonal lamina of sides 25 mm rests on one of its sides on HP. The lamina makes 45° to HP and the side on which it rests makes 30° to VP. Draw its projections.
13. A hexagonal lamina of sides 25 mm rests on one of its corners on HP. The lamina makes 45° to HP and the diagonal passing through the corner on which it rests is inclined at 30° to VP. Draw its projections.
14. Draw the projections of a circular plate of negligible thickness of 50 mm diameter resting on HP on a point A on the circumference, with its plane inclined at 45° to HP and the top view of the diameter passing through the resting point makes 60° with VP.
15. A circular lamina of 50 mm diameter is standing with one of its points on the rim on HP and the lamina inclined at 45° to HP. The diameter at right angles to the diameter which is passing through the point on which the lamina rests is parallel to VP. Draw its projections.
16. A circular lamina of 50 mm diameter rests on HP such that one of its diameters is inclined at 30° to VP and 45° to HP. Draw its top and front views in this position.
17. A rectangular lamina of sides 20 mm × 25 mm has an edge in HP and adjoining edge in VP, is tilted such that the front view appears as a rectangle of 20 mm × 15 mm. The edge, which is in VP, is 30mm from the right profile plane. (a) Draw the top view, front view and the left profile view in this position. (b) Find its inclinations with the corresponding principal planes.

18. A pentagonal lamina of edges 25 mm is resting on VP with one of its sides such that the surface makes an angle of 60° with VP. The edge on which it rests is inclined at 45° to HP. Draw its projections.
19. A hexagonal lamina of 30 mm sides rests on HP with one of its corners touching VP and surface inclined at 45° to it. One of its edges is inclined to HP at 30°. Draw the front and top views of the lamina in its final position.
20. A circular lamina inclined to the VP appears in the front view as an ellipse of major axis 30 mm and minor axis 15 mm. The major axis is parallel to both HP and VP. One end of the minor axis is in both the HP and VP. Draw the projections of the lamina and determine the inclination of the lamina with the VP.

■■■

5

ORTHOGRAPHIC PROJECTIONS OF SOLIDS

INTRODUCTION

- Any object having definite dimensions like length, breadth and height (3 dimensions) is called a solid. The study of the projection of solid is very important in the present day world for the product design. The knowledge is very much essential for 3-D modeling, analysis and animation. It is the basic for the present day technology for any product.
- Solids may be divided into two types: (a) polyhedra, (b) solid of revolution.
- Polyhedra are those bounded by plane surfaces.
- Polyhedra are sub-divided into: (a) regular polyhedra, prisms and pyramids.
- Regular polyhedra are those, who have all faces similar, equal and regular like tetrahedron, cube, octahedron dodecahedron isosahedron.
- Prisms are those, who have two equal and similar faces, parallel to each other joined together with rectangular faces: like square prism, rectangular prism, pentagonal prism hexagonal prism.
- Pyramid are those, who have polygonal plane for the base which connected to a number of triangular faces equal to number of sides of the base connected to a point called as apex of the pyramid: like triangular pyramid, square pyramid, rectangular pyramid, pentagonal pyramid and hexagonal pyramid.
- Solid of revolution are formed by the revolution of plane, which form cylinder, cone, frustum of cones and truncated solids of cones.
- Important point to note all these solids will have axis.
- The position of a solid may have different orientations in space.
- As per first angle projection, the axis may be parallel, perpendicular or inclined to either or both the reference planes (horizontal or vertical planes).
- Positions of solid
  1. Solid axis parallel and perpendicular to reference planes (HP & VP)
     (a) Axis parallel to HP and perpendicular to VP.
     (b) Axis parallel to VP and perpendicular to HP.
  2. Solid axis parallel to both HP & VP.
  3. Solid axis parallel and inclined to reference planes (HP & VP)
     (a) Solid axis parallel to HP and inclined to VP.
     (b) Solid axis parallel to VP and inclined to HP.
     (c) Solid axis parallel to both HP & VP.
  4. Solid axis inclined to both HP & VP.
  5. Solid axis inclined to both HP & VP
     (a) Axis inclination to HP and VP is not equal to 90°.
     (b) Axis inclination to HP and VP is equal to 90°.

System of Notation

1. The actual solid in space is denoted by capital letters A_1, B_1, C_1 and D_1, etc for Base of solid and A, B, C and D, etc for top face of the solid and axis as o_1 and o.
2. The front view (FV) of a solid is denoted by their corresponding lower case letters with dashes as a_1', b_1', c_1' and d_1' etc for base of solid and a′, b′ c′ and d′ etc. for top face of the solid and for axis as o_1' and o′.
3. The top view (TV) of a solid is denoted by their corresponding lower case letters with dashes as a_1, b_1, c_1 and d_1 etc for bottom of solid and a, b c and d, etc. for top face of the solid and for axis as o_1 and o.
4. The side view (SV) of a solid are denoted by their corresponding lower case letters with double dashes as a_1'', b_1'', c_1'' and d_1'' etc for base of the solid and a″, b″, c″ and d″ etc for top face of the solid and for axis as o_1'' and o″.
5. Projectors are always drawn as continuous thin lines.
6. Line with specific thickness for a particular type of line.

In Computer Aided Engineering Graphics for projection of solid following commands are used other than evoking software, opening file, saving file and giving print command. Using these minimum13 commands any type of projection of line problem can be solved they are as follows:

1. Select tool Command.
2. Point command.
3. Poly-Line command.
4. Two Point Line command.
5. Parallel line command.
6. Center Circle command
7. Bisector command.
8. Smart Dimension command.
9. Line Width command.
10. Insert Text command.
11. Move Copy command.
12. Rectangle command.
13. Smart Delete command.

PROBLEM 5.1

A square prism 35 mm side of base and 60 mm axis length rests on HP on one of its edges of the base which is inclined to VP at 30º. Draw the projections of the prism when the axis is inclined to HP at 45º.

SOLUTION

Manual Method

(a) Draw the XY line. Mark VP and HP above and below it.

(b) Draw top view of the square prism i.e., square of 35 mm side below XY line. Name the vertices as a b c d and a_1 b_1 c_1 d_1.

(c) Project the front view and mark the axis as o′ and o_1'.

(d) Redraw the front view with an axis inclined at an angle of 45° to XY line, with a_1' d_1' on XY line.

(e) Draw vertical projectors from second stage front view. Draw horizontal projectors from first stage top view intersect vertical projectors to get second stage top view.

(f) Draw 600 line, redraw second stage top view, such that one of its base edge rests match with 60° line drawn to get third stage top view.

(g) Project vertically upwards from third stage top view. Draw horizontal projectors from second stage front view to intersect vertical projectors to get final front view.

(h) Mark annotations correctly and dimension necessarily.

Computer Aided Drafting Procedure

1. Open the SOFTWARE. Click on the DRAWING in the open dialog box and say OK.

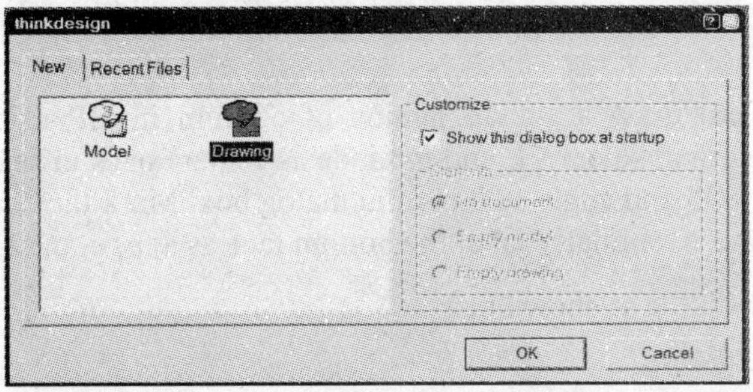

2. To set up the sheet of required size (Ex: A4) by selecting TOOLS from Main Menu Bar and click on OPTIONS/PROPERTIES. Select document properties in dialog box appeared and then select drawing in selection panel. Select the required size say A4, and click OK.

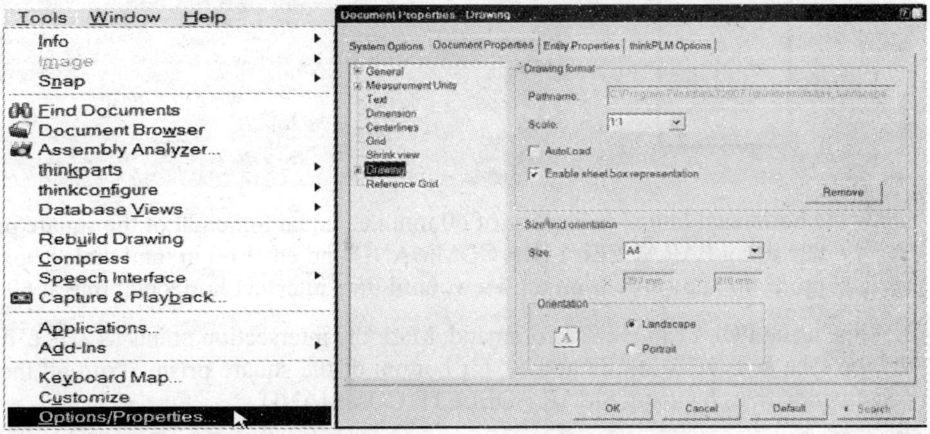

3. To draw XY line, projection lines, dotted lines and top & front view lines. After selecting line command, in format select XY for XY line, PL for projection lines DL for dotted (hidden) lines, AL for axis line and VL for top and front view lines before drawing these lines.

4. Draw the line by using POLYLINE  command from drafting tool bar and in format select XY.

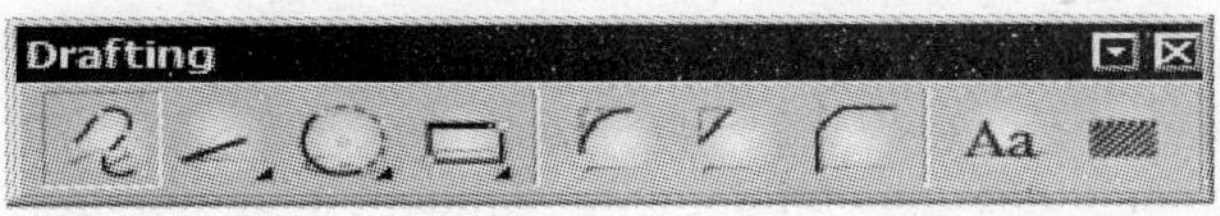

5. Make Annotation X, Y, VP, and HP to the line drawn by using INSERT TEXT Command  from drafting tool bar, just by typing X, Y, VP and HP in Text Box and insert these in the required position by left click of the mouse, as shown below.

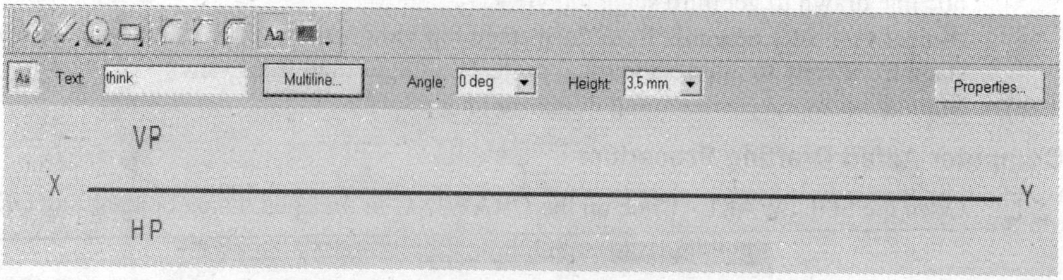

6. As per the problem draw a square lamina of 35 mm in HP using RECTANGLE  command and in format select VL and in mode as center+sizes in selection tree. Now enter X size = 35, Y size = 35 and angle as 0 in mini dialog box. Mark the corner points of top face as a b c d and center as o. similarly label the bottom face as a_1 b_1 c_1 d_1 center as o_1 using INSERT TEXT Command  as shown below.

7. Draw the horizontal line at a distance of 60 mm i.e., equal to height of the square prism above the XY line using PARALLEL LINE COMMAND and enter 60 in mini dialog box. Draw the vertical projection upwards from top view, until they intersect horizontal line at 60 mm above XY line using POLYLINE 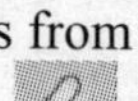 command. Mark the intersection points as a′ b′ c′ d′ and o′ for the top face and a_1' b_1' c_1' d_1' and o_1' for bottom of the square prism. Trim all the unwanted construction lines by using SMART DELETE COMMAND.

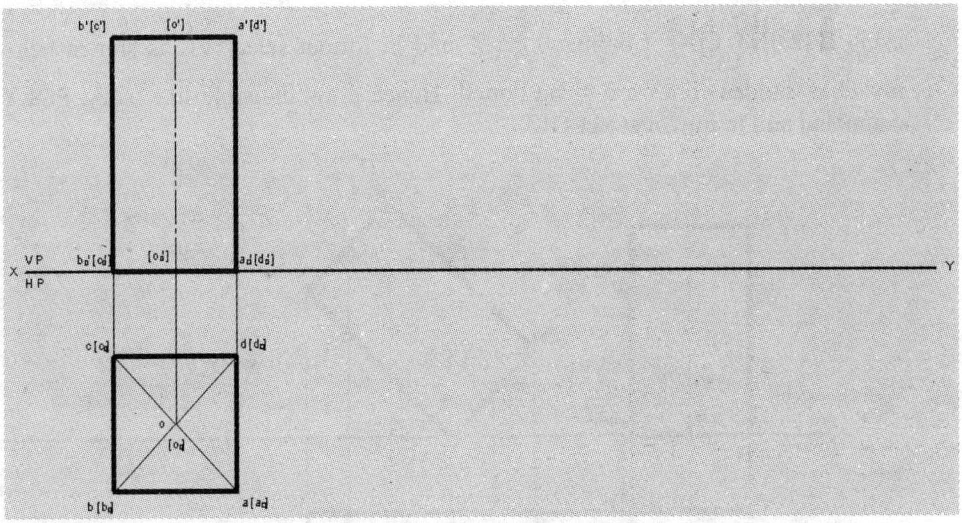

8. Since the square prism axis is inclined at 45° to HP. By using POLYLINE command and in format select PL enter length equal to length of first stage front view and angle as 45 in mini dialog box draw a line of 45°. From edit menu select MOVE COPY command and then select first stage front view. In selection tree right click on the start point and click reset to select the start point any where on the axis of prism to shift on to 45° line drawn. Click and drag the lamina on 45° line. Click or drag to rotate and enter angle as 45 in mini dialog box such that one edge resting on HP and click on OK in selection tree. Mark the annotations as shown below.

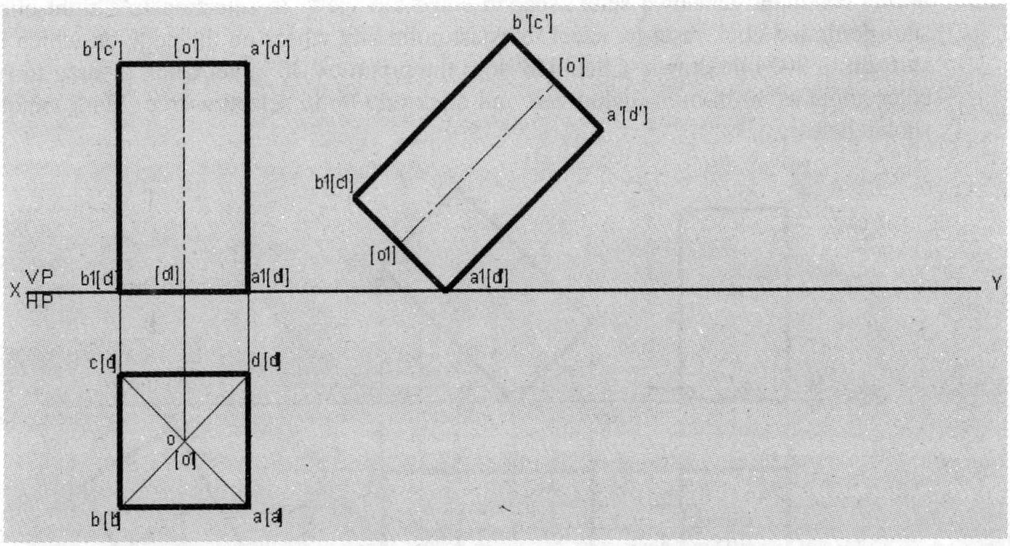

9. Draw vertical projectors downwards from the second stage front view using POLYLINE command and in format select PL. Draw horizontal projectors from top view to intersect vertical projectors to get required second stage top view by joining intersection points by

using 2 POINT LINE Command  and in format select VL as shown below. Note the invisible (hidden) lines are to be dotted. Hence draw invisible line using POLYLINE  command and in format select DL.

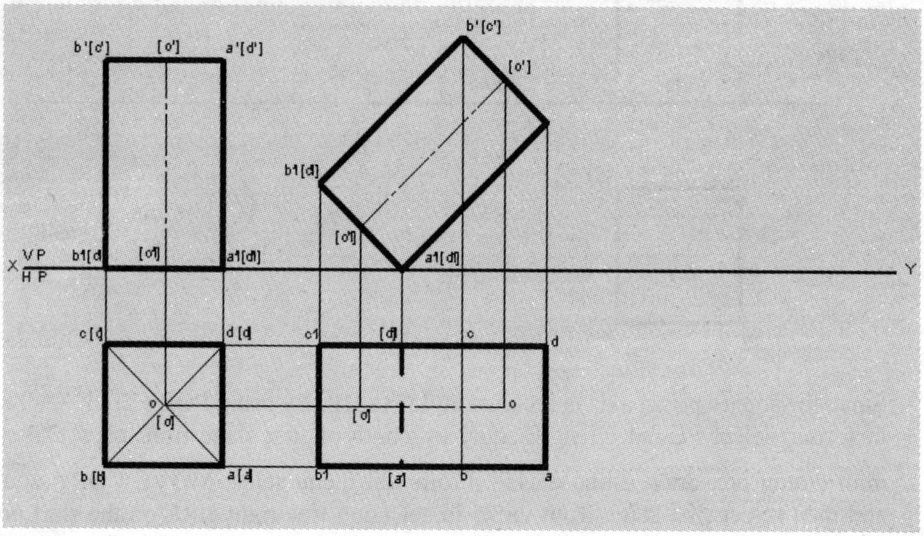

10. Since the edge on which prism rests is inclined to VP at 30°. Draw a line of 30° in HP using POLYLINE  command and in format select PL. From edit menu select MOVE COPY 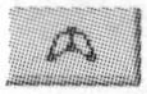 command and then select second stage top view. In selection tree right click on the start point and click reset to select the start point any where on the edge on which it rests to shift on to 30° line drawn. Click and drag the prism on 30° line. Click or drag to rotate and enter angle as 30 in mini dialog box and click on OK in selection tree. Mark annotations as shown below.

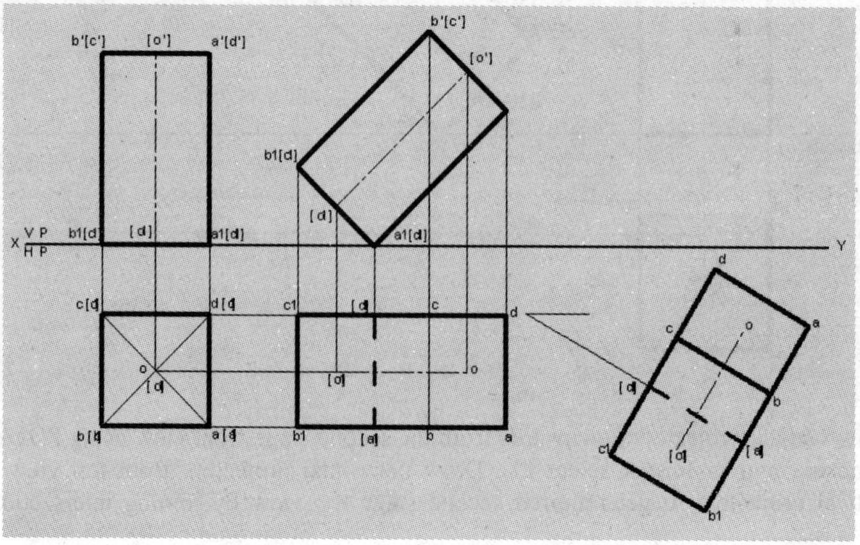

11. Draw the vertical projection upwards from the third stage top view using POLYLINE command and in format select PL. Again draw horizontal projectors from second stage front view to intersect vertical projectors to get the final front view. Join all the intersection points using 2 POINT LINE Command and in format select VL. Trim all the unwanted construction lines by using SMART DELETE COMMAND.

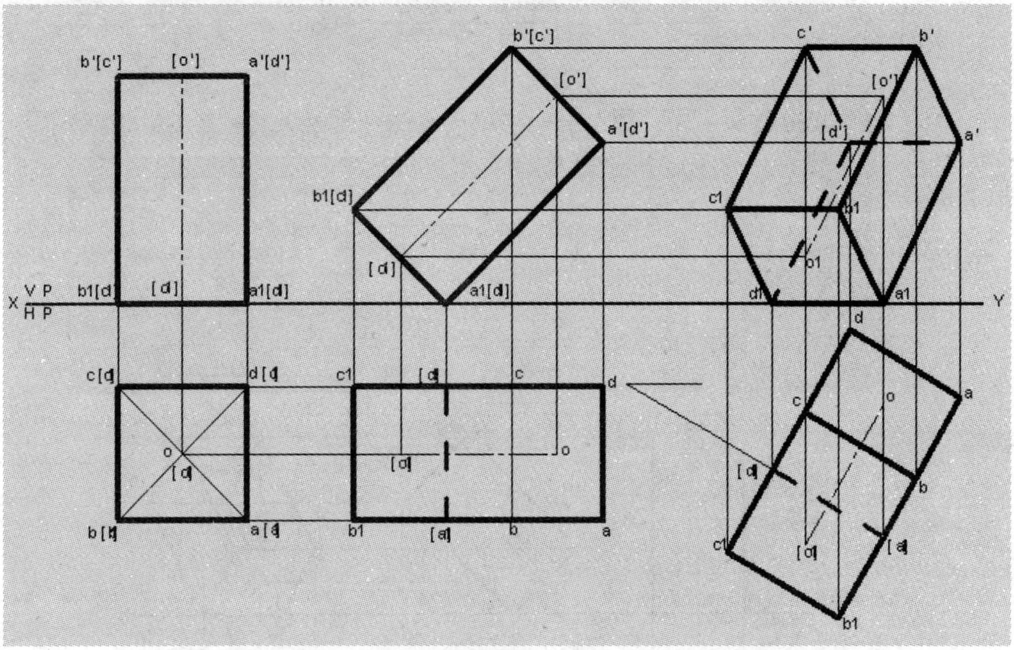

12. Using SMART DIMENSION Command in drawing tool bar dimension the drawing as shown.

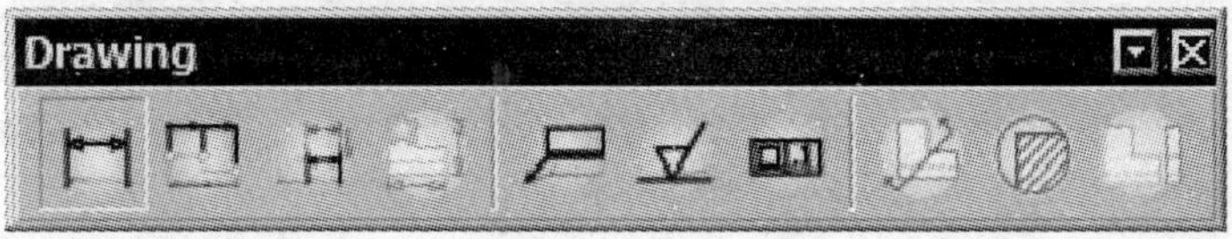

13. To get a Hard Copy of the standard drawing select print from file menu bar. Print dialog window will appear select page and change width to Entities and select the activated button now substitute width 1 as 0.15 mm, width 2 as 0.05 mm, width 3 as 0.5 mm, width 4 as 0.35 mm and say OK. Select print to get a hard copy and finally save the file. The required standard drawing is as shown on next page.

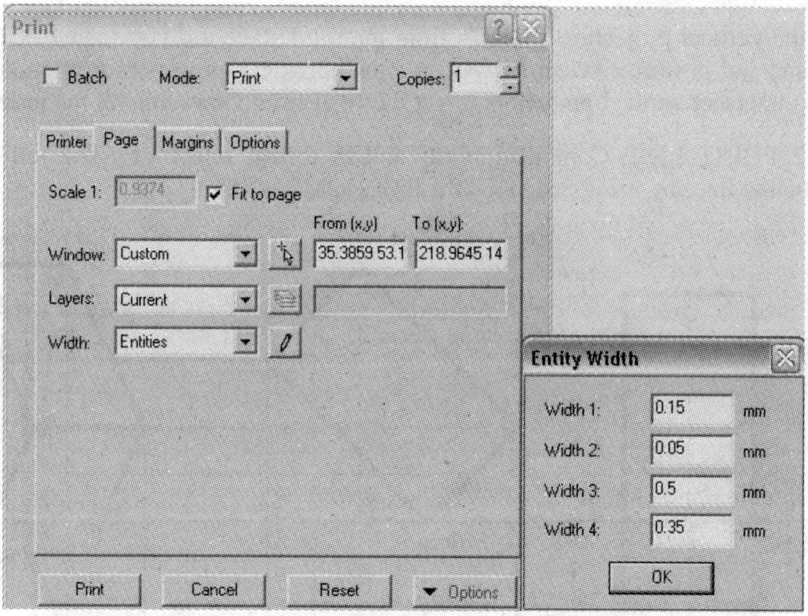

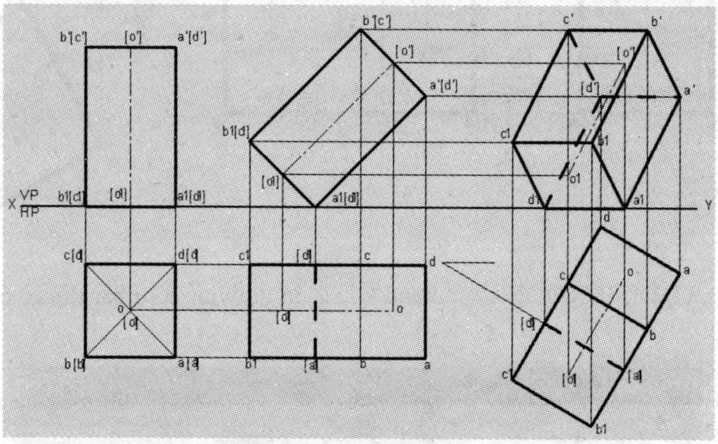

PROBLEM 5.2

A hexagonal prism 25 mm sides of base and 50 mm axis length rests on HP on one of its corners of the base such that the two base edges containing the corner on which it rests make equal inclinations with HP. Draw the projections of the prism when the axis of the prism is inclined to HP at 40º and to VP at 30º.

SOLUTION

Manual Method

(a) Draw the XY line. Mark VP and HP above and below it.

(b) Draw top view of the hexagonal prism i.e., hexagon of 25 mm side below XY line. Name the vertices as a b c d etc and a_1 b_1 c_1 d_1 etc.

(c) Project the front view and mark the axis as o' and o_1'.

(d) Redraw the front view with an axis inclined at an angle of 40° to XY line, with a_1' on XY line.

(e) Draw vertical projectors from second stage front view. Draw horizontal projectors from first stage top view intersect vertical projectors to get second stage top view.

(f) Draw 30° line, mark axis length of first stage and draw locus. With same center mark axis length of second stage to cut locus, on that axis redraw second stage top view, such that axis match with 30° line drawn to get third stage top view.

(g) Project vertically upwards from third stage top view. Draw horizontal projectors from second stage front view to intersect vertical projectors to get final front view.

(h) Mark annotations correctly and dimension necessarily.

Computer Aided Drafting Procedure

1. Open the SOFTWARE. Click on the DRAWING in the open dialog box and say OK.

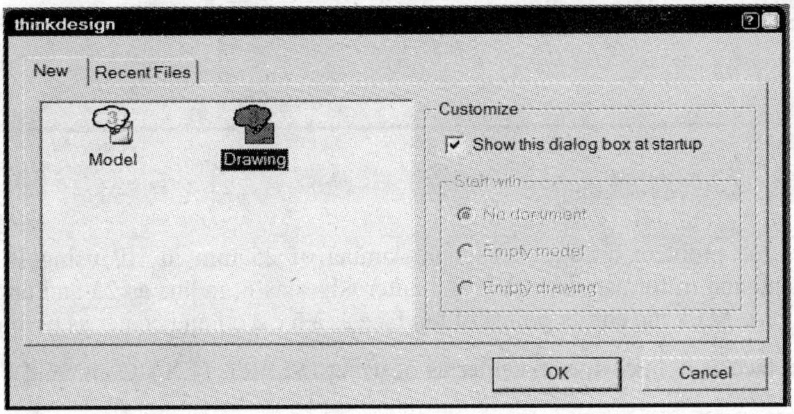

2. To set up the sheet of required size (Ex: A4) by selecting TOOLS from Main Menu Bar and click on OPTIONS/PROPERTIES. Select document properties in dialog box appeared and then select drawing in selection panel. Select the required size say A4, and click OK.

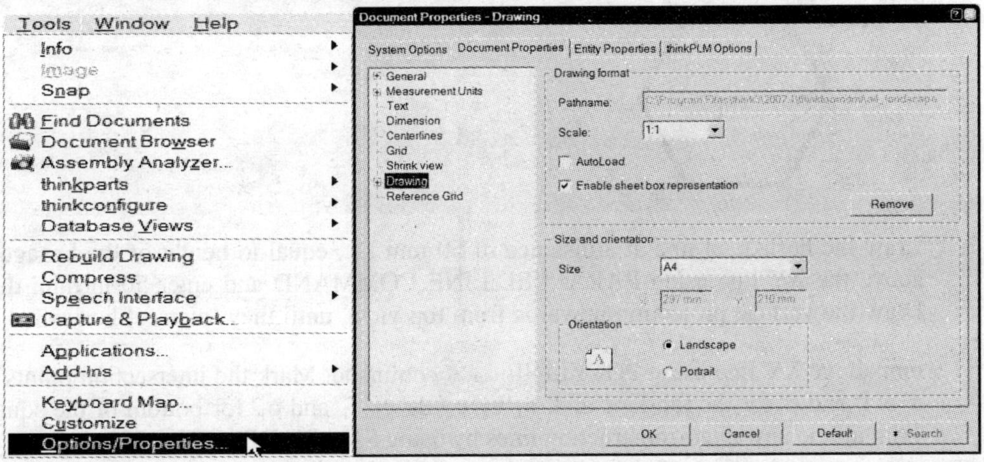

3. To draw XY line, projection lines, dotted lines and top & front view lines. After selecting line command, in format select XY for XY line, PL for projection lines DL for dotted (hidden) lines, AL for axis line and VL for top and front view lines before drawing these lines.

4. Draw the line by using POLYLINE command from drafting tool bar and in format select XY.

5. Make Annotation X, Y, VP, and HP to the line drawn by using INSERT TEXT Command from drafting tool bar, just by typing X, Y, VP and HP in Text Box and insert these in the required position by left click of the mouse, as shown below.

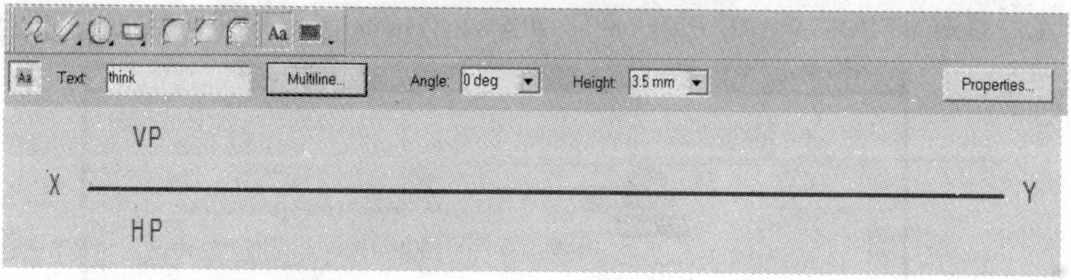

6. As per the problem draw a hexagonal lamina of 25 mm in HP using POLYGON command and in format select VL and enter edges as 6, radius as 25 and angle as 0 in mini dialog box. Mark the corner points of top face as a b c d e f and center as o. Similarly label the bottom face as a_1 b_1 c_1 d_1 e_1 f_1 center as o_1 using INSERT TEXT Command as shown below.

7. Draw the horizontal line at a distance of 50 mm i.e., equal to height of the hexagonal prism above the XY line using PARALLEL LINE COMMAND and enter 50 in mini dialog box. Draw the vertical projection upwards from top view, until they intersect horizontal line at 50 mm above XY line using POLYLINE command. Mark the intersection points as a′ b′ c′ d′ e′ f′ and o′ for the top face and $a_1'b_1'c_1'd_1'e_1'f_1'$ and o_1' for bottom of the square prism. Trim all the unwanted construction lines by using SMART DELETE COMMAND.

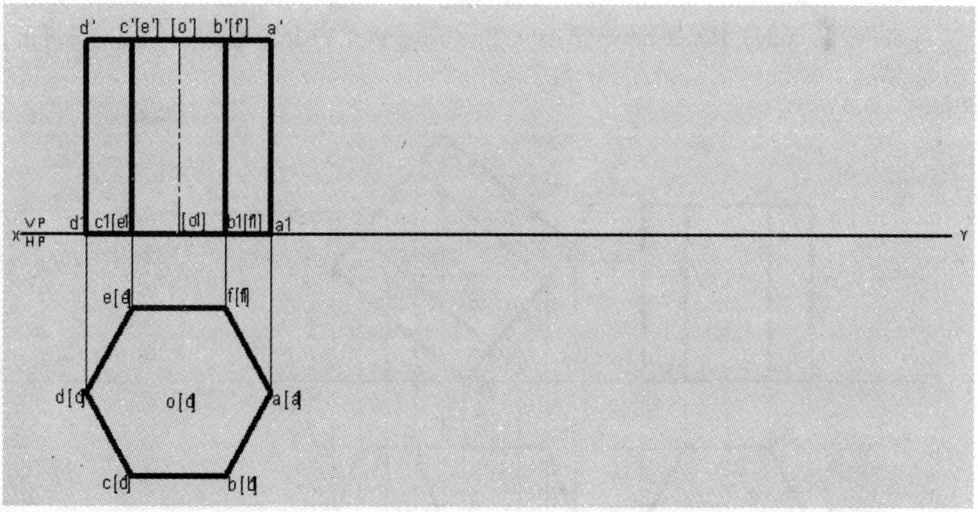

8. Since the hexagonal prism axis is inclined at 40° to HP. By using POLYLINE command and in format select PL enter length equal to length of first stage front view and angle as 40 in mini dialog box to draw a line of 40°. From edit menu select MOVE COPY command and then select first stage front view. In selection tree right click on the start point and click reset to select the start point any where on the axis of prism to shift on to 40° line drawn. Click and drag the lamina on 40° line. Click or drag to rotate and enter angle as 40 in mini dialog box such that one edge resting on HP and click on OK in selection tree. Mark the annotations as shown below.

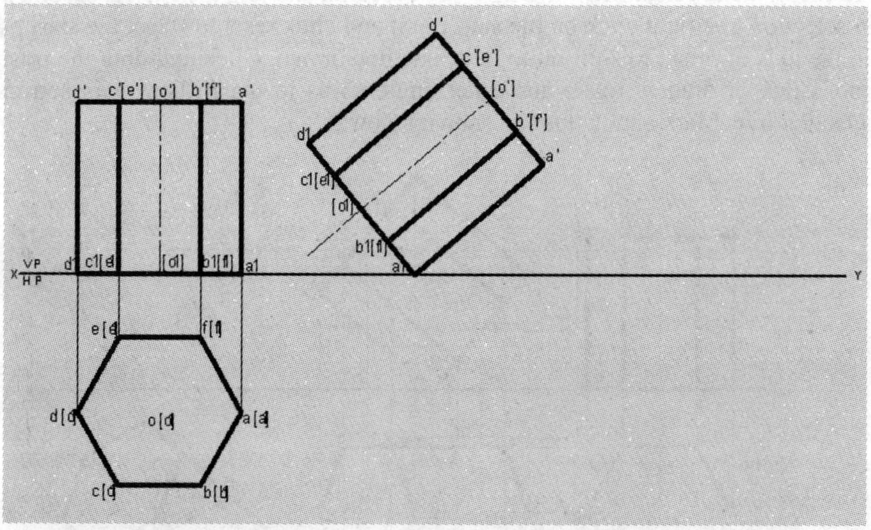

9. Draw vertical projectors downwards from the second stage front view using POLYLINE command and in format select PL. Draw horizontal projectors from top view to intersect vertical projectors to get required second stage top view by joining intersection points by using 2 POINT LINE Command and in format select VL as shown below. Note the invisible (hidden) lines are to be dotted. Hence draw invisible line using POLYLINE  command and in format select DL.

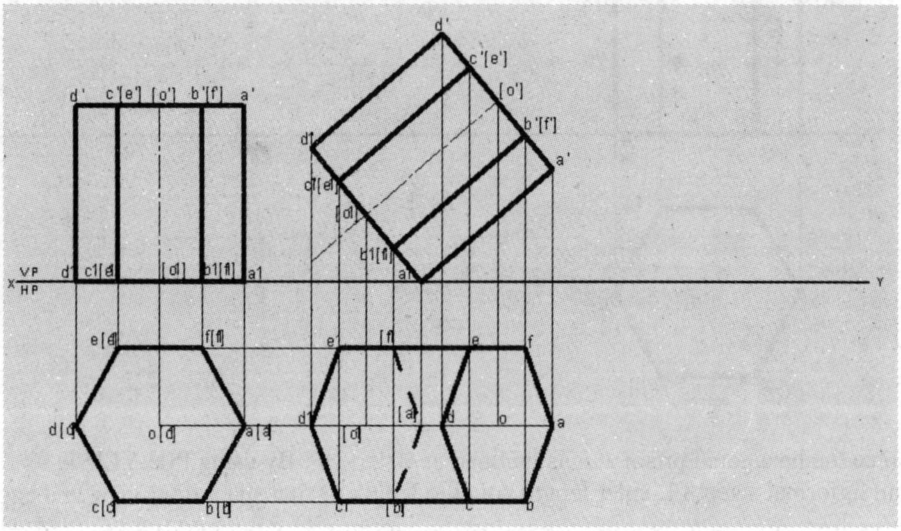

10. As per the problem draw a line of 30° in HP using POLYLINE  command and in format select PL. Draw an arc of radius equal to axis of prism from first stage front view to cut on 30° line drawn. Draw a locus from point o_1, now with radius equal to axis of prism from second stage top view to cut on the locus. Join o o_1 to get the axis of third stage top view. From edit menu select MOVE COPY 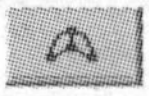 command and then select second stage top view. In selection tree right click on the start point and click reset to select the start point any where on the axis of prism to shift on to new axis line drawn. Click and drag the prism on new axis line. Click or drag to rotate and enter angle so as to match both axis and click on OK in selection tree. Mark annotations as shown below.

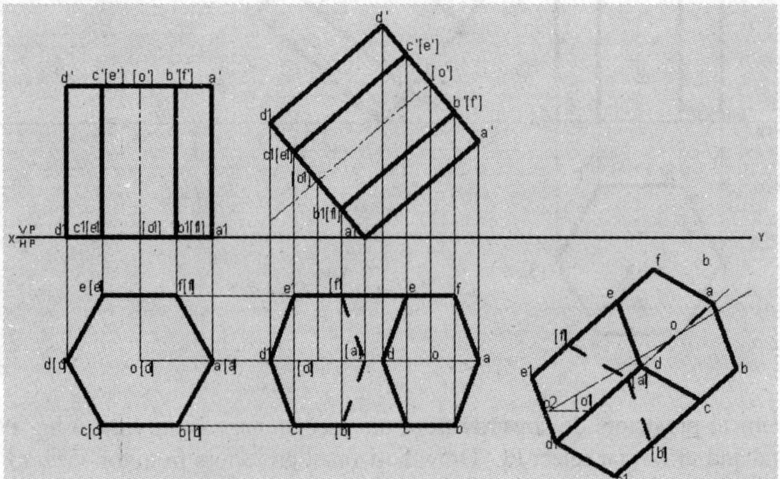

11. Draw the vertical projection upwards from the third stage top view using POLYLINE command and in format select PL. Again draw horizontal projectors from second stage front view to intersect vertical projectors to get the final front view. Join all the intersection points using 2 POINT LINE Command and in format select VL and draw invisible line using POLYLINE command and in format select DL. Trim all the unwanted construction lines by using SMART DELETE COMMAND.

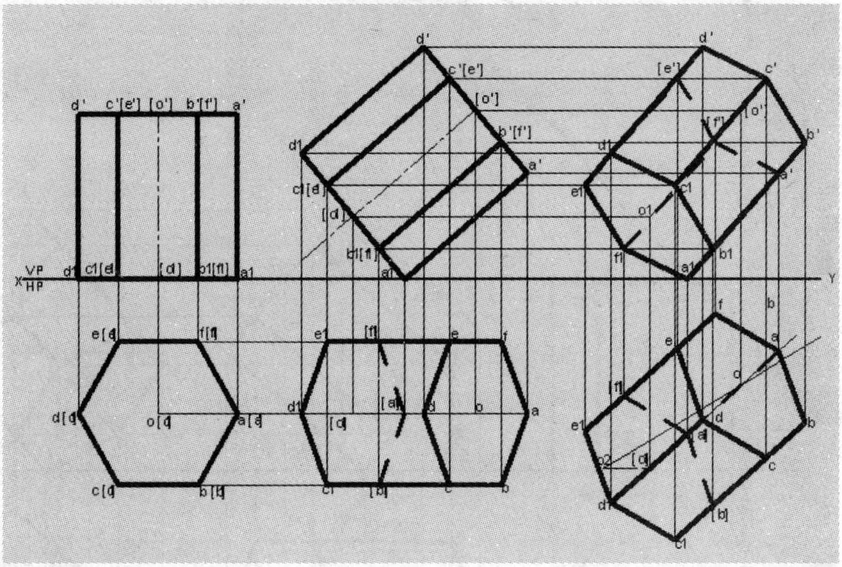

12. Using SMART DIMENSION Command in drawing tool bar dimension the drawing as shown.

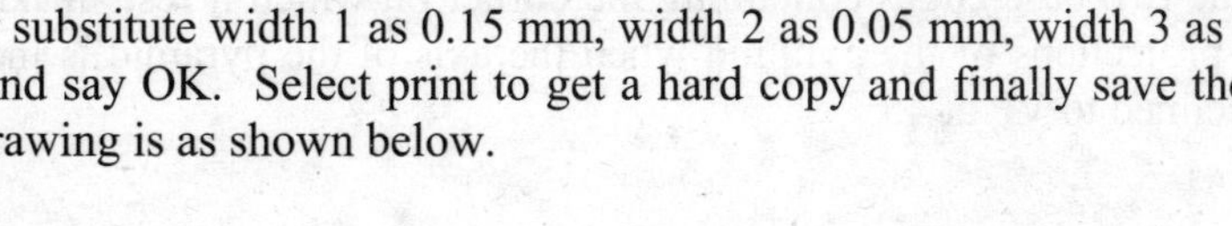

13. To get a Hard Copy of the standard drawing select print from file menu bar. Print dialog window will appear select page and change width to Entities and select the activated button now substitute width 1 as 0.15 mm, width 2 as 0.05 mm, width 3 as 0.5 mm, width 4 as 0.35 mm and say OK. Select print to get a hard copy and finally save the file. The required standard drawing is as shown below.

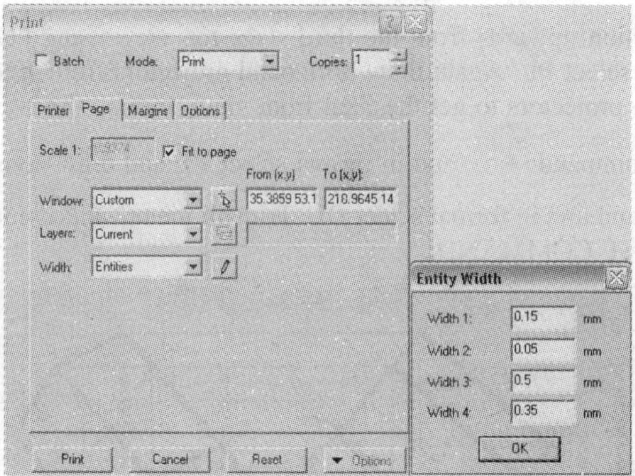

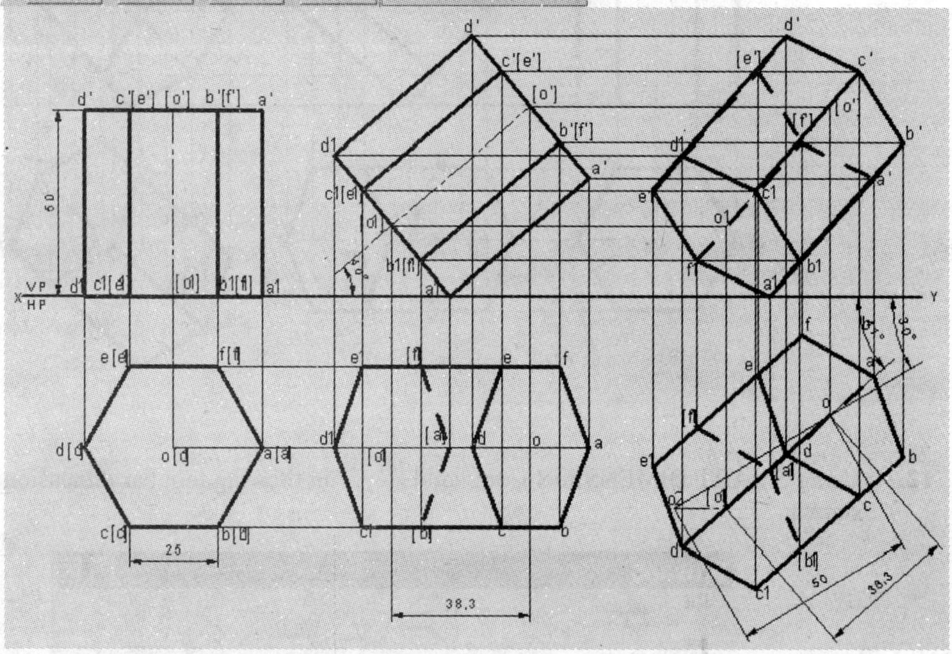

PROBLEM 5.3

A pentagonal pyramid 25 mm sides of base and 50 mm axis length rests on HP on one of its corners of the base such that the two base edges containing the corner on which it rests make equal inclinations with HP. Draw the projections of the pyramid when the axis of the pyramid is inclined to HP at 40º and appears to be inclined to VP at 45º.

SOLUTION

Manual Method

(a) Draw the XY line. Mark VP and HP above and below it.

(b) Draw top view of the pentagonal pyramid i.e., pentagon of 25 mm side below XY line. Name the vertices as a b c d and e. Join a b c d e to enter of pentagon o.

(c) Project the front view and mark the axis as o′ and o_1′.

(d) Redraw the front view with an axis inclined at an angle of 40° to XY line, with a_1′ on XY line.

(e) Draw vertical projectors from second stage front view. Draw horizontal projectors from first stage top view intersect vertical projectors to get second stage top view.

(f) Draw 45° line, redraw second stage top view, such that axis match with 45° line drawn to get third stage top view.

(g) Project vertically upwards from third stage top view. Draw horizontal projectors from second stage front view to intersect vertical projectors to get final front view.

(h) Mark annotations correctly and dimension necessarily.

Computer Aided Drafting Procedure

1. Open the SOFTWARE. Click on the DRAWING in the open dialog box and say OK.

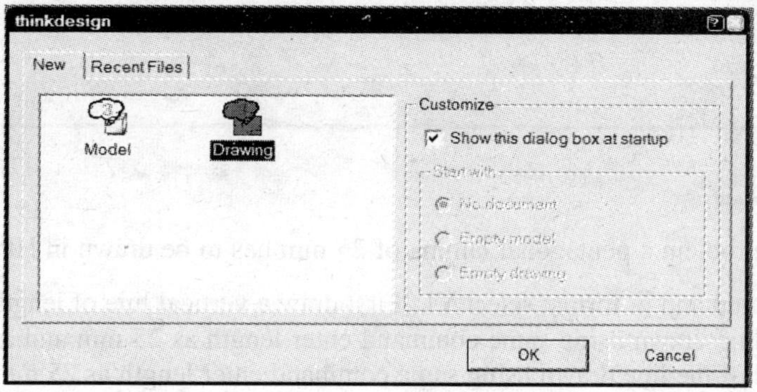

2. To set up the sheet of required size (Ex: A4) by selecting TOOLS from Main Menu Bar and click on OPTIONS/PROPERTIES. Select document properties in dialog box appeared and then select drawing in selection panel. Select the required size say A4, and click OK.

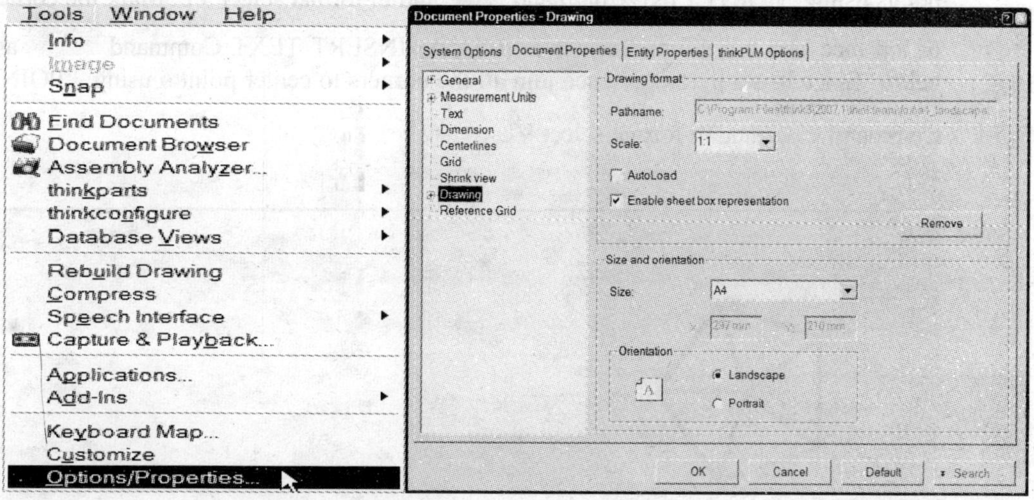

3. To draw XY line, projection lines, dotted lines and top & front view lines. After selecting line command, in format select XY for XY line, PL for projection lines DL for dotted (hidden) lines, AL for axis line and VL for top and front view lines before drawing these lines.

4. Draw the line by using POLYLINE command from drafting tool bar and in format select XY.

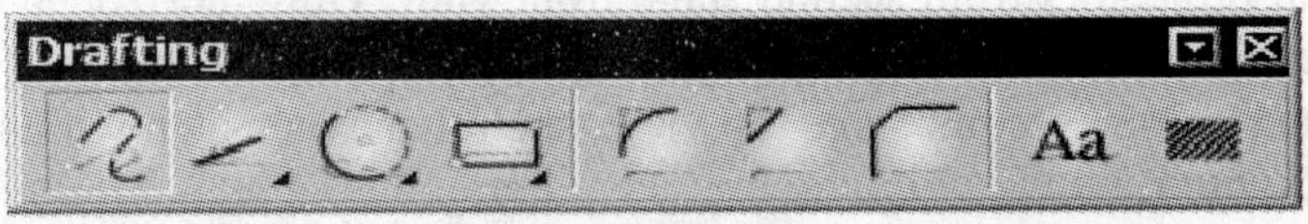

5. Make Annotation X, Y, VP, and HP to the line drawn by using INSERT TEXT Command from drafting tool bar, just by typing X, Y, VP and HP in Text Box and insert these in the required position by left click of the mouse, as shown below.

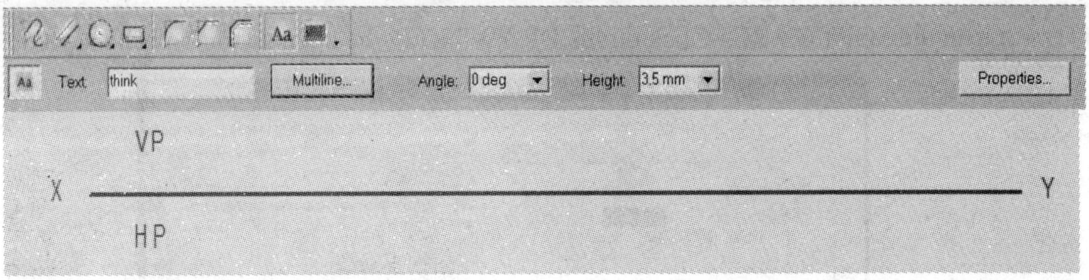

6. As per the problem a pentagonal lamina of 25 mm has to be drawn in HP, using POLYLINE command and in format select VL. First draw a vertical line of length 25 mm, select one end of the line drawn using same command enter length as 25 mm and angle as +18°, select another end of the line drawn using same command enter length as 25 mm and angle as –18°.

   Now from these two new ends draw an arc of radius of 25 mm using CENTER CIRCLE command in drafting tool bar. In mode option select arc, to get final point. Join all these points using 2 POINT LINE Command and in format select VL. Mark the corner points of top face as a b c d e and center as o. Using INSERT TEXT Command as shown below. Since it is a pyramid hence join all the corners to center point o using 2 POINT LINE Command and in format select VL.

7. Draw the vertical projector upwards from corners of the top view. Draw the base of the pyramid on XY line using 2 POINT LINE Command and in format select VL represent as a′ b′ c′

d′ e′ and o_1′. To get the height of pyramid draw vertical projector upwards from center o in top view. Draw axis which is equal to height of pyramid (50 mm). Represent apex at o′. Join all the corners to the apex using 2 POINT LINE Command  and in format select VL. Mark the annotations as shown below. Trim all the unwanted construction lines by using SMART DELETE COMMAND.

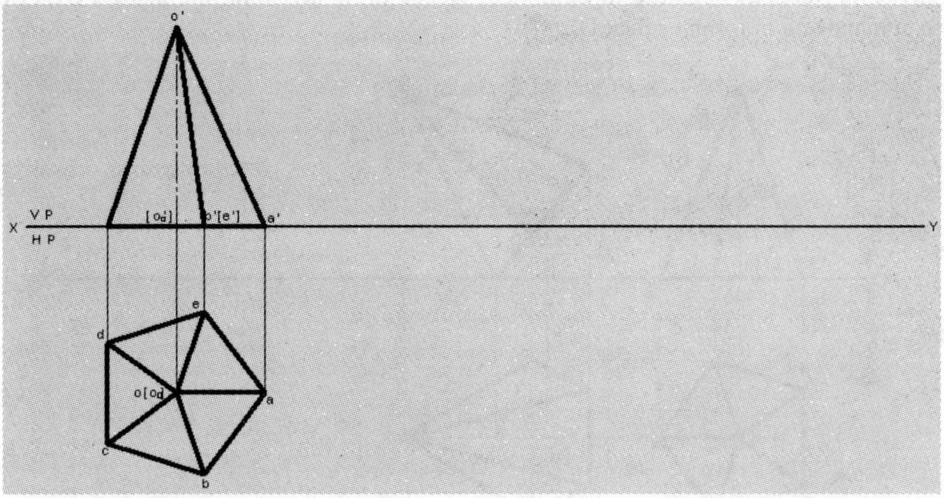

8. Since the pyramid axis is inclined at 40° to HP. By using POLYLINE  command and in format select PL enter length equal to length of first stage front view and angle as 40 in mini dialog box to draw a line of 40°. From edit menu select MOVE COPY 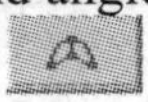 command and then select first stage front view. In selection tree right click on the start point and click reset to select the start point any where on the axis of pyramid to shift on to 40° line drawn. Click and drag the pyramid on 40° line. Click or drag to rotate and enter angle as 40 in mini dialog box such that one corner resting on HP and click on OK in selection tree. Mark the annotations as shown below.

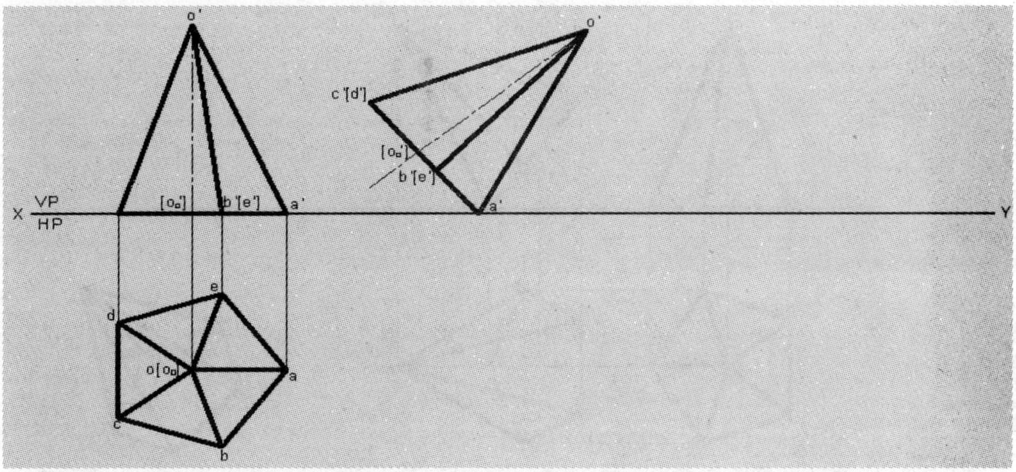

9. Draw vertical projectors downwards from the second stage front view using POLYLINE command and in format select PL. Draw horizontal projectors from top view to intersect vertical projectors to get required second stage top view by joining intersection points by using 2 POINT LINE Command and in format select VL as shown below. Note, the invisible (hidden) lines are to be dotted. Hence draw invisible line using POLYLINE command and in format select DL.

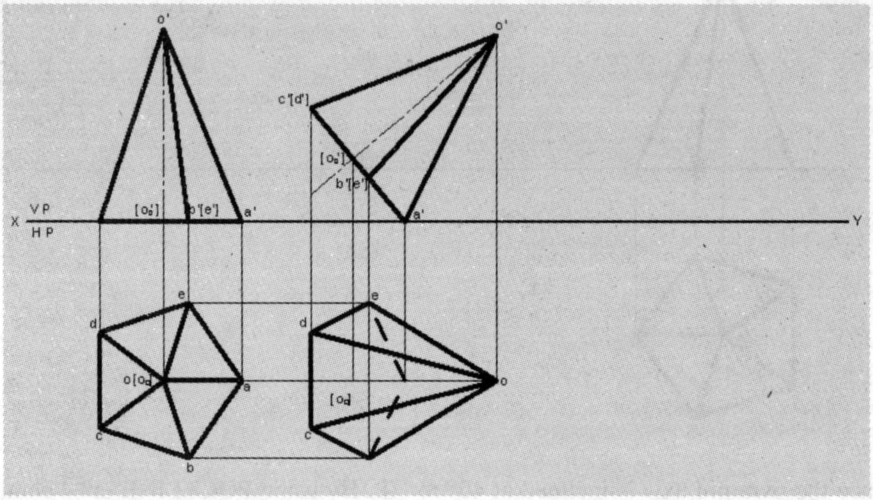

10. Since the prism appears to be inclined to VP at 45°. Draw a line of 45° in HP using POLYLINE command and in format select PL. From edit menu select MOVE COPY command and then select second stage top view. In selection tree right click on the start point and click reset to select the start point any where on the axis of pyramid to shift on to 45° line drawn. Click and drag the prism on 45° line. Click or drag to rotate and enter angle as 45 in mini dialog box and click on OK in selection tree. Mark annotations as shown below.

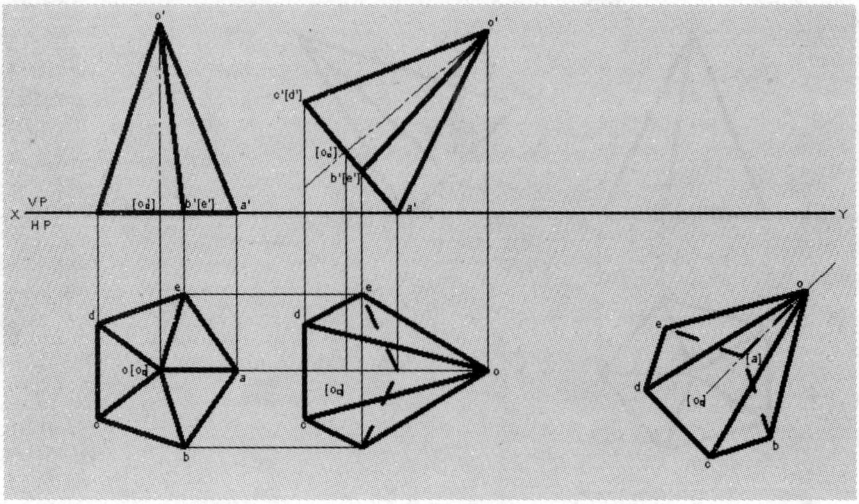

11. Draw the vertical projection upwards from the third stage top view using POLYLINE command and in format select PL. Again draw horizontal projectors from second stage front view to intersect vertical projectors to get the final front view. Join all the intersection points using 2 POINT LINE command and in format select VL. Trim all the unwanted construction lines by using SMART DELETE COMMAND.

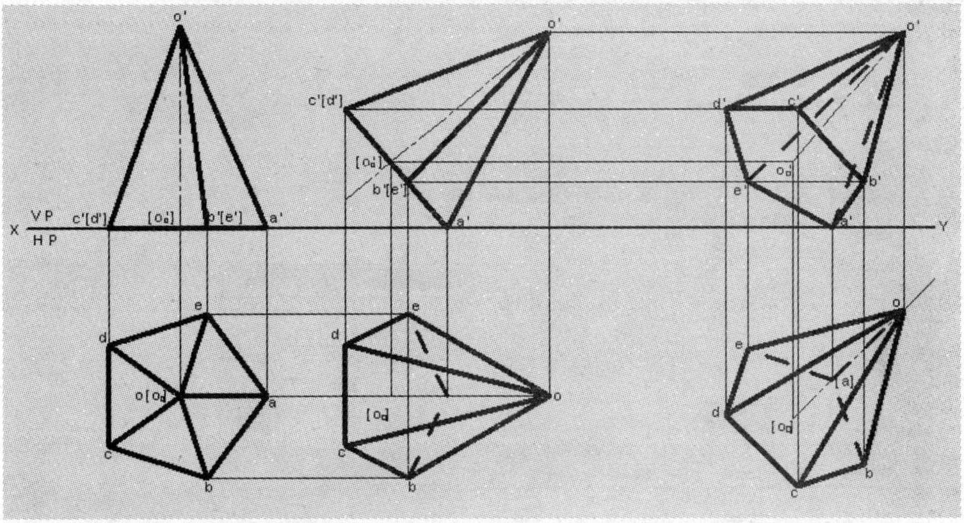

12. Using SMART DIMENSION Command in drawing tool bar dimension the drawing as shown.

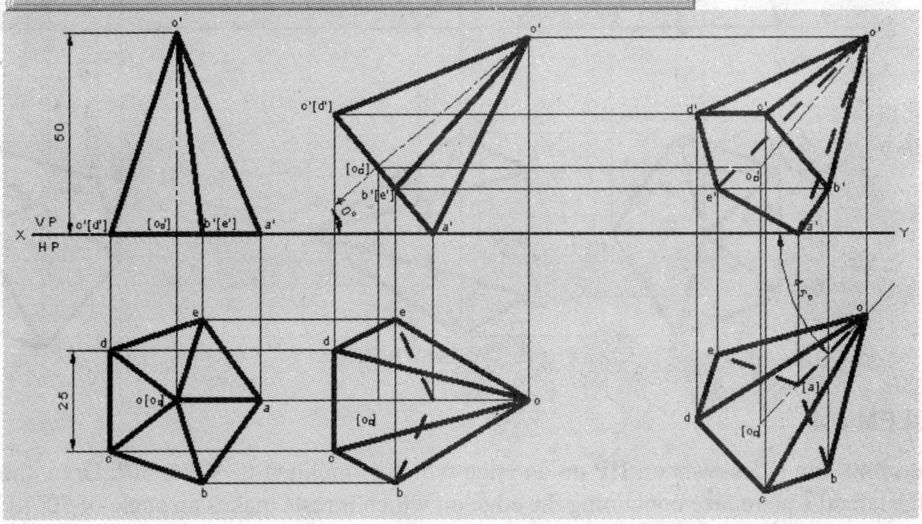

13. To get a Hard Copy of the standard drawing select print from file menu bar. Print dialog window will appear select page and change width to Entities and select the activated button  now substitute width 1 as 0.15 mm, width 2 as 0.05 mm, width 3 as 0.5 mm, width 4 as 0.35 mm and say OK. Select print to get a hard copy and finally save the file. The required standard drawing is as shown below.

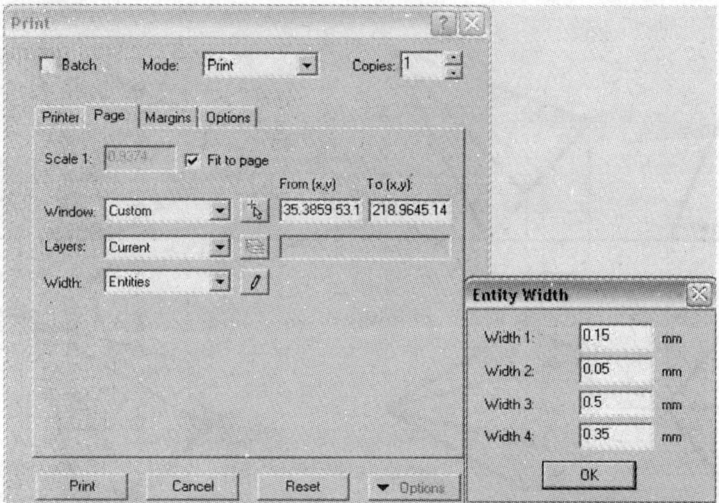

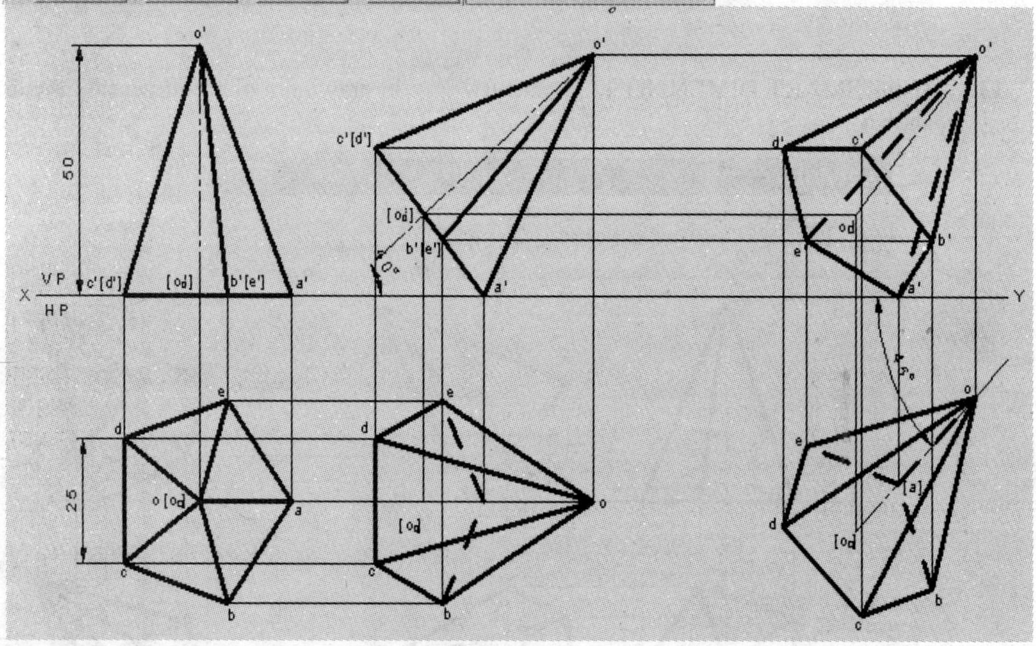

PROBLEM 5.4

A cube of 40 mm sides rests on HP on an edge which is inclined to VP at 30°. Draw the projections when the lateral square face containing the edge on which it rests makes an angle of 50° to HP.

SOLUTION

Manual Method

(a) Draw the XY line. Mark VP and HP above and below it.

(b) Draw top view of the cube i.e., square of 40 mm side below XY line. Name the vertices as a b c d and a_1 b_1 c_1 d_1.

(c) Project the front view and mark the axis as o' and o_1'.

(d) Redraw the front view with an axis inclined at an angle of 50° to XY line, with $a_1'd_1'$ on XY line.

(e) Draw vertical projectors from second stage front view. Draw horizontal projectors from first stage top view intersect vertical projectors to get second stage top view.

(f) Draw 30° line, redraw second stage top view, such that the edge on which it rests match with 30° line drawn to get third stage top view.

(g) Project vertically upwards from third stage top view. Draw horizontal projectors from second stage front view to intersect vertical projectors to get final front view.

(h) Mark annotations correctly and dimension necessarily.

Computer Aided Drafting Procedure

1. Open the SOFTWARE. Click on the DRAWING in the open dialog box and say OK.

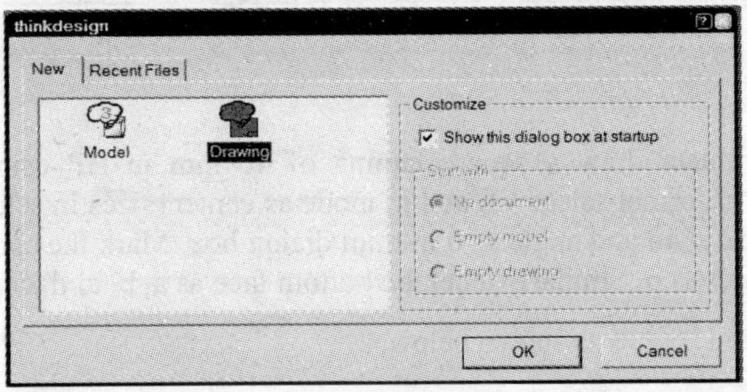

2. To set up the sheet of required size (Ex: A4) by selecting TOOLS from Main Menu Bar and click on OPTIONS/PROPERTIES. Select document properties in dialog box appeared and then select drawing in selection panel. Select the required size say A4, and click OK.

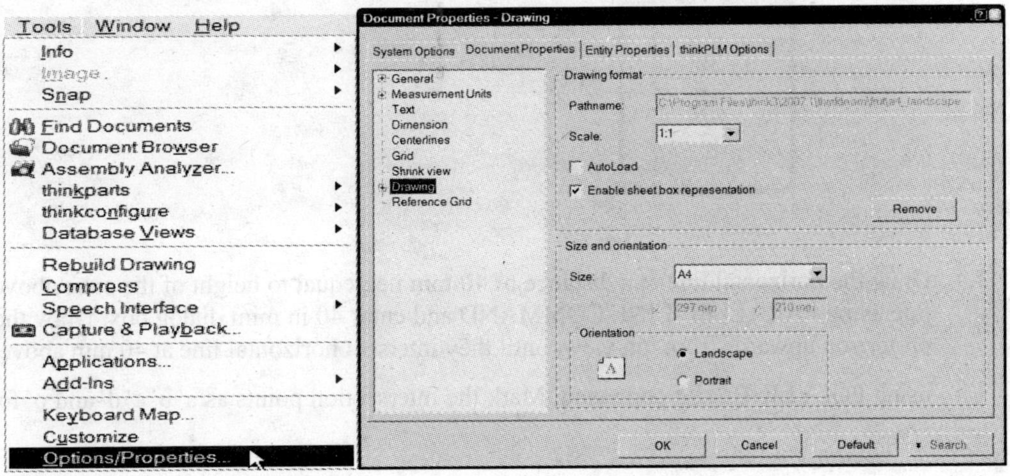

3. To draw XY line, projection lines, dotted lines and top & front view lines. After selecting line command, in format select XY for XY line, PL for projection lines DL for dotted (hidden) lines, AL for axis line and VL for top and front view lines before drawing these lines.

4. Draw the line by using POLYLINE command from drafting tool bar and in format select XY.

5. Make Annotation X, Y, VP, and HP to the line drawn by using INSERT TEXT Command from drafting tool bar, just by typing X, Y, VP and HP in Text Box and insert these in the required position by left click of the mouse, as shown below.

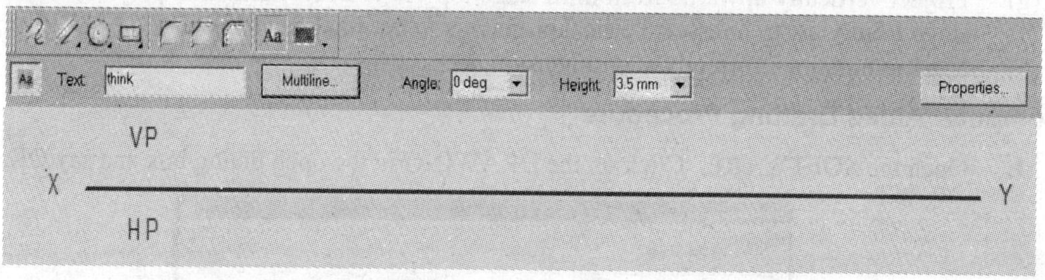

6. As per the problem draw a square lamina of 40 mm in HP using RECTANGLE command and in format select VL and in mode as center+sizes in selection tree. Now enter X size = 40, Y size = 40 and angle as 0 in mini dialog box. Mark the corner points of top face as a b c d and center as o. Similarly label the bottom face as a_1 b_1 c_1 d_1 center as o_1 using INSERT TEXT Command as shown below.

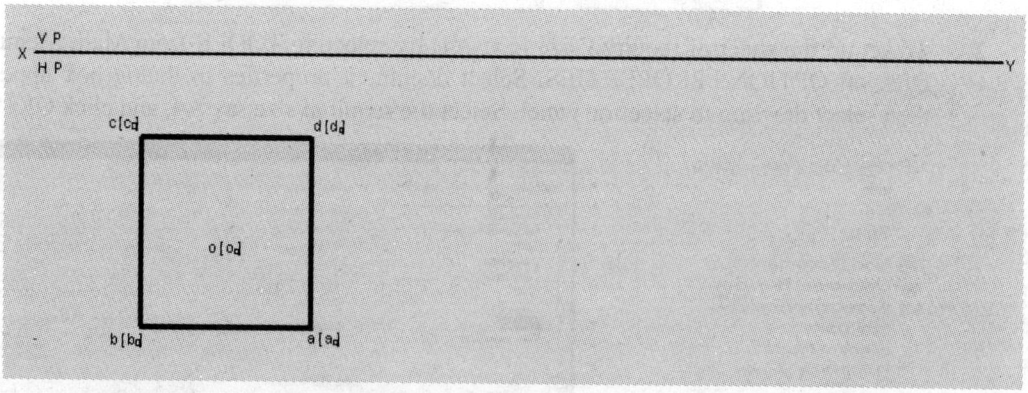

7. Draw the horizontal line at a distance of 40 mm i.e., equal to height of the cube above the XY line using PARALLEL LINE COMMAND and enter 40 in mini dialog box. Draw the vertical projection upwards from top view, until they intersect horizontal line at 40 mm above XY line using POLYLINE command. Mark the intersection points as a′ b′ c′ d′ and o′ for the top

face and $a_1'b_1'c_1'd_1'$ and o_1' for bottom of the cube. Trim all the unwanted construction lines by using SMART DELETE COMMAND.

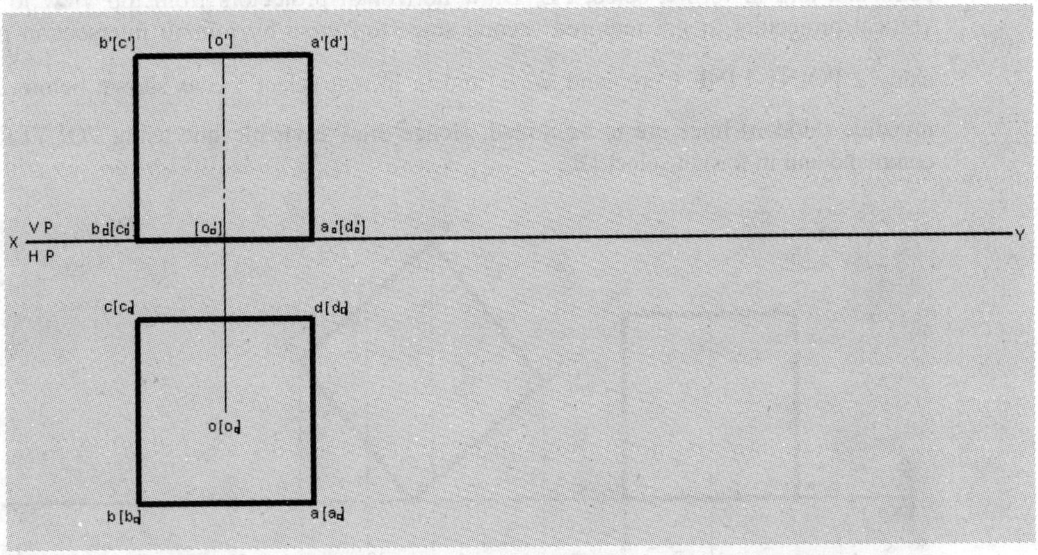

8. Since the axis of cube is inclined at 50° to HP. By using POLYLINE 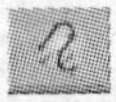 command and in format select PL enter length equal to length of first stage front view and angle as 50 in mini dialog box to draw a line of 50°. From edit menu select MOVE COPY 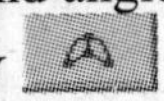 command and then select first stage front view. In selection tree right click on the start point and click reset to select the start point any where on the axis of cube to shift on to 50° line drawn. Click and drag the cube on 50° line. Click or drag to rotate and enter angle as 50 in mini dialog box such that one edge resting on HP and click on OK in selection tree. Mark the annotations as shown below.

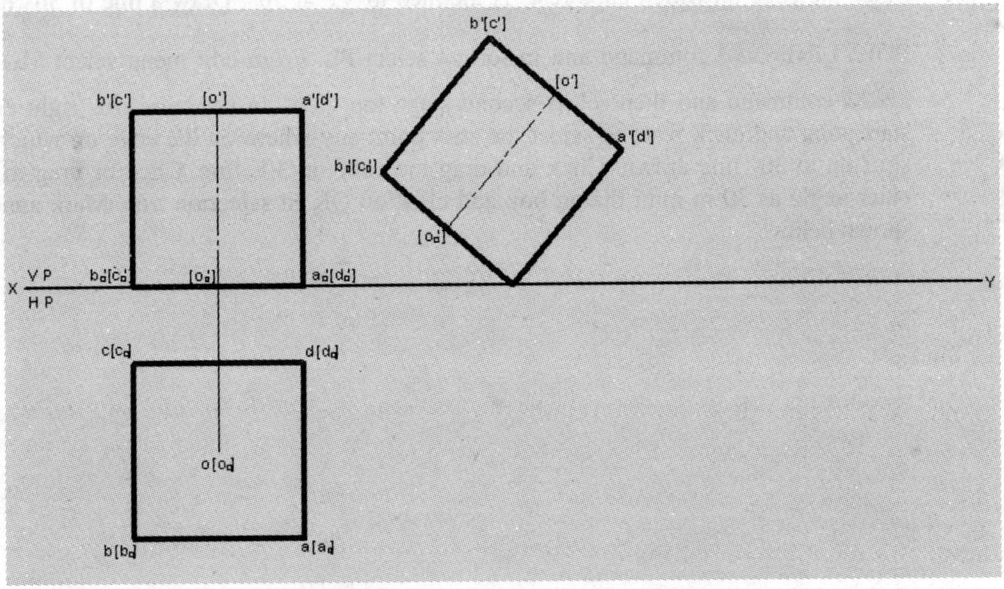

9. Draw vertical projectors downwards from the second stage front view using POLYLINE command and in format select PL. Draw horizontal projectors from top view to intersect vertical projectors to get required second stage top view by joining intersection points by using 2 POINT LINE Command and in format select VL as shown below. Note the invisible (hidden) lines are to be dotted. Hence draw invisible line using POLYLINE command and in format select DL.

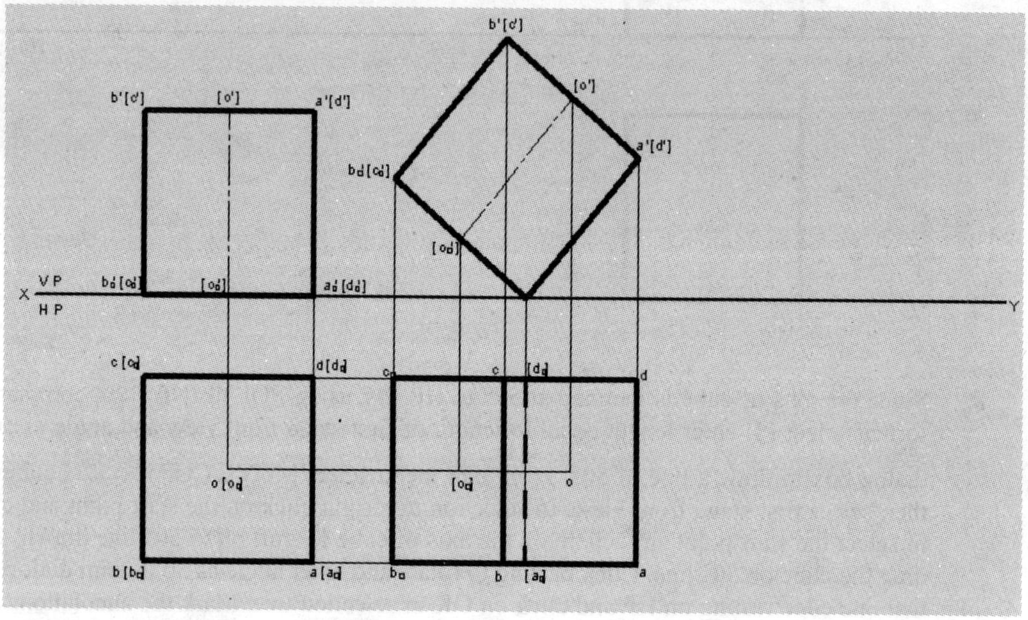

10. Since the edge on which cube rests is inclined to VP at 30°. Draw a line of 30° in HP using POLYLINE command and in format select PL. From edit menu select MOVE COPY command and then select second stage top view. In selection tree right click on the start point and click reset to select the start point any where on the edge on which it rests to shift on to 30° line drawn. Click and drag the cube on 30° line. Click or drag to rotate and enter angle as 30 in mini dialog box and click on OK in selection tree. Mark annotations as shown below.

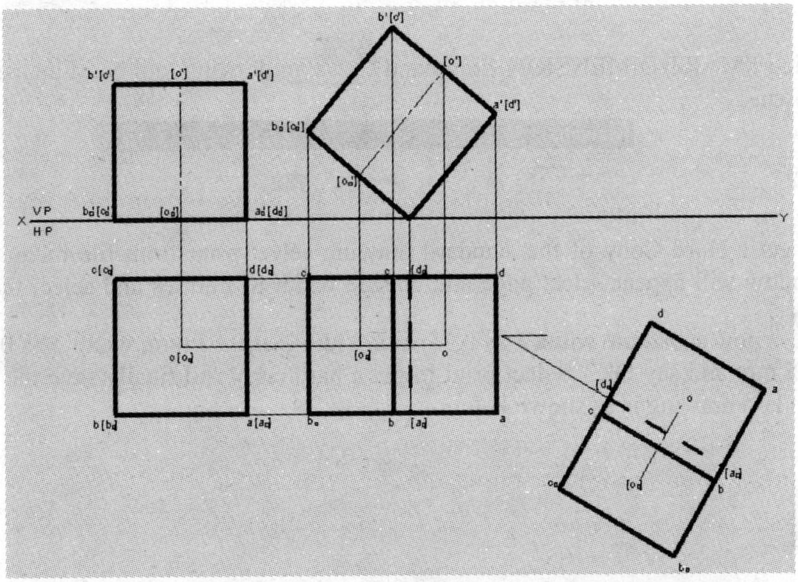

11. Draw the vertical projection upwards from the third stage top view using POLYLINE 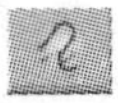 command and in format select PL. Again draw horizontal projectors from second stage front view to intersect vertical projectors to get the final front view. Join all the intersection points

using 2 POINT LINE Command  and in format select VL. Trim all the unwanted construction lines by using SMART DELETE COMMAND.

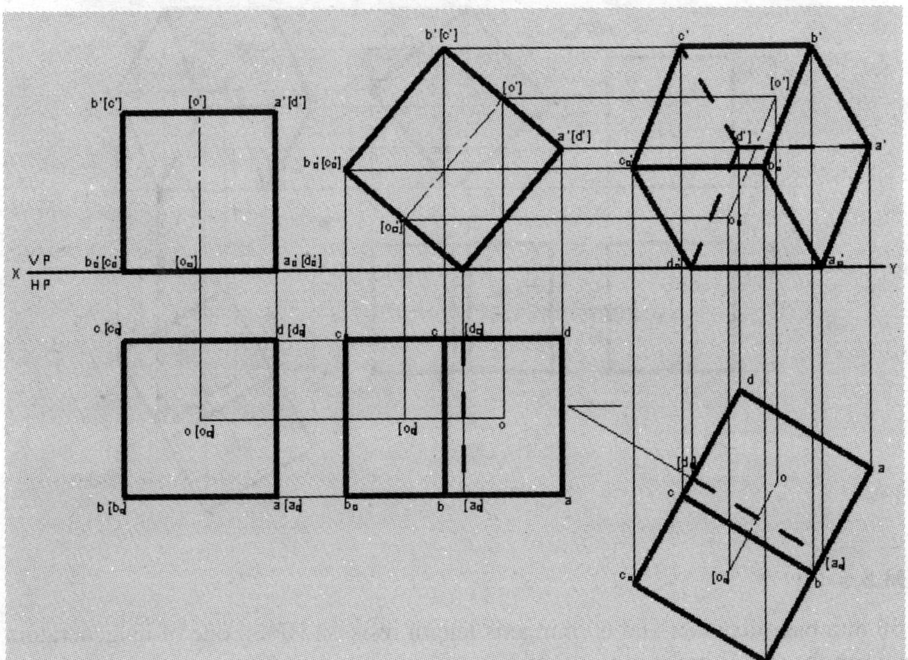

12. Using SMART DIMENSION Command  in drawing tool bar dimension the drawing as shown.

13. To get a Hard Copy of the standard drawing select print from file menu bar. Print dialog window will appear select page and change width to Entities and select the activated button  now substitute width 1 as 0.15 mm, width 2 as 0.05 mm, width 3 as 0.5 mm, width 4 as 0.35 mm and say OK. Select print to get a hard copy and finally save the file. The required standard drawing is as shown below.

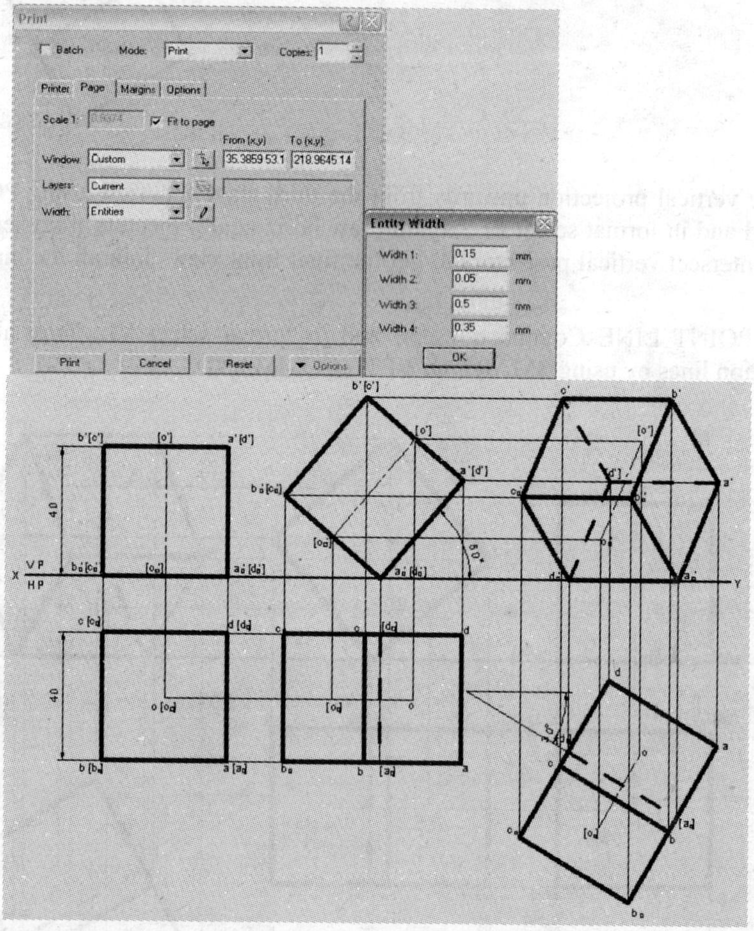

PROBLEM 5.5

A cone of 50 mm base diameter and 60 mm axis length rests on HP on one of its generators. Draw its projections when the axis is inclined to VP at 30º.

SOLUTION

Manual Method

(a) Draw the XY line. Mark VP and HP above and below it.

(b) Draw top view of the cone i.e., circle of diameter 50 mm below XY line. Divide the circle into any number of equal parts. Name as a b c d etc and join all these points to center of circle o.

(c) Project the front view and mark the axis as o′ and o_1′.

(d) Redraw the front view such that one of the generator is on XY line.

(e) Draw vertical projectors from second stage front view. Draw horizontal projectors from first stage top view intersect vertical projectors to get second stage top view.

(f) Draw 30° line, redraw second stage top view, such that axis match with 30° line drawn to get third stage top view.

(g) Project vertically upwards from third stage top view. Draw horizontal projectors from second stage front view to intersect vertical projectors to get final front view.

(h) Mark annotations correctly and dimension necessarily.

Computer Aided Drafting Procedure

1. Open the SOFTWARE. Click on the DRAWING in the open dialog box and say OK.

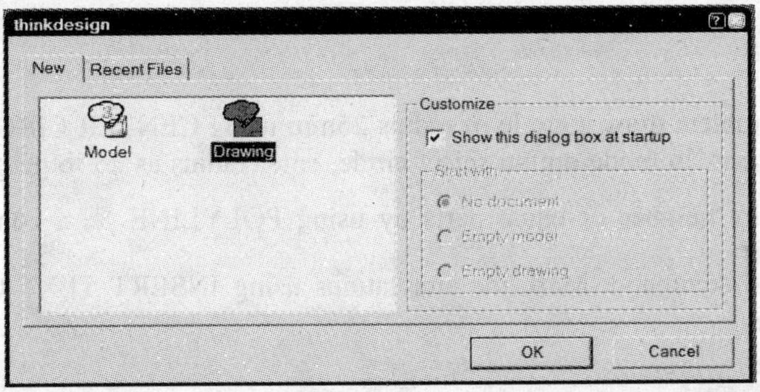

2. To set up the sheet of required size (Ex: A4) by selecting TOOLS from Main Menu Bar and click on OPTIONS/PROPERTIES. Select document properties in dialog box appeared and then select drawing in selection panel. Select the required size say A4, and click OK.

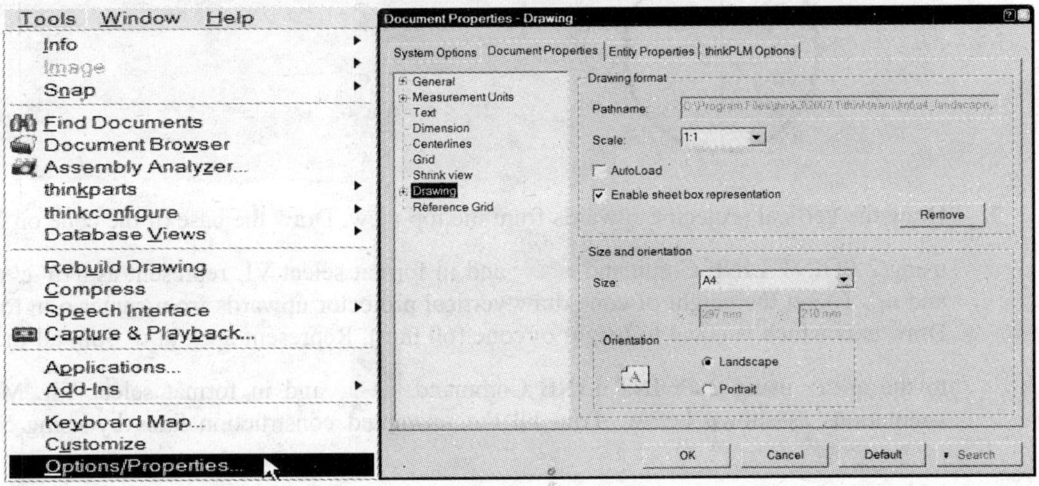

3. To draw XY line, projection lines, dotted lines and top & front view lines. After selecting line command, in format select XY for XY line, PL for projection lines DL for dotted (hidden) lines, AL for axis line and VL for top and front view lines before drawing these lines.

4. Draw the line by using POLYLINE command from drafting tool bar and in format select XY.

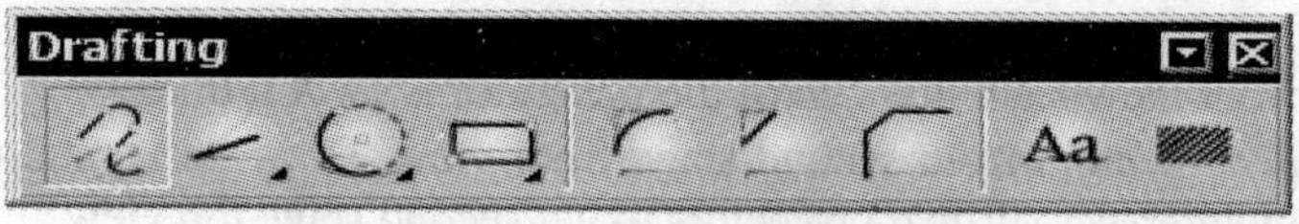

5. Make Annotation X, Y, VP, and HP to the line drawn by using INSERT TEXT Command from drafting tool bar, just by typing X, Y, VP and HP in Text Box and insert these in the required position by left click of the mouse, as shown below.

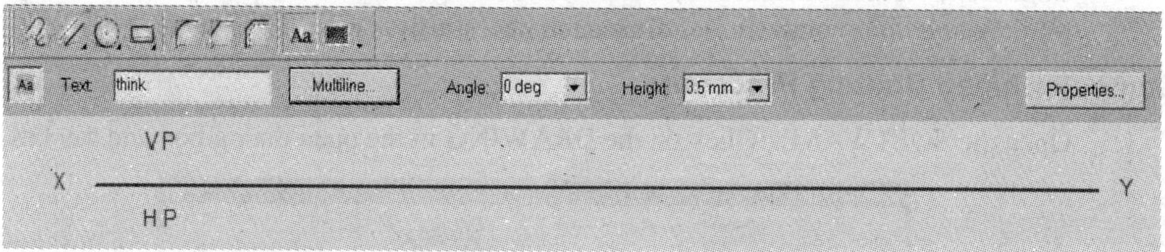

6. As per the problem draw a circle of radius 25mm using CENTER CIRCLE command in drafting tool bar. In mode option select circle, enter radius as 25 to get top view. Divide the circle into any number of equal parts by using POLYLINE command and MOVE COPY command. Mark the annotations using INSERT TEXT Command as shown below.

7. Draw the vertical projector upwards from the top view. Draw the base of the cone on XY line using 2 POINT LINE Command and in format select VL represent as a′ b′ c′ d′ e′ etc and o_1'. To get the height of cone draw vertical projector upwards from center o in top view. Draw axis which is equal to height of cone (60 mm). Represent apex at o′. Join all the points to the apex using 2 POINT LINE Command and in format select VL. Mark the annotations as shown below. Trim all the unwanted construction lines by using SMART

DELETE COMMAND. Draw the axis line using POLYLINE command and in format select AL.

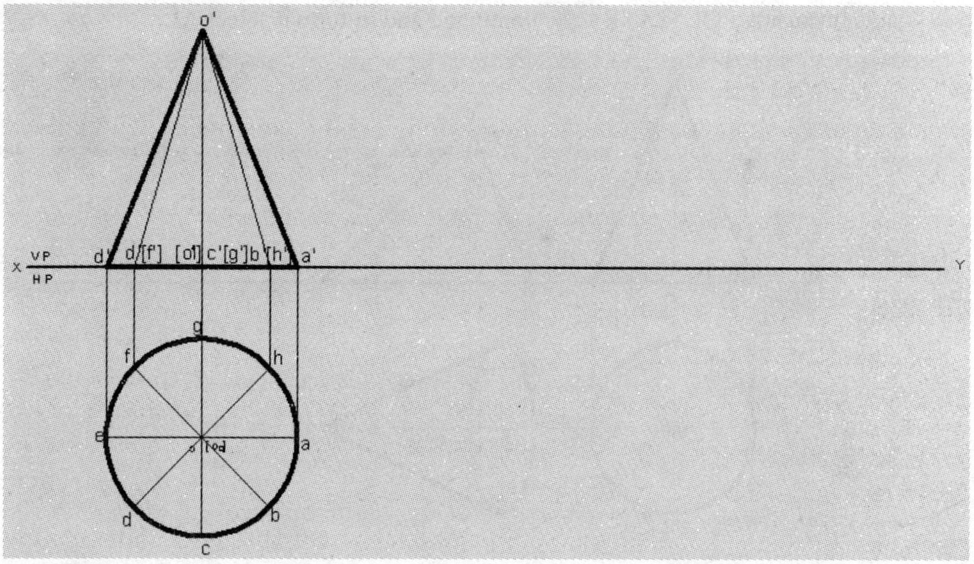

8. Since the cone rests on one of its generators on HP. From edit menu select MOVE COPY command and then select first stage front view. In selection tree right click on the start point and click reset to select the start point any where on one of the generators of cone to shift on to XY line drawn. Click and drag the cone on XY line. Click or drag to rotate and enter angle so as to match one of the generators and XY line and click on OK in selection tree. Mark the annotations as shown below.

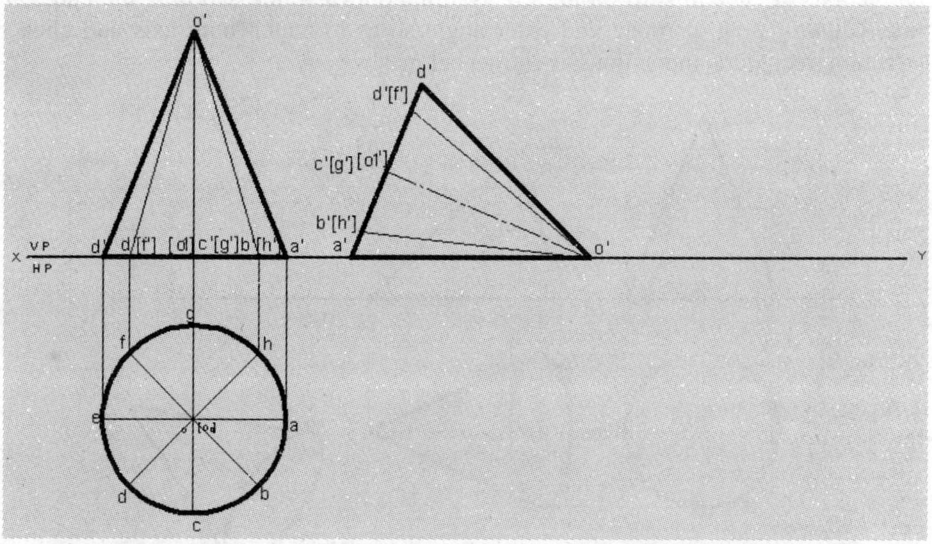

9. Draw vertical projectors downwards from the second stage front view using POLYLINE command and in format select PL. Draw horizontal projectors from top view to intersect vertical projectors to get required second stage top view by joining intersection points by using 2 POINT LINE Command and in format select VL as shown below. Draw the axis line using POLYLINE command and in format select AL.

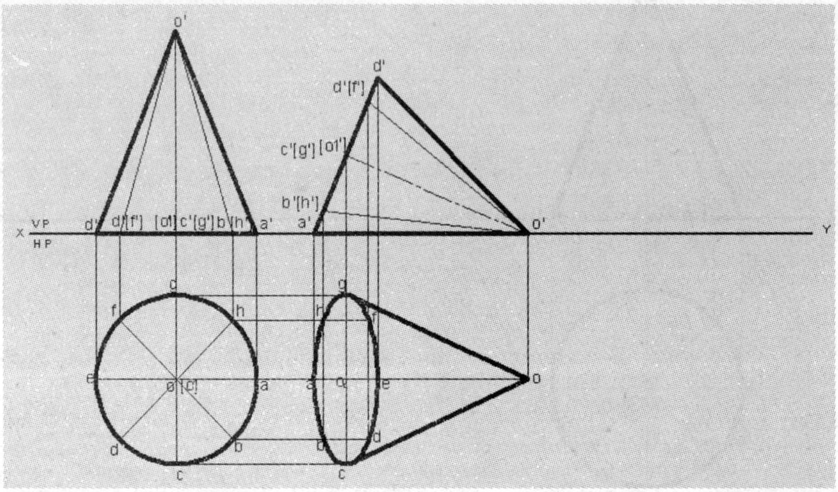

10. Since the cube is inclined to VP at 30°. Draw a line using POLYLINE command and in format select PL. Draw an arc of radius equal to axis of cube from first stage front view to cut on 30° line drawn. Draw a locus from point o_2, now with radius equal to axis of cube from second stage top view to cut on the locus. Join o_2 o_1 to get the axis of third stage top view. From edit menu select MOVE COPY command and then select second stage top view. In selection tree right click on the start point and click reset to select the start point any where on the axis of cube to shift on to new axis line drawn. Click and drag the cube on new axis line. Click or drag to rotate and enter angle so as to match both axis and click on OK in selection tree. Mark annotations as shown below.

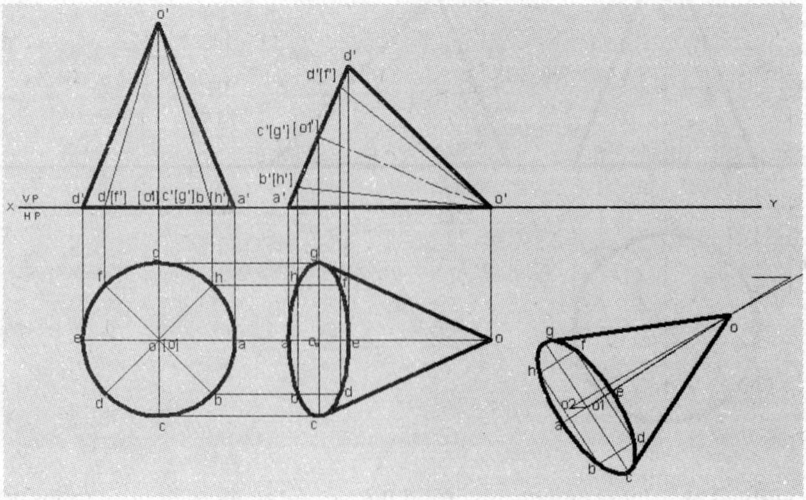

11. Draw the vertical projection upwards from the third stage top view using POLYLINE command and in format select PL. Again draw horizontal projectors from second stage front view to intersect vertical projectors to get the final front view. Join all the intersection points using 2 POINT LINE Command and in format select VL. Trim all the unwanted construction lines by using SMART DELETE COMMAND.

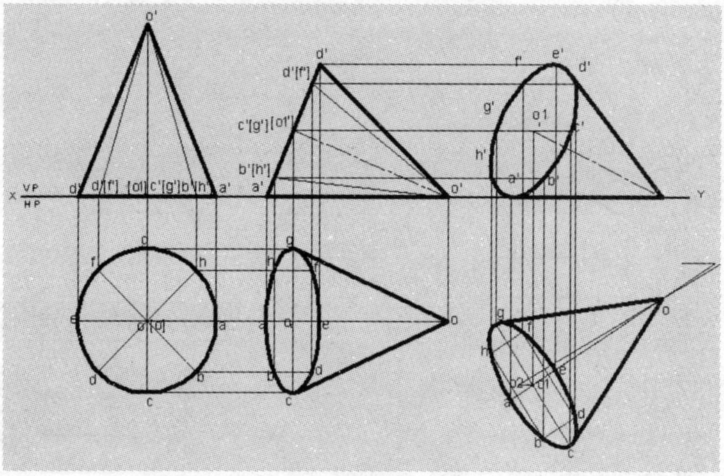

12. Using SMART DIMENSION Command in drawing tool bar dimension the drawing as shown.

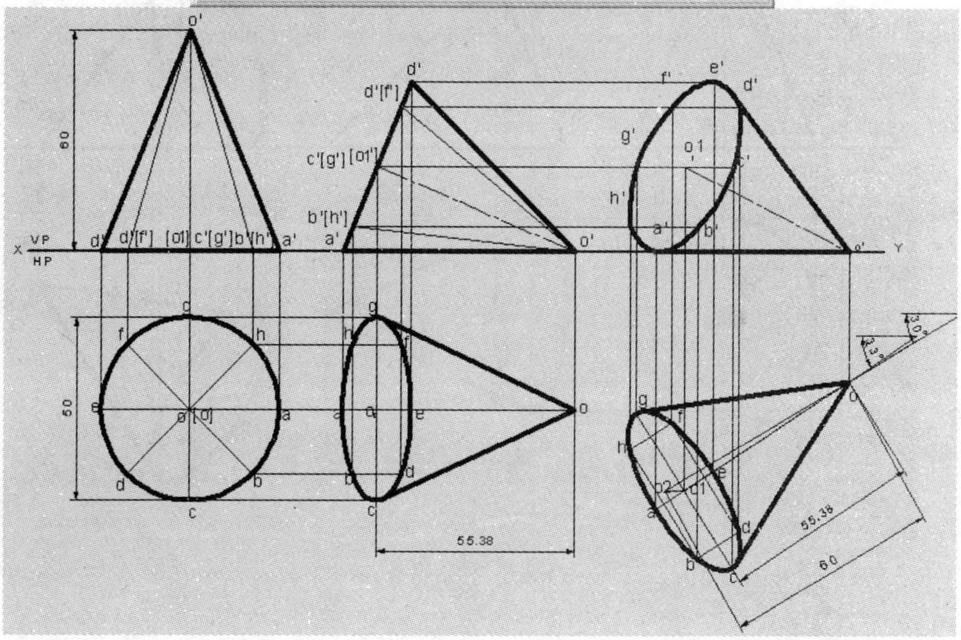

13. To get a Hard Copy of the standard drawing select print from file menu bar. Print dialog window will appear select page and change width to Entities and select the activated button  now substitute width 1 as 0.15 mm, width 2 as 0.05 mm, width 3 as 0.5 mm, width 4 as 0.35 mm and say OK. Select print to get a hard copy and finally save the file. The required standard drawing is as shown below.

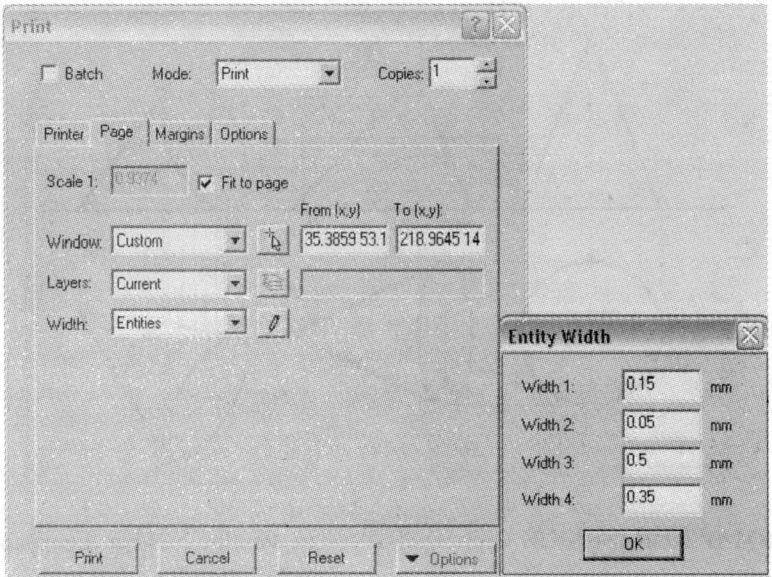

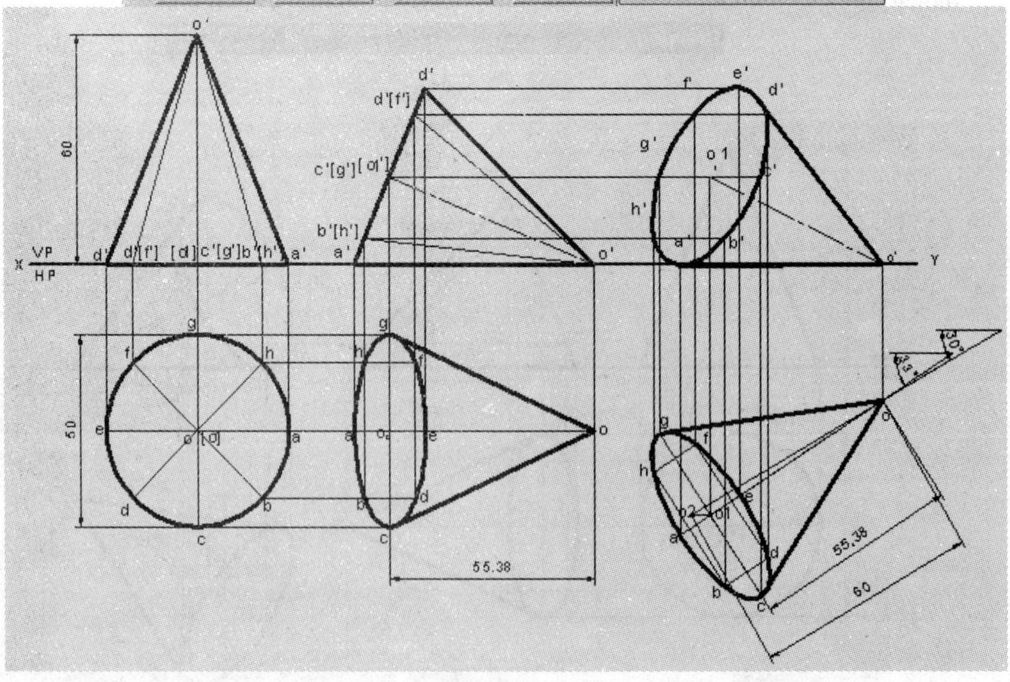

EXERCISE PROBLEMS

1. A square prism 35 mm side of base and 60 mm axis length rests on HP on one of its corners of the base such that the two base edges containing the corner on which it rests make equal inclinations with HP. Draw the projections of the prism when the axis of the prism is inclined to HP at 40° and appears to be inclined to VP at 45°.
2. A square prism 35 mm side of base and 60 mm axis length rests on HP on one of its corners of the base such that the two base edges containing the corner on which it rests make equal inclinations with HP. Draw the projections of the prism when the axis of the prism is inclined to HP at 40° and to VP at 30°.
3. A pentagonal prism 25 mm sides of base and 60 mm axis length rests on HP on one of its edges of the base. Draw the projections of the prism when the axis is inclined to HP at 40° and VP at 30°.
4. A pentagonal prism 25 mm sides of base and 60 mm axis length rests on HP on one of its corners of the base such that the two base edges containing the corner on which it rests make equal inclinations with HP. Draw the projections of the prism when the axis of the prism is inclined to HP at 40° and appears to be inclined to VP at 45°.
5. A hexagonal prism 25 mm sides of base and 50 mm axis length rests on HP on one of its edges. Draw the projections of the prism when the axis is inclined to HP at 45° and appears to be inclined to VP at 40°.
6. A hexagonal prism 25 mm sides of base and 50 mm axis length rests on HP on one of its edges of the base. Draw the projections of the prism when the axis is inclined to HP at 45° and VP at 30°.
7. A square prism 35 mm side of base and 60 mm axis length is suspended freely from one of its corners. Draw the projections of the prism when the axis appears to be inclined to VP at 45°.
8. A pentagonal prism 25 mm sides of base and 60 mm axis length is suspended freely from one of its corners. Draw the projections of the prism when the axis appears to be inclined to VP at 45°.
9. A hexagonal prism 25 mm sides of base and 50 mm axis length is suspended freely from one of its corners. Draw the projections of the prism when the axis appears to be inclined to VP at 45°.
10. A square pyramid 35 mm side of base and 60 mm axis length rests on HP on one of its corners of the base such that the two base edges containing the corner on which it rests make equal inclinations with HP. Draw the projections of the pyramid when the axis of the pyramid is inclined to HP at 40° and appears to be inclined to VP at 45°.
11. A square pyramid 35 mm side of base and 60 mm axis length rests on HP on one of its corners of the base such that the two base edges containing the corner on which it rests make equal inclinations with HP. Draw the projections of the pyramid when the axis of the pyramid is inclined to HP at 40° and to VP at 30°.
12. A pentagonal pyramid 25 mm sides of base and 60 mm axis length rests on HP on one of its edges of the base. Draw the projections of the pyramid when the axis is inclined to HP at 40° and VP at 30°.
13. A pentagonal pyramid 25 mm sides of base and 50 mm axis length rests on HP on one of its corners of the base such that the two base edges containing the corner on which it rests make equal inclinations with HP. Draw the projections of the pyramid when the axis of the pyramid is inclined to HP at 40° and appears to be inclined to VP at 45°.
14. A hexagonal pyramid 25 mm sides of base and 50 mm axis length rests on HP on one of its corners of the base such that the two base edges containing the corner on which it rests make

equal inclinations with HP. Draw the projections of the pyramid when the axis of the pyramid is inclined to HP at 40° and appears to be inclined to VP at 45°.

15. A hexagonal pyramid 25 mm sides of base and 50 mm axis length rests on HP on one of its corners of the base such that the two base edges containing the corner on which it rests make equal inclinations with HP. Draw the projections of the pyramid when the axis of the pyramid is inclined to HP at 40° and to VP at 30°.
16. A square pyramid 35 mm sides of base and 60 mm axis length is suspended freely from a corner of its base. Draw the projections of the pyramid when the axis appears to be inclined to VP at 45°.
17. A square pyramid 35 mm side of base and 60 mm axis length rests on HP on one of its slant edges. Draw the projections of the pyramid when the axis is inclined to VP at 45°.
18. A square pyramid 35 mm side of base and 60 mm axis length rests on HP on one of its slant triangular faces. Draw the projections of the pyramid when the axis appears to be inclined to VP at 45°.
19. A hexagonal pyramid 25 mm sides of base and 50 mm axis length rests on HP on one of its slant edges. Draw the projections of the pyramid when the axis is inclined to VP at 45°.
20. A hexagonal pyramid 25 mm sides of base and 50 mm axis length rests on HP on one of its slant triangular faces. Draw the projections of the pyramid when the axis appears to be inclined to VP at 45°.
21. A cone of base diameter 40 mm and 60 mm axis length rests on HP on one of its generators. Draw the projections of the cone when the axis is inclined to VP at 45°.
22. A cone of base diameter 40 mm and 60 mm axis length rests on HP on its apex. Draw the projections of the cone when the axis is inclined to VP at 45°.
23. A cone of base diameter 40 mm and 60 mm axis length rests on HP Draw the projections of the cone when the axis is inclined to VP at 45° and to HP is 45°.
24. A cylinder of base diameter 40 mm and 60 mm axis length rests on HP on one of its generators. Draw the projections of the cylinder when the axis is inclined to VP at 45°.
25. A cylinder of base diameter 40 mm and 60 mm axis length rests on HP Draw the projections of the cylinder when the axis is inclined to VP at 45° and to HP is 45°.

6

DEVELOPMENT OF LATERAL SURFACES OF SOLIDS

INTRODUCTION

- Development of solid (lateral surfaces of solid) is a graphical method of obtaining the area of the surfaces of a solid. When the lateral surfaces of solid is cut and spread on a plane, the surface of the solid is said to be developed.
- The knowledge of development is for designing and manufacturing of the objects. It is used in sheet metal work.
- There are two methods of development: (a) Parallel line method (b) Radial line method.
- Parallel line method is used for development of surfaces of prisms and cylinders. It is called because two parallel line (stretch-out lines) are drawn from the two ends of the solids and the lateral faces are drawn between these lines.
- Radial line method is used for development of surfaces of pyramids and cones. In this method an arc of radius equal to the slant edge/generator is drawn and lateral faces/angle are marked on this arc drawn.
- Important point to note for all these solids bottom and top face are not drawn.
- As per first angle projection, the solid axis may be parallel to HP and perpendicular to VP (Solid base resting on HP such that axis is parallel to VP).

System of Notation

1. The actual solid in space is denoted by capital letters A_1 , B_1, C_1 and D_1 etc for Base of solid and A, B, C and D etc for top face of the solid and axis as o1 and o.
2. The front view (FV) of a solid is denoted by their corresponding lower case letters with dashes as a1′, b1′, c1′ and d1′ etc for base of solid and a′, b′ c′ and d′ etc for top face of the solid and for axis as o1′ and o′.
3. The top view (TV) of a solid is denoted by their corresponding lower case letters with dashes as a1, b1, c1 and d1 etc for bottom of solid and a, b c and d etc for top face of the solid and for axis as o1 and o.
4. The side view (SV) of a solid are denoted by their corresponding lower case letters with double dashes as a1″, b1″, c1″ and d1″ etc for base of the solid and a″, b″, c″ and d″ etc for top face of the solid and for axis as o1″ and o″.
5. Projectors are always drawn as continuous thin lines.
6. Section line is represented by any two capital letters like AA, BB, CC etc.
7. Developed lateral surface is represented by their corresponding capital letters A1, B1, C1 and D1 etc for Base of solid and A, B, C and D etc for top face of the solid.
8. Line with specific thickness for a particular type of line.

In Computer Aided Engineering Graphics for development of lateral surface following commands are used other than evoking software, opening file, saving file and giving print command. Using these minimum15 commands any type of development of lateral surface problem can be solved they are as follows:

1. Select tool Command.
2. Point command.
3. Poly-Line command.
4. Two Point Line command.
5. Parallel line command.
6. Center Circle command
7. Bisector command.
8. Smart Dimension command.
9. Line Width command.
10. Insert Text command.
11. Rectangle command.
12. Smart Delete command.
13. Cross Hatch command.
14. Offset on Plane command.
15. Curve through Control Points command

PROBLEM 6.1

A rectangular prism of base 40 mm × 25 mm and height 65 mm rests on HP on its base with the longer base side inclined at 30° to VP. It is cut by a plane inclined at 40° to HP, perpendicular to VP cuts the axis at its mid height. Draw the development of the remaining portion of the prism.

SOLUTION

Manual Method

(a) Draw the top and front view of rectangular prism.

(b) Draw 400 line such that it bisects the axis of the rectangular prism in front view. Mark 1′2′3′ and 4′ in front view and 1 2 3 and 4 in top view.

(c) Draw the development of the prism using parallel line method.

(d) Locate the points 1 2 3 and 4 on the development by drawing horizontal projector from 1′2′3′ and 4′.

(e) Join all the points by straight lines and darken the sides corresponding to the retained portion of the solid.

(f) Mark annotations correctly and dimension necessarily.

Computer Aided Drafting Procedure

1. Open the SOFTWARE. Click on the DRAWING in the open dialog box and say OK.

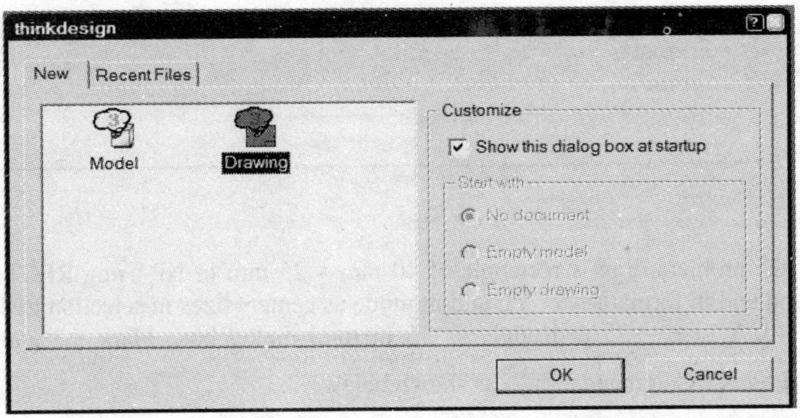

2. To set up the sheet of required size (Ex: A4) by selecting TOOLS from Main Menu Bar and click on OPTIONS/PROPERTIES. Select document properties in dialog box appeared and then select drawing in selection panel. Select the required size say A4, and click OK.

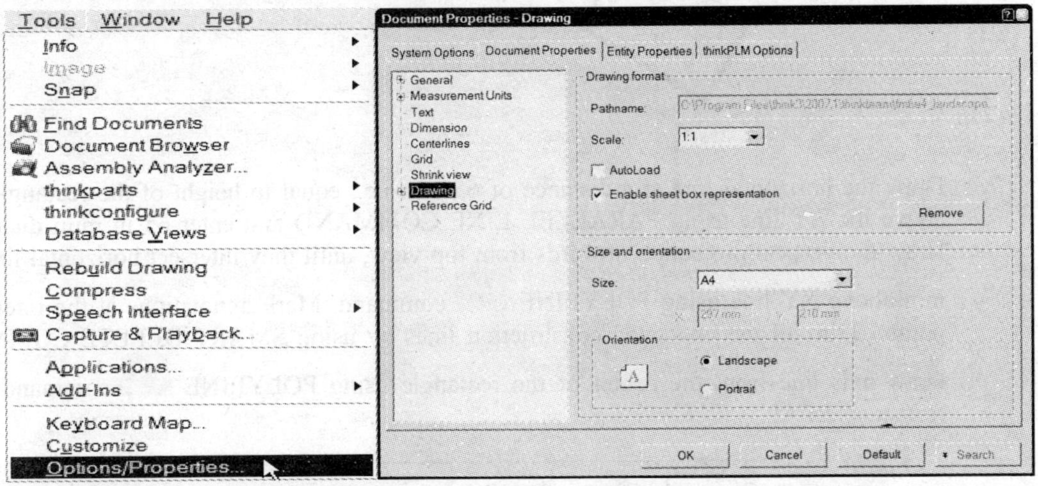

3. To draw XY line, projection lines, dotted lines, axis line, sectional line and top & front view lines. After selecting line command, in format select XY for XY line, PL for projection lines DL for dotted (hidden) lines, AL for axis line SL for section line and VL for top and front view lines before drawing these lines.

4. Draw the line by using POLYLINE  command from drafting tool bar and in format select XY.

5. Make Annotation X, Y, VP, and HP to the line drawn by using INSERT TEXT Command 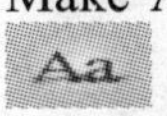

from drafting tool bar, just by typing X, Y, VP and HP in Text Box and insert these in the required position by left click of the mouse, as shown below.

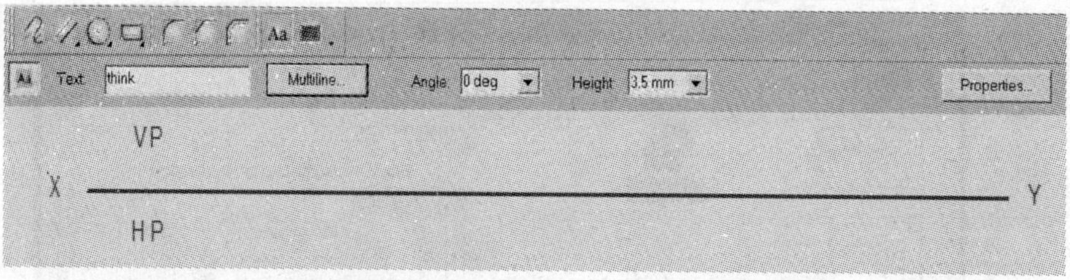

6. As per the problem draw a rectangle of 40 mm × 25 mm in HP using RECTANGLE command and in format select VL and in mode as center+sizes in selection tree. Now enter X size = 40, Y size = 25 and angle as 35 in mini dialog box. Mark the annotations using INSERT TEXT Command as shown below.

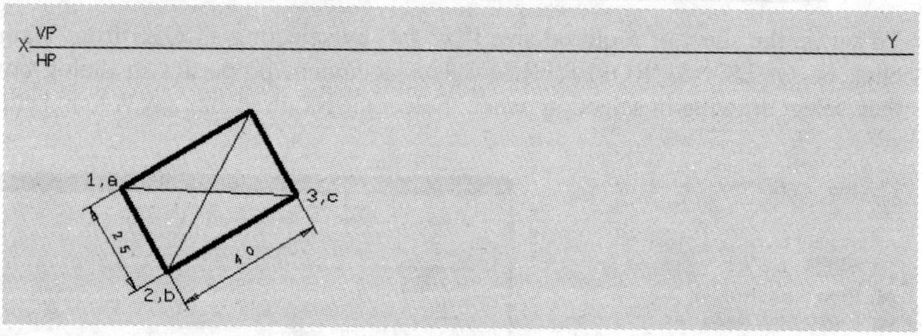

7. Draw the horizontal line at a distance of 65 mm i.e., equal to height of the rectangle prism above the XY line using PARALLEL LINE COMMAND and enter 65 in mini dialog box. Draw the vertical projection upwards from top view, until they intersect horizontal line at 65 mm above XY line using POLYLINE command. Mark annotations at the intersection points. Trim all the unwanted construction lines by using SMART DELETE COMMAND. Draw axis line from the center of the rectangle using POLYLINE command and in format select AL.

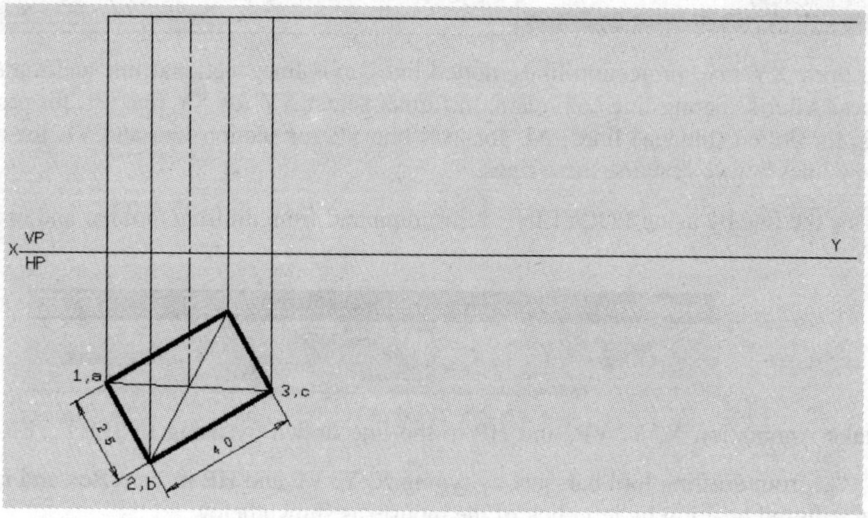

8. As per the problem using POLYLINE command and in format select SL draw a line inclined at 40° such that it bisects the axis. Using INSERT TEXT Command mark 1′2′ 3′ and 4′ where the section plane cuts the prism as shown.

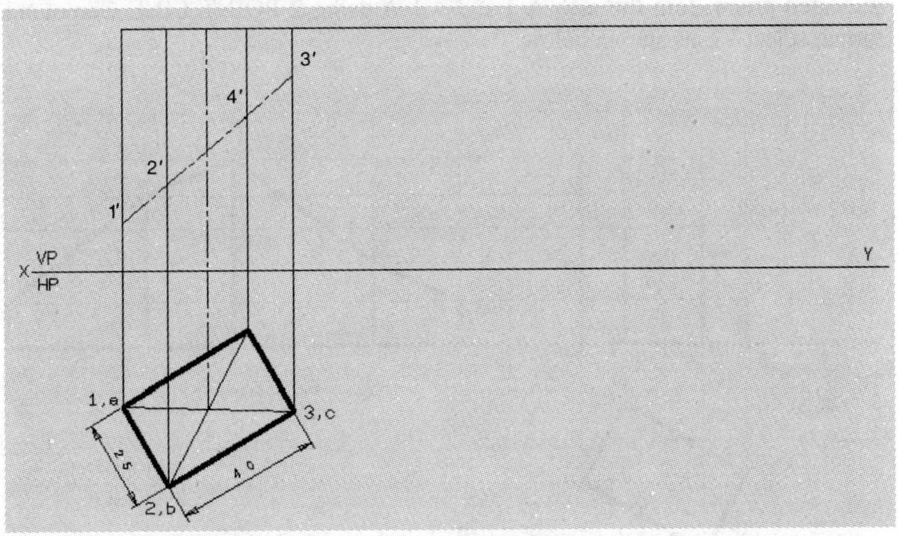

9. Draw downward projectors through 1′2′3′ and 4′ to meet the corners of the rectangle. Hatch the sectioned part in top view using CROSS HATCH COMMAND in drafting tool bar customize the properties if required in the selection tree.

10. To draw a development, draw a line AA length equal to the perimeter of the rectangle. Draw a another horizontal line of length AA above XY line at height equal to height of prism 65 mm (given) AA_1 using POLYLINE command in format select PL and draw AA_1 BB_1 CC_1 DD_1 and AA_1 using POLYLINE command and OFFSET ON PLANE COMMAND enter the distance equal to the each side of the rectangle in mini dialog box as shown.

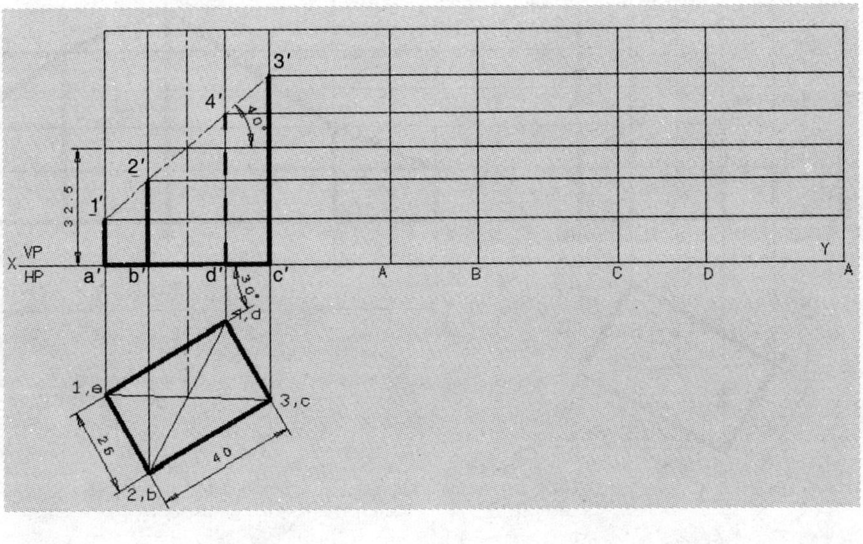

11. Draw the projection points from 1′2′3′ and 4′ on the corresponding development edges. Mark these points as 1 2 3 and 4 respectively by using INSERT TEXT command . The area A 1 2 3 4 1 A, represents the development of lower portion of the lateral surface of the truncated prism. Join the area A 1 2 3 4 1 A using 2 POINT LINE Command  and in format select VL as shown below.

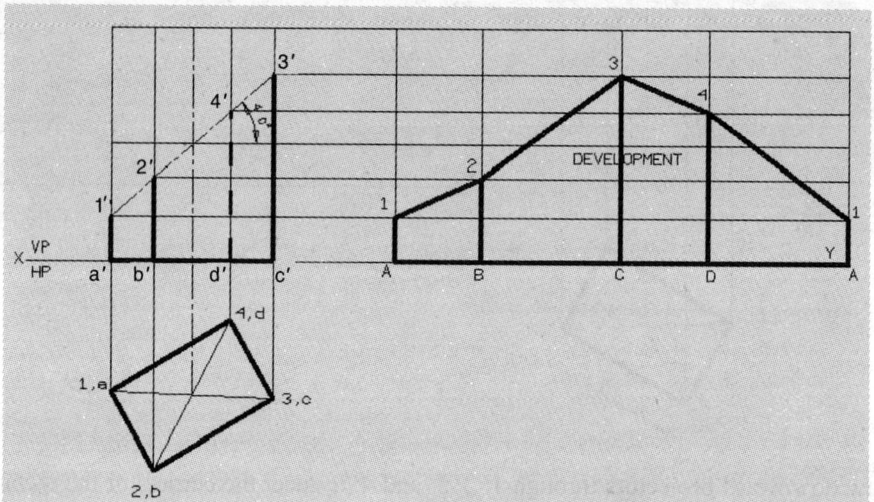

12. Using SMART DIMENSION Command  in drawing tool bar dimension the drawing as shown.

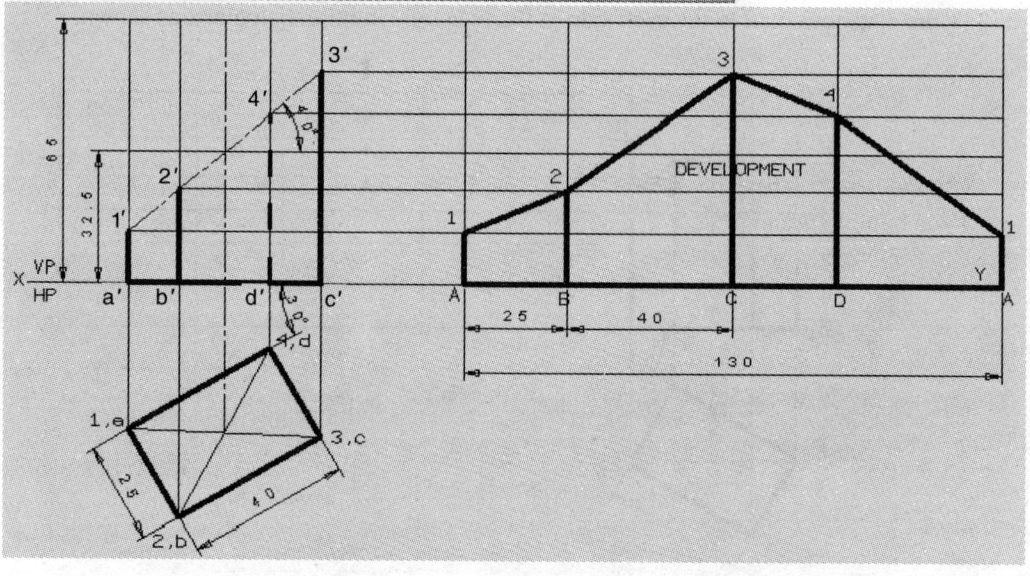

13. To get a Hard Copy of the standard drawing select print from file menu bar. Print dialog window will appear select page and change width to Entities and select the activated button  now substitute width 1 as 0.15 mm, width 2 as 0.05 mm, width 3 as 0.5 mm, width 4 as 0.35 mm and say OK. Select print to get a hard copy and finally save the file. The required standard drawing is as shown below.

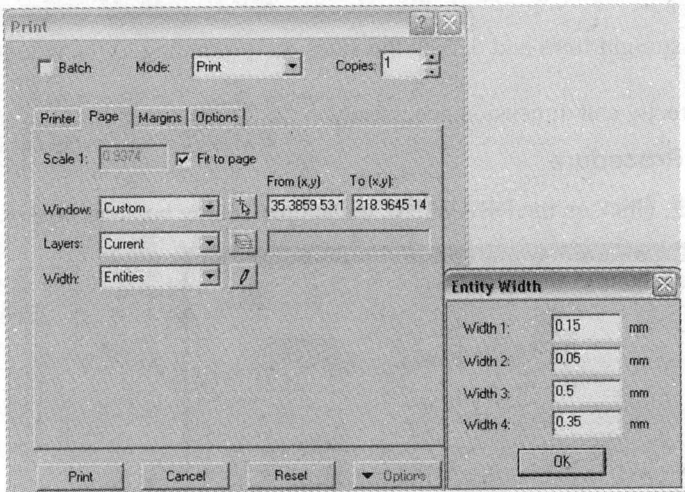

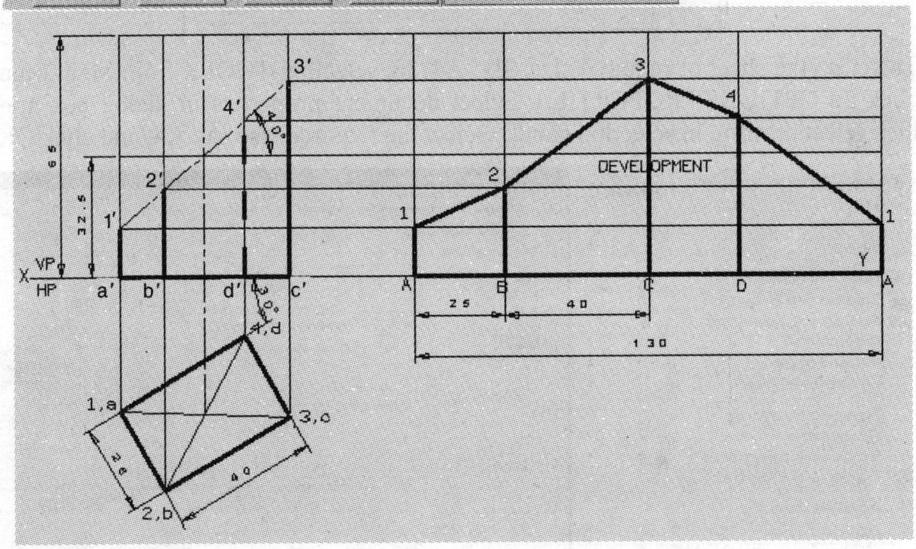

PROBLEM 6.2

Draw the development of the truncated portion of the lateral faces of a pentagonal prism of 20 mm sides of base and 50 mm height standing vertically with one of its rectangular faces parallel to VP and nearer to it so as to produce a one piece development. The inclined face of the truncated prism is 30° to its axis and passes through the right extreme corner of the top face of the prism.

SOLUTION

Manual Method

(a) Draw the top and front view of pentagonal prism.

(b) Draw 30° line such that it passes through the axis and right extreme corner of the top face of the prism. Mark 1′2′3′ etc in front view and 1 2 3 etc in top view.

(c) Draw the development of the prism using parallel line method.

(d) Locate the points 1 2 3 etc on the development by drawing horizontal projector from 1′ 2′ 3′etc.

(e) Join all the points by straight lines and darken the sides corresponding to the retained portion of the solid.

(f) Mark annotations correctly and dimension necessarily.

Computer Aided Drafting Procedure

1. Open the SOFTWARE. Click on the DRAWING in the open dialog box and say OK.

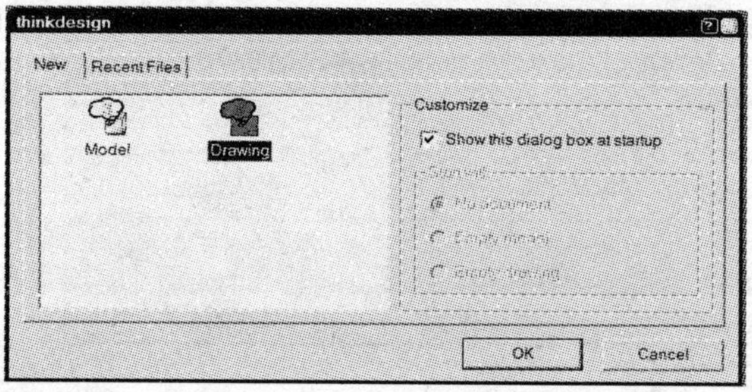

2. To set up the sheet of required size (Ex: A4) by selecting TOOLS from Main Menu Bar and click on OPTIONS/PROPERTIES. Select document properties in dialog box appeared and then select drawing in selection panel. Select the required size say A4, and click OK.

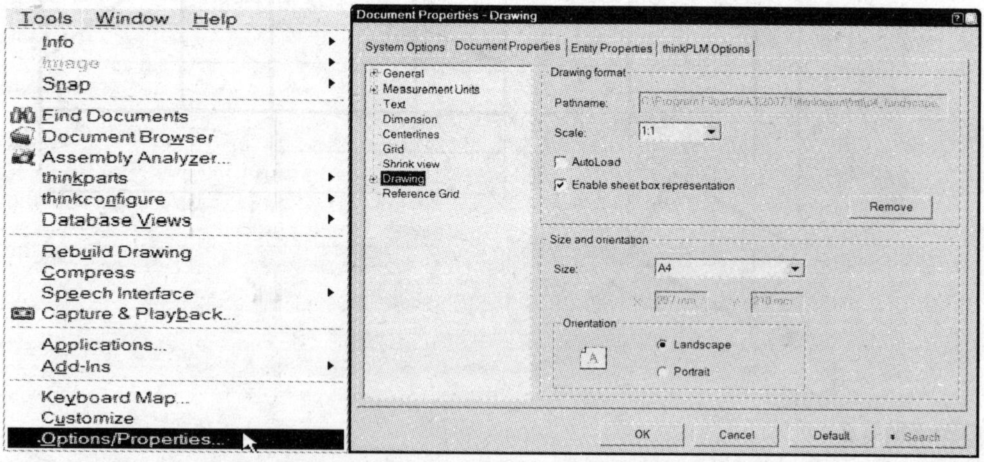

3. To draw XY line, projection lines, dotted lines, axis line, sectional line and top & front view lines. After selecting line command, in format select XY for XY line, PL for projection lines DL for dotted (hidden) lines, AL for axis line SL for section line and VL for top and front view lines before drawing these lines.

4. Draw the line by using POLYLINE command from drafting tool bar and in format select XY.

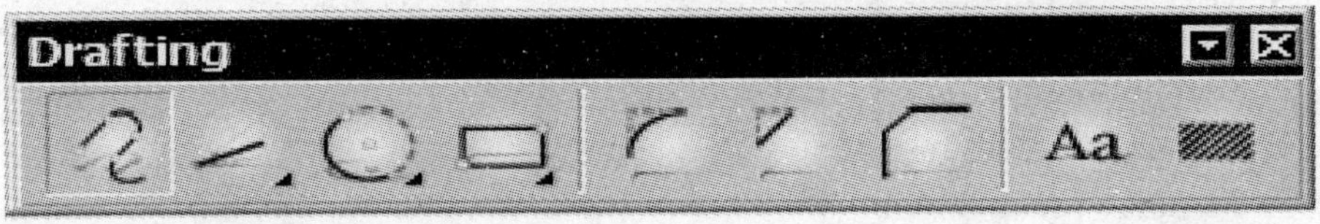

5. Make Annotation X, Y, VP, and HP to the line drawn by using INSERT TEXT Command from drafting tool bar, just by typing X, Y, VP and HP in Text Box and insert these in the required position by left click of the mouse, as shown below.

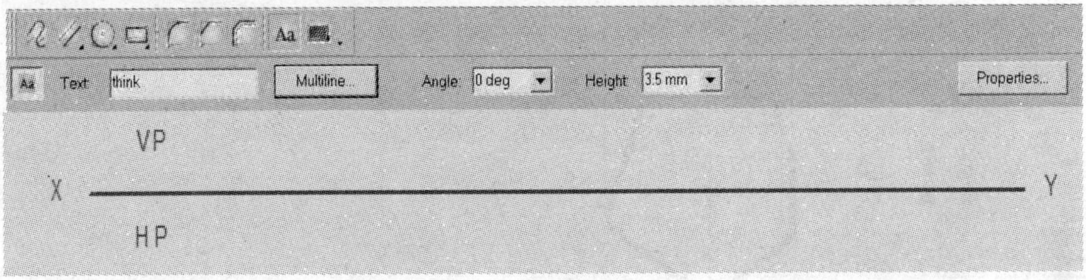

6. As per the problem draw a pentagon of 20 mm in HP using POLYLINE command and in format select VL. Mark the annotations using INSERT TEXT Command .

7. Draw the horizontal line at a distance of 50 mm i.e., equal to height of the pentagonal prism above the XY line using PARALLEL LINE COMMAND and enter 50 in mini dialog box. Draw the vertical projection upwards from top view, until they intersect horizontal line at 50 mm above XY line using POLYLINE command. Mark annotations at the intersection points. Trim all the unwanted construction lines by using SMART DELETE COMMAND. Draw axis line from the center of the prism using POLYLINE command and in format select AL.

8. As per the problem using POLYLINE command and in format select SL draw a 30° line inclined to axis such that it passes through the right extreme corner of the top face of the prism. Using INSERT TEXT Command mark 1′ 2′ 3′ 4′ 5′ and 6′ where the section plane cuts the prism.

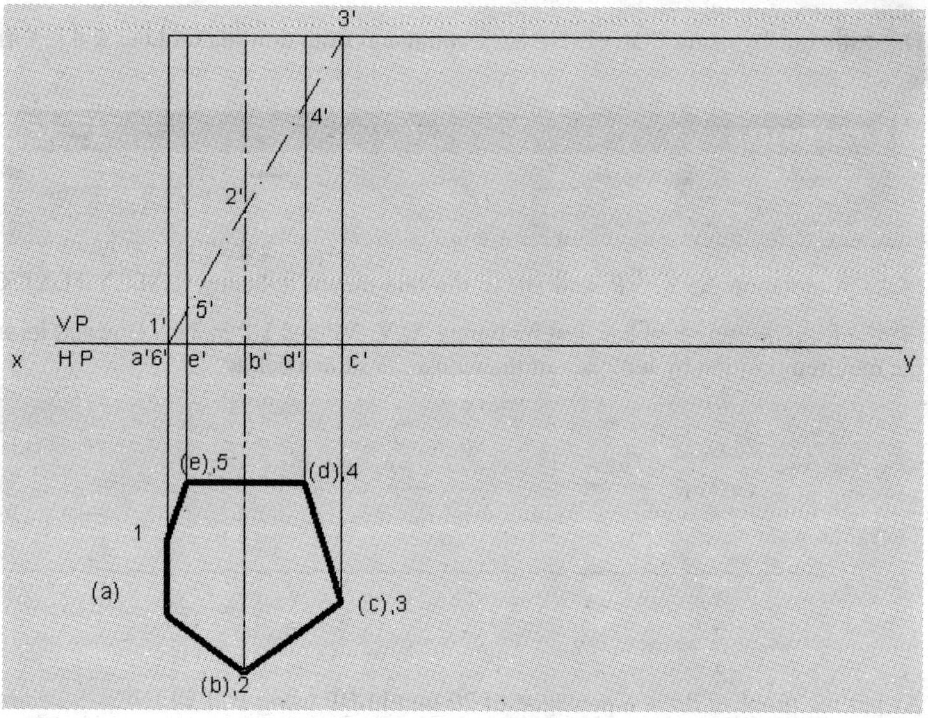

9. Draw downward projectors through 1′ 2′ 3′ 4′ 5′ and 6′ to meet the corners of the rectangle. Hatch the sectioned part in top view using CROSS HATCH COMMAND in drafting tool bar customize the properties if required in the selection tree.

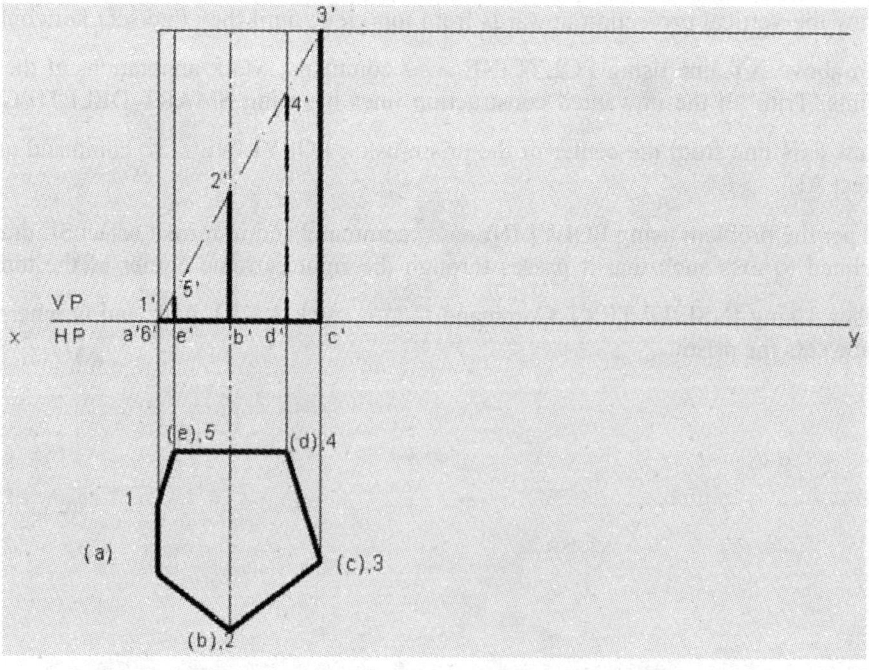

10. To draw a development, draw a line AA length equal to the perimeter of the pentagon. Draw a parallel line of length AA above XY line at height equal to height of prism 65 mm (given) AA_1 using POLYLINE command in format select PL and draw AA_1 BB_1 CC_1 DD_1 EE_1 and AA_1 using POLYLINE command and OFFSET ON PLANE COMMAND enter the distance equal to 20 in mini dialog box as shown.

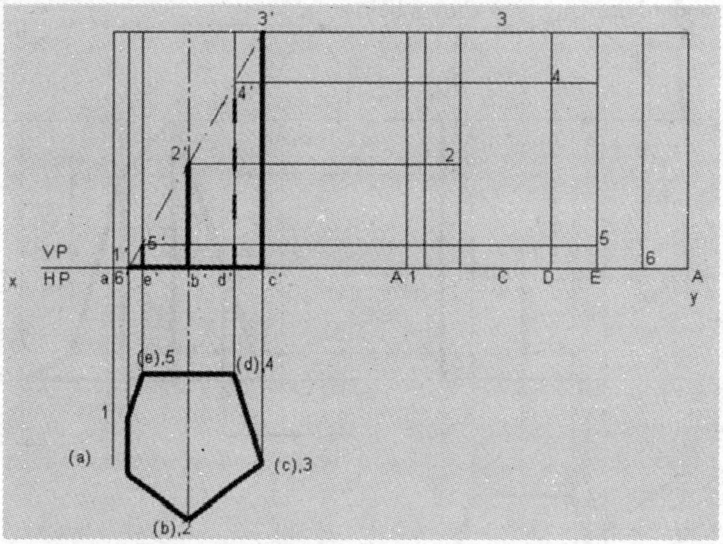

11. Draw the projection points from 1′2′3′4′5′ and 6′ on the corresponding development edges. Mark these points as 1 2 3 4 5 and 6 respectively by using INSERT TEXT command. The area 1 2 3 4 5 6 and 1, represents the development of lower portion of the lateral surface of the truncated prism. Join the area 1 2 3 4 5 6 and 1 using 2 POINT LINE Command and in format select VL as shown below.

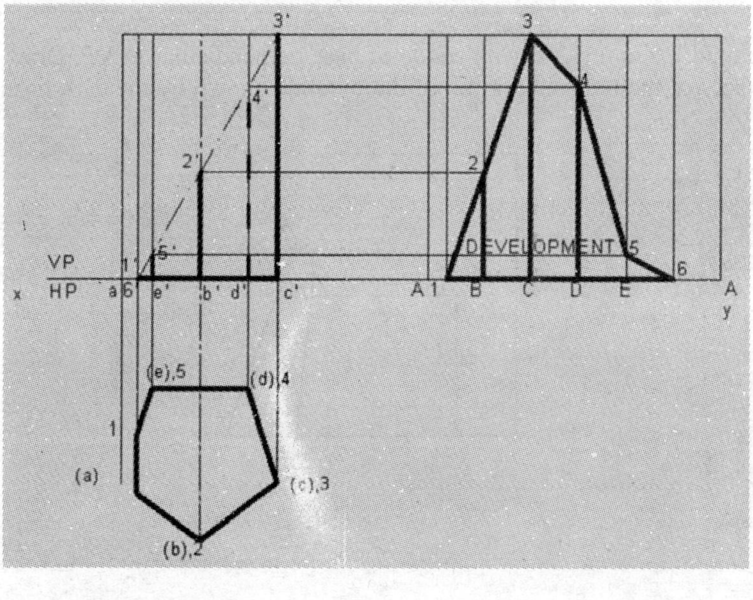

12. Using SMART DIMENSION Command in drawing tool bar dimension the drawing as shown. To get a Hard Copy of the standard drawing select print from file menu bar. Print dialog window will appear select page and change width to Entities and select the activated button now substitute width 1 as 0.15 mm, width 2 as 0.05 mm, width 3 as 0.5 mm, width 4 as 0.35 mm and say OK. Select print to get a hard copy and finally save the file. The required standard drawing is as shown below.

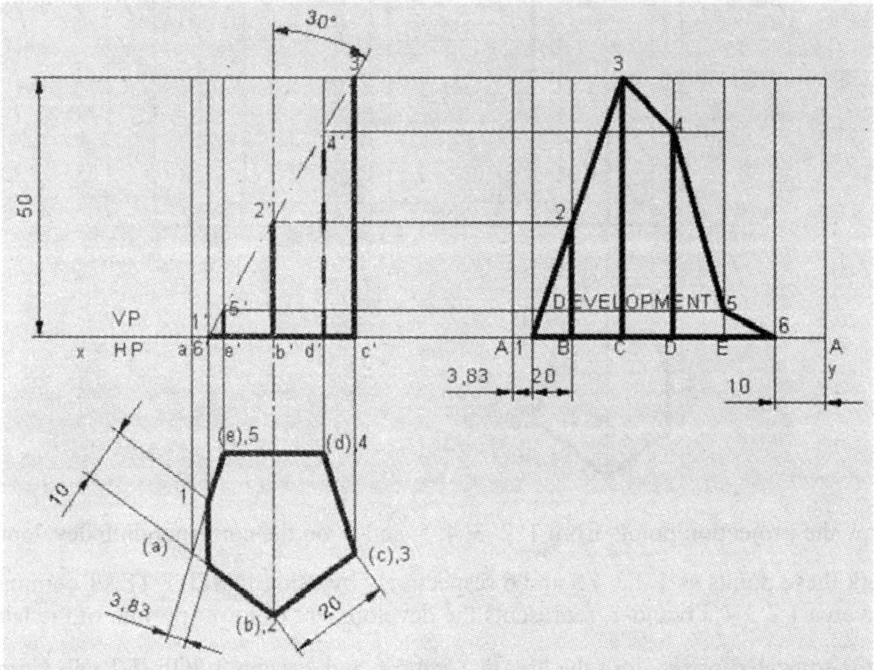

PROBLEM 6.3

A pentagonal pyramid, 30 mm sides, with a side of base perpendicular to VP. Draw the development of the lateral surfaces of the retained portion of the pyramid shown by the dark lines in the following figure.

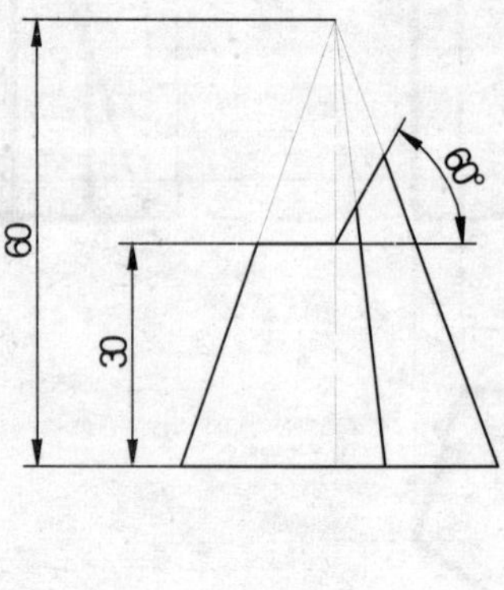

SOLUTION

Manual Method

(a) Draw the top and front view of rectangular pyramid.

(b) Draw 400 line such that it bisects the axis of the rectangular prism in front view. Mark 1′2′3′ and 4′ in front view and 1 2 3 and 4 in top view.

(c) Draw the development of the prism using parallel line method.

(d) Locate the points 1 2 3 and 4 on the development by drawing horizontal projector from 1′2′3′ and 4′.

(e) Join all the points by straight lines and darken the sides corresponding to the retained portion of the solid.

(f) Mark annotations correctly and dimension necessarily.

Computer Aided Drafting Procedure

1. Open the SOFTWARE. Click on the DRAWING in the open dialog box and say OK.

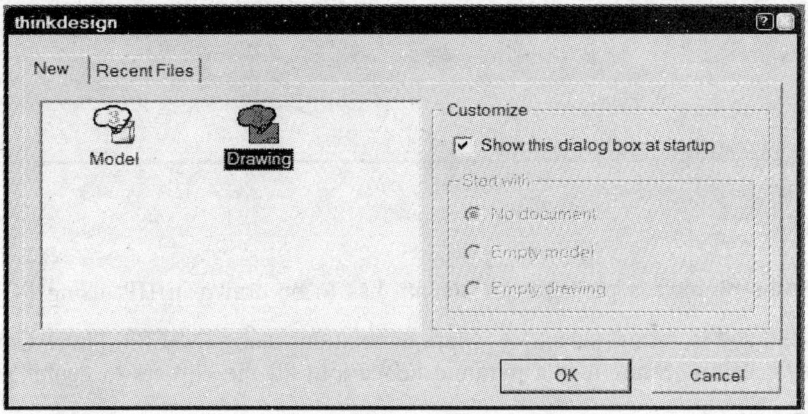

2. To set up the sheet of required size (Ex: A4) by selecting TOOLS from Main Menu Bar and click on OPTIONS/PROPERTIES. Select document properties in dialog box appeared and then select drawing in selection panel. Select the required size say A4, and click OK.

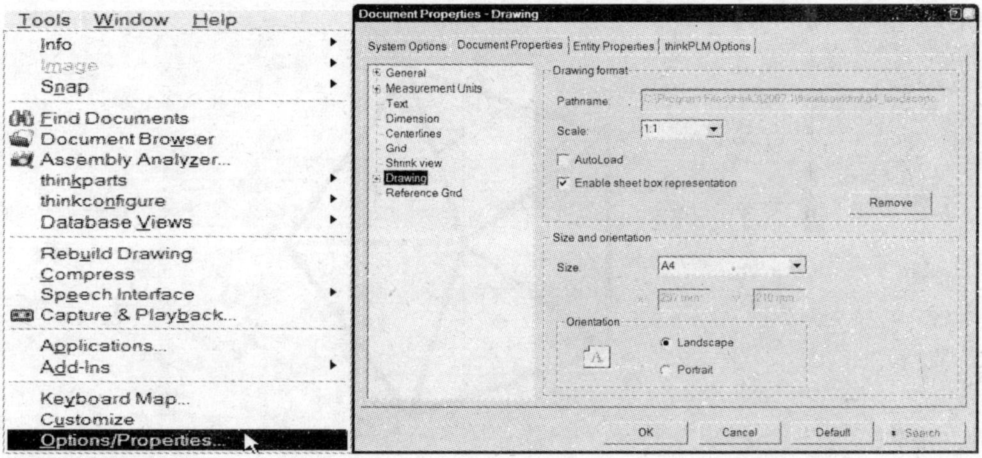

3. To draw XY line, projection lines, dotted lines, axis line, sectional line and top & front view lines. After selecting line command, in format select XY for XY line, PL for projection lines DL for dotted (hidden) lines, AL for axis line SL for section line and VL for top and front view lines before drawing these lines.

4. Draw the line by using POLYLINE  command from drafting tool bar and in format select XY.

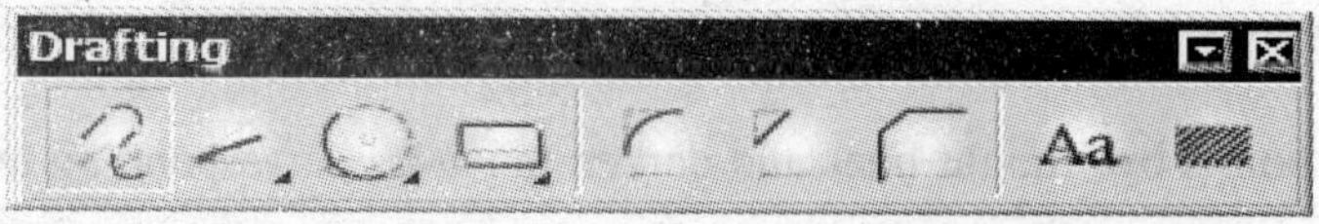

5. Make Annotation X, Y, VP, and HP to the line drawn by using INSERT TEXT Command  from drafting tool bar, just by typing X, Y, VP and HP in Text Box and insert these in the required position by left click of the mouse, as shown below.

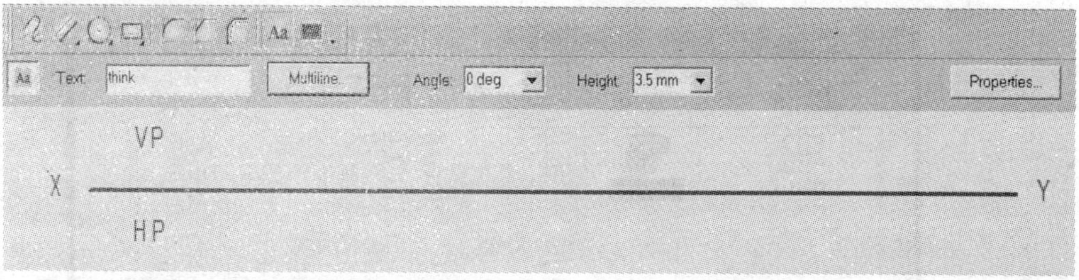

6. As per the problem a pentagon of 30 mm has to be drawn in HP, using POLYLINE  command and in format select VL. Mark annotations using INSERT TEXT Command 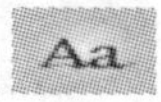 as shown below. Since it is a pyramid hence join all the corners to center point o using 2 POINT LINE Command  and in format select VL.

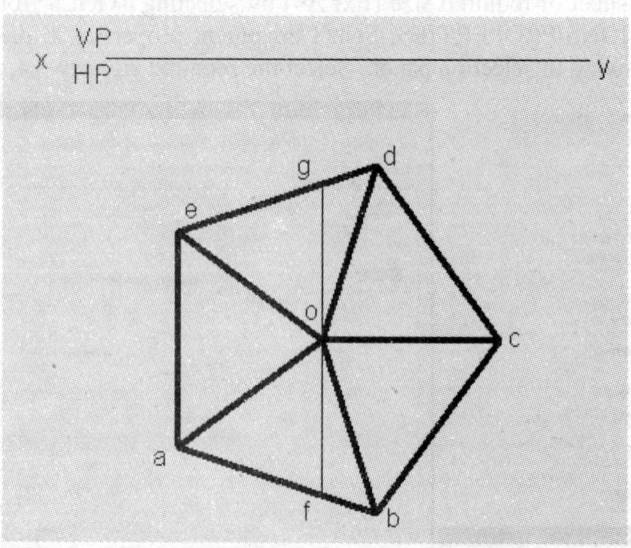

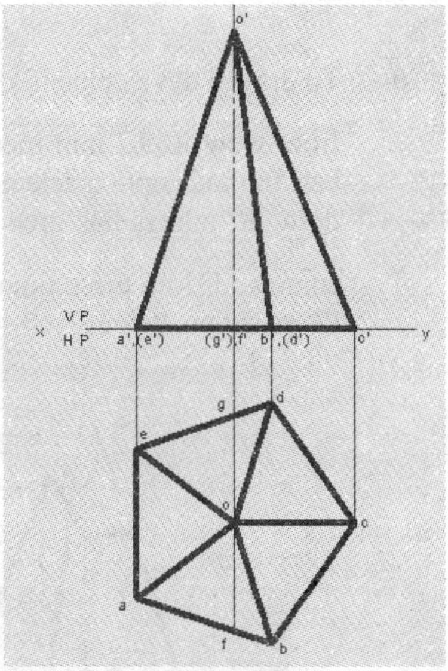

7. Draw the vertical projector upwards from corners of the top view. Draw the base of the pyramid on XY line using 2 POINT LINE Command and in format select VL represent as a′ b′ c′ d′ e′ and o_1′. To get the height of pyramid draw vertical projector upwards from center o in top view. Draw axis which is equal to height of pyramid (60 mm). Represent apex at o′. Join all the corners to the apex using 2 POINT LINE Command and in format select VL. Mark the annotations as shown below. Trim all the unwanted construction lines by using SMART DELETE COMMAND. Draw axis line from the center of the prism using POLYLINE command and in format select ALA.

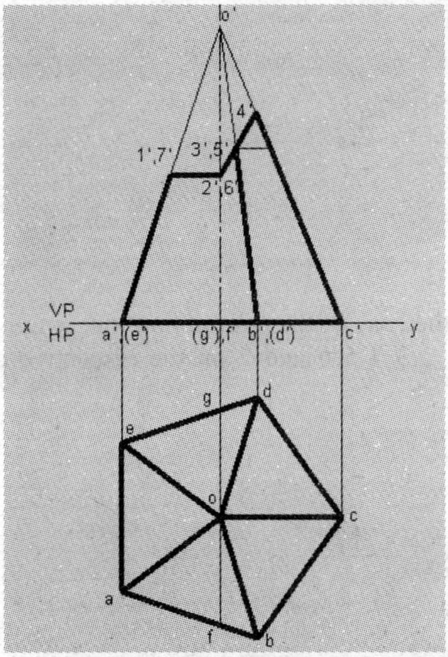

8. As per the problem using POLYLINE command and in format select SL draw a horizontal line which bisects the axis and also draw 600 line inclined to base such that it passes through the horizontal line drawn to the pyramid. Using INSERT TEXT Command mark 1′ 2′ 3′ 4′ 5′ 6′ and 7’ where the section plane cuts the pyramid as shown.

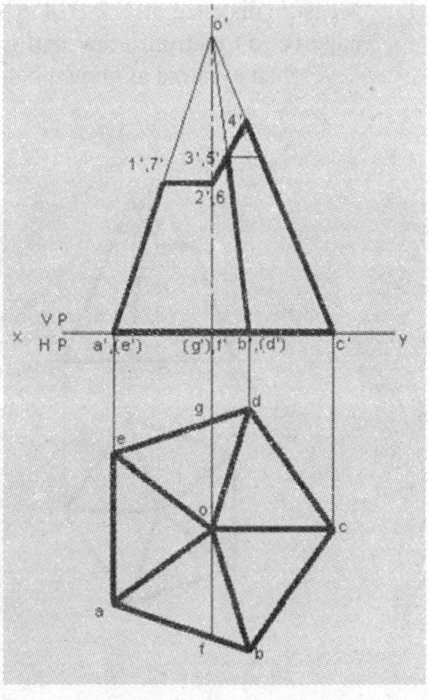

9. Draw downward projectors through 1′ 2′ 3′ 4′ 5′ 6′ and 7′ to meet the corners of the pentagon. Hatch the sectioned part in top view using CROSS HATCH COMMAND in drafting tool bar customize the properties if required in the selection tree.

10. To draw a development, draw an arc with radius equal to true length of slant edge OC (o′c′ in front view) (65.2 mm measured) by using CENTER CIRCLE  command in drafting tool bar. In mode option select arc, enter radius 65.2 mm. Mark a point A on arc. With A as center draw 30 mm radius arcs equal to base side to get the points B C D E and A using same command. Join these points to o using 2 POINT LINE Command  and in format select PL as shown below.

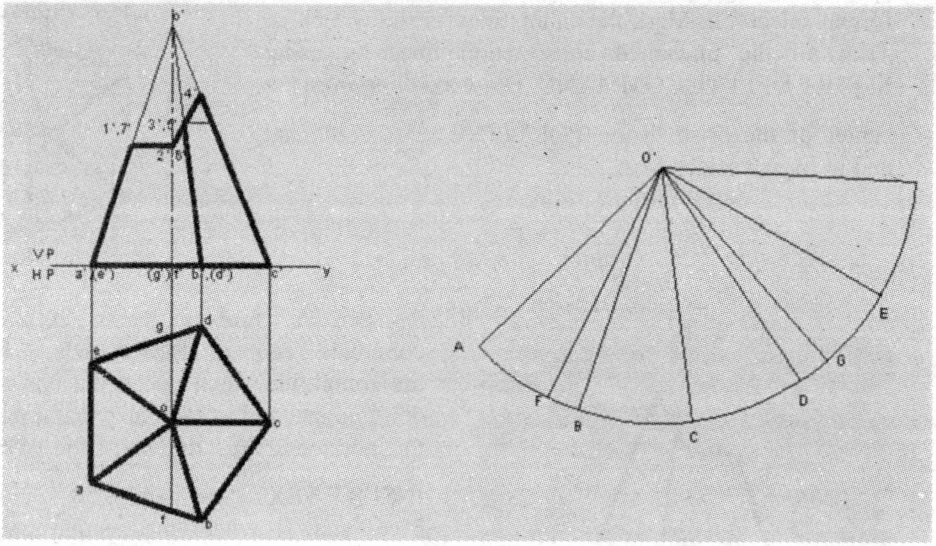

11. Measure distance of 1′2′3′4′5′6′ and 7′ from the base of the pyramid on true length of slant edge (o′ c′) in front view and mark them as 1 2 3 4 5 6 and 7 on the respective edges of developed pyramid as shown below.

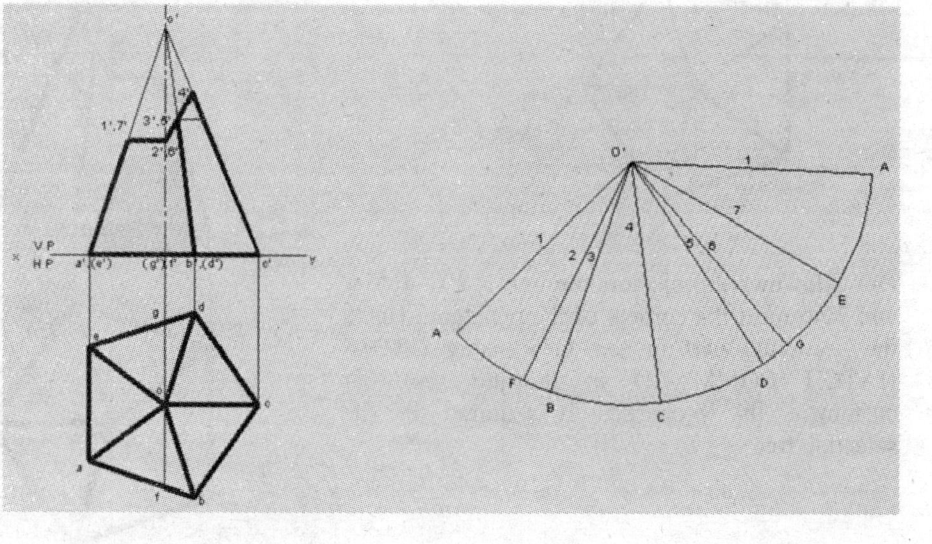

12. Join these marked points by 2 POINT LINE Command and in format select PL. The area A 1 2 3 4 5 6 7 1 and A represents the development of lower portion of the lateral surface of the truncated pentagonal pyramid. Using SMART DIMENSION Command in drawing tool bar dimension the drawing as shown.

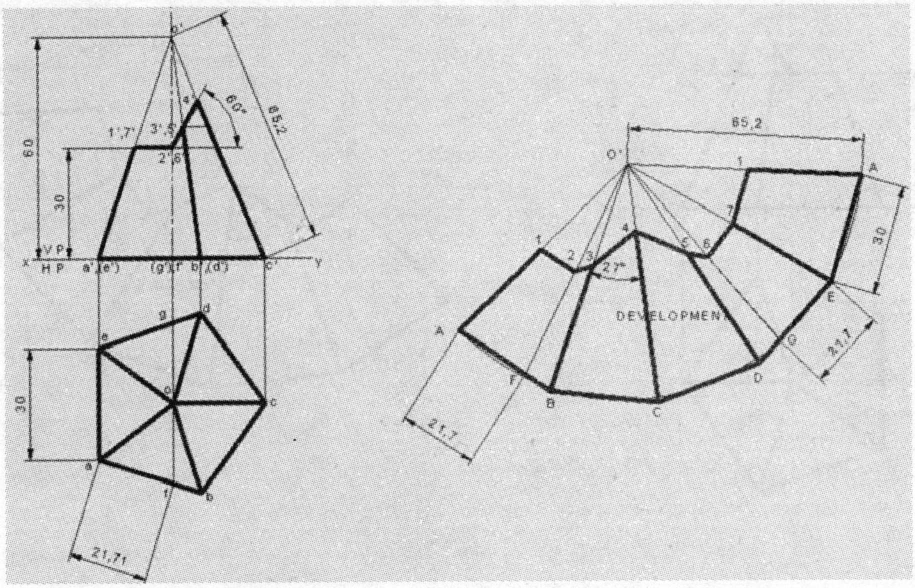

13. To get a Hard Copy of the standard drawing select print from file menu bar. Print dialog window will appear select page and change width to Entities and select the activated button now substitute width 1 as 0.15 mm, width 2 as 0.05 mm, width 3 as 0.5 mm, width 4 as 0.35 mm and say OK. Select print to get a hard copy and finally save the file. The required standard drawing is as shown below.

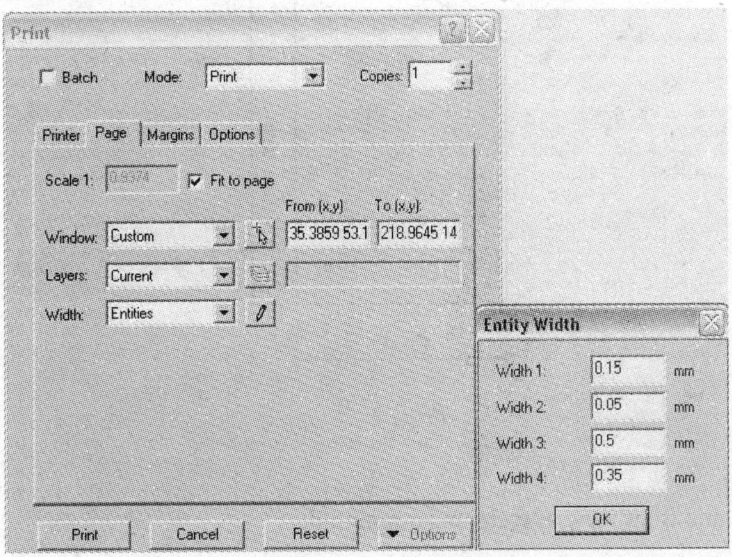

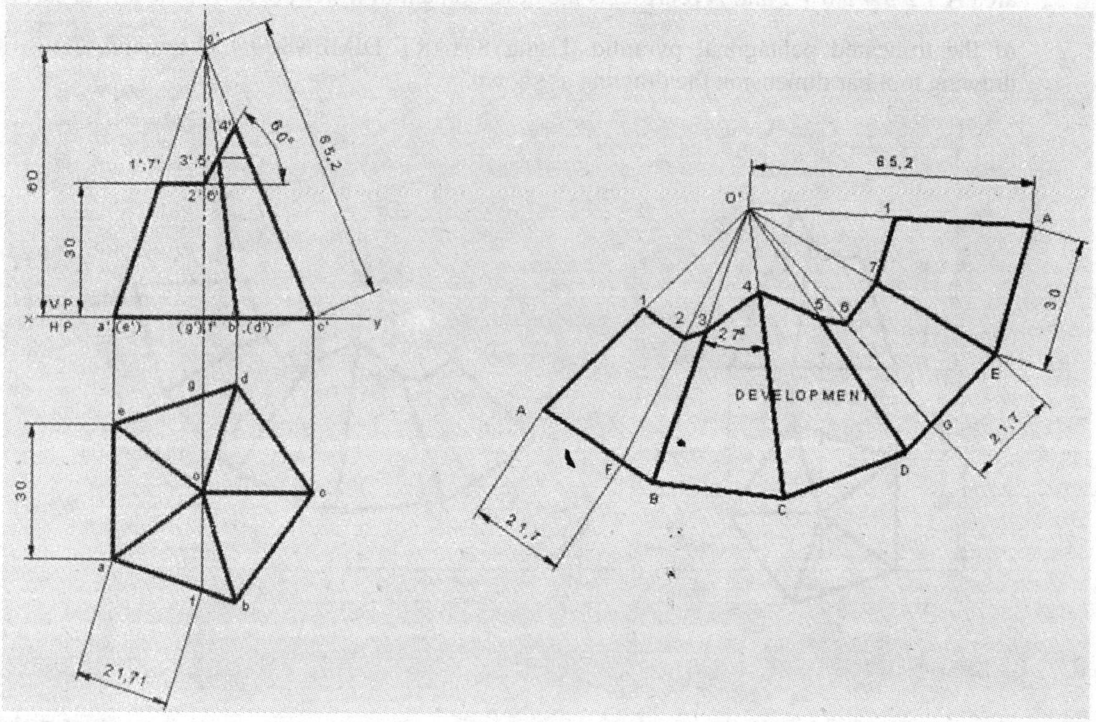

PROBLEM 6.4

Develop the lateral surface of the cylinder of 40 mm diameter and height 60 mm which is cut in the following figure.

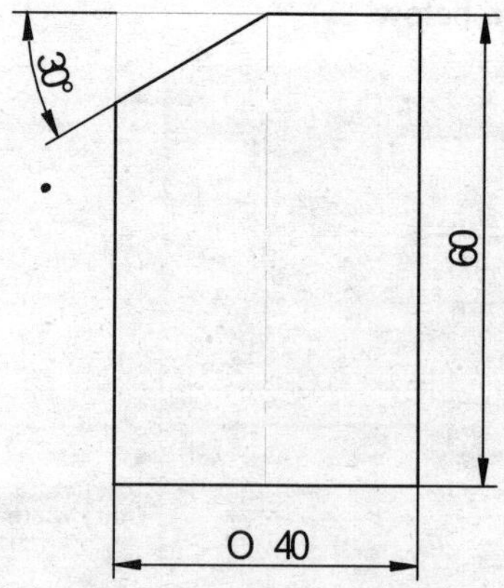

SOLUTION

Manual Method

(a) Draw the top and front view of rectangular pyramid.

(b) Draw 400 line such that it bisects the axis of the rectangular prism in front view. Mark 1′2′3′ and 4′ in front view and 1 2 3 and 4 in top view.

(c) Draw the development of the prism using parallel line method.

(d) Locate the points 1 2 3 and 4 on the development by drawing horizontal projector from 1′2′3′ and 4′.

(e) Join all the points by straight lines and darken the sides corresponding to the retained portion of the solid.

(f) Mark annotations correctly and dimension necessarily.

Computer Aided Drafting Procedure

1. Open the SOFTWARE. Click on the DRAWING in the open dialog box and say OK.

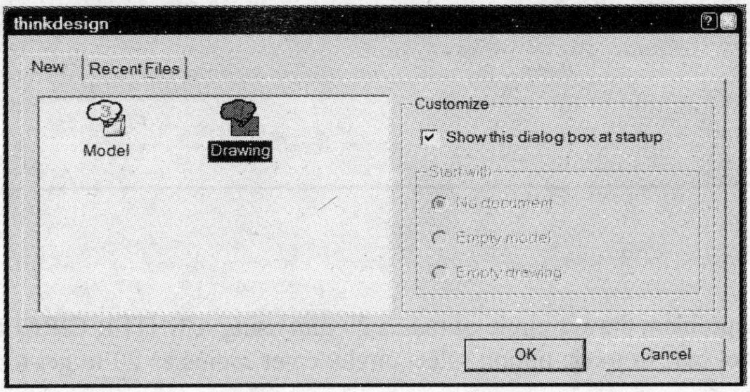

2. To set up the sheet of required size (Ex: A4) by selecting TOOLS from Main Menu Bar and click on OPTIONS/PROPERTIES. Select document properties in dialog box appeared and then select drawing in selection panel. Select the required size say A4, and click OK.

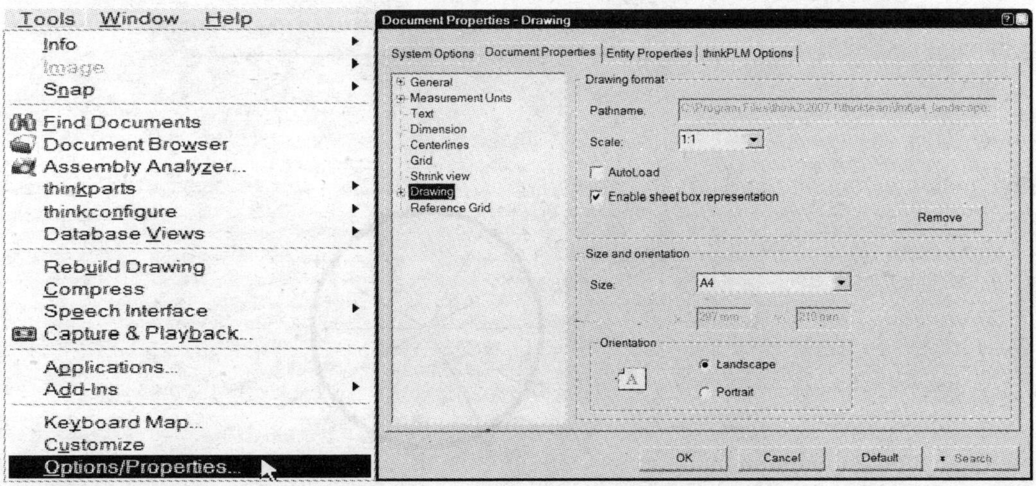

3. To draw XY line, projection lines, dotted lines, axis line, sectional line and top & front view lines. After selecting line command, in format select XY for XY line, PL for projection lines DL for dotted (hidden) lines, AL for axis line SL for section line and VL for top and front view lines before drawing these lines.

4. Draw the line by using POLYLINE  command from drafting tool bar and in format select XY.

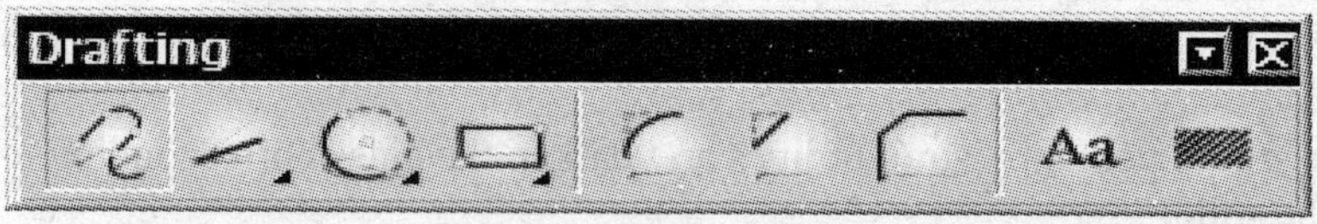

5. Make Annotation X, Y, VP, and HP to the line drawn by using INSERT TEXT Command  from drafting tool bar, just by typing X, Y, VP and HP in Text Box and insert these in the required position by left click of the mouse, as shown below.

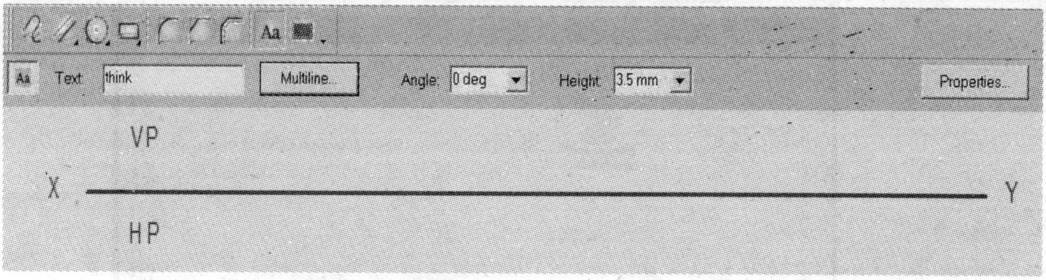

6. As per the problem draw a circle of radius 20 mm using CENTER CIRCLE  command in drafting tool bar. In mode option select circle, enter radius as 20 to get top view. Divide the circle into any number of equal parts by using POLYLINE  command and MOVE COPY  command. Mark the annotations using INSERT TEXT Command  as shown below.

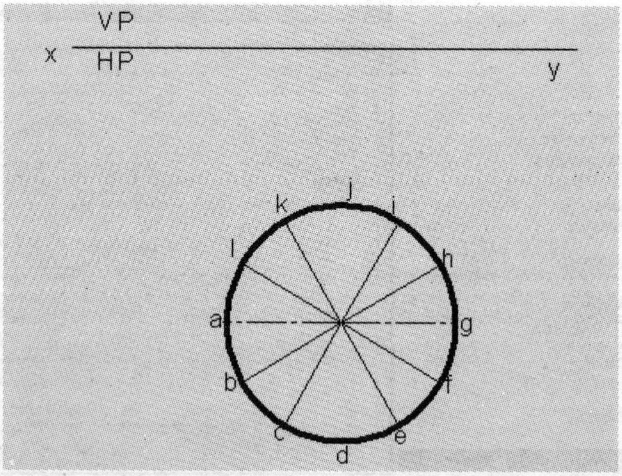

7. Draw the horizontal line at a distance of 60 mm i.e., equal to height of the cylinder above the XY line using PARALLEL LINE COMMAND and enter 60 in mini dialog box. Draw the vertical projection upwards from top view, until they intersect horizontal line at 60 mm above

XY line using POLYLINE  command. Mark the intersection points as shown. Trim all the unwanted construction lines by using SMART DELETE COMMAND.

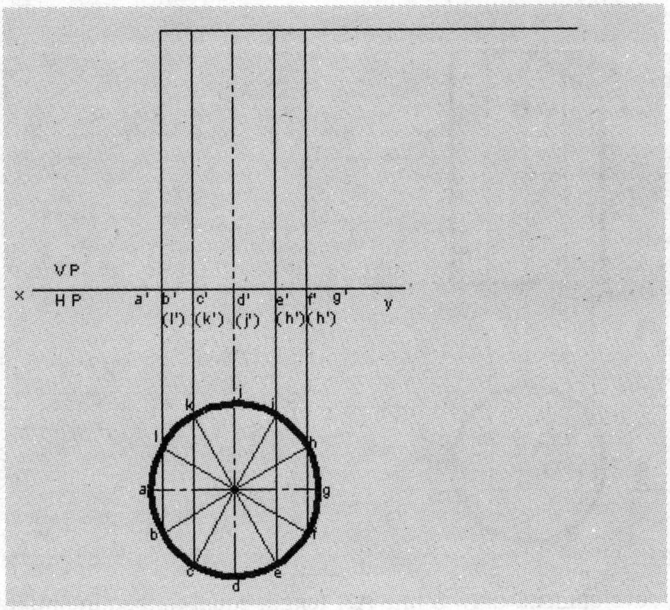

8. As per the problem using POLYLINE  command and in format select SL draw 30° inclined line, such that it passes through the axis on top face. Using INSERT TEXT Command  mark 1′ 2′ 3′ 4′ 5′ 6′ and 7′ where the section plane cuts the cylinder as shown.

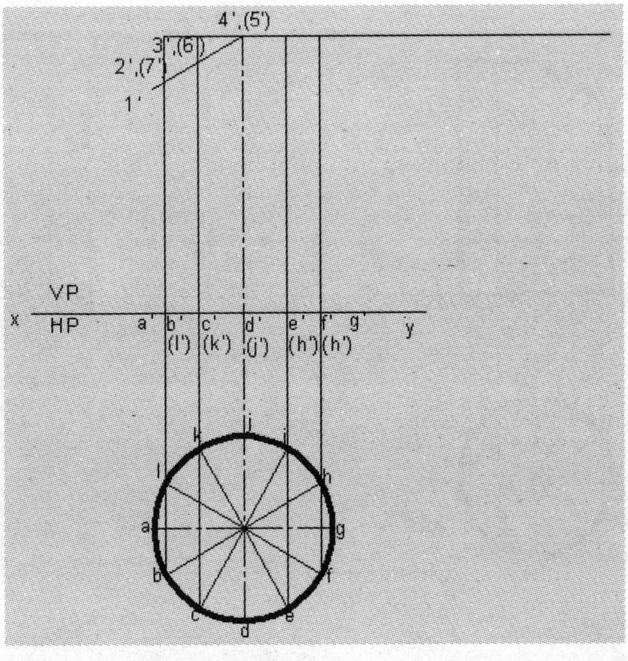

9. Draw downward projectors through 1′2′3′4′5′6′ and 7′ to meet the top view of the cylinder. Hatch the sectioned part in top view using CROSS HATCH COMMAND in drafting tool bar customize the properties if required in the selection tree.

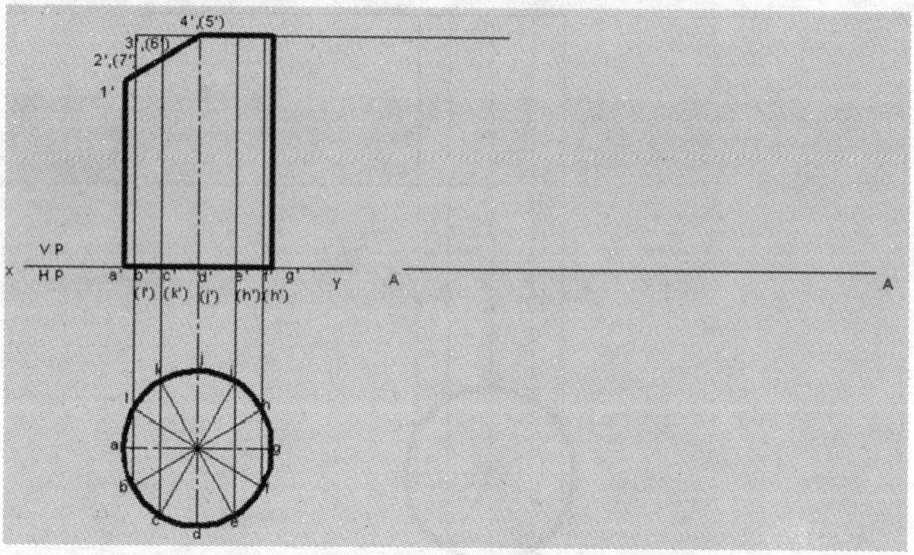

10. To draw a development, draw a line AA length equal to the circumference of the circle (πD). Draw a parallel line of length AA above XY line at height equal to height of cylinder 60mm (given) AA_1 using POLYLINE command in format select PL and draw AA_1 BB_1 CC_1 DD_1 EE_1 etc and AA_1 using POLYLINE command and OFFSET ON PLANE COMMAND enter the distance equal to arc length of the circle divided in mini dialog box as shown.

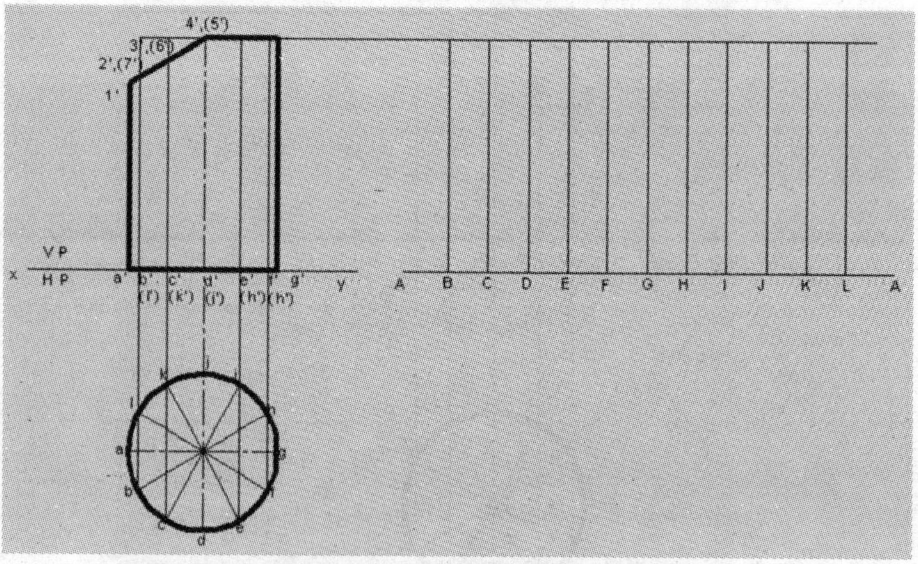

11. Draw the projection points from 1′ 2′ 3′ 4′ 5′ 6′ and 7′ on the corresponding development edges. Mark these points as 1 2 3 4 5 6 and 7 respectively by using INSERT TEXT command 

. The area A 1 2 3 4 5 6 7 1 and A represents the development of lower portion of the lateral surface of the prism. Join the area A 1 2 3 4 5 6 7 1 and A using 2 POINT LINE Command  and in format select VL as shown below.

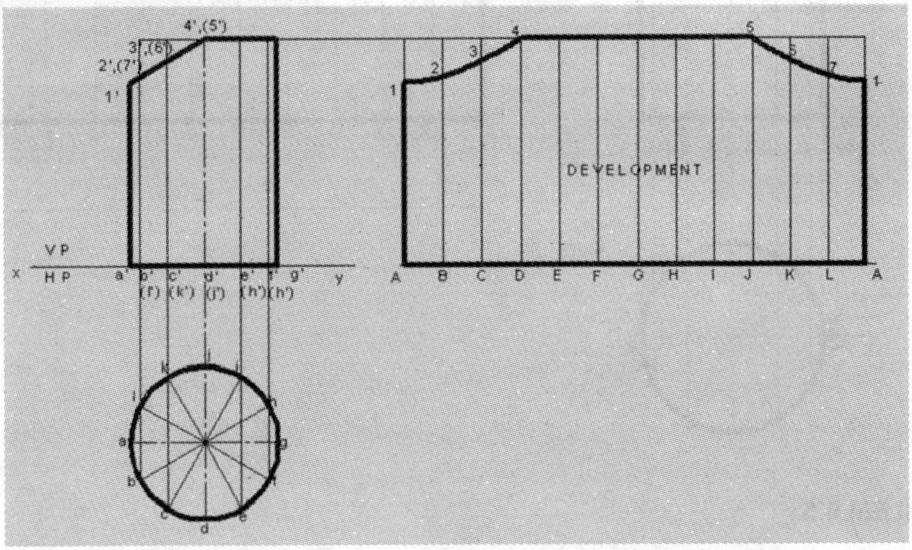

12. Using SMART DIMENSION Command  in drawing tool bar dimension the drawing as shown. To get a Hard Copy of the standard drawing select print from file menu bar. Print dialog window will appear select page and change width to Entities and select the activated button  now substitute width 1 as 0.15 mm, width 2 as 0.05 mm, width 3 as 0.5 mm, width 4 as 0.35 mm and say OK. Select print to get a hard copy and finally save the file. The required standard drawing is as shown below.

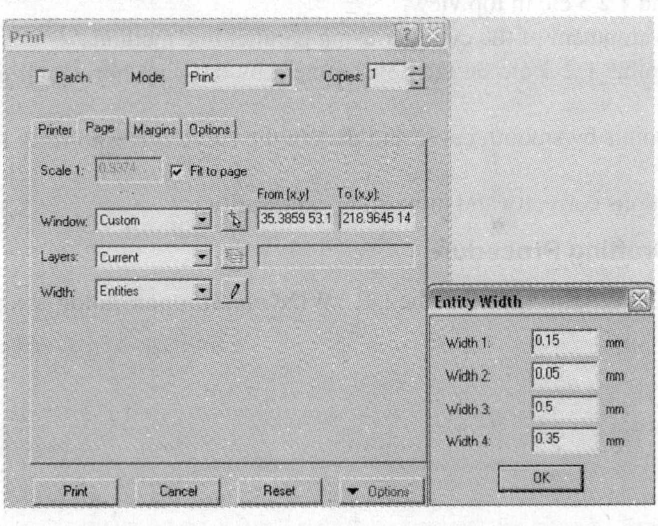

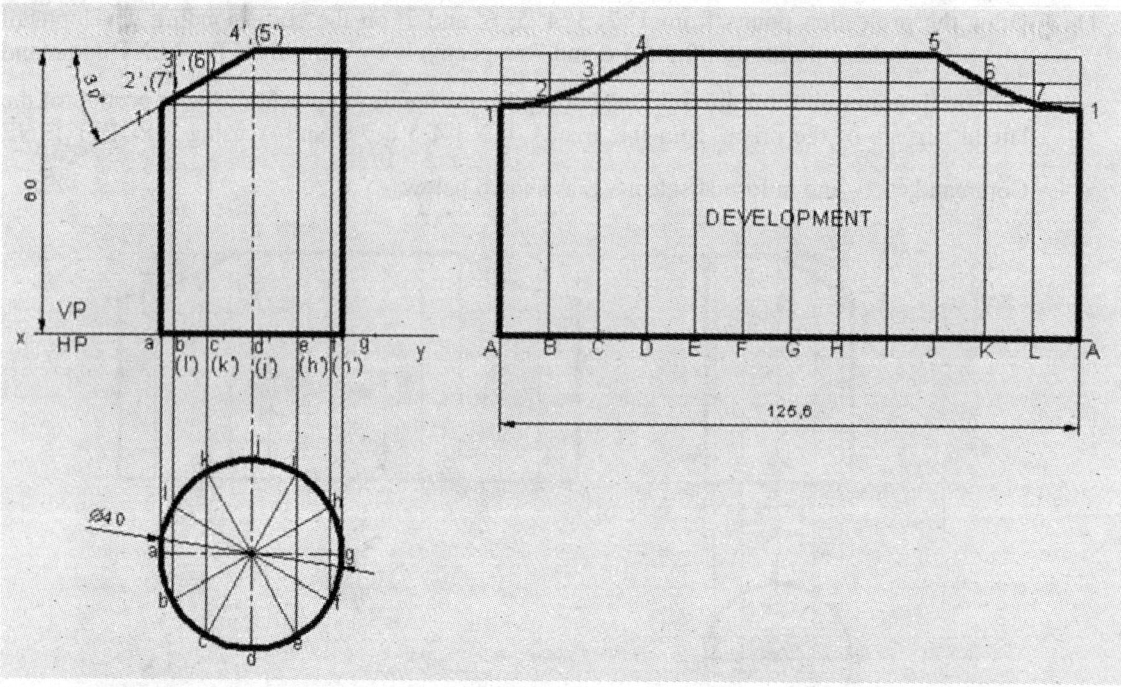

PROBLEM 6.5

Draw the development of the lateral surface of a truncated vertical cylinder, 40 mm diameter of base and height 50mm, the truncated flat surface of the cylinder bisects the axis at 60° to it.

SOLUTION

Manual Method

(a) Draw the top and front view of cylinder.

(b) Draw 60° line such that it bisects the axis of the cylinder in front view. Mark 1′ 2′ 3′ etc in front view and 1 2 3 etc in top view.

(c) Draw the development of the cylinder using parallel line method.

(d) Locate the points 1 2 3 etc on the development by drawing horizontal projector from 1′ 2′ 3′ etc.

(e) Join all the points by smooth curve and darken the curve corresponding to the retained portion of the solid.

(f) Mark annotations correctly and dimension necessarily.

Computer Aided Drafting Procedure

1. Open the SOFTWARE. Click on the DRAWING in the open dialog box and say OK.

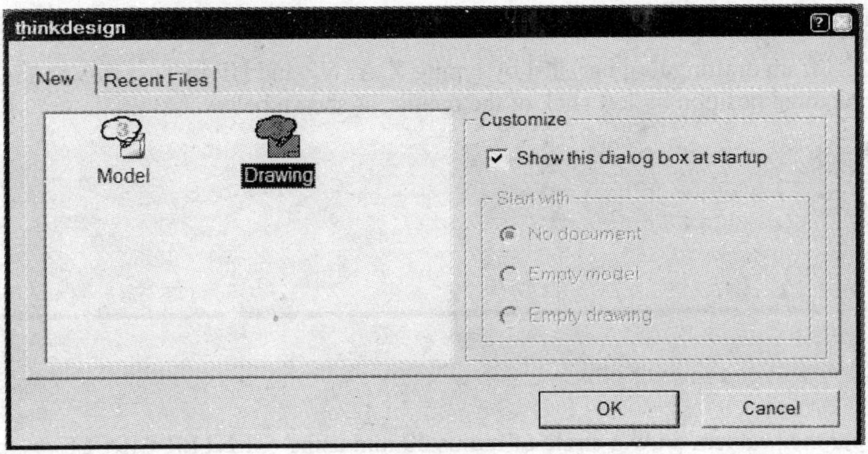

2. To set up the sheet of required size (Ex: A4) by selecting TOOLS from Main Menu Bar and click on OPTIONS/PROPERTIES. Select document properties in dialog box appeared and then select drawing in selection panel. Select the required size say A4, and click OK.

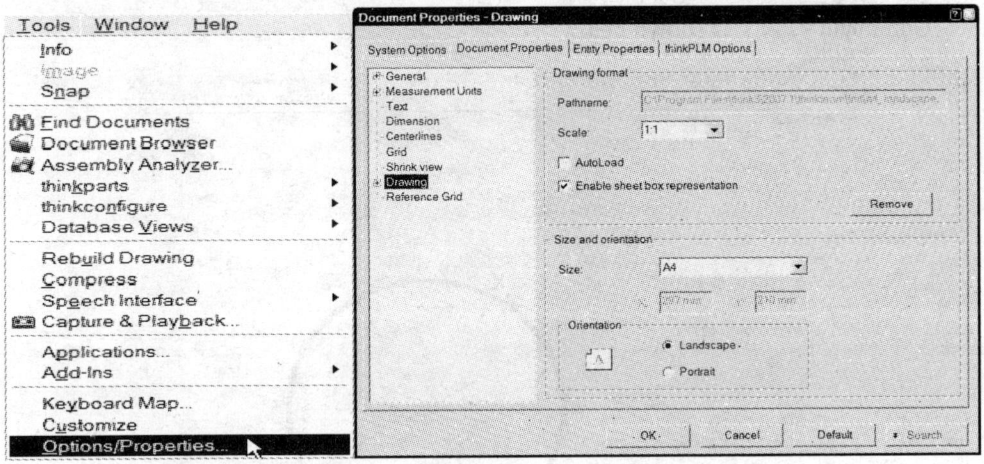

3. To draw XY line, projection lines, dotted lines, axis line, sectional line and top & front view lines. After selecting line command, in format select XY for XY line, PL for projection lines DL for dotted (hidden) lines, AL for axis line SL for section line and VL for top and front view lines before drawing these lines.

4. Draw the line by using POLYLINE  command from drafting tool bar and in format select XY.

5. Make Annotation X, Y, VP, and HP to the line drawn by using INSERT TEXT Command Aa from drafting tool bar, just by typing X, Y, VP and HP in Text Box and insert these in the required position by left click of the mouse, as shown below.

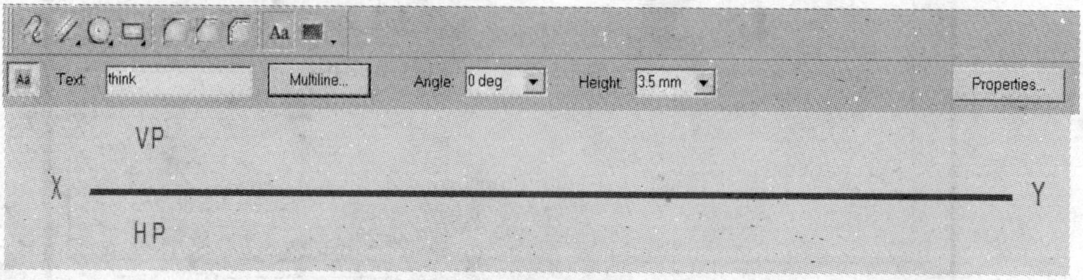

6. As per the problem draw a circle of radius 20 mm using CENTER CIRCLE command in drafting tool bar. In mode option select circle, enter radius as 20 to get top view. Divide the circle into 12 equal parts by using POLYLINE command and MOVE COPY command enter 30 degrees in mini dialog box. Mark the annotations using INSERT TEXT Command Aa as shown below.

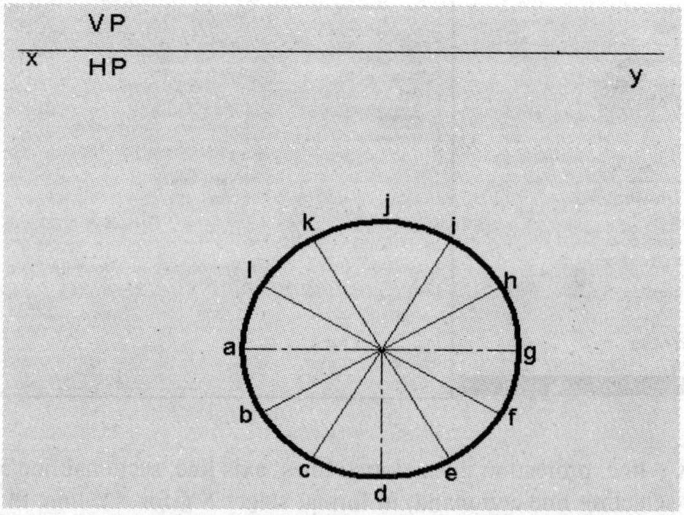

7. Draw the horizontal line at a distance of 50 mm i.e., equal to height of the cylinder above the XY line using PARALLEL LINE COMMAND and enter 50 in mini dialog box. Draw the vertical projection upwards from top view, until they intersect horizontal line at 50 mm above XY line using POLYLINE command. Mark the intersection points as shown. Trim all the unwanted construction lines by using SMART DELET COMMAND.

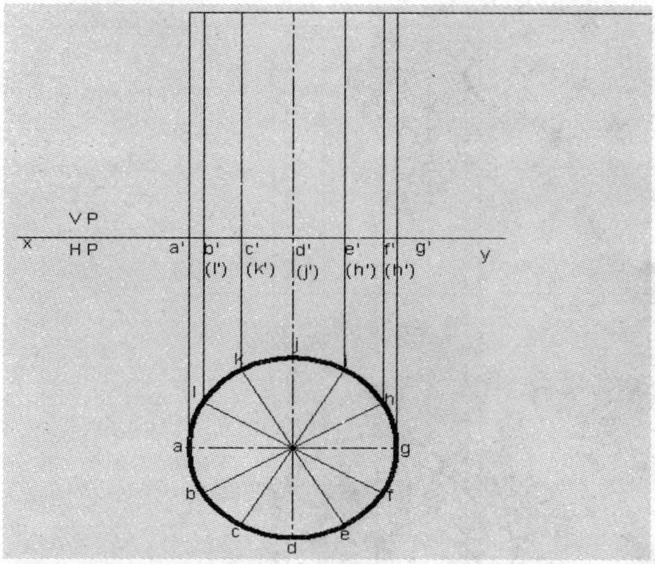

8. As per the problem using POLYLINE command and in format select SL draw 60° inclined line, such that it bisects the axis. Using INSERT TEXT Command mark 1′2′ 3′ etc and 12′ where the section plane cuts the cylinder as shown.

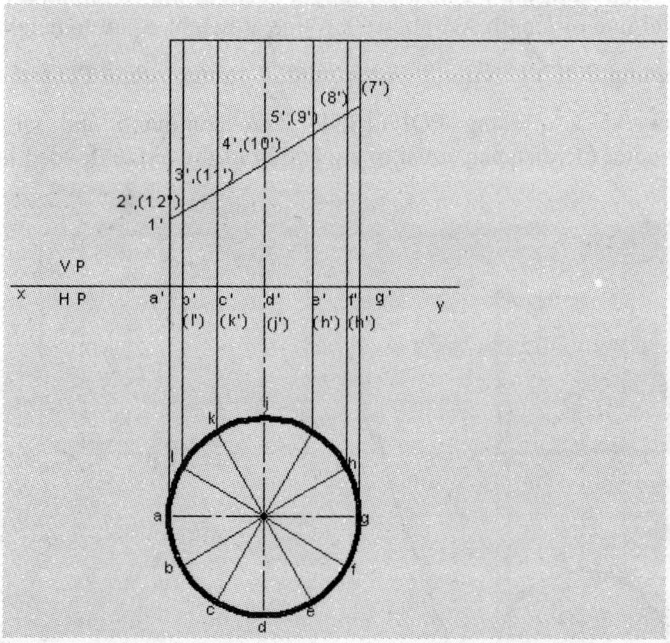

9. Draw downward projectors through 1′ 2′ 3′ etc and 12′ to meet the top view of the cylinder. Hatch the sectioned part in top view using CROSS HATCH COMMAND in drafting tool bar customize the properties if required in the selection tree.

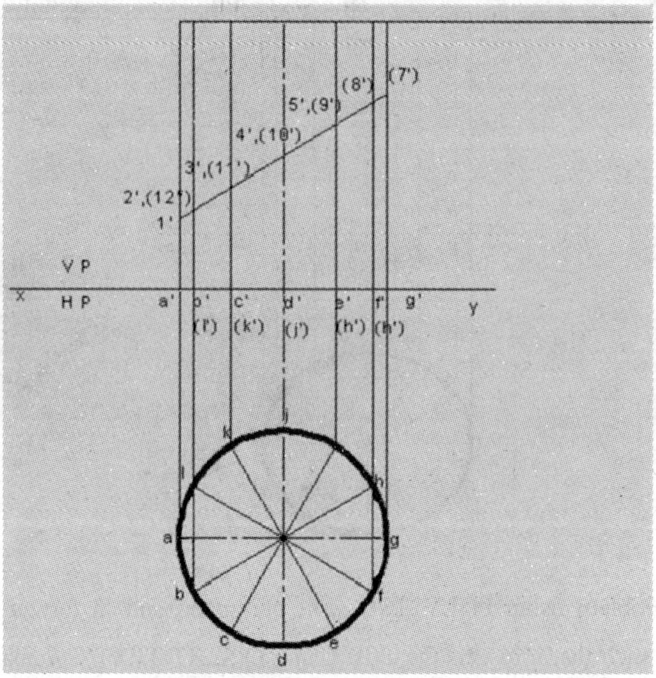

10. To draw a development, draw a line AA length equal to the circumference of the circle (πD). Draw a parallel line of length AA above XY line at height equal to height of cylinder 50 mm (given) AA_1 using POLYLINE command in format select PL and draw AA_1 BB_1 CC_1 DD_1 EE_1 etc and AA_1 using POLYLINE command and OFFSET ON PLANE COMMAND enter the distance equal to arc length of the circle divided in mini dialog box as shown.

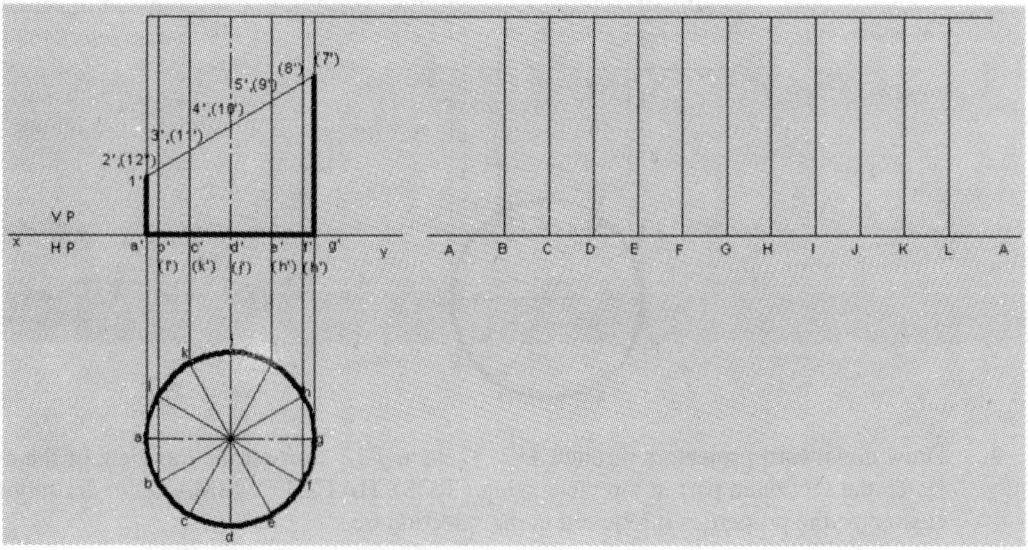

11. Draw the projection points from 1′2′3′ etc and 12′ on the corresponding development edges. Mark these points as 1 2 3 etc and 12 respectively by using INSERT TEXT command 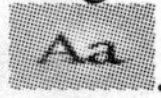. The area A 1 2 3 etc 1 and A represents the development of lower portion of the lateral surface of the cylinder. Join the area A 1 2 3 etc 1 and A using CURVE THROUGH CONTROL POINTS COMMAND in curve tool bar and 2 POINT LINE Command  and in format select VL as shown below.

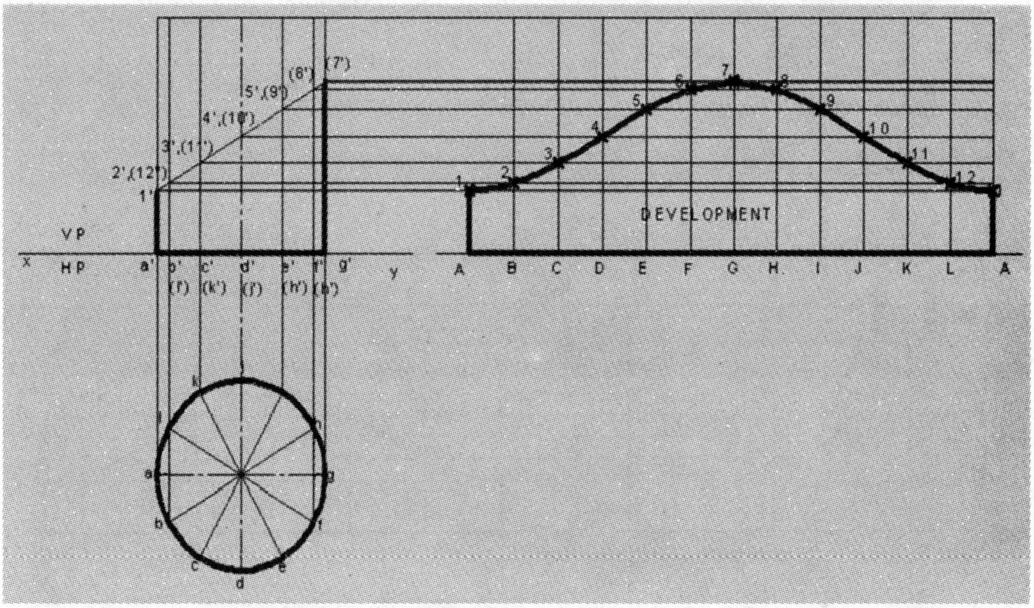

12. Using SMART DIMENSION Command  in drawing tool bar dimension the drawing as shown. To get a Hard Copy of the standard drawing select print from file menu bar. Print dialog window will appear select page and change width to Entities and select the activated button  now substitute width 1 as 0.15 mm, width 2 as 0.05 mm, width 3 as 0.5 mm, width 4 as 0.35 mm and say OK. Select print to get a hard copy and finally save the file. The required standard drawing is as shown below.

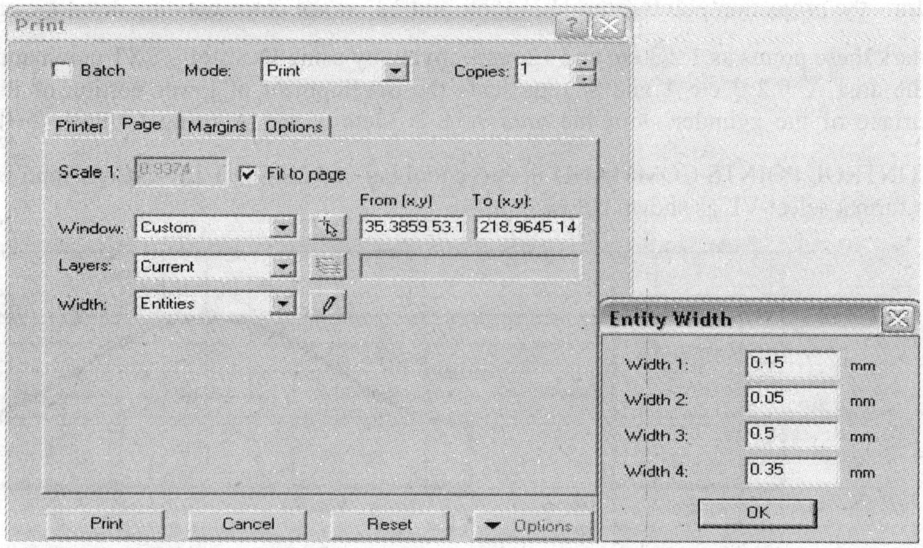

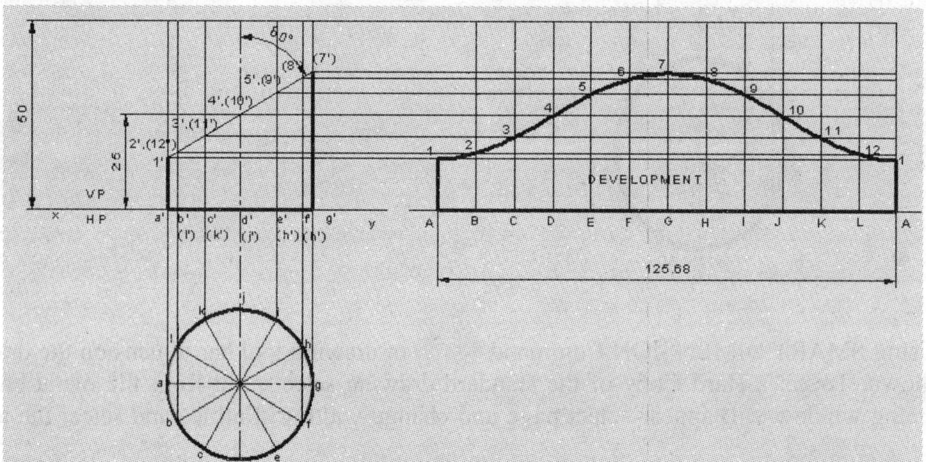

EXERCISE PROBLEMS

1. A square prism of base side 30 mm and axis length 60 mm is resting on HP on its base with all the vertical faces being equally inclined to VP. It is cut by an inclined plane 60° to HP and perpendicular to VP and is passing through a point on the axis at a distance 15 mm from the top face. Draw the development of the lower portion of the prism.
2. A square prism of base side 40 mm and axis length 65 mm is resting on HP on its base with all the vertical faces being equally inclined to VP. It is cut by an inclined plane 60° to HP and perpendicular to VP and is passing through a point on the axis at a distance 15 mm from the top face. Draw the development of the lower portion of the prism.

3. A cube of sides 40 mm is resting on HP with its base on HP such that one of its vertical faces is inclined at 30° to the VP. It is cut by a section plane perpendicular to VP, inclined to HP at an angle 45° and passes through the midpoint of the axis. Draw the development of the lower lateral surface of the cube.
4. A rectangular prism of base 30 mm x 20 mm and height 60 mm rests on HP on its base with the longer base side inclined at 40° to VP. It is cut by a plane inclined at 45° to HP, perpendicular to VP and bisects the axis. Draw the development of the lateral surface of the prism.
5. A pentagonal prism of 30 mm sides of base and height 50 mm lies with its base on HP such that one of the rectangular faces is inclined at 40° to VP. It is cut to the shape of a truncated pyramid with the truncated surface inclined at 30° to the axis so as to pass through a point on it 30 mm above the base. Develop the truncated portion of the prism so as to produce a one piece development.
6. A pentagonal prism of base sides 30 mm and axis length 60 mm rests with its base on HP and an edge of the base inclined at 45° to VP. It is cut by a plane perpendicular to VP, inclined at 40° to HP and passing through a point on the axis, at a distance of 30 mm from the base. Develop the remaining surfaces of the truncated prism.
7. A square pyramid of side of base 45 mm, altitude 70 mm is resting with its base on HP with two sides of the base parallel to VP. The pyramid is cut by a section plane which is perpendicular to the VP and inclined at 40° to the HP. The cutting plane bisects the axis of the pyramid. Obtain the development of the lateral surfaces the truncated pyramid.
8. A square pyramid base 40 mm side and axis 65 mm long has its base on HP and all the edges of the base are equally inclined to VP. It is cut by an inclined section plane so as the truncated surface at 45° to its axis, bisecting it. Draw the development of the truncated pyramid.
9. A regular pentagonal pyramid of side of base 35 mm and altitude 65 mm has its base on HP with a side of base perpendicular to VP. The pyramid is cut by a section plane which is perpendicular to the VP and inclined at 30° to HP. The cutting plane meets the axis of the pyramid at a point 30 mm below the vertex. Obtain the development of the remaining part of the pyramid.
10. A hexagonal pyramid 25 mm side of base and axis 65 mm long is resting on its base on HP with one of the edges of the base parallel to VP. It is cut by a vertical section plane at a distance of 8 mm from the axis towards right side. Develop the lateral surface of the left part of the pyramid.
11. A vertical cylinder of base diameter 45 mm and axis length 60 mm is cut by a plane perpendicular to VP and inclined at 50° to HP, is passing through the centre point of the top face. Draw the development of the lateral surface of the cylinder.
12. A vertical cylinder of base diameter 50 mm and axis length 60 mm is cut by a two planes which are perpendicular to VP and inclined at 45° to HP and passing through either side of the centre point of the top face. Draw the development of the lateral surface of the cylinder.
13. A right cone of 60 mm diameter of base and 75 mm height stands on its base on HP. It is cut to the shape of a truncated cone with its truncated surface inclined at 45° to the axis lying at a distance of 40 mm from the apex of the cone. Obtain the development of the lateral surface of the truncated cone.
14. A right cone of 45 mm diameter of base and 75 mm height stands on its base on HP. It is cut to the shape of a truncated cone with its truncated surface inclined at 30° to the axis lying at a distance of 40 mm from the base of the cone. Obtain the development of the lateral surface of the truncated cone.

15. Draw the development of the lateral surface of a funnel consisting of a cylinder and a frustum of a cone. The diameter of the cylinder is 20 mm and top face diameter of the funnel is 80 mm. The heights of frustum and cylinder are 60 mm and 40 mm respectively.

16. A rectangular prism of base size 25 mm×40 mm and axis length 65 mm is resting on HP on its base with the longer side of base inclined at 30° to VP. It is cut by a plane inclined at 40° to HP and perpendicular to VP and passes through the extreme left corner of base. Draw the development of the lateral surface of the remaining portion of the prism.

17. A regular pentagonal prism of height 60 mm and base edge 30 mm rests with its base on HP. The vertical face closest to VP is 30° to it. Draw the development of the truncated prism with its truncated surface inclined at 60° to its axis and bisecting it.

18. The inside of a hopper of a flour mill is to be lined with thin sheet. The top and bottom of the hopper are regular pentagons with each side equal to 30 mm and 22.5 mm respectively. The height of the hopper is 30 mm. Draw the shape of the sheet to which it is to be cut so as to fit into the hopper.

19. A hexagonal pyramid of sides 35 mm and altitude 65 mm is resting on HP on its base with two of the base sides perpendicular to VP. The pyramid is cut by a plane inclined at 30° to HP and perpendicular to VP and is intersecting the axis at 30 mm above the base. Draw the development of the remaining portion of the pyramid.

20. A funnel is to be made of sheet metal. The funnel tapers from 40 mm to 20 mm diameter to a height of 20 mm and from 20 mm to 15 mm diameter, for the next 20 mm height. The bottom of the funnel is beveled off to a plane inclined at 45° to the axis. Draw the development of the funnel.

■■■

7

ISOMETRIC PROJECTIONS OF COMBINED SOLIDS

INTRODUCTION

- Scales can then be used to draw the edges of a object which are parallel to the axes. How are Isometric projection is one of the three forms of axonometric projection. In isometric projection the angles between the projection of the axes are equal *i.e.* 120º. It is important to appreciate that it is the angles between the projection of the axes that are being discussed and not the true angles between the axes themselves which is always 90º.
- Isometric Scale: Seen how the edges appear shorten (foreshorten) when a view is taken which is not perpendicular to them. So how do we obtain the length of a foreshortened edge in order to draw it on paper? A foreshortened line is a smaller or scaled down version of its true length. Hence, we need to generate a scale to establish the length of the foreshortened edges of an object so that it can then be drawn on paper. In isometric the three angles between the projection of the axes are equal, so the degree of foreshortening along each of the axes is the same. Isometric means "equal measure". This means that only one set of scales is needed to draw an isometric projection of an object. These scales constructed?
- Let us take an isometric view of a cube. In order to see the true lengths of the edges that make up the top of the cube we need to rotate it until we are looking perpendicular to it. Lets rotate it about the line "AC". In its starting position line 'AB' made an angle of 30º with line 'AC'. However, in its final position, which shows the true lengths of the lines 'AB' and 'BC', line 'AB_1' makes an angle of 45º with line 'AC'.

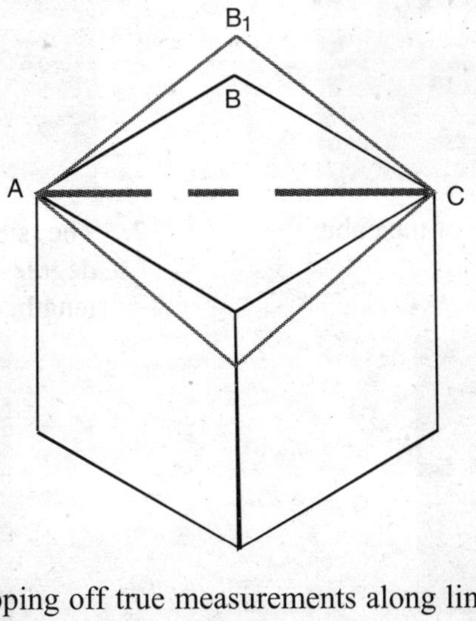

A scale is now constructed by stepping off true measurements along line 'AB_1' which is a true length line. The measurements are then transferred back to line 'AB' to get a smaller scale, in this case an isometric scale (which is the same procedure used in the division of lines). Lines drawn using the isometric scale are approximately 80% of true size. This scale is usually marked off on a piece of paper and used to step off the foreshortened measurements along the projection of axes lines and lines parallel to them. Lines parallel to the projection of axes are known as isometric lines. Lines which are not parallel to theses axes are known as non-isometric lines. It is important to note that you can only use the scales on isometric lines.

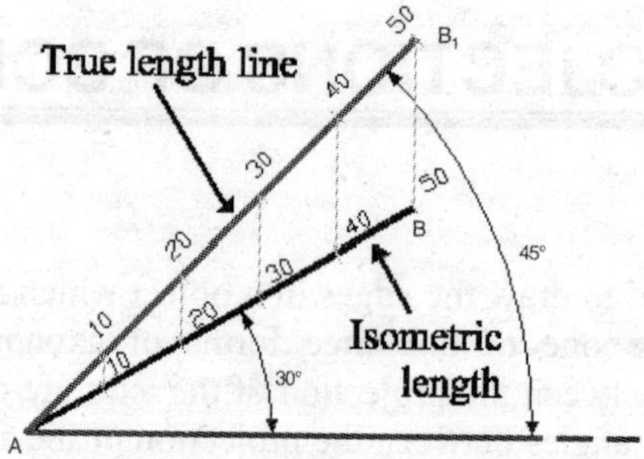

Following are the steps to draw isometric projections:
To draw in isometric you will need a 30 / 60 degree set square (As shown).

A 30 / 60 degree set square

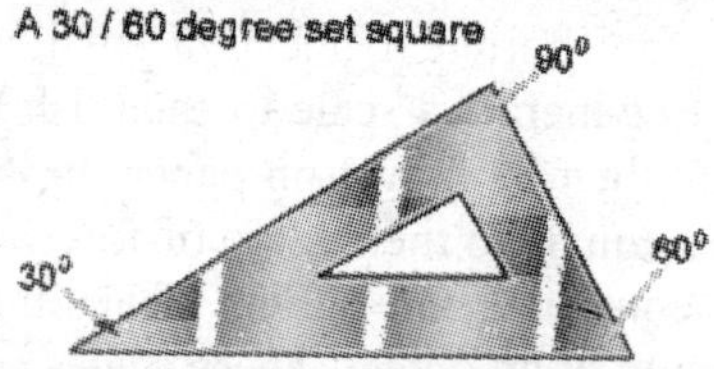

The steps below demonstrate how to draw a 5 cm^3 cube in isometric.

Drawing a box in isometric

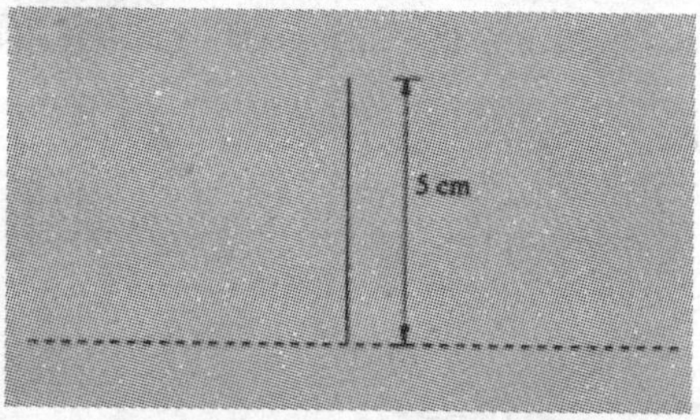

1. Draw the front vertical edge of the cube.

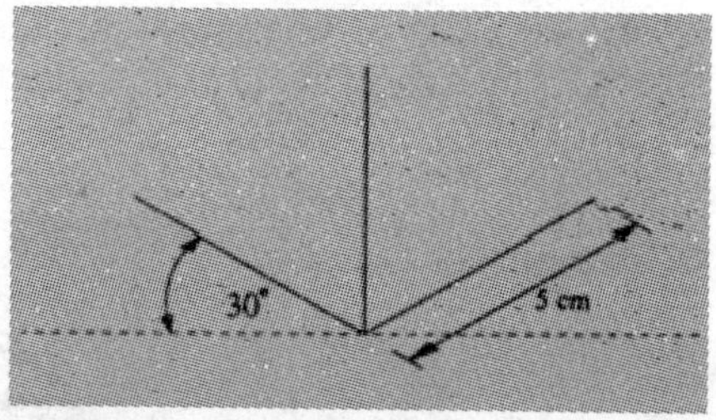

2. The sides of the box are drawn at 30 degrees to the horizontal to the required length. (5cm)

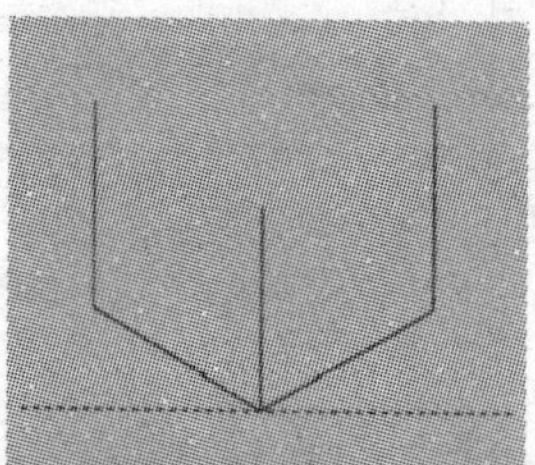

3. Draw all verticals.

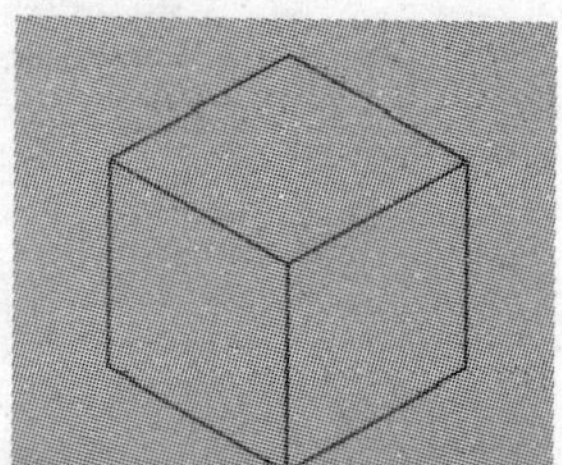

4. Drawn in top view with all lines drawn 30 degrees to the horizontal.

Note: All lengths are drawn as actual lengths in standard isometric.

System of Notation

1. The actual solid in space is denoted by capital letters A_1 , B_1, C_1 and D_1 etc for Base of solid and A, B, C and D etc for top face of the solid and axis as o_1 and o.
2. The front view (FV) of a solid is denoted by their corresponding lower case letters with dashes as a_1', b_1', c_1' and d_1' etc for base of solid and a′, b′ c′ and d′ etc for top face of the solid and for axis as o_1' and o′.
3. The top view (TV) of a solid is denoted by their corresponding lower case letters with dashes as a_1, b_1, c_1 and d_1 etc for bottom of solid and a, b c and d etc for top face of the solid and for axis as o_1 and o.
4. Projectors are always drawn as continuous thin lines.
5. Isometric projection annotations are made with the corresponding letters of the solid.
6. Line with specific thickness for a particular type of line.

In Computer Aided Engineering Graphics for isometric projections following commands are used other than evoking software, opening file, saving file and giving print command. Using these minimum15 commands any type of development of lateral surface problem can be solved they are as follows:

1. Select tool command.
2. Point command.
3. Poly-Line command.
4. Two Point Line command.
5. Parallel line command.
6. Center Circle command
7. Bisector command.
8. Smart Dimension command.
9. Line Width command.
10. Insert Text command.
11. Rectangle command.
12. Smart Delete command.
13. Offset on Plane command.
14. Curve through Control Points command.
15. Trim/Extend Curves command

PROBLEM 7.1

A rectangular pyramid of base 40 mm × 25 mm and height 50 mm is placed centrally on a rectangular slab of sides 100 mm × 60 mm and thickness 20 mm. Draw the isometric projection of the combination.

SOLUTION

Manual Method

(a) As per the problem draw orthographic projection of the combined solid (top and front view)

(b) Construct the isometric scale of suitable length.

(c) Draw reference lines at 300. Draw isometric projection of the rectangular prism base which is a parallelogram, of sides ISO 100 mm × ISO 60 mm on reference lines drawn, build vertical lines of height ISO 20 mm. join all the end points to get rectangular prism.

(d) Mark the center of top face of prism. Draw isometric projection of the rectangular pyramid base which is a parallelogram, of sides ISO 40 mm × ISO 25 mm and from center draw the vertical axis line of height ISO 50 mm and to get the apex of the rectangular pyramid apex.

(e) Join all the end points to apex to get the isometric projection of combined solid.

(f) Construction lines and unnecessary lines can be removed. Mark annotations correctly and dimension necessarily.

Computer Aided Drafting Procedure

1. Open the **SOFTWARE**. Click on the **DRAWING** in the open dialog box and say **OK**.
2. To set up the sheet of required size (Ex: A4) by selecting **TOOLS** from Main Menu Bar and click on **OPTIONS/PROPERTIES**. Select document properties in dialog box appeared and then select drawing in selection panel. Select the required size say A4, and click **OK**.
3. As per the problem draw top and front view of combined solids using suitable commands.

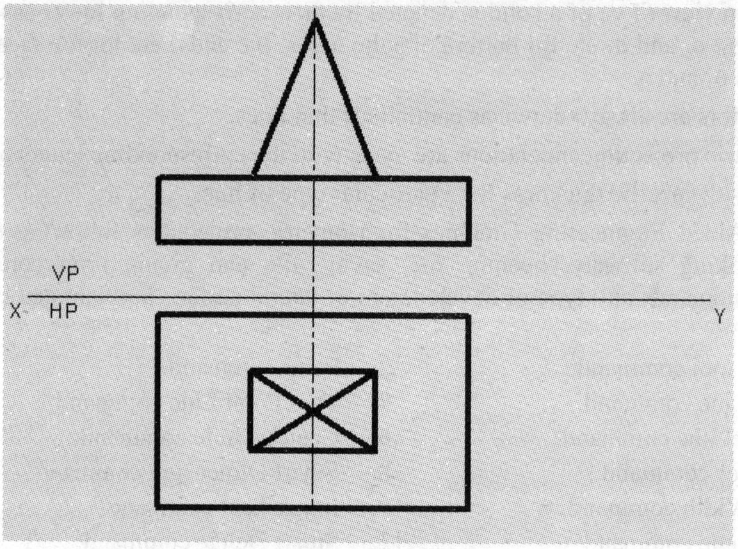

4. Draw the isometric scale, as per the dimensions of the problem.

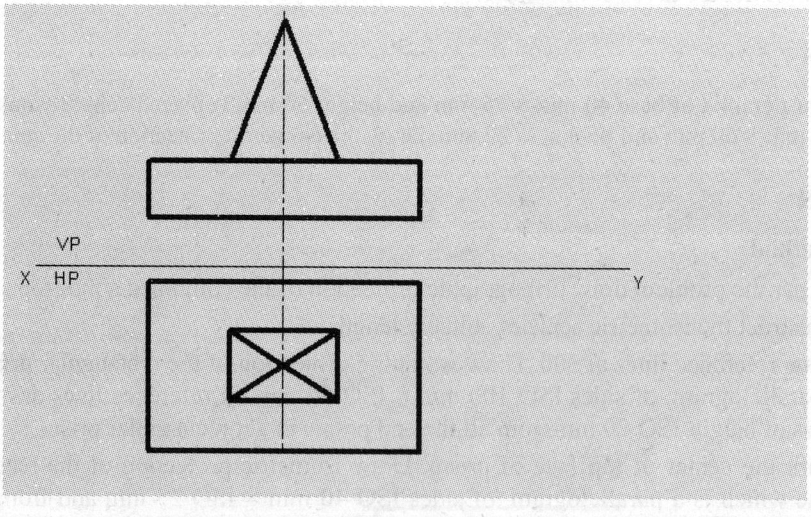

5. Using **POLYLINE**  command and in format select VL for visible edges draw two lines of iso length of 100 mm and 60 mm along 30° line as shown. Draw another two lines, using **PARALLEL LINE COMMAND** and using **TRIM/EXTEND CURVES** so that, they are connected systematically.

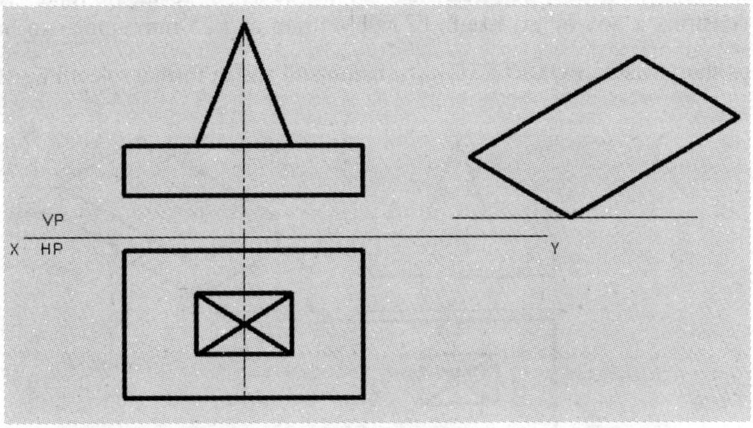

6. Draw the vertical lines at corners of parallelogram equal to isometric height of prism 20 mm using **POLYLINE** command and in format select VL.

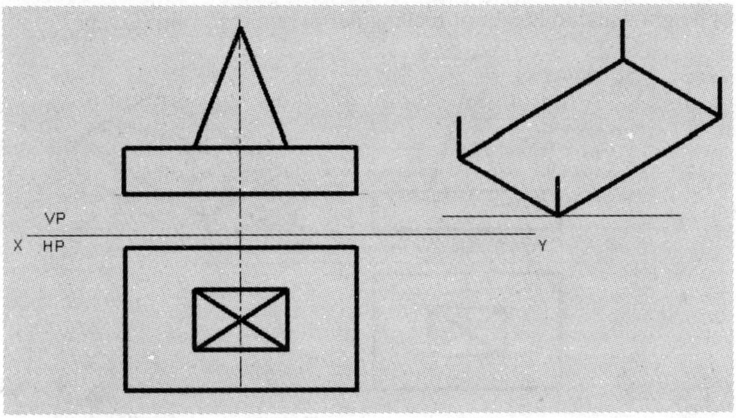

7. Join all the top end points using **2 POINT LINE** Command and in format select VL to get top face of prism as shown below.

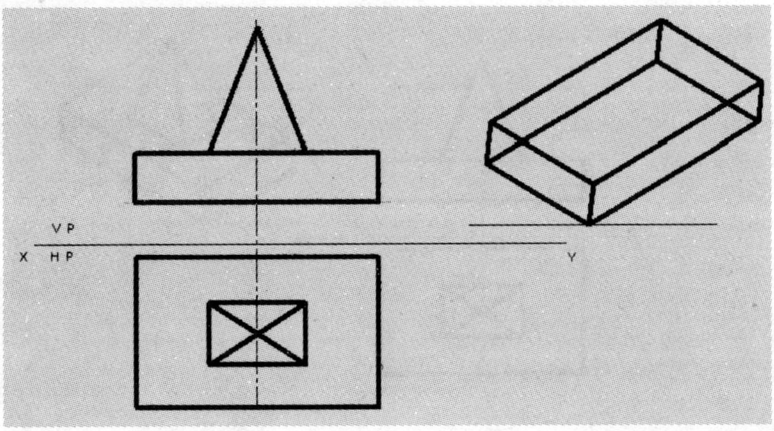

8. Since the axis of solids is collinear, identify the center of rectangle represent it as o. With o as center construct a box of iso length of side 40 mm and 25 mm similar to base rectangle drawn earlier as shown using **POLYLINE** command and in format select PL.

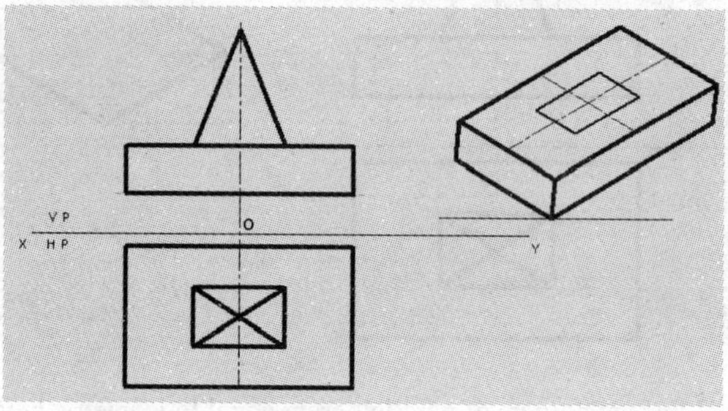

9. Using **POLYLINE** command and in format select AL draw vertical line upwards at the center o of height equal to height of rectangular pyramid 50 mm (given).

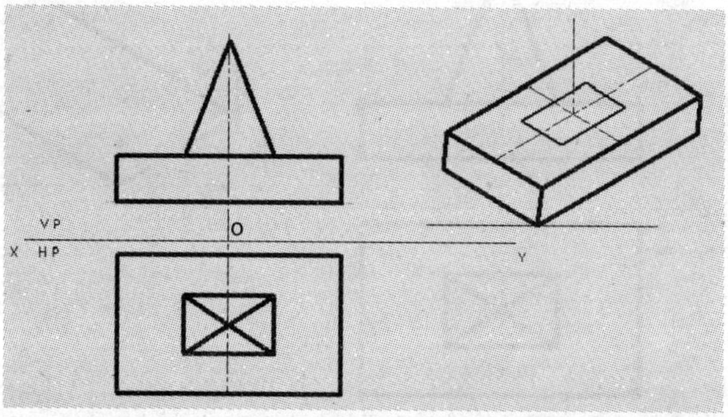

10. Join the base corners of the rectangular pyramid to apex as shown using **POLYLINE** command and in format select VL. Trim all the unwanted construction lines by using **SMART DELET COMMAND.**

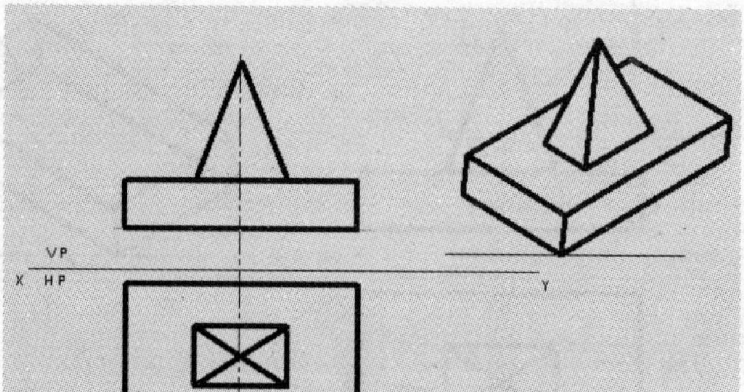

11. Using **SMART DIMENSION** command  in drawing tool bar dimension the drawing as shown. To get a Hard Copy of the standard drawing select print from file menu bar. Print dialog window will appear select page and change width to Entities and select the activated button  now substitute width 1 as 0.15 mm, width 2 as 0.05 mm, width 3 as 0.5 mm, width 4 as 0.35 mm and say **OK.** Select print to get a hard copy and finally save the file. The required standard drawing is as shown below.

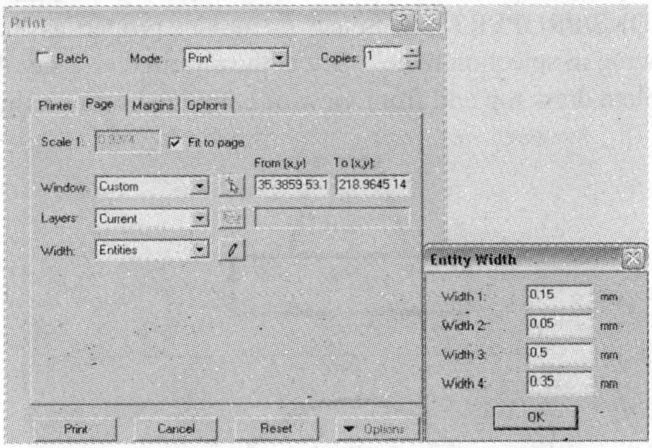

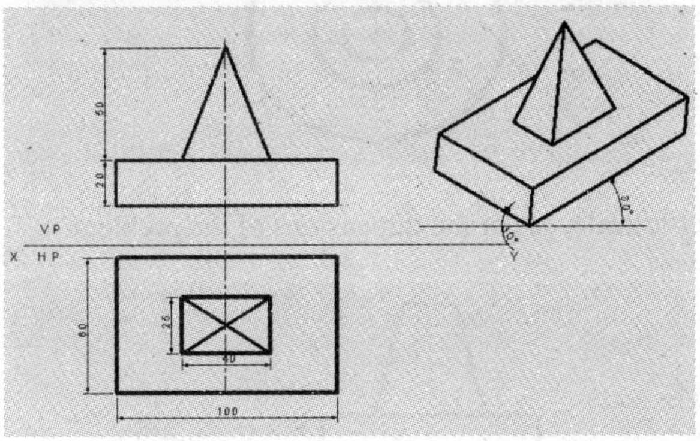

PROBLEM 7.2

A frustum of cone base diameter 50mm, top diameter 25mm and height 50mm is placed centrally on a cylindrical slab of diameter 100mm and thickness 30mm. Draw the isometric projection of combined solids.

SOLUTION

Manual Method:

(a) Draw the XY line. Mark VP above it and HP below it.

(b) Mark a point 40 mm above XY line. This is the front view of P. Name it as a p′.

(c) Draw a vertical projector downwards through p, measure a distance of 30 mm below XY line. This is the top view of P. Name it as p.

(d) Draw a reference line X_1Y_1 perpendicular to XY at a distance of 50 mm from the projector, which intersects at O.

(e) Draw a line passing through O inclined at 45° in HP.

(f) Draw a horizontal projector through p until it meets 45° line, from there draw a vertical projector upwards above XY line.

(g) Draw a horizontal projector through p, which gives lefts side view. Name as p″.

Computer Aided Drafting Procedure

1. Open the **SOFTWARE**. Click on the DRAWING in the open dialog box and say OK.
2. To set up the sheet of required size (Ex: A4) by selecting TOOLS from Main Menu Bar and click on OPTIONS/PROPERTIES. Select document properties in dialog box appeared and then select drawing in selection panel. Select the required size say A4, and click OK.
3. As per the problem draw top and front view of combined solids using suitable commands.

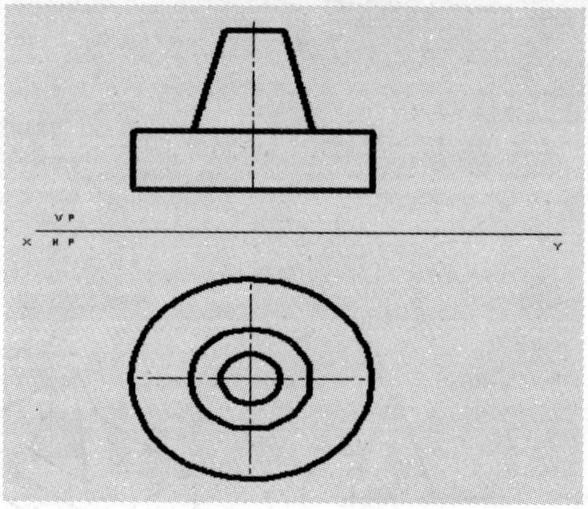

4. Draw the isometric scale, as per the dimensions of the problem.

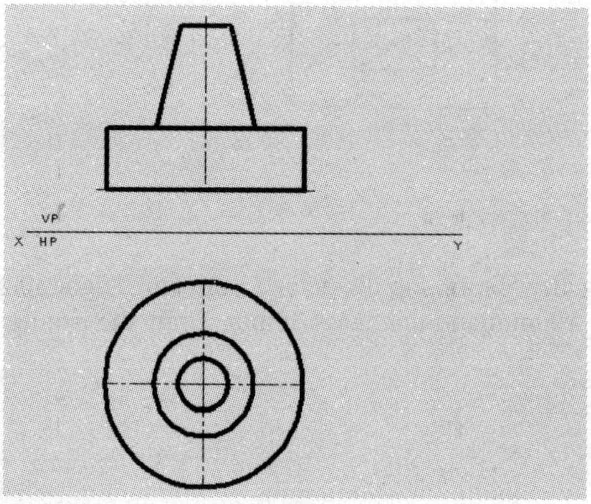

5. Using **POLYLINE** command and in format select PL for construction lines draw two lines, of iso length of 100 mm along 30° line as shown. Draw another two lines, using **PARALLEL LINE COMMAND** and using **TRIM/EXTEND CURVES,** so that they are connected systematically.

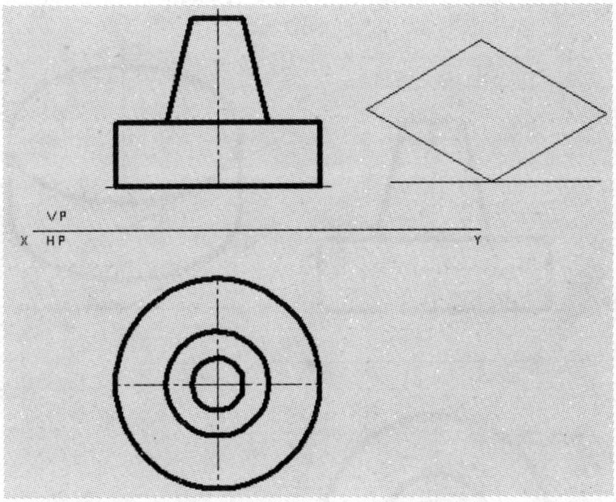

6. Draw the vertical lines at corners of parallelogram equal to isometric height of cylindrical slab of 30 mm using **POLYLINE** command and in format select PL. Using **CENTER CIRCLE** command in drafting tool bar. In mode option select arc, and use four center method draw an ellipse to get the top and bottom of cylindrical slab.

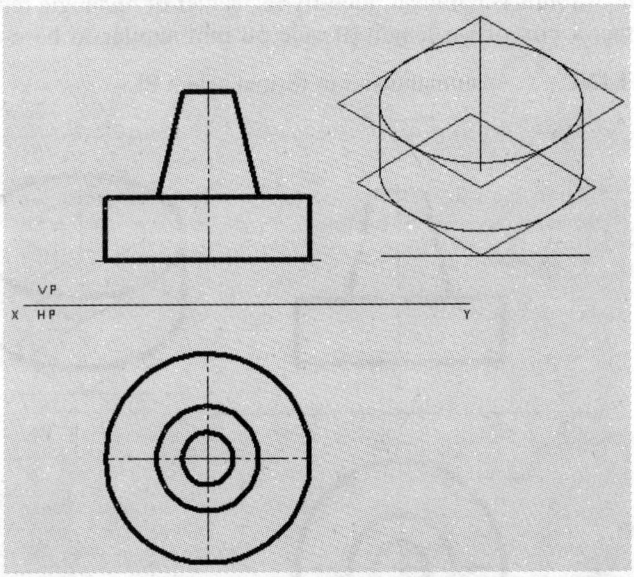

7. Draw two tangential lines on either side, such that to form a cylindrical slab using **2 POINT LINE** command and in format select VL to get complete view.

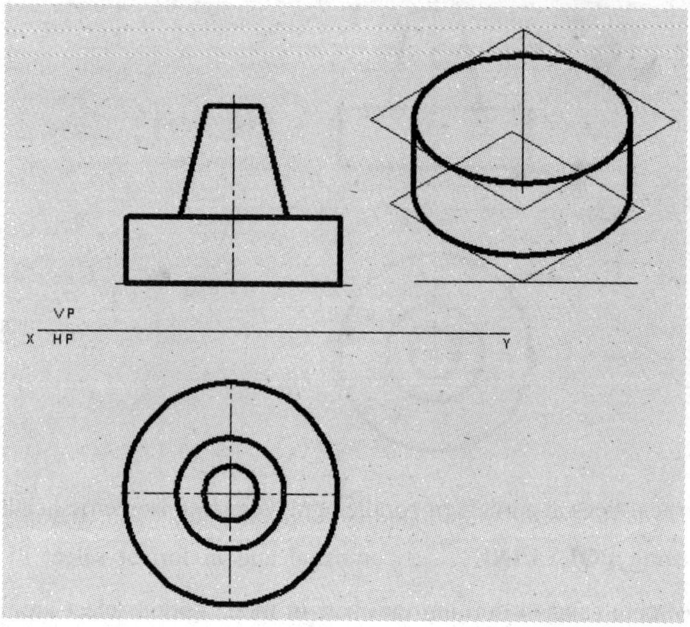

8. Since the axis of solids is collinear, identify the center of rectangle represent it as o. With o as center construct a box of iso length of side 50 mm similar to base drawn earlier as shown using **POLYLINE** command and in format select PL.

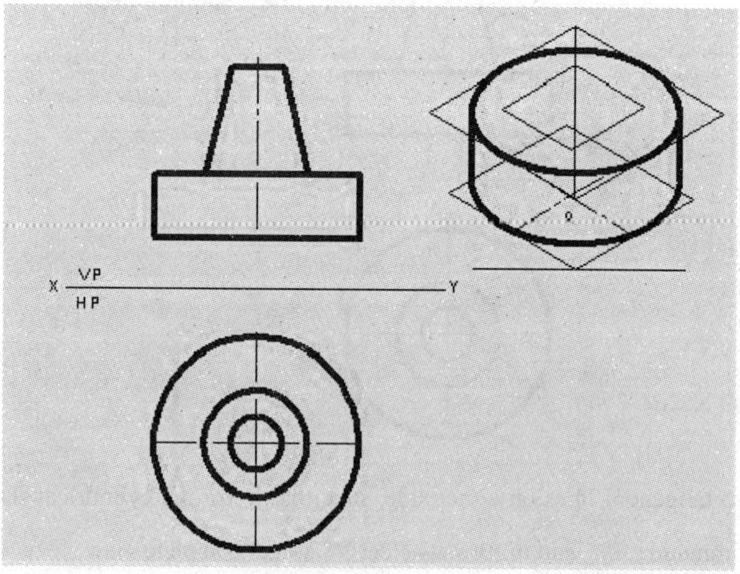

9. Using **CENTER CIRCLE** command in drafting tool bar. In mode option select arc, and use four center method draw an ellipse to get the bottom of frustum of cone.

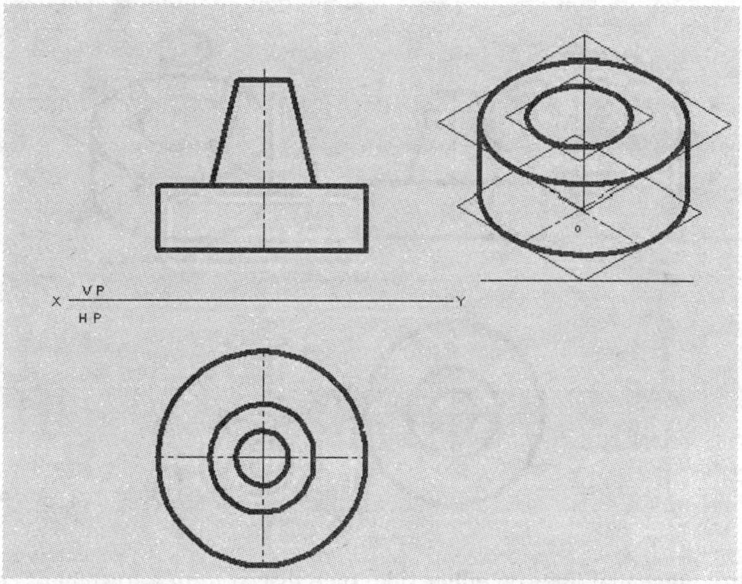

10. Using **POLYLINE** command and in format select AL draw vertical line upwards at the center o of height equal to height of frustum of cone 50 mm (given).

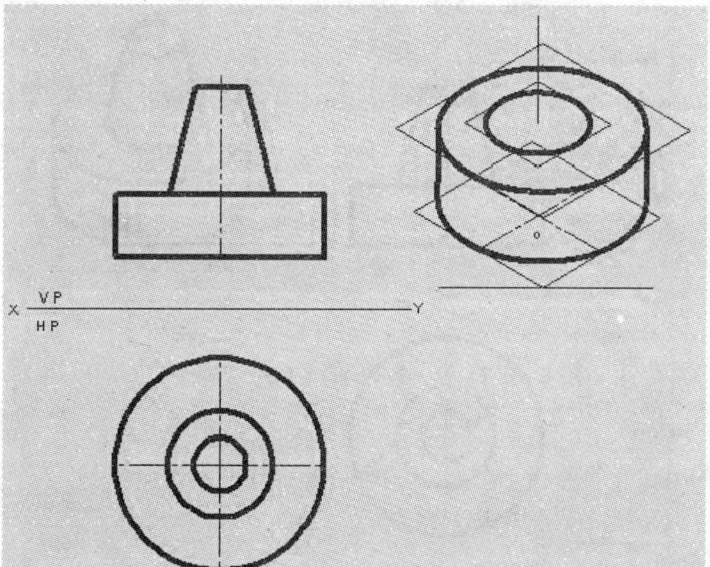

11. Draw a box of iso length of side 25 mm similar to base drawn earlier and using **CENTER CIRCLE** command in drafting tool bar. In mode option select arc, and use four center method draw an ellipse to get the top face of cone.

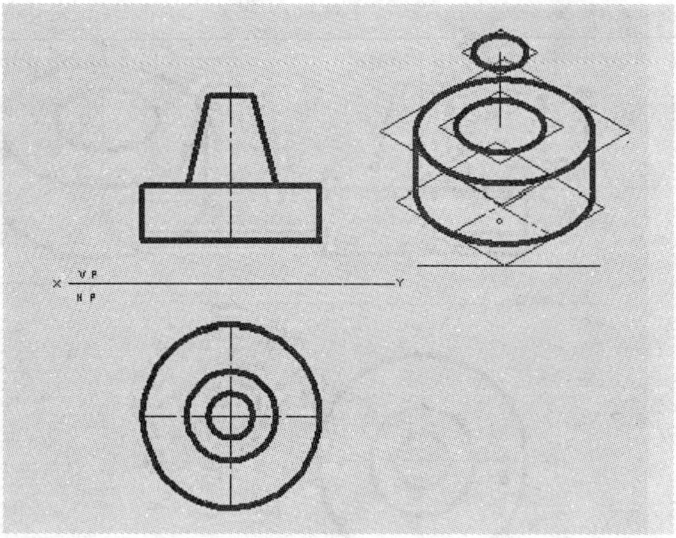

12. Draw two tangential lines on either side, such that to form a frustum of cone using **2 POINT LINE** command  and in format select VL to get complete view. Trim all the unwanted construction lines by using **SMART DELETE COMMAND.**

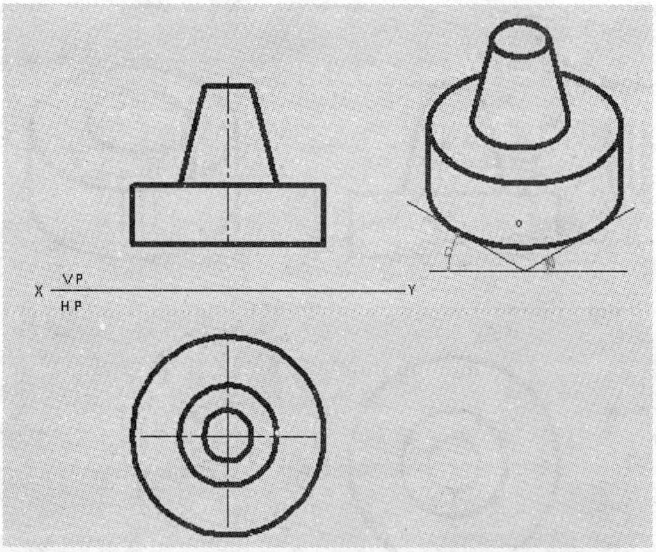

13. Using **SMART DIMENSION** command  in drawing tool bar dimension the drawing as shown. To get a Hard Copy of the standard drawing select print from file menu bar. Print dialog window will appear select page and change width to Entities and select the activated button  now substitute width 1 as 0.15 mm, width 2 as 0.05 mm, width 3 as 0.5 mm, width 4 as 0.35 mm and say **OK.** Select print to get a hard copy and finally save the file. The required standard drawing is as shown below.

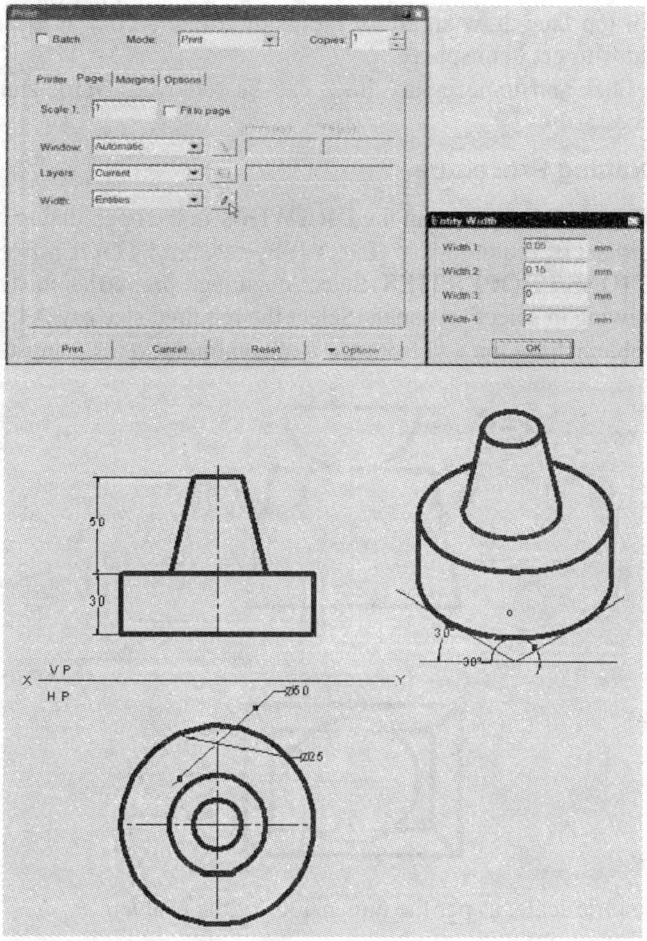

PROBLEM 7.3

A hemisphere diameter 50mm is resting on its curved surface centrally on the top face of frustum of a rectangular pyramid base 80mm x 60mm and top 60mm x 40mm, height 55mm. Draw the isometric projection of combined solids.

SOLUTION

Manual Method

1. As per the problem draw orthographic projection of the combined solid (top and front view)
2. Construct the isometric scale of suitable length.
3. Draw reference lines at 30^0. Draw isometric projection of the rectangular frustum base which is a parallelogram. Draw sides of ISO 80 mm × ISO 60 mm on the vertical line, at this end draw another parallelogram of sides ISO 60 mm × ISO 40 mm and connect corner of base to top to get rectangular frustum.
4. From the center of top face of base solid. Draw a vertical axis of length ISO 25 mm, at this end point construct a parallelogram of ISO 50 mm × ISO 50 mm and inscribe an ellipse which form top face of hemisphere.

5. With center of top face draw an arc of radius of 25mm so that it is tangential to top face of hemisphere draw to get hemisphere.
6. Construction lines and unnecessary lines can be removed. Mark annotations correctly and dimension necessarily.

Computer Aided Drafting Procedure

1. Open the **SOFTWARE**. Click on the **DRAWING** in the open dialog box and say **OK**.
2. To set up the sheet of required size (Ex: A4) by selecting **TOOLS** from Main Menu Bar and click on **OPTIONS/PROPERTIES**. Select document properties in dialog box appeared and then select drawing in selection panel. Select the required size say A4, and click **OK**.
3. As per the problem draw top and front view of combined solids using suitable commands.

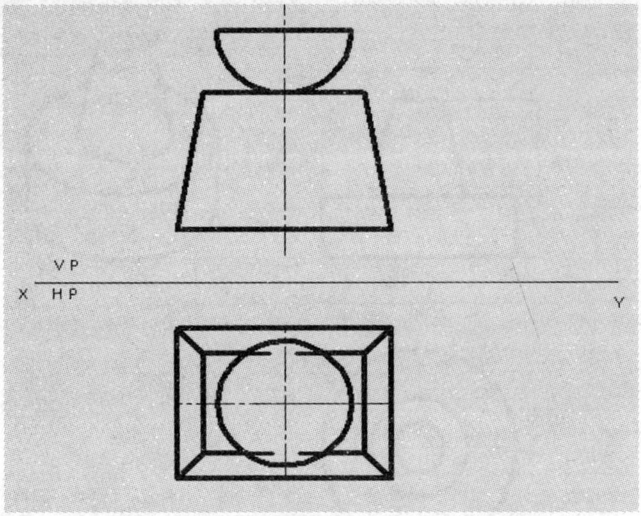

4. Draw the isometric scale, as per the dimensions of the problem.

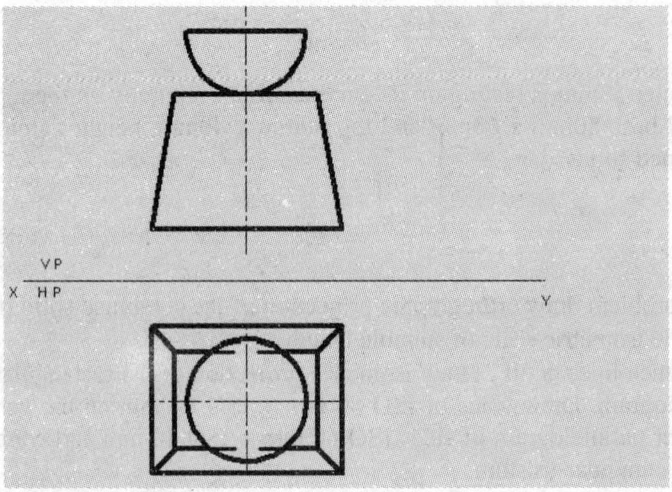

5. Using **POLYLINE** command and in format select VL for visible edges draw two lines of iso length of 80 mm and 60 mm along 30° line as shown. Draw another two lines, using

PARALLEL LINE COMMAND and using **TRIM/EXTEND CURVES** so that, they are connected systematically.

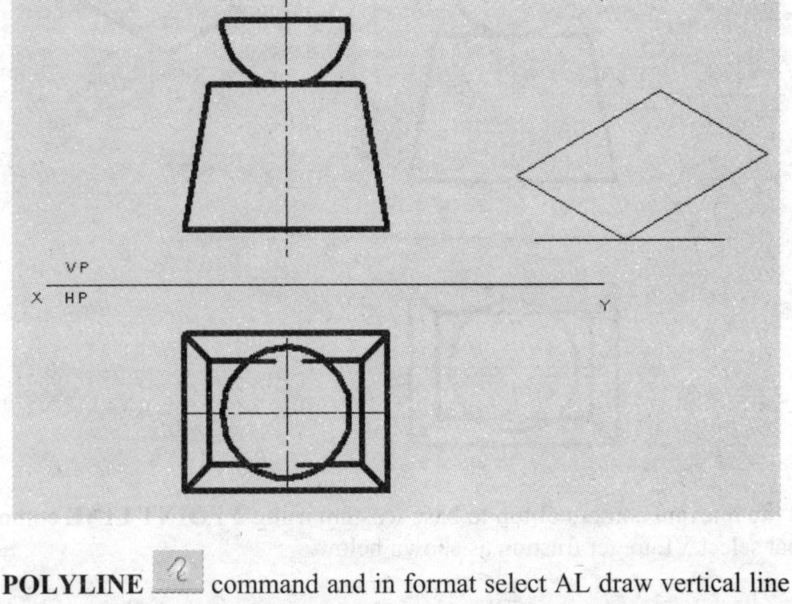

6. Using **POLYLINE**  command and in format select AL draw vertical line upwards at the center of rectangle, equal to the height of rectangular frustum 55 mm (given).

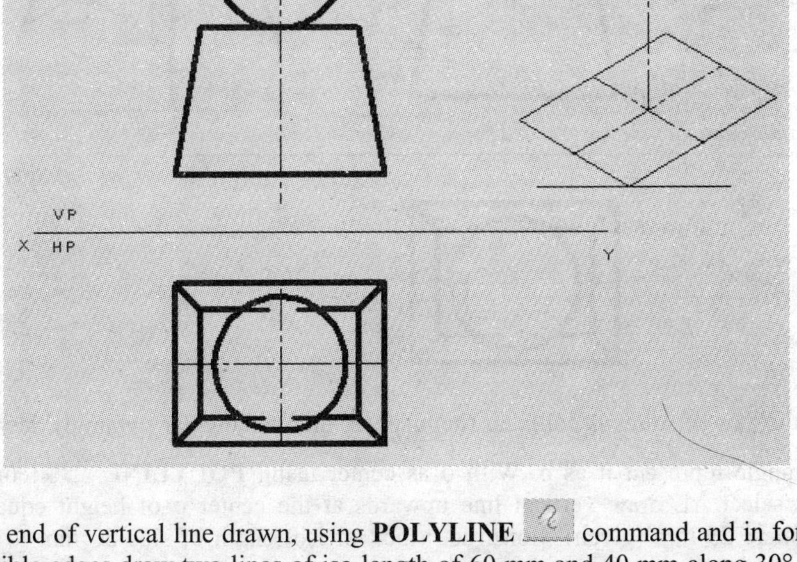

7. At top end of vertical line drawn, using **POLYLINE**  command and in format select VL for visible edges draw two lines of iso length of 60 mm and 40 mm along 30° line as shown. Draw another two lines, using **PARALLEL LINE COMMAND** and using **TRIM/EXTEND CURVES** so that, they are connected systematically.

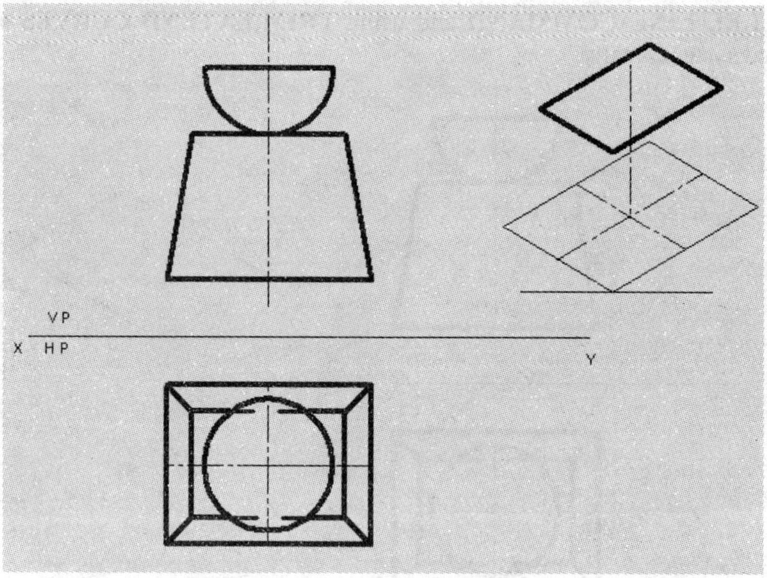

8. Join all the relevant corners of top to base frustum using **2 POINT LINE** command and in format select VL to get frustum as shown below.

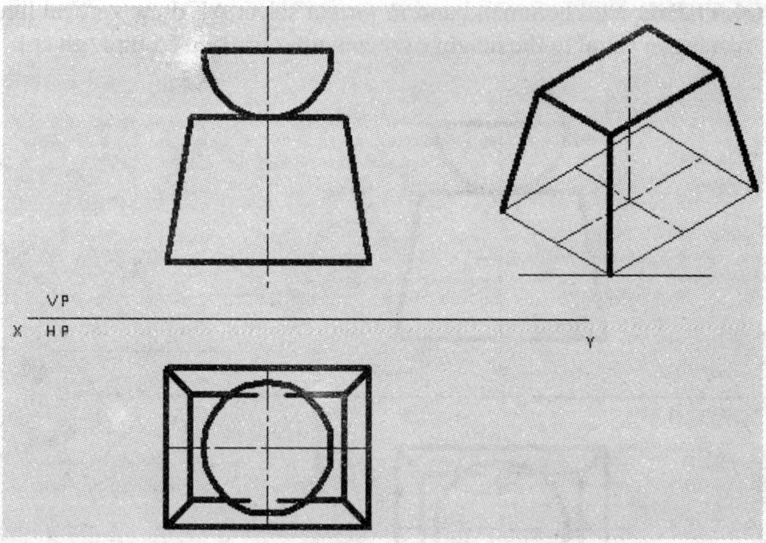

9. Since the axis of solids is collinear (hemisphere and rectangular pyramid), identify the center of rectangle represent it as o. With o as center using **POLYLINE** command and in format select AL draw vertical line upwards at the center o of height equal to height of hemisphere 25 mm (given). Construct a box of iso length of side 50 mm to fit top face of hemisphere using **POLYLINE** command and in format select PL.

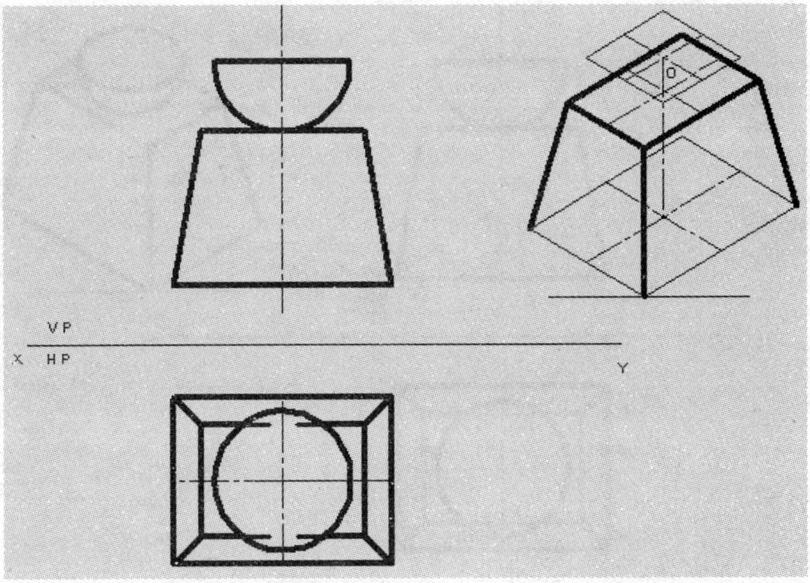

10. Using **3 POINT CIRCLE**  command in drafting tool bar. In mode option select arc, and select 3 points on rectangle draw a top face of hemisphere.

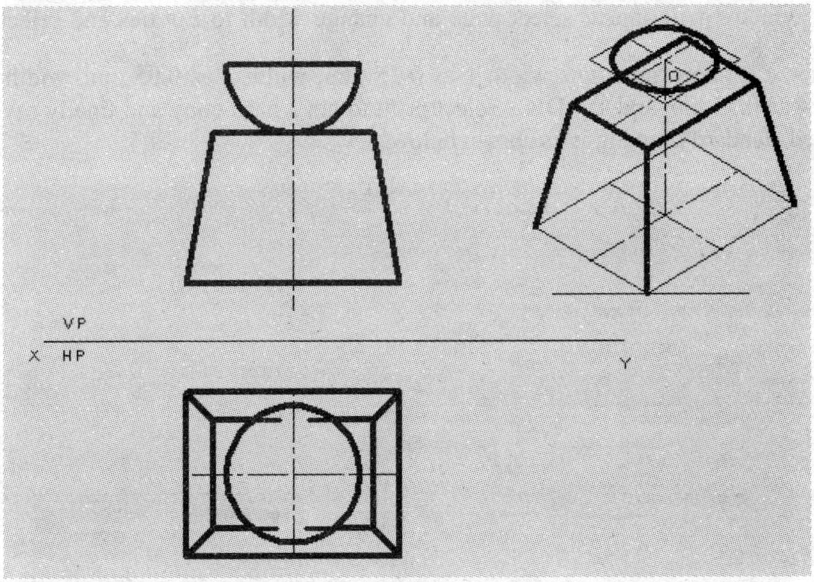

11. Using **CENTER CIRCLE**  command in drafting tool bar. In mode option select arc, with center as center of top face of hemisphere and radius as actual radius of hemisphere draw an arc, so that it touches the top face of hemisphere and passes through the center of top face of the rectangle frustum.

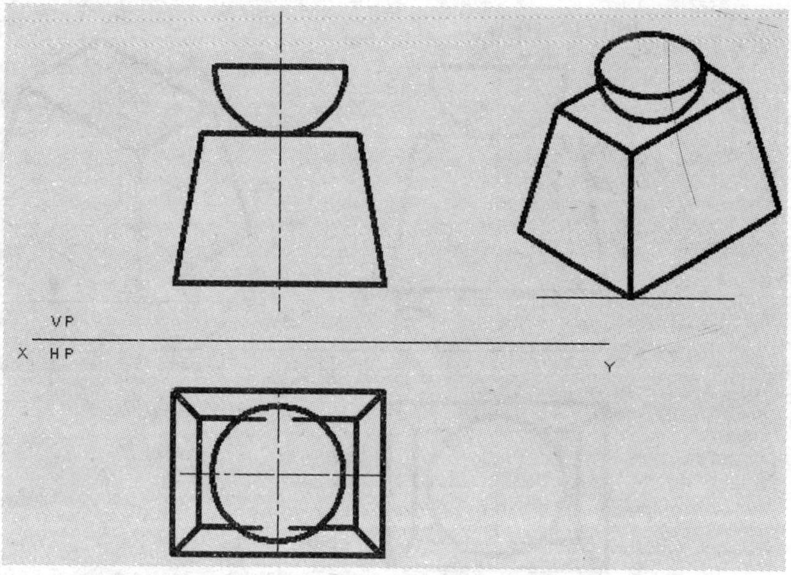

12. Trim all the unwanted construction lines by using **SMART DELETE COMMAND.** Using **SMART DIMENSION** command  in drawing tool bar dimension the drawing as shown.To get a Hard Copy of the standard drawing select print from file menu bar. Print dialog window will appear select page and change width to Entities and select the activated button  now substitute width 1 as 0.15 mm, width 2 as 0.05 mm, width 3 as 0.5 mm, width 4 as 0.35 mm and say **OK.** Select print to get a hard copy and finally save the file. The required standard drawing is as shown below.

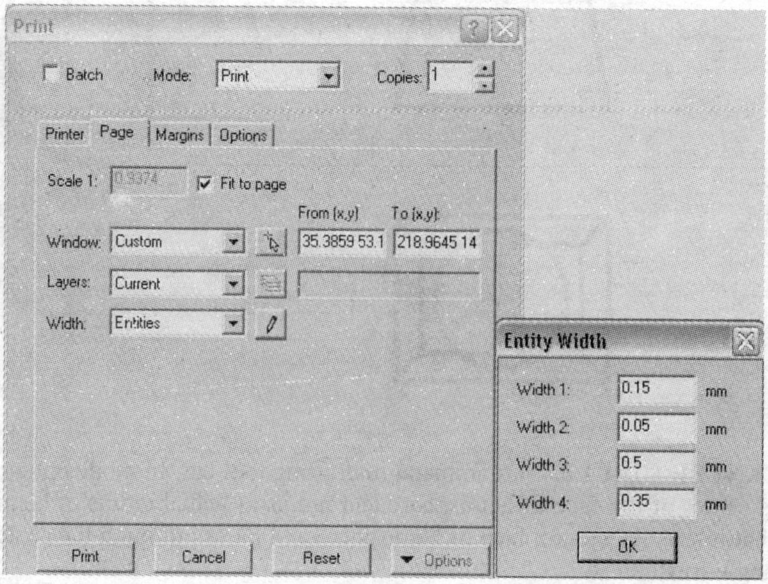

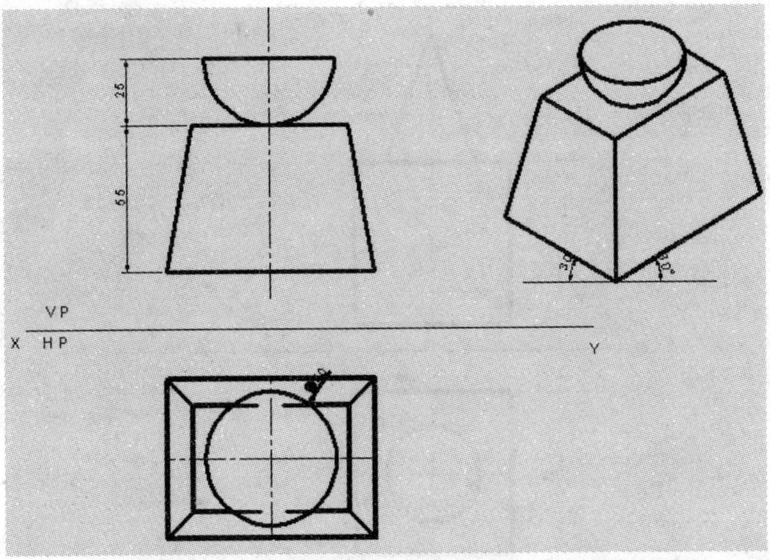

PROBLEM 7.4

A of cone base diameter 30mm and height 40mm rests centrally over a cube of side 50mm. Draw the isometric projection of combination of solids.

Solution

Manual Method:

1. As per the problem draw orthographic projection of the combined solid (top and front view)
2. Construct the isometric scale of suitable length.
3. Draw reference lines at 30°. Draw isometric projection of the square prism base which is a rhombus. Draw sides of ISO 50 mm × ISO 50 mm on reference lines drawn, build vertical lines of height ISO 50 mm at corners. Join all the end points to get square prism.
4. Mark the center of top face of base solid. Draw isometric projection of the cone base which is an ellipse, draw sides of ISO 30 mm × ISO 30 mm, inscribe ellipse. From center draw the vertical axis line of height ISO 40 mm to get apex of cone.
5. Draw two tangential lines on either side from apex to ellipse draw to get cone.
6. Construction lines and unnecessary lines can be removed. Mark annotations correctly and dimension necessarily.

Computer Aided Drafting Procedure

1. Open the **SOFTWARE**. Click on the **DRAWING** in the open dialog box and say **OK**.
2. To set up the sheet of required size (Ex: A4) by selecting **TOOLS** from Main Menu Bar and click on **OPTIONS/PROPERTIES**. Select document properties in dialog box appeared and then select drawing in selection panel. Select the required size say A4, and click **OK**.
3. As per the problem draw top and front view of combined solids using suitable commands..

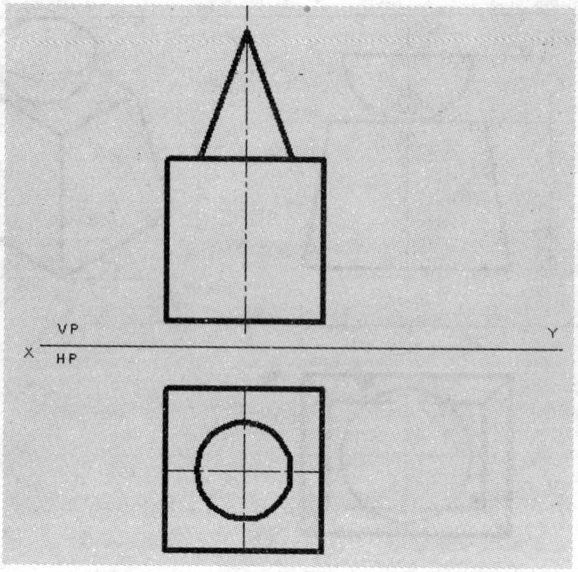

4. Draw the isometric scale, as per the dimensions of the problem.

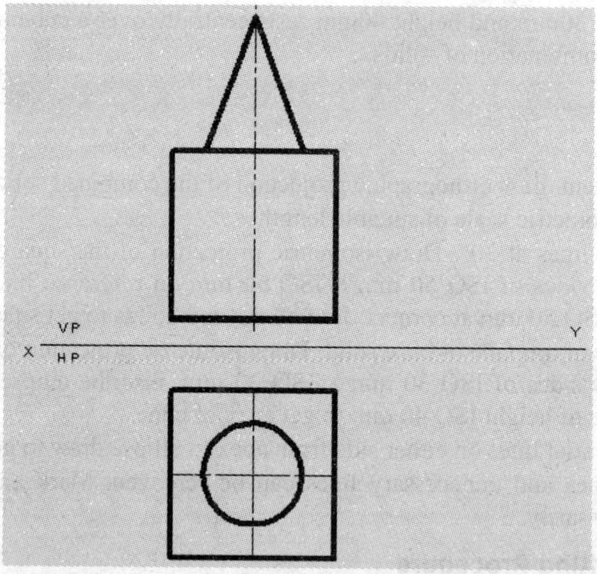

5. Using **POLYLINE** command and in format select PL for construction lines draw two lines of iso length of 50 mm along 30° line as shown. Draw another two lines, using **PARALLEL LINE COMMAND** and using **TRIM/EXTEND CURVES,** so that they are connected systematically.

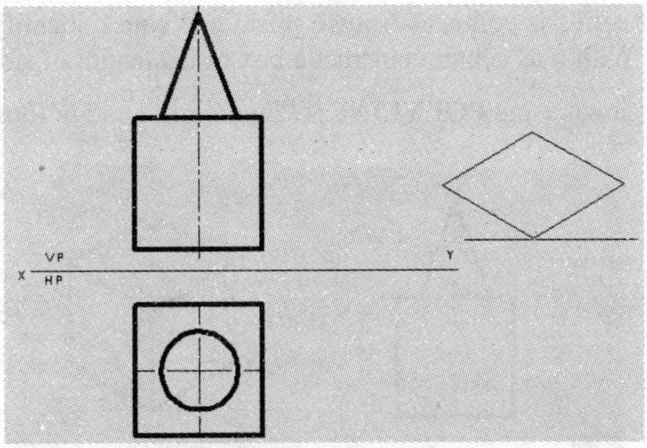

6. Draw the vertical lines at corners of parallelogram equal to isometric height of square prism of 50 mm using **POLYLINE** command and in format select VL.

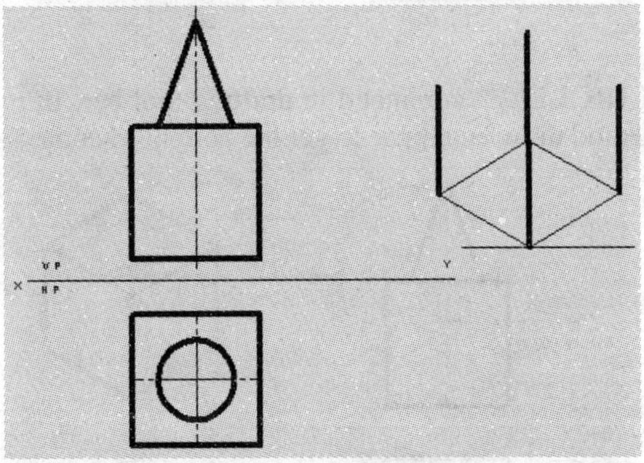

7. Join all the top end points using **2 POINT LINE** Command and in format select PL to get top face as shown below.

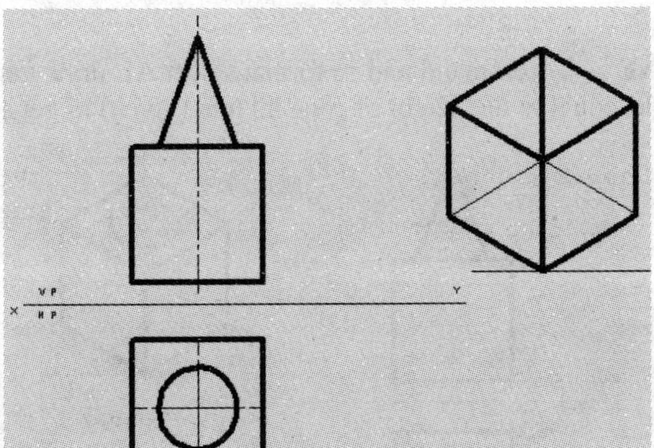

8. Since the axis of solids is collinear (square prism and cone), identify the center of rectangle represent it as o. With o as center construct a box of iso length of side 30 mm similar to base drawn earlier as shown using **POLYLINE** command and in format select PL.

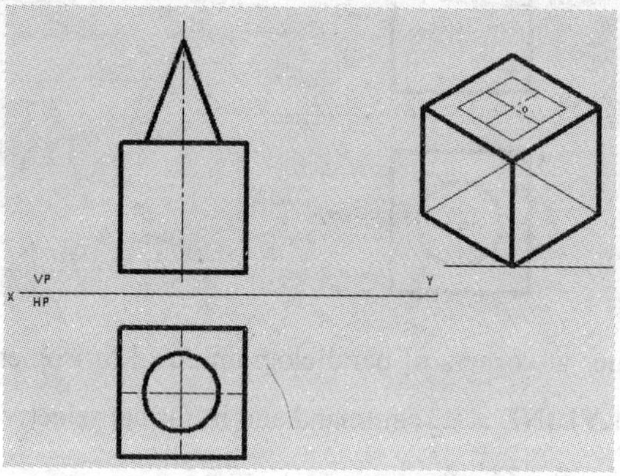

9. Using **3 POINT CIRCLE** command in drafting tool bar. In mode option select arc, and use three center method draw an ellipse to get the bottom of cone.

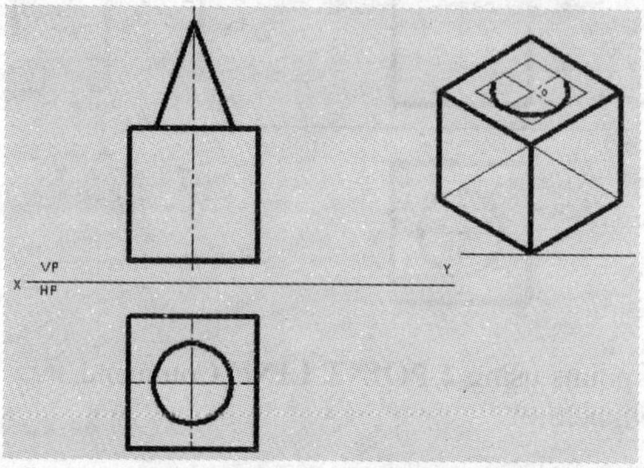

10. Using **POLYLINE** command and in format select AL draw vertical line upwards at the center of rectangle, equal to the height of cone 40 mm (given) to get apex of the cone.

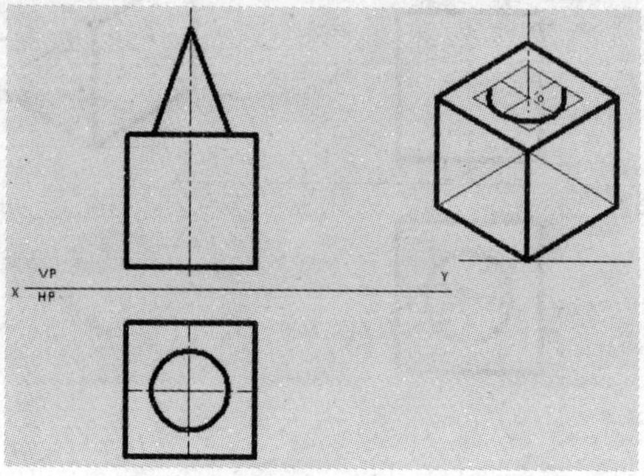

11. Using **POLYLINE**  command and in format select VL draw tangential line from bottom of cone to apex as shown. Trim all the unwanted construction lines by using **SMART DELETE COMMAND.**

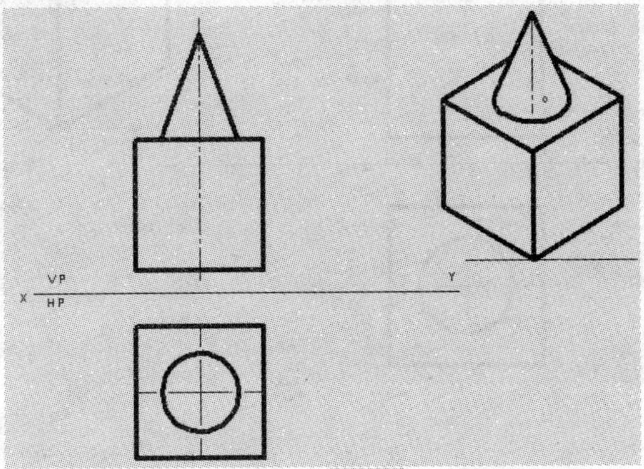

12. Using **SMART DIMENSION** Command  in drawing tool bar dimension the drawing as shown. To get a Hard Copy of the standard drawing select print from file menu bar. Print dialog window will appear select page and change width to Entities and select the activated button  now substitute width 1 as 0.15 mm, width 2 as 0.05 mm, width 3 as 0.5 mm, width 4 as 0.35 mm and say **OK.** Select print to get a hard copy and finally save the file. The required standard drawing is as shown below.

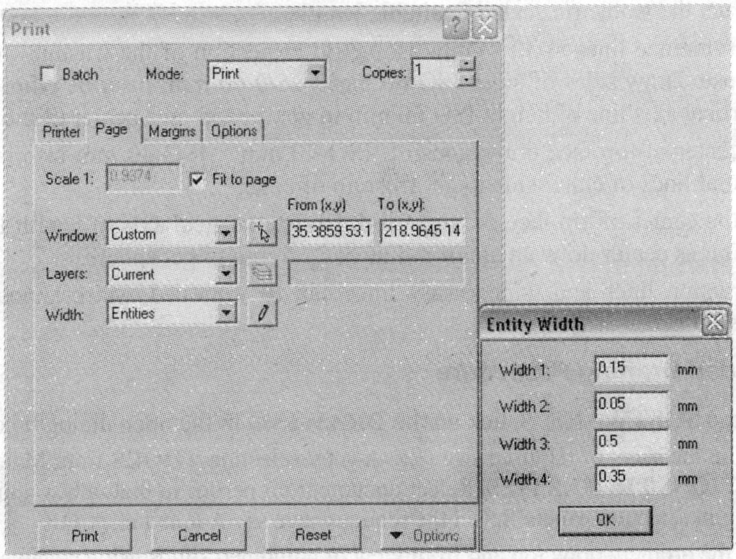

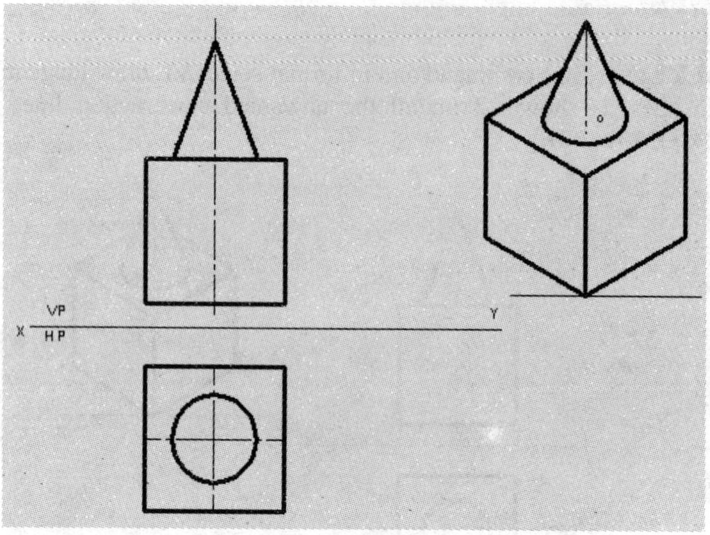

PROBLEM 7.5

A sphere of diameter 45mm rests centrally over a frustum of cone of base diameter 60mm, top diameter 40mm and height 60mm. Draw the isometric projection of combined solids.

SOLUTION

Manual Method:

1. As per the problem draw orthographic projection of the combined solid (top and front view)
2. Construct the isometric scale of suitable length.
3. Draw reference lines at 30°. Draw isometric projection of the frustum of cone base which is an ellipse. Draw sides of sides ISO 60 mm × ISO 60 mm, inscribe ellipse. From center draw the vertical axis line of height ISO 60 mm to get the top face center of the frustum of cone.
4. With center of top face draw sides of ISO 40 mm × ISO 40 mm inscribe ellipse. Draw two tangential lines of either side to get frustum of cone.
5. From the center of top face of base solid. Draw a vertical axis of length ISO 22.5 mm, at this end point as center draw an arc of radius of 22.5 mm to get sphere.
6. Construction lines and unnecessary lines can be removed. Mark annotations correctly and dimension necessarily.

Computer Aided Drafting Procedure

1. Open the **SOFTWARE**. Click on the **DRAWING** in the open dialog box and say **OK**.
2. To set up the sheet of required size (Ex: A4) by selecting **TOOLS** from Main Menu Bar and click on **OPTIONS/PROPERTIES**. Select document properties in dialog box appeared and then select drawing in selection panel. Select the required size say A4, and click **OK**.
3. As per the problem draw top and front view of combined solids using suitable commands.

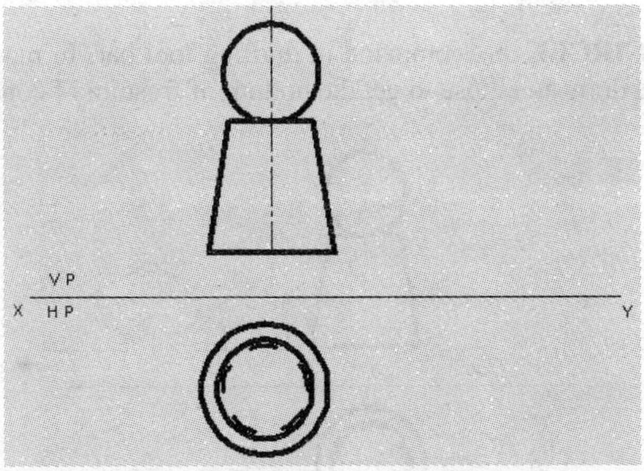

4. Draw the isometric scale, as per the dimensions of the problem.

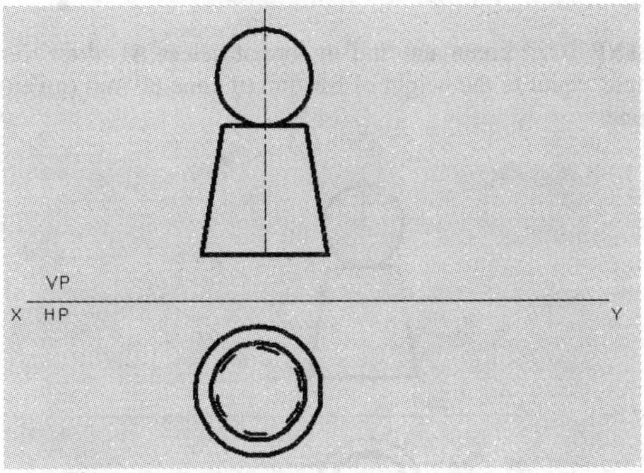

5. Using **POLYLINE**  command and in format select PL for construction lines draw two lines of iso length of 60mm along 30° line as shown. Draw another two lines, using **PARALLEL LINE COMMAND** and using **TRIM/EXTEND CURVES,** so that they are connected systematically.

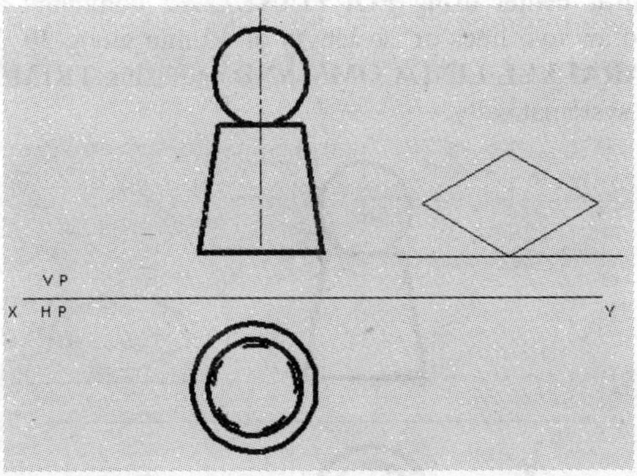

6. Using **CENTER CIRCLE** command in drafting tool bar. In mode option select arc, and use four center method draw an ellipse to get the bottom of frustum of cone in the rectangle drawn.

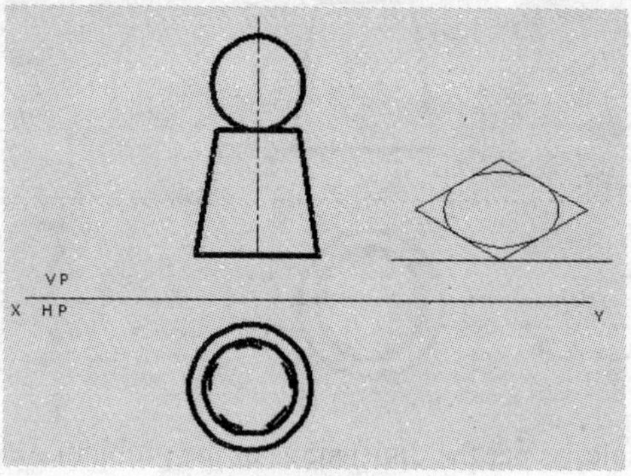

7. Using **POLYLINE** command and in format select AL draw vertical line upwards at the center of rectangle, equal to the height of frustum of cone 60 mm (given) to get center of, top face of frustum of cone.

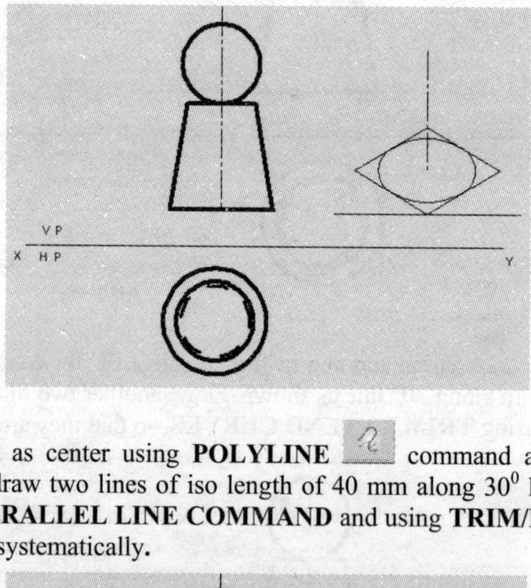

8. At that height and as center using **POLYLINE** command and in format select PL for construction lines draw two lines of iso length of 40 mm along 30^0 line as shown. Draw another two lines, using **PARALLEL LINE COMMAND** and using **TRIM/EXTEND CURVES,** so that they are connected systematically.

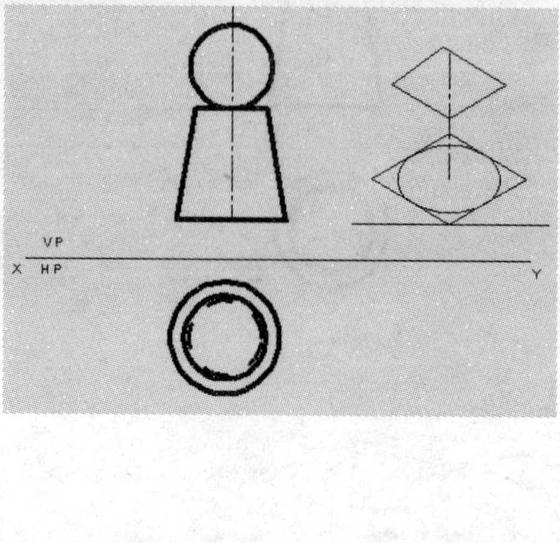

9. Using **CENTER CIRCLE**  command in drafting tool bar. In mode option select arc, and use four center method draw an ellipse to get the top of frustum of cone in the rectangle drawn. Join these top and bottom of frustum of cone by drawing two tangential lines on either side using **2 POINT LINE** Command  and in format select VL to get frustum of cone as shown below.

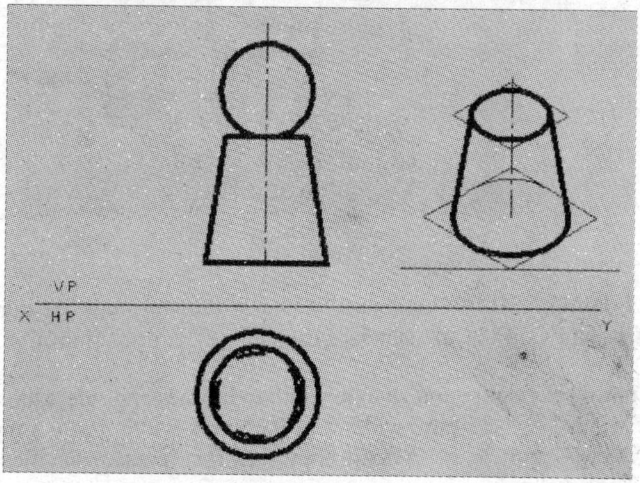

10. Since the axis of solids is collinear (frustum of cone and sphere), identify the center of rectangle represent it as o. With o as center using **POLYLINE**  command and in format select AL draw vertical line upwards at the center of rectangle, equal to the height of iso radius of sphere 22.5 mm (given). At this point with actual radius using **CENTER CIRCLE**  command in drafting tool bar. In mode option select circle, draw a circle to get sphere.

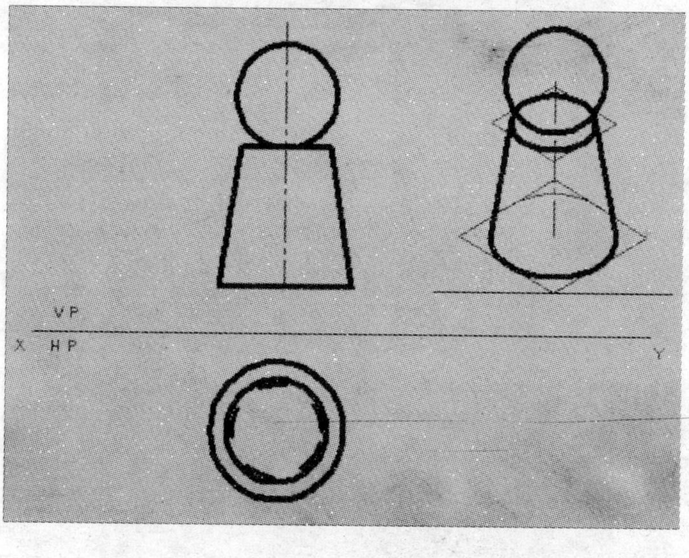

11. Trim all the unwanted construction lines by using **SMART DELET COMMAND.**

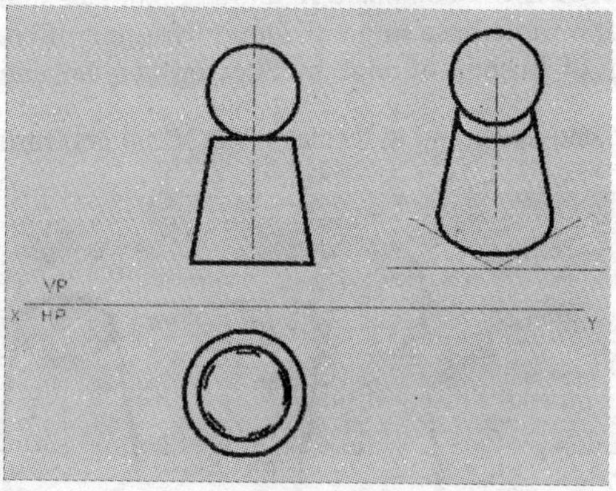

12. Using **SMART DIMENSION** Command  in drawing tool bar dimension the drawing as shown. To get a Hard Copy of the standard drawing select print from file menu bar. Print dialog window will appear select page and change width to Entities and select the activated button  now substitute width 1 as 0.15 mm, width 2 as 0.05 mm, width 3 as 0.5 mm, width 4 as 0.35 mm and say **OK.** Select print to get a hard copy and finally save the file. The required standard drawing is as shown below.

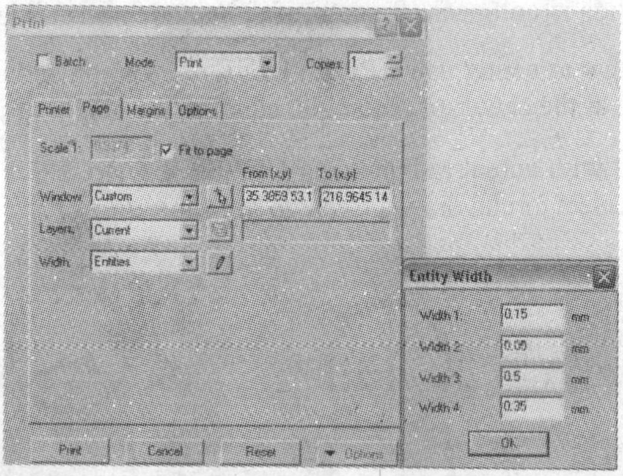

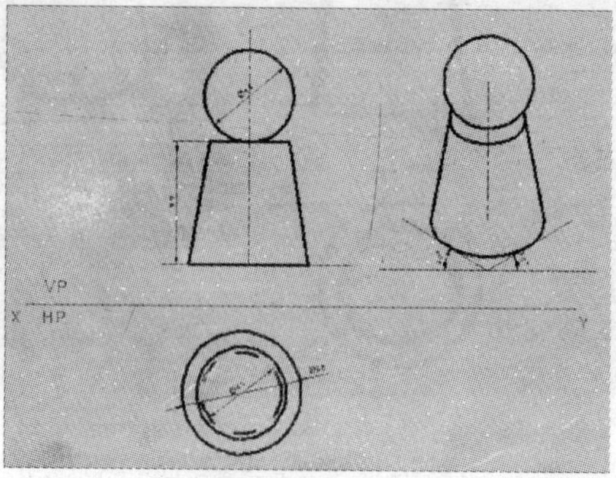

EXERCISE PROBLEMS

1. The frustum of a square pyramid of base side 40 mm, top face side 20 mm and height 60 mm rests on the centre of the top of a square block of side 60 mm and height 20 mm. The base edges of the pyramid are parallel to the top edges of the square block. Draw the isometric projection of the combination of the solids.
2. A square pyramid of base side 40mm and height 70mm rests centrally over a cube of edge 50mm, which itself is placed on a cylinder of diameter 80mm and thickness 30mm. Draw the isometric projection of the solids, if the axes of the three solids are in common line.
3. A regular pentagonal prism of base edge 30mm and axis 60mm is mounted centrally over a cylindrical block of 80mm diameter and 25mm thick. Draw the isometric projection of the combined solid.
4. A sphere of diameter 30mm rests on the frustum of a hexagonal pyramid base 30 mm, top face 18mm side and height 50 mm, such that their axes coincide. Draw the isometric projection of the combined solid.
5. Draw the isometric projection of a hexagonal prism of sides of base 40 mm and height 60 mm with a right circular cone of base 40 mm diameter and altitude 50 mm, resting on its top such that the axes of both the solids are collinear.
6. A hemisphere of diameter 50 mm is centrally resting on top of a square prism of base side 60 mm and height 30 mm such that the curved surface of hemisphere is touching the top face of the prism. Draw its isometric projection.
7. Draw the isometric projection of the combination of solids formed by a frustum of cone and co-axial frustum of pentagonal pyramid. The lower frustum of cone is of 80 mm base diameter, 60 mm top face diameter and height 25 mm. The upper frustum of pyramid is of 30 mm sides of base, 20 mm sides of top face and height 40 mm.
8. A rectangular pyramid of base 40 mm × 25 mm and height 50 mm is placed centrally on a cylindrical slab of diameter 80 mm and thickness 30 mm. Draw the isometric projection of the combination of solids.
9. A square prism base side 40 mm, height 50 mm is placed centrally on a cylindrical slab of diameter 100 mm and thickness 30 mm. Draw the isometric projection of the combination of solids.
10. A square prism base side 40 mm, height 50 mm is placed centrally on a rectangular slab sides 100 mm × 60 mm and thickness 20 mm. Draw the isometric projection of the combination of solids.
11. A frustum of cone base diameter 50 mm, top face diameter 25 mm and height 50 mm is placed centrally on a square slab side 80 mm and thickness 30 mm. Draw the isometric projection of the combination of solids.
12. A hemisphere of diameter 70 mm is placed on the ground on its curved surface. A cone of base diameter 70 mm and height 70 mm is placed centrally on it. Draw the isometric projection of the combination of solids.
13. A sphere of diameter 60 mm is placed centrally on the top face of a hexagonal prism of base side 35 mm and height 50 mm. Draw the isometric projection of the combination.
14. A sphere of diameter 40 mm is placed centrally on the flat face of a hemisphere of diameter 60 mm. Draw the isometric projection of the combination.

15. A triangular pyramid of basc sidc 40 mm and height 50 mm is placed centrally on a square slab side 80 mm and 20 mm thick. Draw the isometric projection of the combination of solids.

16. Two rectangular slabs are placed one above the other co-axially with dimensions (lxbxh) 100 mm x 60 mm × 20 mm and 100 mm × 40 mm × 20 mm such that longer edges are parallel to VP. Draw the isometric projection of the combination of solids.

17. A equilateral triangular prism base sides 30 mm and axis length 70 mm is resting on its rectangular face on top of a square slab of side 70 mm and 25 mm thick. Draw the isometric projection of the combination of solids.

18. Three cubes of sides 60 mm, 40 mm and 20 mm are placed centrally one above the other in the descending order of their sides. Draw the isometric projection of the combination.

19. A cone of base diameter 50 mm and height 50 mm is placed centrally on an equilateral triangular prism of sides 100 mm and 20 mm thick Draw the isometric projection of the combination.

20. A square prism of base side 40 mm and height 70 mm has a full depth co-axial square hole of base side 20 mm, such that edges of both the squares are parallel. Draw the isometric projection of the hollow prism.

■■■